STREET & SMITH'S
GUIDE TO BASEBALL
1995

STREET & SMITH'S GUIDE TO BASEBALL 1995

By the editors of
Street & Smith's

Consulting editor:
Scott Gray

BALLANTINE BOOKS • NEW YORK

Copyright © 1994 by Condé Nast Publications, Inc.

All rights reserved under International and Pan-American Copyright Conventions. Published in the United States of America by Ballantine Books, a division of Random House, Inc., New York, and simultaneously in Canada by Random House of Canada Limited, Toronto.

ISBN 0-345-39353-8

Manufactured in the United States of America

Cover Photo of Ken Griffey, Jr. © Otto Greule/Allsport

The Major League Baseball Club trademarks depicted herein were reproduced with permission from Major League Baseball Properties, Inc.

Major League Baseball player names and images used with permission of the Major League Baseball Players Association and the individual teams.

First Edition: March 1995

10 9 8 7 6 5 4 3 2

Table of Contents

Acknowledgements

It took the combined creative energy of numerous dedicated professionals to bring you this guide. The editors would like to extend our unlimited gratitude to the following individuals.

We are very appreciative of the patient assistance afforded us by Major League Baseball Photos and the staffs of the media relations departments of all twenty-eight major league teams, as well as those of the league offices, who answered our queries and requests quickly and helpfully.

The exceptionl people at Creative Graphics, to whom we extend our fondest thanks, helped shape this guide into a useful tool for baseball fans.

Cathy Repetti, our foresightful editor at Ballantine Books, was crucial to the smooth operation of this complicated project. Others at Ballantine who made immeasurable contributions include George Davidson, Caron Harris, Nora Reichard, Maurice Black, and Alix Krijgsman.

This guide was skillfully typeset by Gioia Di Biase.

The player profiles were created from the detailed reports of the following scouts. Paul Bratt, Richard Gray, Chris Haven, Bruce Hoffacker, Steve Hoffacker, Patrick T. McCarville, Cliff Phillips, David Seideman, Paul Stone, and Gene Taback. Their expertise was invaluable.

Introduction

Winter arrived early for baseball lovers in 1994. The season was officially shut down on August 12 due to a work stoppage, and the absence of our national pastime left many fans in a cranky mood. Just when the pennant races were beginning to percolate under the summer sun—Giants and Dodgers, Indians and White Sox, Reds and Astros—suddenly our collective field of dreams was intruded upon by men in expensive suits bickering over salary caps and replacement players.

We're ready to talk baseball again, and that's what this book is all about. The coming season, whether or not it starts on time, should give fans a chance to forget about the business of strikes and negotiations and to finally see how the revised playoff format is going to take shape. Can the amazing Tony Gwynn make another run at .400? Is it possible that both leagues could feature challenges to Roger Maris's single-season home run record? Hopefully, we'll all have the opportunity to greet the spring on time and learn the answers to such questions in 1995.

This guide will give you all the information you need to get the skinny on your hometown team's outlook for the coming campaign, gain the baseball insider's perpective on the All-Stars and the scrubeenies, or achieve the winning edge in your fantasy/rotisserie league. The following notes should assist you in making the most of this guide.

Statistical projections are based on a two-year performance curve that is adjusted for a player's age and projected games lost to the strike. It's impossible to create a bug-free system for predicting a ballplayer's future, so we've purposely erred on the side of optimism. In other words, though projections for each individual player are within his range of capabilities, it's unlikely that every major leaguer will live up to our formula's expectations. If a player was injured in either 1993 or 1994, or if he was a rookie last year, you'll find a note indicating that there is no projection for him. Keep in mind that these projections were made by a computer, an instrument that does a nice imitation of intelligence, without actually being intelligent enough to take our rigid formula and mold it to fit the infinitely varying circumstances of human performance and potential. In other words, please don't wager the family farm on the basis of our projections.

All team MVPs were chosen by the editors. Some selections are open to argument, such as Paul O'Neill over Jimmy Key, Barry Bonds over Matt Williams, and Kenny Lofton over Albert Belle. We hope that if you don't instantly agree with our MVP pick for your favorite team, the feature profile on the selected player will lend you a fresh point of view, if not a change of heart.

Team rosters and scouting reports were compiled immediately prior to publication of this book. They are subject to numerous changes due to free agency and trades. We've provided an index of all the players profiled, so if you don't find a prominent player in his new team's chapter, try locating him via the index.

Above all, thanks for purchasing this guide. Without you fans who truly love baseball despite the obvious human flaws of those who play and manage the game, we'd have nobody with whom to talk trade.

National League

1994 Recap

NL East

The Expos took hold of first place on July 20 and held on to win the division by six full games. At the time of the work stoppage Montreal was on pace for a 105-victory season. A sizzling 25–8 second half propelled the Expos to the best overall record in the majors.

The Braves found themselves trailing Montreal when the strike spoiled the season, despite the second-best winning percentage in the National League. After a phenomenal fifteen-win April, Atlanta merely played great baseball till the strike. It wasn't enough to keep up with the runaway Expos.

The Mets recovered some measure of pride in 1994, stressing fundamentals and enthusiasm. New York rode the blazing bat of Jeff Kent to early respectability, but the team wasn't ready to challenge the elite of the East. The downfall of Philadelphia allowed the Mets to claim third place.

The Phillies suffered a nightmarish, injury-filled 1994 campaign. The list of disabled Phils included Dykstra, Daulton, Kruk, Hollins, and Greene—all crucial components of the National League's 1993 World Series representatives.

Florida experienced the organization's first trip to the cellar, due largely to a lack of quality starting pitching. The Fish did show improvement in their second year, finishing two games ahead of their inaugural-season pace.

NL Central

Davey Johnson's Reds used an imposing batting order to win the West by half a game over Houston. Cincy won twenty-two games against each of the three divisions, led by Kevin Mitchell's power show and a stingy bullpen.

The Astros struggled when playing on pastoral fields, going 19–20 against the NL West. Inefficiency on grass was a prime reason for Houston's slight season-ending deficit. The team was on pace to set franchise records in every important offensive category.

Jim Leyland worked some serious magic to extract a third-place tie from Pittsburgh's limited talent. A seventeen-win June kept the Pirates' season from being utterly dismal.

St. Louis soared in the early going, flying high on the bat of Ray Lankford, but as the weather warmed, Lankford cooled off—and so did the Cards.

The Cubbies were weak at home, finishing the season nineteen games below .500 at Wrigley, including an atrocious 0–12 start in the no-longer-friendly confines.

NL West
The Dodgers withstood a furious rush by the Giants to end 1994 as division champs, 3.5 games ahead of their Northern California rivals. A rejuvenated bullpen bolstered so-so starting pitching at Dodger Stadium.

San Francisco got a shot in the arm from the mid-season arrival of Darryl Strawberry, but the Giants weren't able to overtake Los Angeles. Despite the offensive fireworks of Matt Williams and Barry Bonds, the Giants were one of the league's poorest-hitting teams.

Colorado finished the 1994 campaign within range of first place in the National League's weakest division. The slugging Rockies were just half a game from the top on July 28, but Andres Galarraga's broken hand proved to be their demise.

San Diego's final record doesn't tell the story of their divided season. After an NL-worst 10–32 start, the Padres posted the fifth-best mark in the National League from May 21 till the work stoppage.

National League Standings

NL CENTRAL	W	L	PCT	GB	HOME	ROAD	vs. EAST	vs. CENT.	vs. WEST
Cincinnati	66	48	.579	—	37–22	29–26	22–18	22–16	22–14
Houston	66	49	.574	5	37–22	29–27	17–13	30–16	19–20
Pittsburgh	53	61	.465	13.0	32–29	21–32	26–21	17–27	10–13
St. Louis	53	61	.465	13.0	23–33	30–28	23–25	16–20	14–16
Chicago	49	64	.434	16.5	20–39	29–25	10–23	19–25	20–16

NL EAST	W	L	PCT	GB	HOME	ROAD	vs. EAST	vs. CENT.	vs. WEST
Montreal	74	40	.649	—	32–20	42–20	21–13	25–13	28–14
Atlanta	68	46	.596	6.0	31–24	37–22	23–16	20–26	25–4
New York	55	58	.487	18.5	23–30	32–28	15–21	21–14	19–23
Philadelphia	54	61	.470	20.5	34–26	20–35	19–19	18–17	17–25
Florida	51	64	.443	23.5	25–34	26–30	16–25	16–28	19–11

NL WEST	W	L	PCT	GB	HOME	ROAD	vs. EAST	vs. CENT.	vs. WEST
Los Angeles	58	56	.509	—	33–22	25–34	19–29	22–14	17–13
San Francisco	55	60	.478	3.5	29–31	26–29	26–22	15–25	14–13
Colorado	53	64	.453	6.5	25–32	28–32	16–24	25–22	12–18
San Diego	47	70	.402	12.5	26–31	21–39	16–33	17–24	14–13

1995 Preview

NL East	NL Central	NL West
1. Atlanta	1. Houston	1. Los Angeles
2. Montreal	2. Cincinnati	2. San Diego
3. Philadelphia	3. Chicago	3. San Francisco
4. New York	4. St. Louis	4. Colorado
5. Florida	5. Pittsburgh	

Playoffs: Houston over Montreal; Atlanta over Los Angeles
Pennant Winner: Houston
World Series Winner: New York over Houston

The East is the NL's most compelling division, featuring the league's two best teams, the Expos and Braves, as well as the unpredictable Phillies. Much will depend on off-season signings, but as of this writing, Atlanta appears to still have the most talented starting pitchers in the division. If Philadelphia is at full strength, there could be a three-team battle for first. New York has added Pete Harnisch and should finish well above the Marlins, but not within striking distance of the Phillies.

The Central Division is ripe for the taking, and Houston stands to garner the spoils—if what remains of their starting rotation holds together. Cincinnati's batting order has men on base in every inning, but the Reds' starting pitching is far from a sure thing. The teams in the bottom three-fifths of the division are at least two years away from contention, with St. Louis and Pittsburgh starved for pitching, while the Cubs have some promising young arms who won't receive much run support in 1995.

The Western Division has parity without strength, as the Dodgers and Giants are of equal quality, while Colorado and San Diego could surprise. The Giants could take a long fall if they lose Bill Swift. San Francisco's rivals to the south can be expected to outlast the rest of the West, but the Dodgers are hardly invincible. The Rockies could have enough power and experience to make one run at a division title.

Atlanta
BRAVES

1995 Scouting Report

Outfielders: Roberto Kelly (CF) sports a sweet glove and an electric bat. David Justice has become a well rounded, dangerous hitter and an solid right fielder. Left field belongs to Ryan Klesko; he makes up for shaky defense by swinging a powerful lefty bat. The team will have to make room for sophomore Tony Tarasco.

Infielders: Second baseman Mark Lemke and shortstop Jeff Blauser are an excellent doubleplay tandem. Lemke is a contact hitter, while Blauser has some power. Chipper Jones lost last season to injury, but the Braves may let go of Blauser to make room for Jones. The Braves have smooth-fielding home run machine Fred McGriff at first base. Terry Pendleton was the leader of the infield, but Jose Oliva is the new man at third base.

Catchers: Javier Lopez has much to learn both at the plate and behind it, but he has the tools to be a star.

Starting Pitchers: The majors' best starting corps. It begins with Greg Maddux, the number-one pitcher in baseball. Tom Glavine is the team's other Cy Young winner. Steve Avery has top-flight stuff and pitching wisdom beyond his years. John Smoltz would be the ace of most teams. Kent Mercker can be dominant; his first start of 1994 was a no-hitter.

Relief Pitchers: Greg McMichael got the save opportunities last year, but Gregg Olson is expected to take over. Steve Bedrosian, Mike Stanton, and Mark Wohlers handle setup duties. Derek Lilliquist joined the Braves in the offseason.

Manager: Bobby Cox (1025–908) is the Braves' winningest manager of the modern era.

1995 Outlook

At first glance, the Braves appear to field the majors' most talented lineup. And at second and third glances as well. The team sent three players (Justice, Maddux, and McGriff) to the All-Star game last season, but they have potential All-Stars at almost every position. The Braves are a baseball alchemist's blend of immense power (137 HRs; first in the NL), seamless fielding (.982 fielding percentage; tied for third in the NL), and the game's finest group of starting pitchers.

Yet the Braves are clearly not invincible—their postseason disappointments have been fully chronicled. The team relies heavily on unproven young phenoms Klesko, Lopez, and Tarasco. The departure of Terry Pendleton will compound the team's inexperience. Another trouble spot could be the bullpen, which has been serviceable, but not unhittable. Still, all of these possible flaws could be turned to the Braves' advantage. Gregg Olson is a quality closer if his arm is sound. The Braves' trio of sophomores could each become stars. And Atlanta still has seasoned leadership in key positions.

But there's another worrisome weakness in Atlanta. The Braves are apparently allergic to plastic grass. The team is built to play in its home park, which is the antithesis of the artificial turf stadiums of the NL Central, against whom the Braves were a lackluster 20–26. That alone accounts for the Expos' edge in '94. If the Braves can play .500 ball on phoney grass, they're still the club to beat in the National league East.

On paper, the Braves have a strong chance to finish with the NL's best record in 1995. They've assembled a perfect mix of young talent and veteran leadership, with a core group of stars in their prime. Of course, if the season were played on paper, Atlanta would probably have won a World Series by now. This is a team that started the 1994 season 13–1, only to finish six games behind the Expos. Nevertheless, they've got incomparable frontline talent. The Braves have baseball's best record over the past four seasons, 27.5 games better than Toronto.

1995 Atlanta Braves Roster

Manager: Bobby Cox
Coaches: Jim Beauchamp, Pat Corrales, Clarence Jones, Leo Mazzone, Jimy Williams, Ned Yost

No.	Pitchers	B	T	HT	WT	DOB	Birthplace
33	Avery, Steve	L	L	6–4	190	4/14/70	Trenton, MI
36	Bedrosian, Steve	R	R	6–3	205	12/6/57	Methuen, MA
47	Glavine, Tom	L	L	6–1	190	3/25/66	Concord, MA
28	Lilliquist, Derek	L	L	5–10	195	2/20/66	Winter Park, FL
31	Maddux, Greg	R	R	6–0	175	4/14/66	San Angelo, TX
38	McMichael, Greg	R	R	6–3	215	12/1/66	Knoxville, TN
50	Mercker, Kent	L	L	6–2	195	2/1/68	Dublin, OH
40	Olson, Gregg	R	R	6–4	210	10/11/66	Scribner, NE
29	Smoltz, John	R	R	6–3	185	5/15/67	Warren, MI
30	Stanton, Mike	L	L	5–10	190	6/2/67	Houston, TX
43	Wohlers, Mark	R	R	6–4	207	1/23/70	Holyoke, MA
—	Woodall, Brad	B	L	6–0	175	6/25/69	Atlanta, GA
	Catchers						
—	Ayrault, Joe	R	R	6–3	190	10/8/71	Rochester, MI
—	Houston, Tyler	L	R	6–2	210	1/17/71	Las Vegas, NV
8	Lopez, Javier	R	R	6–3	185	11/5/70	Ponce, PR
11	O'Brien, Charlie	R	R	6–2	205	5/1/61	Tulsa, OK
	Infielders						
2	Belliard, Rafael	R	R	5–6	160	10/24/61	Pueblo Nuevo Mao, DR
10	Jones, Chipper	B	R	6–3	185	4/24/72	DeLand, FL
20	Lemke, Mark	B	R	5–9	167	8/13/65	Utica, NY
27	McGriff, Fred	L	L	6–3	215	10/31/63	Tampa, FL
—	Mordecai, Mike	B	R	5–11	175	12/13/67	Birmingham, AL
—	Oliva, Jose	R	R	6–1	150	3/3/71	San Pedro Macoris, DR
	Outfielders						
23	Justice, David	L	L	6–3	200	4/14/66	Cincinnati, OH
25	Kelly, Mike	R	R	6–4	195	6/2/70	Los Angeles, CA
14	Kelly, Roberto	R	R	6–2	190	10/1/64	Panama City, Panama
18	Klesko, Ryan	L	L	6–3	220	6/12/71	Westminster, CA
26	Tarasco, Tony	L	R	6–1	205	12/9/70	New York, NY

1995 Schedule

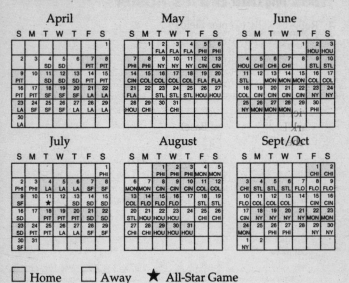

April

S	M	T	W	T	F	S
						1
2	3	4	5 SD	6 SD	7 PIT	8 PIT
9 PIT	10	11 SD	12 SD	13 SD	14 PIT	15 PIT
16 PIT	17 PIT	18 SF	19 SF	20 SF	21 LA	22 LA
23 LA	24 SF	25 SF	26 SF	27 LA	28 LA	29 LA
30 LA						

May

S	M	T	W	T	F	S
	1	2 FLA	3 FLA	4 FLA	5 PHI	6 PHI
7 PHI	8 PHI	9 NY	10 NY	11 NY	12 CIN	13 CIN
14 CIN	15 COL	16 COL	17 COL	18 COL	19 FLA	20 FLA
21 FLA	22	23 STL	24 STL	25 STL	26 HOU	27 HOU
28 HOU	29 CHI	30	31 CHI			

June

S	M	T	W	T	F	S
				1	2 HOU	3 HOU
4 HOU	5 CHI	6 CHI	7 CHI	8	9 STL	10 STL
11 STL	12	13 MON	14 MON	15 MON	16 COL	17 COL
18 COL	19 CIN	20 CIN	21 CIN	22 CIN	23 NY	24 NY
25 NY	26 MON	27 MON	28 MON	29	30 PHI	

July

S	M	T	W	T	F	S
						1 PHI
2 PHI	3 PHI	4 LA	5 LA	6 LA	7 SF	8 SF
9 SF	10	11 ★	12	13 SD	14 SD	15 SD
16 SD	17 PIT	18 PIT	19 PIT	20	21 SD	22 SD
23 SD	24 PIT	25 PIT	26 LA	27 LA	28 SF	29 SF
30 SF	31					

August

S	M	T	W	T	F	S
		1 PHI	2 PHI	3 PHI	4 MON	5 MON
6 MON	7 MON	8 CIN	9 CIN	10 CIN	11 COL	12 COL
13 COL	14 FLO	15 FLO	16 FLO	17	18 STL	19 STL
20 STL	21 HOU	22 HOU	23 HOU	24	25 CHI	26 CHI
27 CHI	28 CHI	29 HOU	30 HOU	31 HOU		

Sept/Oct

S	M	T	W	T	F	S
					1 CHI	2 CHI
3 CHI	4 STL	5 STL	6 STL	7 FLO	8 FLO	9 FLO
10 FLO	11 COL	12 COL	13 COL	14	15 CIN	16 CIN
17 CIN	18 NY	19 NY	20 NY	21 NY	22 MON	23 MON
24 MON	25	26 PHI	27 PHI	28	29 NY	30 NY
1 NY	2					

☐ Home　　☐ Away　　★ All-Star Game

Atlanta–Fulton County Stadium

Capacity: 52,710

Turf: Grass

Dimensions:
LF Line: 330'
RF Line: 330'
Center: 402'
Alleys: 385'

Tickets:
(404) 522-7630

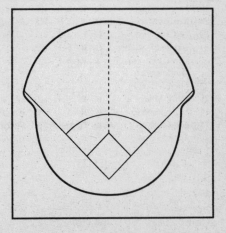

1994 Batting Order

1. Roberto Kelly (Center Field)
2. Jeff Blauser (Shortstop)
3. Ryan Klesko (Left Field)
4. Fred McGriff (First Base)
5. David Justice (Right Field)
6. Terry Pendleton (Third Base)
7. Javier Lopez (Catcher)
8. Mark Lemke (Second Base)
9. Pitcher

1994 Team Record
68–46 (.596); Second in NL East

NL East	W	L	NL Central	W	L	NL West	W	L
Atlanta	—	—	Chicago	4	2	Colorado	8	2
Florida	8	4	Cincinnati	5	5	Los Angeles	6	0
Montreal	4	5	Houston	3	3	San Diego	6	1
New York	5	4	Pittsburgh	3	9	S. Francisco	5	1
Philadelphia	6	3	St. Louis	5	7			
Total	23	16		20	26		25	4

1994 National League Team Rank Batting

Batting Average: Seventh (.267)
Runs Scored: Fifth (542)
Runs Batted In: Fifth (510)
Stolen Bases: Thirteenth (48)
Slugging Percentage: Fifth (.434)
On-Base Percentage: Sixth (.333)

1994 National League Team Rank Pitching

Earned Run Average: Second (3.57)
Bases On Balls: Tenth (378)
Strikeouts: First (865)
Wins: Second (68)
Saves: Twelfth (26)
Complete Games: First (16)

Atlanta Braves MVP

Greg Maddux No. 31/ P

Born: 4/14/66, San Angelo, TX
Height: 6' 0"   **Weight:** 175
Bats: Right   **Throws:** Right
Opp. Batting Average: .207

Maddux is racking up Hall of Fame credentials, having followed two Cy Young seasons with a third in 1994. Maddux has the phenomenal ability to stay ahead in the count while not serving up an easy pitch to hit, and he's a master at inducing opposing hitters to get themselves out on weak ground balls and swinging strikeouts. Maddux has great command of his repertoire, which consists of a ninety-mph fastball, biting slider, split-finger fastball, and his strikeout pitch—the circle change. His K/BB ratio was a remarkable 5/1, easily the best of any starter in the league.

Maddux is a workhorse; he led the league in innings pitched for the fourth year in a row, and he's won more games (123) in the last seven years than any pitcher in baseball. In a year of record-threatening offensive explosions, Maddux compiled the third-best ERA in the majors since 1919. The numbers are a story unto themselves: Maddux ranked first in innings pitched and shutouts, tied for first in wins, and ranked third in strikeouts and fewest walks per nine innings (1.4).

Maddux oozes quiet confidence on the mound, and his teammates always feel invincible when he's on the hill. He's considered an excellent fielder, and he even contributed a .222 batting average at the plate in '94. Maddux is in his prime, and figures to be baseball's premier hurler for years to come.

	G	GS	IP	ERA	H	BB	SO	W	L	SV
1994	25	25	202.0	1.56	150	31	156	16	6	0
Career	273	269	1911.0	3.02	1730	538	1290	131	91	0
Projected	35	35	267.0	2.02	215	47	201	20	9	0

Steve Avery No. 33/ P

Born: 4/14/70, Trenton, MI
Height: 6' 4" **Weight:** 190
Bats: Left **Throws:** Left
Opp. Batting Average: .227

Avery suffered the highest ERA of his career in '94, but was helped by excellent run support (5.8 per game). He improved his strikeout ratio dramatically (.8 per inning, up from .56 in '93). That bodes well for Avery's development, since most great hurlers ring up more Ks as they mature. He's only twenty-five years old, but his fifty-eight wins are fifth most in Braves' history.

	G	GS	IP	ERA	H	BB	SO	W	L	SV
1994	24	24	151.2	4.04	127	55	122	8	3	0
Career	150	149	918.0	3.58	869	279	588	58	39	0
Projected	34	34	213.0	3.38	195	56	140	15	5	0

Jeff Blauser No. 4/ SS

Born: 11/8/65, Los Gatos, CA
Height: 6' 0" **Weight:** 170
Bats: Right **Throws:** Right
1994 OBP: .329 **SLG:** .382

Blauser had a productive yet frustrating '94 season following his breakthrough '93 performance. The ideal number-two hitter, Blauser sprays the ball to all fields and is patient at the plate. But his batting average dropped forty-seven points from the previous season, and he walked almost a third less often per plate appearance. Blauser is an expert at infield positioning.

	G	AB	H	2B	3B	HR	RS	RBI	BB	SB	BA
1994	96	380	98	21	4	6	56	45	38	1	.258
Career	835	2746	744	140	21	70	403	325	316	42	.271
Projected	154	610	189	32	4	14	108	77	80	11	.298

Tom Glavine   No. 47/ P

Born: 3/25/66, Concord, MA
Height: 6' 1"   **Weight:** 190
Bats: Left   **Throws:** Left
Opp. Batting Average: .268

Glavine's ERA increased for the fourth straight season in 1994, and he topped the Braves' starters in walks (2.8 per game), but he still had a .591 winning percentage. He has a great circle change, and he's adept at pitching to zones, but when his control isn't on, he's hittable. Glavine is one of the most intelligent, competitive pitchers in the big leagues.

	G	GS	IP	ERA	H	BB	SO	W	L	SV
1994	25	25	165.1	3.97	173	70	140	13	9	0
Career	233	233	1522.1	3.58	1467	513	904	108	75	0
Projected	35	35	230.0	3.52	232	91	148	20	9	0

David Justice   No. 23/ OF

Born: 4/14/66, Cincinnati, OH
Height: 6' 3"   **Weight:** 200
Bats: Left   **Throws:** Left
1994 OBP: .427   **SLG:** .531

Justice became a complete hitter in '94, increasing his batting average by forty-three points from the previous year. Justice seemed to be concentrating on his discipline at the plate in the first half, and it paid off as he led the Braves in on-base percentage. After the break, he turned on the power stroke, blasting six longballs between July 19 and the strike.

	G	AB	H	2B	3B	HR	RS	RBI	BB	SB	BA
1994	104	352	110	16	2	19	61	59	69	2	.313
Career	657	2307	637	101	14	130	379	419	358	28	.276
Projected	158	92	183	20	4	39	99	118	97	3	.297

Roberto Kelly   No.14/ OF

Born: 10/1/64, Panama City, Panama
Height: 6' 2"   **Weight:** 190
Bats: Right   **Throws:** Right
1994 OBP: .347   **SLG:** .422

Kelly has been through a couple of name changes (Roberto to Bobby to Roberto) and three teams since '92, but he's an explosive talent, combining speed and power in the leadoff spot with great range in center field. Kelly led the Braves in multi-hit games (37) and stolen bases, while raising the level of the Braves' mediocre outfield play with a .985 fielding percentage.

	G	AB	H	2B	3B	HR	RS	RBI	BB	SB	BA
1994	110	434	127	23	3	9	73	45	35	19	.293
Career	826	3031	866	150	18	74	437	338	220	191	.286
Projected	160	648	201	35	5	16	102	69	45	35	.307

Ryan Klesko   No. 18/ OF

Born: 6/12/71, Westminster, CA
Height: 6' 3"   **Weight:** 220
Bats: Left   **Throws:** Left
1994 OBP: .344   **SLG:** .563

Klesko had major league pitchers scrambling through June, hitting at a scorching .322 clip with 14 HRs, but he slumped badly in July and August. His batting eye isn't great, and neither is his glove, but Klesko is young, has tremendous power, and could be a superstar once he gets his sea legs. All seventeen of his round-trippers came off righthanded pitching.

	G	AB	H	2B	3B	HR	RS	RBI	BB	SB	BA
1994	92	245	68	13	3	17	42	47	26	1	.278
Career	127	276	74	14	3	19	45	53	29	1	.268
Projected	142	342	106	19	4	26	62	71	40	1	.297

Mark Lemke No. 20/ 2B

Born: 8/13/65, Utica, NY
Height: 5' 9" **Weight:** 167
Bats: Both **Throws:** Right
1994 OBP: .363 **SLG:** .363

Lemke is one of the league's top defensive second basemen; he's especially quick turning the doubleplay. His .994 fielding percentage was the highest in franchise history for a second baseman. At the plate, Lemke came through in the clutch, hitting .318 with runners in scoring position and less than two out. He's difficult to fan, striking out just once in every 10.6 at bats.

	G	AB	H	2B	3B	HR	RS	RBI	BB	SB	BA
1994	104	350	103	15	0	3	40	31	38	0	.294
Career	678	1891	464	71	9	20	200	162	212	2	.245
Projected	160	566	177	27	0	5	66	55	61	0	.300

Javier Lopez No. 8/ C

Born: 11/5/70, Ponce, PR
Height: 6' 3" **Weight:** 185
Bats: Right **Throws:** Right
1994 OBP: .299 **SLG:** .419

Braves fans have been salivating for Javy Lopez to begin his tenure at and behind the plate in Fulton County. Behind the plate, Lopez threw out only 20% of runners attempting to steal. At the plate, he leapt out to a quick start, showing an impressive ability to pull fastballs out of the yard. But he had only three home runs after May as pitchers preyed on his aggressiveness.

	G	AB	H	2B	3B	HR	RS	RBI	BB	SB	BA
1994	80	277	68	9	0	13	27	35	17	0	.245
Career	97	309	80	12	1	14	31	39	17	0	.259
Projected	123	426	107	14	0	18	39	50	24	0	.240

Fred McGriff   No. 27/ 1B

Born: 10/31/63, Tampa, FL
Height: 6' 3"   **Weight:** 215
Bats: Left   **Throws:** Left
1994 OBP: .389   **SLG:** .623

McGriff is a devastating slugger who had his best season in '94. The keys to his power are perfect mechanics and the willingness to wait for a pitch he can drive. McGriff is remarkably consistent; he's averaged thirty dingers per season since beating out Cecil Fielder as Toronto's full-time first baseman in 1988. McGriff has soft hands and smooth reactions at first base.

	G	AB	H	2B	3B	HR	RS	RBI	BB	SB	BA
1994	113	424	135	25	1	34	81	94	50	7	.318
Career	1147	3984	1136	202	16	262	703	710	679	45	.285
Projected	156	584	180	32	2	43	115	117	76	7	.306

Greg McMichael   No. 38/ P

Born: 12/1/66, Knoxville, TN
Height: 6' 3"   **Weight:** 215
Bats: Right   **Throws:** Right
Opp. Batting Average: .280

McMichael is as difficult for fans to figure out as he is for hitters. After coming from nowhere to be Atlanta's stopper in '93, he began last season with a 1.91 ERA and 13 saves through early June. But hitters seemed to be belting his change-up with authority by August, and McMichael's role for '95 may be middle relief, with Gregg Olson closing.

	G	GS	IP	ERA	H	BB	SO	W	L	SV
1994	51	0	58.2	3.84	66	19	47	4	6	21
Career	125	0	150.1	2.75	134	48	136	6	9	40
Projected	71	0	86.0	2.75	76	27	77	3	5	23

Kent Mercker No. 50/ P

Born: 2/1/68, Dublin, OH
Height: 6' 2" **Weight:** 195
Bats: Left **Throws:** Left
Opp. Batting Average: .220

Despite once again entering the season with uncertainty about his role, Mercker no-hit the Dodgers in his first start of '94. It looked as if he had finally established a permanent spot in the Braves' rotation, but Mercker's lack of reliable complements to his ninety-six-mph heat continued to be a concern, and by year's end he was making appearances in middle relief.

	G	GS	IP	ERA	H	BB	SO	W	L	SV
1994	20	17	112.1	3.45	90	45	111	9	4	0
Career	204	28	372.2	3.24	300	181	324	24	17	19
Projected	35	13	98.0	3.23	79	45	94	7	3	0

Terry Pendleton No. 9/ 3B

Born: 7/16/60, Los Angeles, CA
Height: 5' 9" **Weight:** 195
Bats: Both **Throws:** Right
1994 OBP: .280 **SLG:** .398

Pendleton had a difficult '94 season and may be reaching the end of an interesting career. A mediocre performer in St. Louis, Pendleton became an MVP in Atlanta in 1991. But last season he cleared the fence just twice from June 5 through the season's end. The Braves elected not to re-sign Pendleton for '95, opting for promising Jose Oliva at the hot corner.

	G	AB	H	2B	3B	HR	RS	RBI	BB	SB	BA
1994	77	309	78	18	3	7	25	30	12	2	.252
Career	1478	5601	1524	279	37	111	702	747	380	121	.272
Projected	140	542	138	29	2	14	60	64	27	4	.260

John Smoltz   No. 29/ P

Born: 5/15/67, Warren, MI
Height: 6' 3"   **Weight:** 185
Bats: Right   **Throws:** Right
Opp. Batting Average: .239

Smoltz, who has the best pure stuff on the Braves' formidable staff, had a difficult season that ended with elbow surgery. Extremely tough on righties, Smoltz can make batters look inept with his hard slider. Still looking for consistency, Smoltz has yet to fulfill the high expectations of Braves fans, but his control improved last season, and he's poised to have a career year.

	G	GS	IP	ERA	H	BB	SO	W	L	SV
1994	21	21	134.2	4.14	120	48	113	6	10	0
Career	202	202	1358.0	3.59	1180	500	1059	78	75	0
Projected	32	32	213.0	3.80	184	83	181	12	12	0

Tony Tarasco   No. 26/ OF

Born: 12/9/70, New York, NY
Height: 6' 1"   **Weight:** 205
Bats: Left   **Throws:** Right
1994 OBP: .313   **SLG:** .432

Tarasco joined the Braves as an undrafted free agent, but has worked his way through the minors and played his first full season in '94. He was productive in a platoon role, and he should get more playing time, despite the Braves' crowded outfield picture. Tarasco has a ton of ability and can be a solid everyday player, with an outside chance at stardom.

	G	AB	H	2B	3B	HR	RS	RBI	BB	SB	BA
1994	87	132	36	6	0	5	16	19	9	5	.273
Career	111	167	44	8	0	5	22	21	9	5	.263
Projected	134	210	63	10	0	8	27	32	15	8	.284

Chicago
CUBS

1995 Scouting Report

Outfielders: Sammy Sosa leads the Cubs at the plate and in center field. Glenallen Hill in right and Derrick May in left provide offensive punch, but their defense won't win any awards. Eddie Zambrano, Karl Rhodes, and Kevin Roberson will compete for playing time.

Infielders: The retirement of Ryne Sandberg leaves slick-fielding Rey Sanchez at second base. Shawon Dunston will try to stay healthy at shortstop. The Cubs have great defense at the corners with veterans Mark Grace (1B) and Steve Buechele (3B).

Catchers: Rick Wilkins should rebound from last season's hitting woes.

Starting Pitchers: Wrigley Field is a torture garden for pitchers when the wind is blowing out. Yet the Cubs' starters actually fared better at home than outside the friendly confines. The staff is in disarray; Willie Banks and Jose Guzman haven't come close to fulfilling their potential. But there is hope; young guns Steve Trachsel and Kevin Foster looked promising in '94. The fifth spot should go to Frank Castillo.

Relief Pitchers: The Cubs' relievers saw a lot of action in '94. Randy Myers continues to deliver as the late-inning stopper. Setup men include Dan Plesac, Chuck Crim, Jose Bautista, and Dave Otto.

Manager: New manager Jim Riggleman signed a two-year deal in October, coming to Chicago from San Diego. His first year as the Cubbies' skipper might feel like trying to steer a dinghy in a gale. He'll call on his youthful starting rotation to lead the Cubs to respectability.

1995 Outlook

The Cubs are attempting to revamp their organization from the top, having named Andy MacPhail as president and CEO, and Jim Riggleman as manager. No team in baseball was more in need of change than the troubled Cubbies, who used seventy-four different lineups in 1994 and endured the worst home start in the National League in the twentieth century (0–12).

It's impossible to predict a winning season for the Cubs, but they've got a decent shot at staying out of the NL Central cellar. By way of encouragement, the team unearthed some promising young arms—Kevin Foster and Steve Trachsel have the makeup of potential aces. Catcher Rick Wilkins is certain to improve on his '94 offensive performance. The team isn't devoid of veterans who know how winning feels. And the infield defense is excellent.

Of course, the ivy grows in the other direction as well, and the Cubs have some serious deficiencies. The starting staff lives on the edge, and the dropoff is precipitous—Foster and Trachsel combined for an ERA of 3.09, while the next three pitchers in the rotation put together a 5.21 ERA.

Alarmingly, the Cubs had no advantage at home in 1994. That's a problem considering the unique features of Wrigley Field. The first task of the new management is to begin acquiring personnel suited to make the most of playing eighty-one games in the friendly confines. Specifically, control-type pitchers who induce grounders (to minimize big innings) and hitters with high on-base percentages who can sustain a long-sequence offense.

If the Cubs can begin making studied progress toward rebuilding around their young guns, Trachsel and Foster, while maintaining their core contributors on offense (Sosa, Grace, et al.), they should be able to win sixty-five to seventy games this year.

1995 Chicago Cubs Roster

Manager: Jim Riggleman
Coaches: Dave Bialas, Fergie Jenkins, Tony Muser, Max Olivares, Dan Radison, Billy Williams

No.	Pitchers	B	T	HT	WT	DOB	Birthplace
35	Banks, Willie	R	R	6–1	203	2/27/69	Jersey City, NJ
38	Bautista, Jose	R	R	6–2	205	7/26/64	Bani, DR
52	Bullinger, Jim	R	R	6–2	185	8/21/65	New Orleans, LA
49	Castillo, Frank	R	R	6–1	190	4/1/69	El Paso, TX
31	Foster, Kevin	R	R	6–1	160	1/13/69	Evanston,IL
29	Guzman, Jose	R	R	6–3	195	4/9/63	Santa Isabel, PR
—	Hickerson, Bryan	L	L	6–2	203	10/13/63	Bemidji, MN
36	Morgan, Mike	R	R	6–2	220	10/8/59	Tulare, CA
28	Myers, Randy	L	L	6–1	230	9/19/62	Vancouver, WA
53	Otto, Dave	L	L	6–7	210	11/12/64	Chicago, IL
46	Trachsel, Steve	R	R	6–4	205	10/31/70	Oxnard, CA
13	Wendell, Turk	B	R	6–2	190	5/19/67	Pittsfield, MA
16	Young, Anthony	R	R	6–2	210	1/19/66	Houston, TX
	Catchers						
2	Wilkins, Rick	L	R	6–2	210	6/4/67	Jacksonville, FL
	Infielders						
24	Buechele, Steve	R	R	6–2	200	9/26/61	Lancaster, CA
12	Dunston, Shawon	R	R	6–1	180	3/21/63	Brooklyn, NY
18	Hernandez, Jose	R	R	6–1	180	7/14/69	Vega Alta, PR
11	Sanchez, Rey	R	R	5–9	170	10/5/67	Rio Piedras, PR
	Outfielders						
4	Hill, Glenallen	R	R	6–2	220	3/22/65	Santa Cruz, CA
27	May, Derrick	L	R	6–4	225	7/14/68	Rochester, NY
25	Rhodes, Karl	L	L	6–0	195	8/21/68	Cincinnati, OH
19	Roberson, Kevin	B	R	6–4	210	1/29/68	Decatur, IL
21	Sosa, Sammy	R	R	6–0	185	11/12/68	San Pedro Macoris, PR
22	Zambrano, Eddie	R	R	6–3	200	2/1/66	Maricaibo, VZ

1995 Schedule

April

S	M	T	W	T	F	S
						1 TEX
2	3 CIN	4 CIN	5 CIN	6 CIN	7 NY	8 NY
9 NY	10	11 CIN	12 CIN	13 NY	14 NY	15 NY
16 NY	17 PHI	18 PHI	19 PHI	20 MON	21 MON	22 MON
23 MON	24 PHI	25 PHI	26 PHI	27 MON	28 MON	29 MON
30 MON						

May

S	M	T	W	T	F	S
	1 HOU	2 HOU	3	4	5 PIT	6 PIT
7 PIT	8 STL	9 STL	10 STL	11	12 SD	13 SD
14 SD	15 SF	16 SF	17 SF	18	19 LA	20 LA
21 LA	22 COL	23 COL	24 COL	25	26 FLA	27 FLA
28 FLA	29 ATL	30	31 ATL			

June

S	M	T	W	T	F	S
				1 FLA	2 FLA	3 FLA
4 FLA	5 ATL	6 ATL	7 ATL	8 COL	9 COL	10 COL
11 COL	12	13 SF	14 SF	15 SF	16 LA	17 LA
18 LA	19 SD	20 SD	21 SD	22 HOU	23 HOU	24 HOU
25 HOU	26 PIT	27 PIT	28 PIT	29 STL	30 STL	

July

S	M	T	W	T	F	S
						1 STL
2 STL	3	4 NY	5 NY	6 NY	7 PHI	8 PHI
9 PHI	10	11 ★	12	13 CIN	14 CIN	15 CIN
16 CIN	17 NY	18 NY	19 MON	20 MON	21 CIN	22 CIN
23 CIN	24 MON	25 MON	26 MON	27	28 PHI	29 PHI
30 PHI	31					

August

S	M	T	W	T	F	S
		1 PIT	2 PIT	3 PIT	4 STL	5 STL
6 STL	7	8 SD	9 SD	10 SD	11 SF	12 SF
13 SF	14 LA	15 LA	16 LA	17 COL	18 COL	19 COL
20 COL	21	22 FLA	23 FLA	24 FLA	25 ATL	26 ATL
27 ATL	28 ATL	29 FLA	30 FLA	31 FLA		

Sept/Oct

S	M	T	W	T	F	S
					1 ATL	2 ATL
3 ATL	4 COL	5	6 COL	7	8 SF	9 SF
10 SF	11 LA	12 LA	13 LA	14	15 SD	16 SD
17 SD	18 HOU	19 HOU	20 HOU	21 PIT	22 PIT	23 PIT
24 PIT	25 STL	26 STL	27 STL	28 HOU	29 HOU	30 HOU
1	2					

☐ Home   ☐ Away   ★ All-Star Game

Wrigley Field

Capacity: 38,719

Turf: Grass

Dimensions:
LF Line: 355'
RF Line: 353'
Center: 400'
Alleys: 368'

Tickets:
(312) 404-2827

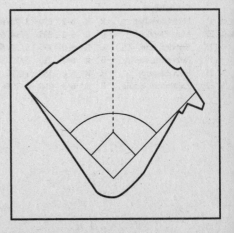

1994 Batting Order

1. Karl Rhodes (Center Field)
2. Ryne Sandberg (Second Base)
3. Mark Grace (First Base)
4. Derrick May (Left Field)
5. Sammy Sosa (Right Field)
6. Rick Wilkins (Catcher)
7. Steve Buechele (Third Base)
8. Shawon Dunston (Shortstop)
9. Pitcher

1994 Team Record
49–64 (.434); Fifth in NL Central

NL East	W	L	NL Central	W	L	NL West	W	L
Atlanta	2	4	Chicago	—	—	Colorado	6	6
Florida	4	5	Cincinnati	5	7	Los Angeles	3	3
Montreal	2	4	Houston	4	8	San Diego	6	3
New York	1	4	Pittsburgh	5	5	S. Francisco	5	4
Philadelphia	1	6	St. Louis	5	5			
Total	10	23		19	25		20	16

1994 National League Team Rank Batting

Batting Average: Eleventh (.259)
Runs Scored: Eleventh (500)
Runs Batted In: Eleventh (464)
Stolen Bases: Ninth (69)
Slugging Percentage: Eighth (.404)
On-Base Percentage: Eleventh (.325)

1994 National League Team Rank Pitching

Earned Run Average: Tenth (4.47)
Bases On Balls: Eleventh (392)
Strikeouts: Seventh (717)
Wins: Thirteenth (49)
Saves: Ninth (27)
Complete Games: Tenth (5)

© Rich Pilling/MLB Photos

Chicago Cubs MVP

Sammy Sosa   No. 21/ OF

Born: 11/12/68, San Pedro Macoris, DR
Height: 6' 0"   **Weight:** 185
Bats: Right   **Throws:** Right
1994 OBP: .339   **SLG:** .545

Sosa is an electrifying talent, with possibly the quickest bat in the majors, and he's now entering his prime. He was the Cubs' leader in batting average, home runs, and runs batted in, giving him a team Triple Crown for 1994.

A streak hitter, Sosa tends to hit longballs in pairs—he had four two-homer games last season, giving him eleven for his career. Remarkably, Sosa collected nearly 30% of his total RBIs for '94 in just five games. Though he still has no concept of discipline at the plate, resulting in a disappointing on-base percentage, he made enough contact to end the season with a .300 batting average, a thirty-nine-point increase from '93. And his numbers were not inflated by playing at Wrigley. Sosa actually hit slightly better on the road than at home in '94.

Sosa has forty-eight career outfield assists, an outstanding average of twelve assists per 162 games, playing both right and center fields. He gets to the ball quickly and has a strong arm.

An archetypical blend of power and speed, Sosa is a thrilling player to watch, and yet the national media and fans have been slow to fully credit his fine all-around accomplishments. Sosa is the only Cub in history to follow a 30/30 season with a 20/20 season.

	G	AB	H	2B	3B	HR	RS	RBI	BB	SB	BA
1994	159	426	128	17	6	25	59	70	25	22	.300
Career	658	2317	587	93	24	95	330	304	140	125	.253
Projected	160	643	193	27	7	38	99	107	41	38	.288

Willie Banks   No. 35/ P

Born: 2/27/69, Jersey City, NJ
Height: 6' 1"   **Weight:** 203
Bats: Right   **Throws:** Right
Opp. Batting Average: .261

As a flyball pitcher prone to control problems, Banks seemed to be out of place at Wrigley Field after being traded by Minnesota. Banks was selected third overall in the '87 amateur draft, and he has shown glimpses of dominance. He took a no-hitter into the eighth inning versus Philly on May 30. But he also went winless in his final eight starts with an 8.04 ERA.

	G	GS	IP	ERA	H	BB	SO	W	L	SV
1994	23	23	138.1	5.40	139	56	91	8	12	0
Career	75	68	398.0	4.88	426	183	282	24	29	0
Projected	31	30	176.0	4.65	186	77	131	11	14	0

Jose Bautista   No. 38/ P

Born: 7/26/64, Bani, DR
Height: 6' 2"   **Weight:** 205
Bats: Right   **Throws:** Right
Opp. Batting Average: .284

Bautista continues to be a workhorse for the Cubs' overworked bullpen staff; his fifty-eight relief appearances tied for second most in the majors. Bautista has exemplary command of his forkball. He allowed just one unintentional walk every 6.9 innings last season. All those innings may have taken a toll; Bautista finished the year in a tailspin.

	G	GS	IP	ERA	H	BB	SO	W	L	SV
1994	58	0	69.1	3.89	75	17	45	4	5	1
Career	191	42	462.2	4.18	476	116	232	24	28	3
Projected	68	4	106.0	3.24	105	26	63	8	5	2

Steve Buechele   No. 24/ 3B

Born: 9/26/61, Lancaster, CA
Height: 6' 2"   **Weight:** 200
Bats: Right   **Throws:** Right
1994 OBP: .325   **SLG:** .404

Buechele possesses great range at third, and he committed only five errors last season. He may be the most unrecognized great fielder in the game. He's also got an active bat, generating excellent linedrive power in a lineup that desperately needs it. Buechele was prone to slumps in '94, but the Cubs can feel relatively secure at the hot corner for at least one more year.

	G	AB	H	2B	3B	HR	RS	RBI	BB	SB	BA
1994	104	339	82	11	1	14	33	52	39	1	.242
Career	1293	4136	1023	181	21	136	491	538	393	17	.247
Projected	146	484	120	23	2	17	51	69	52	1	.254

Frank Castillo   No. 49/ P

Born: 4/1/69, El Paso, TX
Height: 6' 1"   **Weight:** 190
Bats: Right   **Throws:** Right
Opp. Batting Average: .278

The Cubs have openings in their starting rotation, and Castillo has been expected to fill one for the past two seasons, but he's struggled to establish himself. Castillo changes speeds well and throws a fine change-up; he compiled promising strikeout numbers in the minor leagues. He threw a complete game August 6 last season, allowing just one unearned run.

	G	GS	IP	ERA	H	BB	SO	W	L	SV
1994	4	4	23.0	4.30	25	5	19	2	1	0
Career	84	80	481.1	4.11	473	140	311	23	27	0
Projected	17	15	85.0	4.77	97	23	54	4	5	0

Shawon Dunston   No. 12/ SS

Born: 3/21/63, Brooklyn, NY
Height: 6' 1"   **Weight:** 180
Bats: Right   **Throws:** Right
1994 OBP: .313   **SLG:** .435

After undergoing back surgery twice in the past two years, Dunston still has plenty of pop for a shortstop. Though he hit .333 batting leadoff for the final thirty-one games, his patience at the plate is minimal, and his attempts at base stealing are doing more harm than good. Before the injuries, Dunston was poised to be the majors' number-one slugging shortstop.

	G	AB	H	2B	3B	HR	RS	RBI	BB	SB	BA
1994	88	331	92	19	0	11	38	35	16	3	.278
Career	1013	3674	959	178	38	84	448	379	153	136	.261
Projected	135	491	141	31	0	16	60	54	23	4	.284

Kevin Foster   No. 31/ P

Born: 1/13/69, Evanston, IL
Height: 6' 1"   **Weight:** 160
Bats: Right   **Throws:** Right
Opp. Batting Average: .234

Foster actually had a better '94 season than his fine record indicates. In four of his six no-decisions, he left the game with the Cubs leading. A hard thrower with fairly good control, Foster has the stuff and makeup of an ace. The fans in Chicago have to be excited about this local product who had consecutive ten-strikeout outings versus Cincinnati.

	G	GS	IP	ERA	H	BB	SO	W	L	SV
1994	13	13	81.0	2.89	70	35	75	3	4	0
Career	15	14	87.2	3.80	83	42	81	3	5	0
Projected			No projection. Player was a rookie in 1994.							

Mark Grace   No. 17/ 1B

Born: 6/28/64, Winston-Salem, NC
Height: 6' 2"   **Weight:** 190
Bats: Left   **Throws:** Left
1994 OBP: .370   **SLG:** .414

Grace had the least productive campaign of his life after having a career year in '93. Never a power hitter, Grace notched just one homer for every sixty-seven at bats last season. His judgement of the strike zone is nearly flawless; he's walked 460 times in his career, while fanning only 301. Grace has the highest career fielding percentage in Cub history (.994).

	G	AB	H	2B	3B	HR	RS	RBI	BB	SB	BA
1994	106	403	120	23	3	6	55	44	48	0	.298
Career	1012	3804	1153	210	25	66	511	497	460	49	.303
Projected	158	608	195	38	4	12	87	87	73	5	.317

Jose Guzman   No. 29/ P

Born: 4/9/63, Santa Isabel, PR
Height: 6' 3"   **Weight:** 195
Bats: Right   **Throws:** Right
Opp. Batting Average: .289

When Guzman is healthy, which hasn't been often in the past two years, he has one of the nastiest repertoires in the game. Last season, Guzman underwent shoulder surgery; he'll be a large question mark in the Cubs' rotation for '95. Guzman tantalized Cubs rooters when he opened the '93 season by taking a no-hitter into the ninth inning versus Atlanta.

	G	GS	IP	ERA	H	BB	SO	W	L	SV
1994	4	4	19.2	9.15	22	13	11	2	2	0
Career	193	186	1224.1		1193	482	889	80	74	0
Projected				No projection. Player was injured in 1994.						

Glenallen Hill   No. 4/ OF

Born: 3/22/65, Santa Cruz, CA
Height: 6' 2"   **Weight:** 220
Bats: Right   **Throws:** Right
1994 OBP: .365   **SLG:** .461

Hill had a productive '94 campaign at the plate, striking a nice balance of speed and power. Though it was May 6 before he drove in a run, blasting an upper-deck shot in Pittsburgh, Hill batted .316 in his final 171 at-bats. He was much more patient than he's been in the past, greatly increasing both his frequency of walks and his batting average.

	G	AB	H	2B	3B	HR	RS	RBI	BB	SB	BA
1994	89	269	80	12	1	10	48	38	29	19	.297
Career	463	1432	370	61	9	64	199	198	110	52	.259
Projected	117	337	97	17	2	16	52	17	30	17	.284

Derrick May   No. 27/ OF

Born: 7/14/68, Rochester, NY
Height: 6' 4"   **Weight:** 225
Bats: Left   **Throws:** Right
1994 OBP: .340   **SLG:** .420

May hasn't lived up to organizational expectations, but he did progress last season in terms of fielding (just one error in a hundred games) and plate discipline. He hasn't hit for much power in the past two years, and he stopped stealing bases in '94, but he's the Cubs' best lefthanded bat, and he struck out just once in every 11.1 at-bats, the sixth-best ratio in the NL.

	G	AB	H	2B	3B	HR	RS	RBI	BB	SB	BA
1994	100	345	98	19	2	8	43	51	30	3	.284
Career	384	1244	351	60	4	28	150	187	79	19	.282
Projected	141	521	163	29	3	12	70	86	41	9	.302

Randy Myers   No. 28/ P

Born: 9/19/62, Vancouver, WA
Height: 6' 1"   **Weight:** 230
Bats: Left   **Throws:** Left
Opp. Batting Average: .260

As his control improved, Myers actually became more hittable as the season progressed. He's still tough on lefties, but he needs to spot the ball more at this point in his career—he can't just lean back and throw heat. He's been one of the best, but his career may be winding down. Myers has struck out exactly one batter per inning in 654 career innings pitched.

	G	GS	IP	ERA	H	BB	SO	W	L	SV
1994	38	0	40.1	3.79	40	16	32	1	5	21
Career	486	12	654.0	3.11	543	291	654	33	47	205
Projected	62	0	64.0	3.36	58	23	66	2	5	41

Rey Sanchez   No. 11/ 2B

Born: 10/5/67, Rio Piedras, PR
Height: 5' 9"   **Weight:** 170
Bats: Right   **Throws:** Right
1994 OBP: .345   **SLG:** .337

Sanchez filled in after Ryne Sandberg, one of the five greatest second basemen ever, retired in mid-season. The Cubs will miss Ryno's leadership as much as they'll struggle to replace his glove and bat. Sanchez made just two errors in 275 total chances. He has little punch at the plate, but he did show some ability to get on base, batting .337 in his last twenty-eight games.

	G	AB	H	2B	3B	HR	RS	RBI	BB	SB	BA
1994	96	291	83	13	1	0	26	24	20	2	.285
Career	288	913	250	38	6	1	86	73	49	5	.274
Projected	126	415	127	16	2	0	41	35	24	2	.295

Steve Trachsel   No. 46/ P

Born: 10/31/70, Oxnard, CA
Height: 6' 4"   **Weight:** 205
Bats: Right   **Throws:** Right
Opp. Batting Average: .242

Trachsel (pronounced TRACK-s'l) is very poised and focused, but he'll need to cut down on the number of walks he allows, especially in Wrigley Field, where bases on balls can quickly turn into three-run home runs. Trachsel finished with a rush (1.88 ERA in his last seventy-two innings), and he pitched great on the road, going 8–0 in ten starts.

	G	GS	IP	ERA	H	BB	SO	W	L	SV
1994	22	22	146.0	3.21	133	54	108	9	7	0
Career	25	25	165.2	3.37	149	57	122	9	9	0
Projected			No projection. Player was a rookie in 1994.							

Rick Wilkins   No. 2/ C

Born: 6/4/67, Jacksonville, FL
Height: 6' 2"   **Weight:** 210
Bats: Left   **Throws:** Right
1994 OBP: .317   **SLG:** .387

In 1993 Rick Wilkins started the season ice cold, then exploded to finish with thirty homers. Last year he duplicated the abysmal start, but never got the fuse lit. Wilkins should be in his prime, and it's hard to imagine that his '93 numbers were a fluke; he figures to come back strong this year. His defense and handling of pitchers are solid.

	G	AB	H	2B	3B	HR	RS	RBI	BB	SB	BA
1994	100	313	71	25	2	7	44	39	40	4	.227
Career	405	1206	317	66	4	51	163	156	13	9	.263
Projected	145	485	142	32	2	25	81	74	60	4	.282

Cincinnati
REDS

1995 Scouting Report

Outfielders: Right fielder Reggie Sanders has a center fielder's range. He also has 30/30 potential at the plate. Kevin Mitchell (LF) possesses limited fielding skills, but he slugged .681 with a .326 batting average. Deion Sanders brings speed to the center field and leadoff slots. Brian R. Hunter is the utility outfielder.

Infielders: Barry Larkin is a perennial All-Star shortstop. Bret Boone is a future All-Star at second base. Hal Morris is a potential batting champion, but he provides vitually no power for a first baseman. Tony Fernandez, a former shortstop, has excellent tools at third base, though he compounds the Reds' power shortage at the corners.

Catchers: Eddie Taubensee drove the ball with authority after being dealt from Houston. The Reds picked up Damon Berryhill over the winter.

Starting Pitchers: The ace is Jose Rijo, who's a good bet to eventually become the first Cy Young winner in team history. John Smiley is still effective, but not to the degree he was in '91 when he won twenty games. Erik Hanson also has slipped a notch from his past excellence, though he could surprise. John Roper endured some growing pains as a rookie, but he's still a top prospect.

Relief Pitchers: Journeyman Jeff Brantley was better than many big-name ninth-inning specialists last year. Hector Carrasco is a solid setup man and possible future closer. Lefthander Chuck McElroy compiled a 2.34 ERA in fifty-two appearances.

Manager: Davey Johnson (714–530) signed a two-year deal in October that will move him into the front office after the 1995 season.

1995 Outlook

When spring training began, the Reds weren't expected to finish the season higher than third place. But the club exploded to lead the National League in both slugging and on-base percentage, while compiling the league's third-best ERA. The Reds could well have been on their way to claiming a championship banner when the season was cut short.

Cincy is loaded with heavy hitters. The Reds' batting order is so potent that their number-seven hitter, Bret Boone, batted .320 with twelve homers at the age of twenty-four. The lineup features two potential batting champions (Larkin and Morris), a potential MVP (Mitchell), and a probable 30/30 man (Reggie Sanders).

Possible trouble spots in the batting order include a lack of power at the corner positions and uncertainty about the leadoff spot, with unproven Deion Sanders having a lifetime batting average under .265.

The pitching isn't as formidable as the offense, but the Reds aren't nearly as desperate for good arms as most teams. Jose Rijo is one of the NL's five best starters year in and year out. The rest of the staff is solid enough to keep the offensive machine from having to overwork itself.

But there are some doubts on the mound at Riverfront. Erik Hanson has never put together strong seasons back-to-back, and John Smiley isn't a twenty-game winner anymore. Cincinnati may need to import another arm if they're going to keep pace with the pitching-rich Braves, Astros, and Expos.

The Reds are undoubtably one of the National League's four best teams. If the pitching doesn't fall apart, they've got enough firepower to gain at least a wild-card berth. It's too bad that either the Reds, Astros, Expos, or Braves are going to miss the playoffs.

1995 Cincinnati Reds Roster

Manager: Dave Johnson
Coaches: Don Gullett, Grant Jackson, Ray Knight, Hal McRae, Joel Youngblood

No.	Pitchers	B	T	HT	WT	DOB	Birthplace
32	Browning, Tom	L	L	6–1	195	4/28/60	Casper, WY
61	Bushing, Chris	R	R	6–0	190	11/4/67	Rockville Center, NY
58	Carrasco, Hector	R	R	6–2	175	10/22/69	San Pedro Macoris, DR
64	Ferry, Mike	R	R	6–3	185	7/26/69	Appleton, WI
39	Hanson, Erik	R	R	6–6	215	5/18/65	Kinnelon, NJ
36	Holman, Brian	R	R	6–4	190	1/25/65	Denver, CO
—	McElroy, Chuck	L	L	6–0	195	10/1/67	Port Arthur, TX
55	Powell, Ross	L	L	6–0	180	1/24/68	Grand Rapids, MI
40	Pugh, Tim	R	R	6–6	225	1/26/67	Lake Tahoe, CA
27	Rijo, Jose	R	R	6–2	210	5/13/65	San Cristobal, DR
44	Roper, John	R	R	6–0	175	11/21/71	Southern Pines, NC
47	Ruffin, Johnny	R	R	6–3	175	7/29/71	Butler, AL
34	Service, Scott	R	R	6–6	235	2/26/67	Cincinnati, OH
57	Smiley, John	L	L	6–4	200	3/17/65	Phoenixville, PA
48	Spradlin, Jerry	B	R	6–7	220	6/14/67	Fullerton, CA
53	Wickander, Kevin	L	L	6–3	200	1/4/65	Fort Dodge, IA
	Catchers						
—	Berryhill, Damon	B	R	6–0	205	12/3/63	South Laguna, CA
33	Dorsett, Brian	R	R	6–4	220	4/9/61	Terre Haute, IN
10	Taubensee, Eddie	L	R	6–4	205	10/31/68	Beeville, TX
	Infielders						
29	Boone, Bret	R	R	5–10	180	4/6/69	El Cajon, CA
20	Branson, Jeff	L	R	6–0	180	1/26/67	Waynesboro, MS
18	Costo, Tim	R	R	6–5	230	2/16/69	Melrose Park, IL
12	Greene, Willie	L	R	5–11	180	9/23/71	Milledgeville, GA
29	Harris, Lenny	L	R	5–10	220	10/28/64	Miami, FL
11	Larkin, Barry	R	R	6–0	190	4/28/64	Cincinnati, OH
23	Morris, Hal	L	L	6–4	215	4/9/65	Fort Rucker, AL
9	Stillwell, Kurt	R	R	5–11	185	6/4/65	Glendale, CA
	Outfielders						
50	Gordon, Keith	R	R	6–1	200	1/22/69	Bethesda, MD
22	Howard, Thomas	B	R	6–2	205	12/11/64	Middletown, OH
30	Hunter, Brian R.	R	L	6–0	195	3/4/68	El Toro, CA
7	Mitchell, Kevin	R	R	5–11	210	1/13/62	San Diego, CA
21	Sanders, Deion	L	L	6–1	195	8/9/67	Ft. Myers, FL
16	Sanders, Reggie	R	R	6–1	180	12/1/67	Florence, SC

1995 Schedule

April

S	M	T	W	T	F	S
						1
2	3 CHI	4 CHI	5 CHI	6 CHI	7 SD	8 SD
9 SD	10 SD	11 CHI	12 CHI	13 SF	14 SF	15 SF
16 SF	17	18 LA	19 LA	20 LA	21 SD	22 SD
23 SF	24 LA	25 LA	26 LA	27 SD	28 SD	29 SD
30 SD						

May

S	M	T	W	T	F	S
	1	2 PHI	3 PHI	4 PHI	5 NY	6 NY
7 NY	8	9 FLO	10 FLO	11 ATL	12 ATL	13 ATL
14 ATL	15	16 MON	17 MON	18	19 COL	20 COL
21 COL	22 HOU	23 HOU	24 HOU	25	26 STL	27 STL
28 STL	29	30 PIT	31 PIT			

June

S	M	T	W	T	F	S
				1 PIT	2 STL	3 STL
4 STL	5 PIT	6 PIT	7 PIT	8 HOU	9 HOU	10 HOU
11 MON	12 COL	13 COL	14 COL	15	16 MON	17 FLO
18 MON	19 ATL	20 ATL	21 ATL	22 FLO	23 FLO	24 FLO
25 FLO	26	27 PHI	28 PHI	29 PHI	30 NY	

July

S	M	T	W	T	F	S
						1 NY
2 NY	3	4 SF	5 SF	6 SF	7 LA	8 LA
9 LA	10	11 ★	12	13 CHI	14 CHI	15 CHI
16 CHI	17 SD	18 SD	19 SD	20	21 CHI	22 CHI
23 CHI	24 SD	25 SD	26 SF	27 SF	28 LA	29 LA
30 LA	31					

August

S	M	T	W	T	F	S
		1 NY	2 NY	3 NY	4 PHI	5 PHI
6 PHI	7	8 ATL	9 ATL	10 ATL	11 FLO	12 FLO
13 FLO	14 COL	15 COL	16 COL	17	18 HOU	19 HOU
20 HOU	21 STL	22 STL	23 STL	24 STL	25 PIT	26 PIT
27 PIT	28 STL	29 STL	30 STL	31 PIT		

Sept/Oct

S	M	T	W	T	F	S
					1 PIT	2 PIT
3 PIT	4 HOU	5 HOU	6 HOU	7	8 COL	9 COL
10 COL	11 FLO	12 FLO	13 FLO	14	15 ATL	16 ATL
17 ATL	18 MON	19 MON	20 MON	21	22 PHI	23 PHI
24 PHI	25 NY	26 NY	27 NY	28 MON	29 MON	30 MON
1 MON	2					

☐ Home ☐ Away ★ All-Star Game

Riverfront Stadium

Capacity: 52,952

Turf: Artificial

Dimensions:
LF Line: 330'
RF Line: 330'
Center: 404'
Alleys: 375'

Tickets:
(513) 421-7337

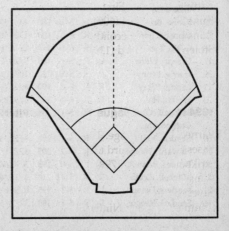

1994 Batting Order

1. Deion Sanders (Center Field)
2. Barry Larkin (Shorstop)
3. Hal Morris (First Base)
4. Kevin Mitchell (Left Field)
5. Reggie Sanders (Right Field)
6. Tony Fernandez (Third Base)
7. Bret Boone (Second Base)
8. Eddie Taubensee (Catcher)
9. Pitcher

1994 Team Record
66–48 (.579); First in NL Central

NL East	W	L	NL Central	W	L	NL West	W	L
Atlanta	5	5	Chicago	7	5	Colorado	4	4
Florida	7	5	Cincinnati	—	—	Los Angeles	3	6
Montreal	4	2	Houston	4	6	San Diego	8	2
New York	2	4	Pittsburgh	9	3	S. Francisco	7	2
Philadelphia	4	2	St. Louis	2	2			
Total	22	18		22	16		22	14

1994 National League Team Rank Batting

Batting Average: First (.286)
Runs Scored: First (609)
Runs Batted In: Second (569)
Stolen Bases: Third (119)
Slugging Percentage: First (.449)
On-Base Percentage: First (.350)

1994 National League Team Rank Pitching

Earned Run Average: Third (3.78)
Bases On Balls: Third (339)
Strikeouts: Fourth (799)
Wins: Third (66)
Saves: Ninth (27)
Complete Games: Ninth (6)

Cincinnati Reds MVP

Kevin Mitchell   No. 7/ OF

Born: 1/13/62, San Diego, CA
Height: 5' 11"   **Weight:** 210
Bats: Right   **Throws:** Right
1994 OBP: .429   **SLG:** .681

Combine the looping, powerful swing of Harmon Killebrew with the weight shift of Cecil Fielder, and you'll have quite a hitter. Kevin Mitchell is that hitter. If not for assorted foot injuries, Mitchell would be one of baseball's most consistent sluggers. As it stands, he's a true titan when healthy.

In 1989, Mitchell blasted forty-seven homers playing in an awful park for hitters, Candlestick Park. His current home field, Riverfront Stadium, is friendly to sluggers, and Mitchell was on a pace to hit fifty last season.

Mitchell finished in the NL top ten in batting average (fifth), home runs (sixth), walks (eighth), on-base percentage (third), and slugging percentage (second).

His hitting strategy versus lefties is to drive the ball into the right field gap, often lining a rope over the wall. Against righthanders, Mitchell will spray the ball to all fields, pulling the inside fastball into the stands. Clearly, if Mitchell is motivated and healthy, he's in the unique class of hitters, such as Albert Belle and Frank Thomas, who can maintain a batting average over .300 without suffering a concurrent loss of power.

As a fielder, Mitchell is considered a liability, though he isn't nearly the worst in the league. He made four errors in '94.

	G	AB	H	2B	3B	HR	RS	RBI	BB	SB	BA
1994	95	310	101	18	1	30	57	77	59	2	.326
Career	1088	3742	1070	201	24	220	582	689	436	29	.286
Projected	146	482	154	29	3	37	84	105	63	2	.327

Bret Boone   No. 29/2B

Born: 4/6/69, El Cajon, CA
Height: 5' 10"   **Weight:** 180
Bats: Right   **Throws:** Right
1994 OBP: .368   **SLG:** .491

Hoping for a fresh start with former slugging second baseman Davey Johnson's Reds, after not seeing eye-to-eye with Lou Piniella in Seattle, Bret Boone outshone all expectations by making consistent contact while maintaining the power stroke on which his reputation was based. Boone's play in the field needs work; he made twelve errors at second base in '94.

	G	AB	H	2B	3B	HR	RS	RBI	BB	SB	BA
1994	108	381	122	5	2	12	59	68	24	3	.320
Career	217	781	215	21	4	28	105	121	45	6	.275
Projected	160	590	186	16	4	23	85	100	39	5	.303

Hector Carrasco   No. 58/P

Born: 10/22/62, San Pedro Macoris, DR
Height: 6' 2"   **Weight:** 175
Bats: Right   **Throws:** Right
Opp. Batting Average: .210

Carrasco was one of the National League's more impressive middle relievers last year. The Reds hope he can harness his excellent stuff and cut down on the high number of free passes he allowed. He's adept at pitching his way out of trouble, which helped keep his ERA low, despite the walks. Carrasco gave up just three homers in '94.

	G	GS	IP	ERA	H	BB	SO	W	L	SV
1994	45	0	56.1	2.24	42	30	41	5	6	6
Career	45	0	56.1	2.24	42	30	41	5	6	6
Projected			No projection. Player was a rookie in 1994.								

Tony Fernandez 3B

Born: 8/6/62, San Pedro Macoris, DR
Height: 6' 2" **Weight:** 175
Bats: Both **Throws:** Right
1994 OBP: .361 **SLG:** .426

After allowing Chris Sabo to file for free agency, the Reds installed former Blue Jays shortstop Tony Fernandez at third base. Fernandez did solidify the position defensively. He didn't duplicate his past production on the basepaths, stealing at a dismal 63% success rate. Winter trade rumors suggested that he could be a Yankee in 1995.

	G	AB	H	2B	3B	HR	RS	RBI	BB	SB	BA
1994	105	366	102	18	6	8	50	50	44	12	.279
Career	1575	6024	1714	292	87	61	790	593	496	214	.285
Projected	151	534	143	24	10	8	68	67	59	19	.274

Erik Hanson No. 39/ P

Born: 5/18/65, Kinnelon, NJ
Height: 6' 6" **Weight:** 215
Bats: Right **Throws:** Right
Opp. Batting Average: .283

Five years removed from an eighteen-win season, Hanson enters this year with consistency as his goal. Possessor of a debilitating curveball, Hanson has struggled with injuries and lack of confidence, but he did finish strongly in '94 after a rocky start. Striking out four for every walk allowed, Hanson pitched better than his ERA reflected.

	G	GS	IP	ERA	H	BB	SO	W	L	SV
1994	22	21	122.2	4.11	137	23	101	5	5	0
Career	167	164	1090.0	3.74	1086	308	841	61	59	0
Projected	30	29	192.0	3.71	200	47	150	9	10	0

Barry Larkin   No. 11/ SS

Born: 4/28/64, Cincinnati, OH
Height: 6' 0"   **Weight:** 190
Bats: Right   **Throws:** Right
1994 OBP: .369   **SLG:** .419

Larkin's demeanor is quiet, but his bat and glove speak volumes. He's a patient hitter with great bat control, quick wrists, and decent power. His stolen-base percentage in '94 was so high (93%) that he probably should be making more attempts. His great range afield has led to high error totals in past seasons, but he makes plays that most shortstops wouldn't even imagine.

	G	AB	H	2B	3B	HR	RS	RBI	BB	SB	BA
1994	110	427	119	23	5	9	78	52	64	26	.279
Career	1045	3933	1164	193	38	87	613	471	388	188	.296
Projected	160	624	188	33	6	13	105	80	89	31	.299

Hal Morris   No. 23/ 1B

Born: 4/9/65, Fort Rucker, AL
Height: 6' 4"   **Weight:** 215
Bats: Left   **Throws:** Left
1994 OBP: .385   **SLG:** .491

Though he often appears awkward and uncomfortable due to his use of a timing mechanism that entails constant movent in the batters box, Morris is a classic lefty high-average hitter. Last season he avoided injury and put together career bests in RBI and HR rates, to go with the fourth-highest batting average in the National League.

	G	AB	H	2B	3B	HR	RS	RBI	BB	SB	BA
1994	112	436	146	30	4	10	60	78	34	6	.335
Career	601	2035	637	124	11	44	274	279	181	33	.313
Projected	160	618	206	37	3	13	83	97	52	6	.330

Tim Pugh   No. 40/ P

Born: 1/26/67, Lake Tahoe, CA
Height: 6' 6"   **Weight:** 225
Bats: Right   **Throws:** Right
Opp. Batting Average: .314

Looking at the tall, lanky Pugh, you might figure him as a Randy Johnson type, but in fact Pugh relies on finesse and control. In 1994, control was what he lacked; Pugh walked more batters than he struck out. The Reds have been tantalized by Pugh's occassional brushes with unhittability, but he'll need to be more consistent in 1995.

	G	GS	IP	ERA	H	BB	SO	W	L	SV
1994	10	9	47.2	6.04	60	26	24	3	3	0
Career	48	43	257.1	4.93	307	98	136	17	20	0
Projected	22	19	115.0	5.43	141	46	64	7	10	0

Jose Rijo   No. 27/ P

Born: 5/13/65, San Cristobal, DR
Height: 6' 2"   **Weight:** 210
Bats: Right   **Throws:** Right
Opp. Batting Average: .265

Rijo is perhaps second only to Greg Maddux in the upper echelon of NL starters. With his past injuries no longer a factor, the consistent Rijo had a fine '94 season, though he did see his ERA finish above 3.00 for the first time since 1988. Rijo collects Ks in bunches when his change-up (the NL's best) is working. He finished second in the NL in strikeouts per nine innings (8.9).

	G	GS	IP	ERA	H	BB	SO	W	L	SV
1994	26	26	172.1	3.08	177	52	171	9	6	0
Career	318	246	1717.0	3.13	1526	612	1494	106	83	3
Projected	35	35	244.0	2.72	225	65	227	13	9	0

John Roper   No. 44/ P

Born: 11/21/71, Southern Pines, NC
Height: 6' 0"   **Weight:** 175
Bats: Right   **Throws:** Right
Opp. Batting Average: .255

Roper has been the talk of the Reds' minor league system, and though he'd been called up for a cup of coffee in '93, last year was his first extended taste of the major league brew. The results were mixed but hopeful. Roper has a fine curveball, but if it hangs or doesn't find the strikezone, he's vulnerable to the longball. Roper is a good bet to keep developing.

	G	GS	IP	ERA	H	BB	SO	W	L	SV
1994	16	15	92.0	4.50	90	30	51	6	2	0
Career	32	30	172.0	5.03	182	66	105	8	7	0
Projected	19	18	100.0	5.03	106	39 .	61	5	4	0

Johnny Ruffin   No. 47/ P

Born: 7/29/71, Butler, AL
Height: 6' 3"   **Weight:** 175
Bats: Right   **Throws:** Right
Opp. Batting Average: .223

1994's rookie-appearances leader, Ruffin was everything the Reds hoped he would be. He showed good command of his above-average fastball-curveball-slider repertoire, and should find a place in the starting rotation soon. Ruffin has been favorably compared to Dwight Gooden (circa 1985). Ruffin was first signed by the White Sox when he was sixteen years old.

	G	GS	IP	ERA	H	BB	SO	W	L	SV
1994	51	0	70.0	3.09	57	27	44	7	2	1
Career	72	0	108.0	3.26	93	38	74	9	3	3
Projected	44	0	67.0	3.26	57	23	46	6	2	2

Deion Sanders   No. 21/ OF

Born: 8/9/67, Fort Meyers, FL
Height: 6' 1"   **Weight:** 195
Bats: Left   **Throws:** Left
1994 OBP: .341   **SLG:** .381

His upward potential as a baseball player is difficult to measure because he combines a formidable package of physical skills with an obvious lack of exclusive commitment to professional baseball. Sanders has Ferrari-type speed and a quick bat, but he isn't on base enough to be a first-rate leadoff man. Clearly, Sanders is the best defensive back in the Reds' outfield.

	G	AB	H	2B	3B	HR	RS	RBI	BB	SB	BA
1994	92	375	106	17	4	4	58	28	32	38	.283
Career	409	1240	326	46	28	27	201	113	94	103	.263
Projected	118	426	129	24	7	7	68	38	33	39	.291

Reggie Sanders   No. 16/ OF

Born: 12/1/67, Florence, SC
Height: 6' 1"   **Weight:** 180
Bats: Right   **Throws:** Right
1994 OBP: .332   **SLG:** .480

An intriguing combination of amazing raw skills makes it tempting to project the talented Sanders as an inevitable superstar, but it remains to be seen if he will be able to fill the holes in his explosive swing. He hit .147 in his last sixty-eight at-bats before the work stoppage, and his strikeout totals were on a par with Cecil Fielder (about one for every four at-bats).

	G	AB	H	2B	3B	HR	RS	RBI	BB	SB	BA
1994	107	400	105	20	8	17	66	62	41	21	.263
Career	370	1321	353	62	18	50	224	184	140	65	.267
Projected	149	567	165	24	8	24	103	95	61	32	.280

John Smiley   No. 57/ P

Born: 3/17/65, Phoenixville, PA
Height: 6' 4"   **Weight:** 200
Bats: Left   **Throws:** Left
Opp. Batting Average: .275

The veteran Smiley won twenty games in 1991, but he hasn't shown that form in quite awhile, largely do to a bone spur that cost him much of the '93 campaign. Last year, Smiley showed flashes of his past effectiveness, especially in his 3/1 K/BB ratio. If his arm holds up, Smiley could take another step forward in 1995, possibly reaching the fifteen-win mark.

	G	GS	IP	ERA	H	BB	SO	W	L	SV
1994	24	24	158.2	3.86	169	37	112	11	10	0
Career	272	193	1359.1	3.70	1278	362	869	90	70	4
Projected	25	25	158.0	4.56	170	40	102	8	11	0

Eddie Taubensee No. 10/ C

Born: 10/31/68, Beeville, TX
Height: 6' 4"   **Weight:** 205
Bats: Left   **Throws:** Right
1994 OBP: .332   **SLG:** .476

Taubensee, who was traded by the Astros after they gave up Kenny Lofton to acquire him, played very well for Cincinnati in Joe Oliver's absence. Taubensee is a low-ball hitter with extra-base pop. His arm is below average for a catcher. The Reds signed Damon Berryhill during the winter, so Taubensee may have to battle for a starting job.

	G	AB	H	2B	3B	HR	RS	RBI	BB	SB	BA
1994	66	187	53	8	2	8	29	21	15	2	.283
Career	290	838	207	36	4	22	83	99	72	5	.247
Projected	98	302	86	13	2	11	36	42	24	2	.274

Colorado
ROCKIES

1995 Scouting Report

Outfielders: Dante Bichette (RF) was the Rockies' lone All-Star last season. Mike Kingery stepped in to play center field when exciting Ellis Burks went on the DL for seventy games. Kingery was outstanding in every respect. Eric Young brings good range to left field, though he may not be a full-time outfielder in '95.

Infielders: Second base will be a potpourri of Roberto Mejia, Pedro Castellano, and Vinny Castilla. Walt Weiss anchored the infield from his shortstop position. Third baseman Charlie Hayes is error prone, but he almost makes up for it at the plate. Andres Galarraga (1B) has terrorized opposing pitchers for the past two years.

Catchers: Joe Girardi has a fine reputation for handling pitchers, and his glove and arm are both above average. He hits just enough to play everyday.

Starting Pitchers: The starting staff was awful last season, but there was improvement made from 1993, and there could be more progress this year. Marvin Freeman was the rotation's success story, leading the NL in winning percentage (.833). David Nied showed glimpses of fulfilling his ace-type potential. Armando Reynoso, who started on Opening Day last season, will try to come back from elbow surgery. The other slots will be filled by Lance Painter, Kevin Ritz, or Greg W. Harris, each of whom pitched inauspiciously in '94.

Relief Pitchers: The job of lefty closer falls to veteran Bruce Ruffin. Setup is handled by Mike Munoz and Willie Blair. There's room for improvement if someone develops.

Manager: Don Baylor (120–159) has done wonders for the Rockies' sluggers, especially Andres Galarraga.

1995 Outlook

The Rockies have made a conscious committment to providing their fans with a team of established major leaguers, as opposed to building with youthful prospects. It's hard to knock a strategy that has produced record attendance numbers—the team was on pace to draw 4,687,840 fans in 1994, which would have smashed the single-season attendance mark the Rockies had set in '93, but there's an on-field price to pay.

The Rockies don't resemble a typical expansion team. They actually have the personnel of a club in decline, with the average age of the batting order being 30.5 years old, an age at which most hitters are past their peak. Nevertheless, the two oldest members of the lineup, Galarraga and Kingery, who are both thirty-three, put together career seasons for the Rockies last season.

The Colorado pitching staff allowed twelve earned runs the day before the work stoppage, putting them solidly into last place in team ERA for the year. Playing in hitters' heaven, Mile High Stadium, didn't help. The only impressive starter was former Atlanta setup man Marvin Freeman, and the prospects are scarce. The Rockies desperately need a breakthrough season from David Nied, who has yet to live up to his status as the team's first pick in the expansion draft.

The Rockies' offense is fun to watch. They've got the ideal atmosphere for explosive run scoring—the air is thin in Denver, and the ball carries very well. Colorado has a lineup of sluggers who thrive in a park that's conducive to the longball, and it's arguable that the careers of Hayes, Bichette, and Galarraga were rescued in part by the light air molecules in Denver. The team is geared toward big innings with the bat and damage control in the field.

We suspect that the Rockies might soon begin paying for their investment in older players, but anything can happen in the NL West, where no team is a clear favorite.

1995 Colorado Rockies Roster

Manager: Don Baylor
Coaches: Larry Bearnarth, Gene Glynn, Ron Hassey, Art Have,
Rick Mathews, Bill Plummer, Don Zimmer

No.	Pitchers	B	T	HT	WT	DOB	Birthplace
19	Blair, Willie	R	R	6–1	185	12/18/65	Paintsville, KY
44	Freeman, Marvin	R	R	6–7	222	4/10/63	Chicago, IL
27	Harris, Greg W.	R	R	6–2	195	12/1/63	Greensboro, NC
48	Hawblitzel, Ryan	R	R	6–2	170	4/30/71	W. Palm Beach, FL
40	Holmes, Darren	R	R	6–0	199	4/25/66	Asheville, NC
45	Leskanic, Curt	R	R	6–0	180	4/2/68	Homestead, PA
54	Moore, Marcus	B	R	6–5	195	11/2/70	Oakland, CA
43	Munoz, Mike	L	L	6–2	200	7/12/65	Baldwin Park, CA
17	Nied, David	R	R	6–2	185	12/22/68	Dallas, TX
28	Painter, Lance	L	L	6–1	195	7/21/67	Bedford, England
39	Reed, Steve	R	R	6–2	202	3/1/66	Los Angeles, CA
42	Reynoso, Armando	R	R	6–0	186	5/1/66	San Luis Potosi, Mexico
18	Ruffin, Bruce	B	L	6–2	209	10/4/63	Lubbock, TX
	Catchers						
7	Girardi, Joe	R	R	5–11	195	10/14/64	Peoria, IL
33	Owens, Jayhawk	R	R	6–1	200	2/10/69	Cincinnati, OH
5	Tatum, Jim	R	R	6–2	200	10/9/67	San Diego, CA
	Infielders						
15	Castellano, Pedro	R	R	6–1	175	3/11/70	Lara, Venezuela
9	Castilla, Vinny	R	R	6–1	175	7/4/67	Oaxaca, Mexico
14	Galarraga, Andres	R	R	6–3	235	6/18/61	Caracas, Venezuela
13	Hayes, Charlie	R	R	6–0	207	5/29/65	Hattiesburg, MS
8	Mejia, Roberto	R	R	5–11	160	4/14/72	Hato Mayor, DR
23	Vander Wal, John	L	L	6–2	190	4/29/66	Grand Rapids, MI
22	Weiss, Walt	B	R	6–0	175	11/28/63	Tuxedo, NY
	Outfielders						
10	Bichette, Dante	R	R	6–3	225	11/18/63	W. Palm Beach, FL
26	Burks, Ellis	R	R	6–2	205	9/11/64	Vicksburg, MS
12	Kingery, Mike	L	L	6–0	185	3/29/61	St. James, MN
21	Young, Eric	R	R	5–9	180	11/26/66	Jacksonville, FL

1995 Schedule

April

S	M	T	W	T	F	S
						1
2	3	4	5	6	7 PHI	8 PHI
9 PHI	10 MON	11 MON	12	13 PHI	14 PHI	15 PHI
16 PHI	17 MON	18 MON	19	20 HOU	21 HOU	22 HOU
23 HOU	24 NY	25 NY	26 NY	27 HOU	28 HOU	29 HOU
30 HOU						

May

S	M	T	W	T	F	S
	1 SD	2 SD	3 SD	4	5 LA	6 LA
7 LA	8	9 SF	10 SF	11 SF	12 FLO	13 FLO
14 FLO	15 ATL	16 ATL	17 ATL	18 ATL	19 CIN	20 CIN
21 CIN	22 CHI	23 CHI	24 CHI	25	26 PIT	27 PIT
28 PIT	29 STL	30 STL	31 STL			

June

S	M	T	W	T	F	S
				1	2 PIT	3 PIT
4 PIT	5 STL	6 STL	7 STL	8 CHI	9 CHI	10 CHI
11 CHI	12 CIN	13 CIN	14 CIN	15	16 ATL	17 ATL
18 ATL	19 FLO	20 FLO	21 FLO	22 SD	23 SD	24 SD
25 SD	26	27 SF	28 SF	29 LA	30 LA	

July

S	M	T	W	T	F	S
						1 LA
2 LA	3 HOU	4 HOU	5 MON	6 MON	7 MON	8 MON
9 MON	10	11 ★	12	13 NY	14 NY	15 NY
16 NY	17 PHI	18 PHI	19 PHI	20	21 NY	22 NY
23 NY	24 PHI	25 PHI	26 HOU	27 HOU	28 MON	29 MON
30 MON	31 MON					

August

S	M	T	W	T	F	S
		1 LA	2 LA	3 LA	4 SD	5 SD
6 SD	7	8 FLO	9 FLO	10 FLO	11 ATL	12 ATL
13 ATL	14 CIN	15 CIN	16 CIN	17 CHI	18 CHI	19 CHI
20 CHI	21	22 PIT	23 PIT	24 PIT	25 STL	26 STL
27 STL	28 PIT	29 PIT	30 PIT	31		

Sept/Oct

S	M	T	W	T	F	S
					1 STL	2 STL
3 STL	4 CHI	5	6 CHI	7	8 CIN	9 CIN
10 CIN	11 ATL	12 ATL	13 ATL	14	15 FLO	16 FLO
17 FLO	18 SD	19 SD	20 SD	21 SF	22 SF	23 SF
24 SF	25 LA	26 LA	27 LA	28 SF	29 SF	30 SF
1 SF	2					

 Home   Away   ★ All-Star Game

Coors Field

Capacity: 50,000

Turf: Grass

Dimensions:
LF Line: 347'
RF Line: 350'
Center: 415'
Left CF: 420'
Right CF: 424'

Tickets:
(303) 762-5437

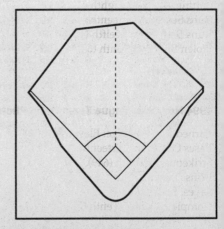

1994 Batting Order

1. Walt Weiss (Shortstop)
2. Eric Young (Left Field)
3. Dante Bichette (Right Field)
4. Andres Galarraga (First Base)
5. Charlie Hayes (Third Base)
6. Mike Kingery (Center Field)
7. Joe Girardi (Catcher)
8. Nelson Liriano (Second Base)
9. Pitcher

1994 Team Record
53–64 (.453); Third in NL West

NL East	W	L	NL Central	W	L	NL West	W	L
Atlanta	2	8	Chicago	6	6	Colorado	—	—
Florida	3	9	Cincinnati	4	4	Los Angeles	4	6
Montreal	4	2	Houston	5	5	San Diego	5	5
New York	5	1	Pittsburgh	2	3	S. Francisco	3	7
Philadelphia	2	4	St. Louis	8	4			
Total	16	24		25	22		12	18

1994 National League Team Rank Batting

Batting Average: Eighth (.266)
Runs Scored: Thirteenth (468)
Runs Batted In: Twelfth (451)
Stolen Bases: Eleventh (65)
Slugging Percentage: Eleventh (.396)
On-Base Percentage: Tenth (.330)

1994 National League Team Rank Pitching

Earned Run Average: Eleventh (4.50)
Bases On Balls: Thirteenth (428)
Strikeouts: Twelfth (649)
Wins: Twelfth (51)
Saves: Fourth (30)
Complete Games: Tenth (5)

Colorado Rockies MVP

Andres Galarraga   No. 14/1B

Born: 6/18/61, Caracas, Venezuela
Height: 6' 3"   **Weight:** 245
Bats: Right   **Throws:** Right
1994 OBP: .356   **SLG:** .592

Continuing from where he left off in '93, "The Big Cat" had as many round-trip shots through June of last year as he'd had in the entire previous season (22). He finished the short season with the best home run total of his career. Galarraga's open stance, taught to him in '92 by Don Baylor when Baylor was the batting coach in St. Louis, allows Galarraga to spray the ball to all fields, accounting for his .346 batting average over the past two seasons combined.

Galarraga went from stardom in 1988 to almost slumping his way out of the majors in '92. He's as impatient as ever, striking out nearly five times as often as he walks, but he makes more contact now than before the stance adjustment. If he does get ahead in the count and can look for the fastball, he's as dangerous as anyone in professional baseball. For such a free swinger, Galarraga is as consistent as a mountain. He went hitless in two consecutive games only three times all season. Galarraga finished in the NL's top ten in RBIs, home runs, total bases, extra-base hits, and slugging.

There's no reason to expect a dramatic decline in Galarraga's production anytime soon, and his smooth glovework has always been an asset. The return to excellence of Andres Galarraga, thanks in part to Don Baylor, has been one of baseball's remarkable comeback stories.

	G	AB	H	2B	3B	HR	RS	RBI	BB	SB	BA
1994	103	417	133	21	0	31	77	85	19	8	.319
Career	1165	4294	1216	238	20	169	580	655	278	69	.283
Projected	139	543	180	34	2	32	89	110	26	6	.339

Dante Bichette   No. 10/ OF

Born: 11/19/63, West Palm Beach, FL
Height: 6' 3"   **Weight:** 235
Bats: Right   **Throws:** Right
1994 OBP: .334   **SLG:** .548

Bichette has established surprising consistency power hitter. In 1994 he increased his longball frequency to one in every eighteen at-bats (from one in every twenty-five in '93), while hitting over .300 and stealing twenty-one bases at a respectable rate of success (72%). Bichette has a much-talked-about throwing arm, and he tied for third in the NL in outfield assists.

	G	AB	H	2B	3B	HR	RS	RBI	BB	SB	BA
1994	116	484	147	33	2	27	74	95	19	21	.304
Career	681	2387	661	145	13	86	311	360	107	75	.277
Projected	150	604	189	45	4	29	100	110	28	21	.310

Ellis Burks   No. 26/ OF

Born: 9/11/64, Vicksburg, MS
Height: 6' 2"   **Weight:** 205
Bats: Right   **Throws:** Right
1994 OBP: .388   **SLG:** .678

Burks shot from the gate like a thoroughbred; he was hitting .354 with 12 HRs when he sprained his left wrist on May 17, forcing him onto the DL till August. A prototype power/speed player, Burks hasn't stayed healthy enough to be a star, but he's extremely valuable when he's in the lineup. At the time of the injury, Burks was slugging .738.

	G	AB	H	2B	3B	HR	RS	RBI	BB	SB	BA
1994	42	149	48	8	3	13	33	24	16	3	.322
Career	910	3442	970	192	34	123	548	485	327	102	.282
Projected	65	227	67	11	3	11	39	35	27	3	.291

Marvin Freeman No. 44/ P

Born: 4/10/63, Chicago, IL
Height: 6' 7" **Weight:** 222
Bats: Right **Throws:** Right
Opp. Batting Average: .262

A recurring theme for the Rockies was played beautifully by Freeman. His '94 success was completely out of context with his dismal past. He missed qualifying for league recognition by 4.1 innings, but led the NL in winning percentage and was third in ERA. Consistent mechanics and a marked improvement in control made all the difference.

	G	GS	IP	ERA	H	BB	SO	W	L	SV
1994	19	18	112.2	2.80	113	23	67	10	2	0
Career	172	36	367.1	3.77	339	150	250	25	12	5
Projected	23	10	79.0	3.36	79	19	53	7	1	0

Joe Girardi No. 7/ C

Born: 10/14/64, Peoria, IL
Height: 5' 11" **Weight:** 200
Bats: Right **Throws:** Right
1994 OBP: .321 **SLG:** .364

Girardi has made the most of his limited abilities, and he managed to stay in the Rockies' lineup on an everyday basis, unlike in his injury-plagued three previous seasons. Girardi hasn't got much pop, but he was willing to take some bases on balls in '94, doubling his walks from '93. He's respected by scouts as an intelligent handler of pitchers.

	G	AB	H	2B	3B	HR	RS	RBI	BB	SB	BA
1994	93	330	91	9	4	4	47	34	21	3	.276
Career	484	1533	415	62	12	10	155	135	98	19	.271
Projected	143	517	149	19	7	6	67	53	37	7	.286

Greg W. Harris   No. 46/ P

Born: 12/1/63, Greensboro, NC
Height: 6' 2"   **Weight:** 191
Bats: Right   **Throws:** Right
Opp. Batting Average: .300

Somewhere inside the body of Greg Harris, an excellent pitcher is trapped. One of baseball's enigmas, he hasn't been the same since arriving in Colorado in mid-season of '93. He's endured (gulp) twenty losses to go with four wins since joining the Rockies. Harris still throws a nifty curveball, but scouts say his velocity has decreased.

	G	GS	IP	ERA	H	BB	SO	W	L	SV
1994	29	19	130.0	6.65	154	52	82	3	12	1
Career	236	103	876.2	3.80	833	287	584	45	59	16
Projected	37	31	204.0	5.34	226	70	118	8	17	1

Charlie Hayes   No. 13/ 3B

Born: 5/29/65, Hattiesburg, MS
Height: 6' 0"   **Weight:** 224
Bats: Right   **Throws:** Right
1994 OBP: .348   **SLG:** .433

Hayes was productive, if unspectacular, following his surprising '93 performance. He's not an easy out, and though he suffered a slight power outage in comparison to the previous season, he can still pull the fastball a long way. Hayes hit .317 at home, .260 on the road. At third base Hayes is erratic, one of the worst percentage fielders in the league.

	G	AB	H	2B	3B	HR	RS	RBI	BB	SB	BA
1994	113	423	122	23	4	10	46	50	36	3	.288
Career	800	2841	758	145	10	83	300	367	162	27	.267
Projected	158	591	180	41	4	21	81	89	47	8	.301

Mike Kingery No. 12/ OF

Born: 3/29/61, St. James, MN
Height: 6' 0" **Weight:** 185
Bats: Left **Throws:** Left
1994 OBP: .402 **SLG:** .532

He's lasted through fifteen seasons of pro ball and five big league teams, but 1994 was Kingery's breakthrough campaign. He set personal bests for average, runs, and doubles. He finished third in the league in triples. Kingery is very versatile, batting from various spots in the order and filling in for Ellis Burks in center field. He's a useful player, even if he doesn't hit .349 again.

	G	AB	H	2B	3B	HR	RS	RBI	BB	SB	BA
1994	105	301	105	27	8	4	56	41	30	5	.349
Career	583	1408	384	78	20	19	194	155	123	30	.273
Projected			No projection. Player was not in the majors in 1993.								

Nelson Liriano No. 4/ 2B

Born: 6/3/64, Puerta Plata, DR
Height: 5' 10" **Weight:** 178
Bats: Both **Throws:** Right
1994 OBP: .357 **SLG:** .396

Liriano returned from baseball's netherworld to assume a starting spot in mid-May. He hit just a buck fifty from the right side of the plate, .274 from the left, and he was one of the few Rockies not helped by his home park. He's a decent second baseman, but not the same player who started for Toronto in 1989. Liriano has signed with the Pittsburgh Pirates for 1995.

	G	AB	H	2B	3B	HR	RS	RBI	BB	SB	BA
1994	87	255	65	17	5	3	39	31	42	0	.255
Career	516	1635	424	73	24	16	234	161	168	55	.259
Projected	134	407	113	23	8	5	47	68	61	6	.276

David Nied   No. 17/ P

Born: 12/22/68, Dallas, TX
Height: 6' 2"   **Weight:** 188
Bats: Right   **Throws:** Right
Opp. Batting Average: .287

Colorado was hoping that Nied (pronounced like "need") would make progress
and remain healthy in '94, and that's gen-
erally what they got. The first pick in the '92 expansion draft,
Nied came out of the pitching-rich Atlanta farm system. He had
trouble with walks last year, and lefthanders tended to feast on
his fastball when he had control problems.

	G	GS	IP	ERA	H	BB	SO	W	L	SV
1994	22	22	122.0	4.80	137	47	74	9	7	0
Career	44	40	232.0	4.58	246	94	139	17	16	0
Projected	23	23	125.0	4.95	141	53	72	8	10	0

Armando Reynoso   No. 42/ P

Born: 5/1/66, San Luis Potosi, Mexico
Height: 6' 0"   **Weight:** 196
Bats: Right   **Throws:** Right
Opp. Batting Average: .278

The Rockies played Reynoso's arm to the
tune of thirty starts in 1993, then heard the
sour note as he lost most of 1994 to elbow
surgery. When his arm is sound, Reynoso has a virtual one-man
band's repertoire, changing speeds, deliveries, and pitches at
will. The Rockies are hoping for Reynoso to come back as their
number-three starter.

	G	GS	IP	ERA	H	BB	SO	W	L	SV
1994	9	9	52.1	4.82	54	22	25	3	4	0
Career	48	45	272.1	4.36	297	97	154	18	16	1
Projected				No projection. Player was injured in 1994.						

Kevin Ritz   No. 30/ P

Born: 6/8/65, Eatontown, NJ
Height: 6' 4"   **Weight:** 220
Bats: Right   **Throws:** Right
Opp. Batting Average: .303

Ritz is just one of a group of contenders for a spot in the Rockies' rotation. His best outing of the '94 season was a 1–0 victory in the team's rain-shortened season finale. Ritz seems to have recovered from elbow surgery that wiped out his '93 campaign. He doesn't have extraordinary stuff, but he's got as good a shot as anyone to start for the Rockies.

	G	GS	IP	ERA	H	BB	SO	W	L	SV
1994	15	15	73.2	5.62	88	35	53	5	6	0
Career	65	47	250.2	5.78	282	159	178	11	24	0
Projected			No projection. Player was injured in 1993.							

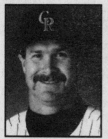

Bruce Ruffin   No. 18/ P

Born: 10/4/63, Lubbock, TX
Height: 6' 2"   **Weight:** 212
Bats: Both   **Throws:** Left
Opp. Batting Average: .253

Ruffin is a well-traveled veteran, but last year was his best season. He ranked sixth in the majors in appearances and tied for eighth in the NL in saves. Ruffin had the rare distinction of pitching better at Mile High than on the road, due to his ability to avoid giving up the longball. He doesn't fit anyone's vision of a stopper, but he's put together back-to-back decent campaigns.

	G	GS	IP	ER	H	BB	SO	W	L	SV
1994	56	0	55.2	4.04	55	30	65	4	5	16
Career	338	152	1142.1	4.25	1246	499	715	53	74	21
Projected	67	7	114.0	3.91	116	58	111	6	6	10

Walt Weiss   No. 22/ SS

Born: 11/28/63, Tuxedo, NY
Height: 6' 0"   **Weight:** 175
Bats: Both   **Throws:** Right
1994 OBP: .336   **SLG:** .303

Weiss probably isn't cut out to be a leadoff hitter, but he was the only Rockies' player to garner at least fifty walks last season. Weiss doesn't so much slap at the ball as offer at it—he's clubbed two homers in his last 1,385 at-bats. His contribution to the team is made with the glove; Weiss is a smart shortstop with good range and a reliable arm.

	G	AB	H	2B	3B	HR	RS	RBI	BB	SB	BA
1994	110	423	106	11	4	1	58	32	56	12	.251
Career	796	2531	634	85	13	10	286	201	294	51	.250
Projected	159	553	146	15	4	1	65	43	82	11	.262

Eric Young   No. 21/ OF

Born: 5/18/67, Jacksonville, FL
Height: 5' 9"   **Weight:** 170
Bats: Right   **Throws:** Right
1994 OBP: .378   **SLG:** .430

The franchise's all-time leader in stolen bases, Young doubled his home run output in half as many at-bats from '93 to last season. Offensively, the upside of Young's potential is to become the next Devon White, minus the Gold Glove defense. He came up as a second baseman, so he's still learning the tricks of good outfield play, but his tools are solid.

	G	AB	H	2B	3B	HR	RS	RBI	BB	SB	BA
1994	90	228	62	13	1	7	37	30	38	18	.272
Career	283	850	228	30	9	11	128	83	109	66	.268
Projected	141	451	132	19	6	7	78	47	66	39	.281

Florida
MARLINS

1995 Scouting Report

Outfielders: Chuck Carr isn't on base enough to take full advantage of his speed, but he's a human highlight film in center field. Jeff Conine (LF) made the All-Star team in just his second full season. Gary Sheffield (RF) is simply the best hitter in Marlins history.

Infielders: Bret Barberie is a solid second baseman, and he's adept at getting on base. Kurt Abbott plays hard at shortstop and has some pop at the plate, but he is strikeout prone. Greg Colbrunn's (1B) injuries have prevented him from playing a full season. Jerry Browne was acquired for his veratility, but he started at third base for most of the second half. Dave Magadan plays well at both corner positions.

Catchers: Benito Santiago still has one of baseball's best arms. He's also good for ten to fifteen home runs each year.

Starting Pitchers: Chris Hammond spent non-arm-related time on the DL, but he could be ready for a big season in 1995. Mark Gardner is masterful in one start, not so in the next. Ryan Bowen will try to return from a shoulder injury. Pat Rapp posted the lowest ERA in the Marlins' brief history at 3.85. Rich Scheid looked good in five starts after being called up from Triple-A Edmonton. After a rocky second half, David Weathers will have to re-earn a place in the rotation.

Relief Pitchers: Florida's bullpen, minus injured stopper Bryan Harvey, converted thirty of thirty-six save opportunities. Robb Nen was a perfect fifteen-for-fifteen.

Manager: Rene Lachemann (115–162) has been granted a contract extension to manage the Marlins through 1997.

1995 Outlook

The Marlins delayed payment of their expansion dues in 1993, but last season the organization had its first cellar-dwelling experience. The good news is that the Fish finished two games ahead of their previous season's pace.

Florida originally took the build-from-within approach to constructing their club. But since the expansion draft, the Marlins have dealt for Gary Sheffield and Benito Santiago. Sheffield should be a perennial All-Star, while Santiago will be a solid everyday backstop until the homegrown talent has a chance to develop.

The Marlins' home field, Joe Robbie Stadium, was reported to be unfriendly to sluggers, but that speculation wasn't supported by the data in 1994. Unfortunately, the M's were out-homered at home (46–70) and on the road (48–50). The Marlins finished eleventh in the league in home runs. Florida's record in games in which they went deep was a respectable 29–31. The Fish were 22–33 minus the longball.

Interestingly, two of the majors' worst ballclubs were extremely efficient in games decided by a single run. Milwaukee was 18–10 (.643) in such contests, while the Marlins were 23–13 (.639). Such trends are often the result of blind luck, though a strong bullpen (which the Marlins have) certainly is beneficial in close games.

Florida is facing a classic problem common to all expansion teams. They have some nice talent in limited areas (quality bullpen, two All-Star position players), but their weaknesses are serious. The Fish have little starting pitching and below-average quality at both corner positions. The team doesn't have many defining characteristics; Florida isn't particularly fast or powerful, the team doesn't play solid defense (.978, the second-worst [tied] percentage in the league), and the pitching staff hasn't taken shape. The growth process will continue for the Marlins in 1995.

1995 Florida Marlins Roster

Manager: Rene Lachemann
Coaches: Rusty Kuntz, Jose Morales, Cookie Rojas, Larry Rothchild,
Rick Williams

No.	Pitchers	B	T	HT	WT	DOB	Birthplace
27	Aquino, Luis	R	R	6–1	190	5/19/65	Santurce, PR
—	Barnes, Brian	L	L	5–9	170	3/25/67	Roanoke Rapids, NC
46	Bowen, Ryan	R	R	6–0	185	2/10/68	Hanford, CA
56	De La Hoya, Javier	R	R	6–0	162	2/21/70	Durango, Mexico
50	Drahman, Brian	R	R	6–3	231	11/7/66	Kenton, KY
11	Hammond, Chris	L	L	6–1	195	1/21/66	Atlanta, GA
34	Harvey, Brian	R	R	6–2	212	6/2/63	Chattanooga, TN
42	Hernandez, Jeremy	R	R	6–6	205	7/6/66	Burbank, CA
58	Klink, Joe	R	L	5–11	175	2/3/62	Hollywood, FL
24	Lewis, Richie	R	R	5–10	175	1/25/66	Muncie, IN
44	Miller, Kurt	R	R	6–5	205	8/24/72	Tucson, AZ
31	Nen, Robb	R	R	6–4	200	11/28/69	San Pedro, CA
48	Rapp, Pat	R	R	6–3	205	7/13/67	Jennings, LA
54	Turner, Matt	R	R	6–5	215	2/18/67	Lexington, KY
35	Weathers, Dave	R	R	6–3	205	9/25/69	Lawrenceburg, TN
38	Whisenant, Matt	B	L	6–3	200	6/8/71	Los Angeles, CA
45	Vaughn, Kip	R	R	6–0	180	7/20/69	Walnut Creek, CA
	Catchers						
13	Natal, Bob	R	R	5–11	190	11/13/65	Long Beach, CA
16	O'Halloran, Greg	L	R	6–2	205	5/21/68	Toronto, Canada
9	Santiago, Benito	R	R	6–1	185	3/9/65	Ponce, PR
	Infielders						
26	Arias, Alex	R	R	6–3	185	11/20/67	New York, NY
8	Barberie, Bret	B	R	5–11	180	8/16/67	Long Beach, CA
4	Colbrunn, Greg	R	R	6–0	200	7/26/69	Fontana, CA
39	Destrade, Orestes	B	R	6–4	230	5/8/62	Santiago, Cuba
18	Magadan, Dave	L	R	6–3	205	9/30/62	Tampa, FL
6	Renteria, Rick	R	R	5–9	175	12/25/61	Harbor City, CA
	Outfielders						
21	Carr, Chuck	B	R	5–10	165	8/10/68	San Bernadino, CA
25	Carrillo, Matias	L	L	5–11	190	2/24/63	Los Mochis, Mexico
14	Clark, Tim	L	R	6–3	210	2/10/69	Philadelphia, PA
19	Conine, Jeff	R	R	6–1	220	6/27/66	Tacoma, WA
7	Moore, Kerwin	B	R	6–1	190	10/29/70	Detroit, MI
10	Sheffield, Gary	R	R	5–11	190	11/18/68	Tampa, FL
17	Whitmore, Darrell	L	R	6–1	210	11/18/68	Front Royal, VA
30	Wilson, Nigel	L	L	6–1	185	1/12/70	Oshawa, Canada

1995 Schedule

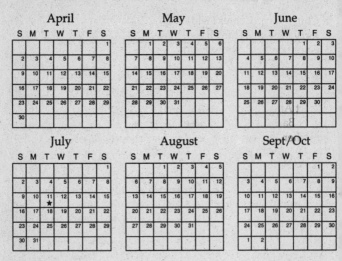

The Marlins were unable to provide a schedule by press time.

Joe Robbie Stadium

Capacity: 43,909

Turf: Grass

Dimensions:
LF Line: 335 '
RF Line: 345'
Center: 410'
Alleys: 380'

Tickets:
(305) 930-7800

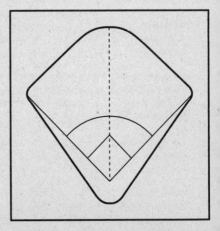

1994 Batting Order

1. Chuck Carr (Center Field)
2. Jerry Browne (Third Base)
3. Gary Sheffield (Right Field)
4. Jeff Conine (Left Field)
5. Greg Colbrunn (First Base)
6. Benito Santiago (Catcher)
7. Kurt Abbott (Shortstop)
8. Bret Barberie (Second Base)
9. Pitcher

1994 Team Record
51–64 (.443); Fifth in NL East

NL East	W	L	NL Central	W	L	NL West	W	L
Atlanta	4	8	Chicago	5	4	Colorado	9	3
Florida	—	—	Cincinnati	5	7	Los Angeles	3	3
Montreal	2	7	Houston	2	4	San Diego	5	1
New York	6	4	Pittsburgh	1	6	S. Francisco	2	4
Philadelphia	4	6	St. Louis	3	7			
Total	16	25		16	28		19	11

1994 National League Team Rank Batting

Batting Average: Eighth (.266)
Runs Scored: Thirteenth (468)
Runs Batted In: Twelfth (451)
Stolen Bases: Eleventh (65)
Slugging Percentage: Eleventh (.396)
On-Base Percentage: Tenth (.330)

1994 National League Team Rank Pitching

Earned Run Average: Eleventh (4.50)
Bases On Balls: Thirteenth (428)
Strikeouts: Twelfth (649)
Wins: Twelfth (51)
Saves: Fourth (30)
Complete Games: Tenth (5)

© Rich Pilling/MLB Photos

Florida Marlins MVP

Gary Sheffield   No. 10/ OF

Born: 11/18/68, Tampa, FL
Height: 5' 11"   **Weight:** 190
Bats: Right   **Throws:** Right
1994 OBP: .380   **SLG:** .584

Despite missing twenty-eight games on the disabled list, due to two attempts to make diving catches, Sheffield established himself as the most prolific slugger in Marlins history. Sheffield's twenty-seven homers erased the previous club record of twenty, set in 1993 by Orestes Destrade.

Sheffield entered the majors as an American Leaguer in 1988, already famous for being Dwight Gooden's nephew and for having rare natural ability. Great things were expected from the beginning, but the young "Sheff" needed time to mature and to learn major league pitching. The Brewers weren't willing to wait, so they traded him to San Diego (for Ricky Bones), where Sheffield had a breakthrough season in 1992.

Not a typical power hitter, Sheffield doesn't accumulate many walks or strikeouts. His lightning-quick stroke generates home run distance without sacrificing his ability to make contact. When his timing is right, Sheffield is a very tough out—during one April stretch of home games last year, he went deep in eight of nine games, including five consecutive.

Though his maturity has often been questioned in the past, the Marlins are pleased with Sheffield's performance so far. He's in his prime as an athlete, even though he's played almost 1,000 professional games (majors and minors).

	G	AB	H	2B	3B	HR	RS	RBI	BB	SB	BA
1994	87	322	89	16	1	27	61	78	51	12	.276
Career	667	2483	705	131	12	101	353	384	143	77	.284
Projected	137	512	159	23	4	31	84	99	64	19	.298

Kurt Abbott   No. 7/ SS

Born: 6/2/69, Zanesville, OH
Height: 6' 0"   **Weight:** 185
Bats: Right   **Throws:** Right
1994 OBP: .291   **SLG:** .394

Abbott was formerly a prospect in the Oakland system. Last year was his first full season in the majors, and it was a productive one. Abbott doesn't have much star potential, but he's a scrappy shortstop with decent power. His two grand slams in '94 tied for most in the league. Abbott's strikeouts-to-walks ratio was 6/1, a situation that is likely to stunt his development.

	G	AB	H	2B	3B	HR	RS	RBI	BB	SB	BA
1994	101	345	86	17	3	9	41	33	16	3	.249
Career	121	406	101	18	3	12	52	42	19	5	.249
Projected	155	542	146	25	4	17	72	58	26	7	.259

Brett Barberie   No. 8/ 2B

Born: 8/16/67, Long Beach, CA
Height: 5' 11"   **Weight:** 180
Bats: Both   **Throws:** Right
1994 OBP: .356   **SLG:** .406

There's a strong possibility that Barberie will have a career year in '95. He's at the right age, twenty-seven, and he finished with a rush last year, hitting .335 in his final 221 at-bats. He smacked twenty-seven extra-base hits last year and hit .371 with two outs and runners in scoring position. Barberie grounded into just four doubleplays in 1994.

	G	AB	H	2B	3B	HR	RS	RBI	BB	SB	BA
1994	107	372	112	20	2	5	40	31	23	2	.301
Career	374	1168	330	59	6	13	127	106	123	15	.283
Projected	160	603	189	30	3	8	71	54	47	3	.301

Jerry Browne　　No. 14/ 3B

Born: 2/3/66, St. Croix, VI
Height: 5' 10"　**Weight:** 170
Bats: Both　**Throws:** Right
1994 OBP: .392　**SLG:** .398

Though it seems like he's been around forever, Browne is only twenty-nine years old. The upside of his potential is to be the next Tony Phillips, a versatile fielder and a clutch hitter. Browne played five positions for the Marlins before taking over the starting job at third base. His .392 on-base percentage set a Marlins club record.

	G	AB	H	2B	3B	HR	RS	RBI	BB	SB	BA
1994	101	329	97	17	4	3	42	30	52	3	.295
Career	905	3006	819	131	25	22	410	271	368	72	.272
Projected	155	538	160	28	4	5	66	47	70	7	.286

Chuck Carr　　No. 21/ OF

Born: 8/10/68, San Bernardino, CA
Height: 5' 10"　**Weight:** 165
Bats: Both　**Throws:** Right
1994 OBP: .305　**SLG:** .330

The Marlins' all-time leader in stolen bases and runs scored, Carr was successful in 80% of his attempts last season. He stole thirty of his thirty-two bases while playing on grass. His K/BB ratios aren't good for a leadoff hitter. Carr is a thrilling defensive center fielder who makes jaw-dropping catches on a regular basis.

	G	AB	H	2B	3B	HR	RS	RBI	BB	SB	BA
1994	106	433	114	19	2	2	61	30	22	32	.263
Career	286	1061	277	41	4	6	145	75	80	102	.261
Projected	151	623	179	25	3	4	90	47	47	59	.276

Jeff Conine   No. 19/ OF

Born: 6/27/66, Tacoma, WA
Height: 6' 1"   **Weight:** 220
Bats: Right   **Throws:** Right
1994 OBP: .373   **SLG:** .525

Conine was the Marlins' lone All-Star representative in his second full season. He hit righties and southpaws equally well (.321 and .316 respectively). Conine finished strong, batting .332 in his last 250 at-bats. His final average (.319) was good for tenth in the league. He led the Marlins in extra-base hits and runs batted in.

	G	AB	H	2B	3B	HR	RS	RBI	BB	SB	BA
1994	115	451	144	27	6	18	60	82	40	1	.319
Career	314	1157	346	58	11	30	148	172	102	3	.299
Projected	161	632	208	32	6	19	85	101	58	2	.316

Mark Gardner   No. 38/ P

Born: 3/1/62, Los Angeles, CA
Height: 6' 1"   **Weight:** 205
Bats: Right   **Throws:** Right
Opp. Batting Average: .276

A chaotic season for Gardner was exemplified by a no-decision start in which the Marlins came back from a 9–3 deficit. Gardner has a fine curveball that tends to fade in and out from start to start. His ERA in four wins was 1.98. In four losses, Gardner compiled a 6.23 ERA. Gardner tied a club record by striking out ten batters versus Montreal on June 26.

	G	GS	IP	ERA	H	BB	SO	W	L	SV
1994	20	14	92.1	4.87	97	30	57	4	4	0
Career	131	117	711.0	4.37	662	273	506	36	43	0
Projected	22	18	109.0	5.54	112	39	65	5	6	0

Chris Hammond   No. 11/ P

Born: 1/21/66, Atlanta, GA
Height: 6' 1"   **Weight:** 195
Bats: Left   **Throws:** Left
Opp. Batting Average: .281

Hammond's season was aborted by two non-arm-related injuries, but he seems to have made progress in attacking hitters aggressively. His ERA through May 21 was 1.70. Hammond allowed just one homer in his last forty innings. Amazingly, each of his four wins were shutouts (one complete game). Hammond needs to throw strikes and bust hitters inside to be effective.

	G	GS	IP	ERA	H	BB	SO	W	L	SV
1994	13	13	73.1	3.07	79	23	40	4	4	0
Career	96	92	522.2	4.24	540	204	281	29	35	0
Projected	25	25	145.0	4.22	157	49	81	8	9	0

Bryan Harvey   No. 34/ P

Born: 6/2/63, Chattanooga, TN
Height: 6' 2"   **Weight:** 212
Bats: Right   **Throws:** Right
Opp. Batting Average: .279

Harvey's injury-riddled campaign included season-ending abdominal surgery. When healthy, he's a stopper. Harvey's career strikeouts-per-nine-innings ratio is 10.4. A former fast-pitch softball star, his fastball reaches ninety-two mph, setting up the best forkball of any reliever in the majors. If he's healthy, Harvey will always be among the league leaders in saves.

	G	GS	IP	ERA	H	BB	SO	W	L	SV
1994	12	0	10.1	5.23	12	4	10	0	0	6
Career	321	0	387.0	2.42	276	143	448	17	25	177
Projected	38	0	42.0	2.17	30	9	44	1	3	27

Jeremy Hernandez   No. 42/ P

Born: 7/6/66, Burbank, CA
Height: 6' 6"   **Weight:** 210
Bats: Right   **Throws:** Right
Opp. Batting Average: .205

A season of tragic proportions took Hernandez to the peak of success, then brought him crashing down. Filling in for injured closer Bryan Harvey, Hernandez led the Marlins in saves before being placed on the disabled list with a herniated disk and a spinal cord compression in his neck. Hernandez missed the final four months of the season.

	G	GS	IP	ERA	H	BB	SO	W	L	SV
1994	21	0	23.1	2.70	16	14	13	3	3	9
Career	126	0	186.0	3.39	179	64	117	10	14	20
Projected	49	0	73.0	3.48	71	26	45	5	5	9

Robb Nen   No. 31/ P

Born: 11/28/69, San Pedro, CA
Height: 6' 4"   **Weight:** 200
Bats: Right   **Throws:** Right
Opp. Batting Average: .222

Injuries to Bryan Harvey and Jeremy Hernandez created an opportunity for Nen, who took over as the club's closer. Nen converted his first fifteen save chances, the longest streak of its kind since blown saves were first tracked in 1988. Nen allowed only one of twenty-eight inherited runners to score, a phenomenal feat. Nen held lefties to a .161 average.

	G	GS	IP	ERA	H	BB	SO	W	L	SV
1994	44	0	58.0	2.95	46	17	60	5	5	15
Career	68	4	114.0	4.82	102	63	99	7	6	15
Projected	41	2	69.0	4.82	66	38	60	4	4	9

Pat Rapp No. 48/ P

Born: 7/13/67, Jennings, LA
Height: 6' 3" **Weight:** 205
Bats: Right **Throws:** Right
Opp. Batting Average: .266

Rapp posted the lowest ERA for a starter in the Marlins' brief history. He also became the first Marlin to hurl back-to-back complete games. Generally, Rapp is either very good or bad, depending on his command of the strikezone. His ERA was 1.30 in his wins, 5.29 in his seventeen other appearances. Rapp isn't overpowering; he needs good location to be effective.

	G	GS	IP	ERA	H	BB	SO	W	L	SV
1994	24	23	133.1	3.85	132	69	75	7	8	0
Career	43	41	237.1	4.06	241	117	135	11	16	0
Projected	24	23	136.0	3.92	140	65	79	7	8	0

Benito Santiago No. 9/ C

Born: 3/9/65, Ponce, PR
Height: 6' 1" **Weight:** 185
Bats: Right **Throws:** Right
1994 OBP: .322 **SLG:** .424

Santiago has his faults (his plate discipline is such that statisticians should count his pitches taken instead of his walks drawn). But when he's comfortable, Santiago is a dynamic player. He eliminated 43% of would-be basestealers and reached double figures in home runs for the eighth straight season. Past expectations aside, Santiago is still a valuable major league catcher.

	G	AB	H	2B	3B	HR	RS	RBI	BB	SB	BA
1994	101	337	92	14	2	11	35	41	25	1	.273
Career	1029	3678	958	157	23	109	396	466	201	73	.260
Projected	147	499	126	21	5	15	53	57	39	7	.251

Rich Scheid   No. 37/ P

Born: 2/3/65, Staten Island, NY
Height: 6' 3"   **Weight:** 195
Bats: Left   **Throws:** Left
Opp. Batting Average: .269

Marlins batters scored a whopping one run for Scheid in his four starts. His one win came in relief. Scheid was released by Houston in 1993, but he pitched great at Triple-A Edmonton last year, leading the Pacific Coast League in strikeouts when he was called to Florida on July 6. Scheid could still emerge as a quality starting pitcher.

	G	GS	IP	ERA	H	BB	SO	W	L	SV
1994	8	5	32.1	3.34	35	8	17	1	3	0
Career	15	6	44.1	4.06	49	14	25	1	4	0
Projected			No projection. Player was a rookie in 1994.							

Dave Weathers   No. 35/ P

Born: 9/25/69, Lawrenceburg, TN
Height: 6' 3"   **Weight:** 205
Bats: Right   **Throws:** Right
Opp. Batting Average: .306

Weathers started '94 hotter than the Florida sun, winning four games and posting a 2.10 ERA in April. He seems to be beyond the health problems that slowed him in '92. Weathers is one of the National League's quickest workers. His last five starts were a negative image of his impressive April showing; he compiled a 12.13 ERA and five losses.

	G	GS	IP	ERA	H	BB	SO	W	L	SV
1994	24	24	135.0	5.27	166	59	72	8	12	0
Career	55	30	198.2	5.26	243	91	122	11	15	0
Projected	23	18	110.0	5.23	135	44	64	6	9	0

Houston
ASTROS

1995 Scouting Report

Outfielders: Speed is essential when covering the deep power alleys in the Astrodome, and the Astros have burners at all three outfield positions. Luis Gonzalez in left, James Mouton in right, and Steve Finley (subject of winter trade talks) in center, all can fill the gaps. On the basepaths, the trio combined for fifty-two steals last season. Look for phenom Brian L. Hunter to break through in '95; he's a prototype Astros outfielder—a young, fast linedrive hitter.

Infielders: The Astros sport an offensively explosive and defensively solid infield. All-Star Craig Biggio (2B) and NL MVP Jeff Bagwell (1B) are both in their prime, while Andujar Cedeno (SS) is still developing as a hitter and fielder. Ken Caminiti provides veteran leadership and an outstanding arm at third, though winter trade rumors had him headed to Boston for Scott Cooper.

Catchers: Tony Eusebio is the future behind the plate. Scott Servais was reliable in '94.

Starting Pitchers: If they find consistency and can progress to the next level, the Astros' starters could rival the Braves'. Doug Drabek and Greg Swindell are polished veterans; both can be counted on for at least twelve wins. Darryl Kile, Pete Harnisch, and Shane Reynolds combined for a .76 strikeouts-per-inning average. Reynolds could turn out to be the best of the lot.

Relief Pitchers: The Astros bullpen may finally have found an anchor in last year's rookie flamethrower John Hudek. Middle relief is handled by Dave Veres, spot starter Brian Williams, and Todd Jones.

Manager: Second-year manager Terry Collins (66–49) will look to build on his inaugural-season success.

1995 Outlook

With the organization's best pitching staff since the 1980 team that featured Joe Niekro, and a prolific offense led by 1994 MVP Jeff Bagwell, the Astros have the best collection of talent in the NL Central. They had more players named to last year's All-Star team than any other club. The team's starting lineup averages 26.6 years of age—they're just entering their prime.

Astros management has made some brilliant trades (Jeff Bagwell from Boston for Larry Andersen; Pete Harnisch and Steve Finley for Glenn Davis), giving up essentially nothing, while acquiring top talent. They've drafted wisely (Craig Biggio, Luis Gonzalez, Darryl Kile) and had success with free agent signees such as Doug Drabek and Greg Swindell. The result is a balanced roster that should be in top form for several seasons.

Houston ranked second in the NL in slugging and on-base percentage, behind division rival Cincinnati in both categories. The batting order errupted for at least ten runs on nine separate occasions. Look for the Astros' production to increase with a full season's worth of at-bats from sophomore catcher Tony Eusebio and rookie outfielder Brian L. Hunter. The Astros have terrific speed throughout the lineup (second in the league in steals), which is especially crucial defensively, playing on the fast turf of the Astrodome.

One possible obstacle to the Astros' quest for a division title, in addition to the formidable Reds, is a heavy reliance on erratic, live-armed starting pitcher Darryl Kile, who struggled with his control in '94. With GM Bob Watson being forced to unload the large salary of Pete Harnisch, due partially to the expensive contracts granted to Bagwell and Biggio, the rotation could be either dominant or unstable, depending on the performance of Kile. There are also rumors that Greg Swindell won't be in Houston much longer, so the Astros' starting staff could go from a strength to a concern by the time spring rolls around.

1995 Houston Astros Roster

Manager: Terry Collins
Coaches: Jesse Barfield, Matt Galante, Steve Henderson, Julio Linares,
   Mel Stottlemyre

No.	Pitchers	B	T	HT	WT	DOB	Birthplace
49	Dougherty, Jim	R	R	6–0	210	3/8/68	Brentwood, NY
15	Drabek, Doug	R	R	6–1	185	7/25/62	Victoria, TX
44	Gallaher, Kevin	R	R	6–3	190	8/1/66	Fairfax, VA
38	Hampton, Mike	R	L	5–10	180	9/9/72	Brooksville, FL
27	Harnisch, Pete	R	R	6–0	207	9/23/66	Commack, NY
35	Hudek, John	S	R	6–1	200	8/8/66	Tampa, FL
42	Jean, Domingo	R	R	6–2	175	1/9/69	San Pedro Macoris, DR
59	Jones, Todd	L	R	6–3	200	4/24/68	Marietta, GA
57	Kile, Darryl	R	R	6–5	185	12/2/68	Garden Grove, CA
51	Morman, Alvin	L	L	6–3	210	1/6/69	Rockingham, NC
52	Powell, Ross	L	L	6–0	180	1/24/69	Grand Rapids, MI
37	Reynolds, Shane	R	R	6–3	210	3/26/68	Bastrop, LA
21	Swindell, Greg	R	L	6–3	225	1/2/65	Fort Worth, TX
43	Veres, Dave	R	R	6–2	195	10/19/66	Montgomery, AL
53	Williams, Brian	R	R	6–2	195	2/15/69	Lancaster, SC
	Catchers						
20	Eusebio, Tony	R	R	6–2	180	4/27/67	San Jose Los Lamos, DR
9	Servais, Scott	R	R	6–2	195	6/5/67	LaCrosse, WI
36	Tucker, Scooter	R	R	6–2	205	11/18/66	Greenville, MS
	Infielders						
5	Bagwell, Jeff	R	R	6–0	195	5/27/68	Boston, MA
7	Biggio, Craig	R	R	5–11	180	12/14/65	Smithtown, NY
11	Caminiti, Ken	S	R	6–0	200	4/21/63	Hanford, CA
10	Cedeno, Andujar	R	R	6–1	168	8/21/69	La Romana, DR
3	Donnels, Chris	L	R	6–0	185	2/21/66	Los Angeles, CA
24	Miller, Orlando	R	R	6–1	180	1/13/69	Changuinola, Panama
4	Stankiewicz, Andy	R	R	5–9	165	8/10/64	Inglewood, CA
	Outfielders						
12	Finley, Steve	L	L	6–2	180	3/12/65	Union City, TN
26	Gonzalez, Luis	L	R	6–2	180	9/3/67	Tampa, FL
60	Hatcher, Chris	R	R	6–3	220	1/7/69	Anaheim, CA
19	Hunter, Brian L.	R	R	6–4	180	3/5/71	Portland, OR
18	Mouton, James	R	R	5–9	175	12/29/68	Denver, CO
62	White, Jimmy	L	R	6–1	170	12/1/72	Tampa, FL

1995 Schedule

April

S	M	T	W	T	F	S
						1
2	3	4 SF	5 SF	6 LA	7 LA	8 LA
9 LA	10	11 SF	12 SF	13 LA	14 LA	15 LA
16 LA	17 SD	18 SD	19 COL	20 COL	21 COL	22 COL
23 COL	24	25 SD	26 SD	27 COL	28 COL	29 COL
30 COL						

May

S	M	T	W	T	F	S
	1	2 CHI	3 CHI	4 STL	5 STL	6 STL
7 STL	8 PIT	9 PIT	10 PIT	11 PIT	12 PHI	13 PHI
14 PHI	15	16 NY	17 NY	18 NY	19 MON	20 MON
21 MON	22 CIN	23 CIN	24 CIN	25 QC	26 ATL	27 ATL
28 ATL	29 FLO	30	31 FLO			

June

S	M	T	W	T	F	S
				1 ATL	2 ATL	3 ATL
4 ATL	5 FLO	6 FLO	7 FLO	8 CIN	9 CIN	10 CIN
11 CIN	12	13 PHI	14 PHI	15 PHI	16 NY	17 NY
18 NY	19 MON	20 MON	21 MON	22 CHI	23 CHI	24 CHI
25 CHI	26 STL	27 STL	28 STL	29	30 PIT	

July

S	M	T	W	T	F	S
						1 PIT
2 PIT	3 COL	4 COL	5 COL	6 SD	7 SD	8 SD
9 SD	10	11 ★	12	13 SF	14 SF	15 SF
16 SF	17 LA	18 LA	19	20 SF	21 SF	22 SF
23 SF	24 LA	25 LA	26 COL	27 COL	28 COL	29
30 SD	31 SD					

August

S	M	T	W	T	F	S
		1 STL	2 STL	3 STL	4 PIT	5 PIT
6 PIT	7	8 MON	9 MON	10 MON	11 NY	12 NY
13 NY	14	15 PHI	16 PHI	17 PHI	18 CIN	19 CIN
20 CIN	21 ATL	22 ATL	23 ATL	24	25 FLO	26 FLO
27 FLO	28 FLO	29 ATL	30 ATL	31 ATL		

Sept/Oct

S	M	T	W	T	F	S
					1 FLO	2 FLO
3 FLO	4 CIN	5 CIN	6 CIN	7	8 PHI	9 PHI
10 PHI	11	12 NY	13 NY	14 NY	15 MON	16 MON
17 MON	18 CHI	19 CHI	20 CHI	21	22 STL	23 STL
24 STL	25 PIT	26 PIT	27 PIT	28	29 CHI	30 CHI
1 CHI	2					

 Home   □ Away   ★ All-Star Game

The Astrodome

Capacity: 53,821

Turf: Artificial

Dimensions:
LF Line: 330'
RF Line: 330'
Center: 400'
Alleys: 375'

Tickets:
(713) 799-9555

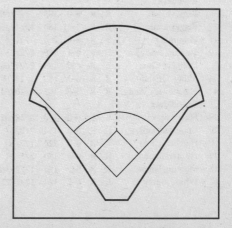

1994 Batting Order

1. James Mouton (Right Field)
2. Steve Finley (Center Field)
3. Craig Biggio (Second Base)
4. Jeff Bagwell (First Base)
5. Luis Gonzalez (Left Field)
6. Ken Caminiti (Third Base)
7. Scott Servais (Catcher)
8. Andujar Cedeno (Shortstop)
9. Pitcher

1994 Team Record
66–49 (.574); Second in NL Central

NL East	W	L	NL Central	W	L	NL West	W	L
Atlanta	3	3	Chicago	8	4	Colorado	5	5
Florida	4	2	Cincinnati	6	4	Los Angeles	1	8
Montreal	2	4	Houston	—	—	San Diego	5	5
New York	3	3	Pittsburgh	8	4	S. Francisco	8	2
Philadelphia	5	1	St. Louis	8	4			
Total	17	13		30	16		19	20

1994 National League Team Rank Batting

Batting Average: Second (.278)
Runs Scored: Second (602)
Runs Batted In: First (573)
Stolen Bases: Second (124)
Slugging Percentage: Second (.445)
On-Base Percentage: Second (.347)

1994 National League Team Rank Pitching

Earned Run Average: Fifth (3.97)
Bases On Balls: Sixth (367)
Strikeouts: Fifth (739)
Wins: Third (66)
Saves: Sixth (29)
Complete Games: Third (9)

Houston Astros MVP

Jeff Bagwell   No. 5/ 1B

Born: 5/27/68, Boston, MA
Height: 6' 0"   **Weight:** 195
Bats: Right   **Throws:** Right
1994 OPB: .451   **SLG:** .750

No limits. That's the only tag you can put on Bagwell's future after his MVP-winning 1994 offensive explosion. Homering once every ten at-bats, while driving in runs at a rate of more than one per game, Bagwell made his acquisition from Boston for Larry Andersen into a Ruthian blunder for the Red Sox.

The ball jumps off Bagwell's bat, reminiscent of Don Mattingly circa 1985. Bagwell blasted more homers in the Astrodome (23), where the ball doesn't carry well, than on the road (16). His slugging percentage at home was an eye-popping .816. He hit two home runs in one inning, then hit another in the next inning, versus the Dodgers in Houston on June 24. Bagwell destroyed lefthanders (.457 BA and 18 HRs in 105 ABs). He became the first National Leaguer since Willie Mays (1955) to finish in the top two in batting average, runs, runs batted in, and home runs.

Though he won a Gold Glove, Bagwell ranked eighth among NL first basemen in fielding percentage (.991). Bagwell is improving each year, and he has the quick reactions and solid footwork to eventually justify being considered the NL's elite first sacker.

Bagwell has suffered a broken left hand in two consecutive seasons, due to pitchers trying to move him off the plate. Barring injury, Bagwell will no doubt be making room on his mantel for one or two more MVP Awards before he hangs up his spikes.

	G	AB	H	2B	3B	HR	RS	RBI	BB	SB	BA
1994	110	400	147	32	2	39	104	116	65	15	.368
Career	570	2075	641	129	16	92	346	382	286	45	.309
Projected	151	583	214	45	4	38	117	132	82	18	.354

Craig Biggio   No. 7/ 2B

Born: 12/14/65, Smithtown, NY
Height: 5' 11"   **Weight:** 180
Bats: Right   **Throws:** Right
1994 OBP: .411   **SLG:** .483

Biggio has transformed himself into the ideal spark plug, concentrating on being in position to score when the big bats come up behind him. Biggio tied for the NL lead in doubles, also tying the Astros' single-season record. With the NL's sixth-highest (tied) OBP, plus thirty-nine steals in forty-three tries, Biggio may be the the NL's number-one offensive catalyst.

	G	AB	H	2B	3B	HR	RS	RBI	BB	SB	BA
1994	114	439	139	44	5	6	88	56	62	39	.318
Career	914	3327	938	191	22	57	492	312	395	163	.282
Projected	158	639	207	54	6	17	118	76	88	34	.311

Ken Caminiti   No. 11/ 3B

Born: 4/21/63, Hanford, CA
Height: 6' 0"   **Weight:** 200
Bats: Both   **Throws:** Right
1994 OBP: .352   **SLG:** .495

Caminiti weathered a job-threatening early season slump (.200 BA through April), then hit .372 in May and finished the year with solid power numbers. He's getting better each year, even though he's the elder statesman of the young Astros lineup. Caminiti regularly makes spectacular diving stops at the hot corner, and his arm is a shotgun.

	G	AB	H	2B	3B	HR	RS	RBI	BB	SB	BA
1994	143	543	142	31	0	13	75	75	49	8	.262
Career	948	3441	896	180	13	75	409	445	298	39	.260
Projected	152	572	158	36	1	19	84	91	56	7	.274

Andujar Cedeno   No. 10/ SS

Born: 8/21/69, La Romana, DR
Height: 6' 1"   **Weight:** 168
Bats: Right   **Throws:** Right
1994 OBP: .334   **SLG:** .418

Astros management cringes when Cedeno swings for the fences. Cedeno garnered seven of his nine big flies in the season's first two months, but as the hitless games mounted he began to concentrate on not trying to pull every pitch. His average did level out, albeit twenty points below the previous year. He's still a raw talent, and could make big strides in '95.

	G	AB	H	2B	3B	HR	RS	RBI	BB	SB	BA
1994	98	342	90	26	0	9	38	49	29	1	.263
Career	392	1326	332	76	8	31	149	154	100	16	.250
Projected	150	540	164	33	3	13	72	70	52	7	.289

Doug Drabek   No. 15/ P

Born: 7/25/62, Victoria, TX
Height: 6' 1"   **Weight:** 185
Bats: Right   **Throws:** Right
Opp. Batting Average: .220

Drabek came into the '94 season determined to justify the Astros' faith (and big contract) after a mediocre '93 campaign. He got off to an 8–2 start, with a (H+BB)/IP ratio of just 1.01, to establish himself as the staff ace. Though he doesn't knock the bat out of a hitter's hands, he changes speeds brilliantly and mixes his pitches like an artist. Expect Drabek to maintain his current level of excellence.

	G	GS	IP	ERA	H	BB	SO	W	L	SV
1994	23	23	164.2	2.84	132	45	121	12	6	0
Career	283	274	1896.2	3.17	1727	492	1174	120	94	0
Projected	32	32	229.0	3.40	212	60	158	12	14	0

Tony Eusebio   No. 20/ C

Born: 4/27/67, San Jose Los Lamos, DR
Height: 6' 2"   **Weight:** 180
Bats: Right   **Throws:** Right
1994 OBP: .320   **SLG:** .459

Eusebio showed star potential in forty-four starts as a rookie in '94. He hit safely in fifteen of his last seventeen games, batting .379. Eusebio has a large platoon-differential; he clobbered lefties at a .426 rate, but he struggled against righthanders (.214). He's got a powerful arm, gunning down 40% of baserunners trying to steal.

	G	AB	H	2B	3B	HR	RS	RBI	BB	SB	BA
1994	55	159	47	9	1	5	18	30	8	0	.296
Career	65	178	49	10	1	5	22	30	14	0	.275
Projected		No projection. Player was a rookie in 1994.									

Steve Finley   No. 12/ OF

Born: 3/12/65, Union City, TN
Height: 6' 2"   **Weight:** 180
Bats: Left   **Throws:** Left
1994 OBP: .329   **SLG:** .434

Finley started hot, but slumped through May and June before missing three weeks with a broken hand. He came off the DL to hit .310 in his next thirty-four games. Finley's value is in center field, where he positions himself well and uses his excellent speed to chase down seemingly uncatchable balls. There's a chance he'll be traded to make room for Brian Hunter.

	G	AB	H	2B	3B	HR	RS	RBI	BB	SB	BA
1994	94	373	103	16	5	11	64	33	28	13	.276
Career	780	2802	768	109	47	37	382	248	203	149	.274
Projected	143	563	155	19	11	12	82	48	35	20	.273

Luis Gonzalez   No. 26/ OF

Born: 9/3/67, Tampa, FL
Height: 6' 2"   **Weight:** 180
Bats: Left   **Throws:** Right
1994 OBP: .353   **SLG:** .429

Though last season wasn't the great leap forward the Astros were expecting, Gonzalez did increase his frequency of doubles (finishing tenth in the league), didn't suffer any prolonged slumps, and demonstrated improved ability to draw walks. Gonzalez's basestealing was a negative (54% success rate). He committed only two errors in left field for a .991 percentage.

	G	AB	H	2B	3B	HR	RS	RBI	BB	SB	BA
1994	112	392	107	29	4	8	57	67	49	15	.273
Career	537	1813	487	112	19	46	231	263	162	52	.269
Projected	157	572	179	40	4	15	89	89	61	22	.300

Pete Harnisch   No. 27/ P

Born: 9/23/66, Commack, NY
Height: 6' 0"   **Weight:** 207
Bats: Right   **Throws:** Right
Opp. Batting Average: .269

The Astros anticipated dominance from Harnisch, but he often struggled to reach the middle innings. He spent time on the DL due to a tear in his bicep. Harnisch depends on hard heat and a wicked slider; if he gets behind in the count, hitters sit on his fastball and treat his offerings like batting practice. Houston dealt him to the Mets during the winter.

	G	GS	IP	ERA	H	BB	SO	W	L	SV
1994	17	17	95.0	5.40	100	39	62	8	5	0
Career	168	167	1041.0	3.73	921	424	785	61	55	0
Projected	28	28	174.0	3.71	151	66	137	13	8	0

John Hudek No. 35/ P

Born: 8/8/66, Tampa, FL
Height: 6' 1" **Weight:** 200
Bats: Both **Throws:** Right
Opp. Batting Average: .174

Hudek became the fifth player in major league history to begin the season in the minors, yet still be named to the All-Star team. He was nearly unhittable against righties, handcuffing them to a .164 batting average. Hudek actually had just three bad outings in forty-two appearances; minus those three, his season ERA was 0.71.

	G	GS	IP	ERA	H	BB	SO	W	L	SV
1994	42	0	39.1	2.97	24	18	39	0	2	16
Career	42	0	39.1	2.97	24	18	39	0	2	16
Projected			No projection. Player was a rookie in 1994.							

Brian L. Hunter No. 19/ OF

Born: 3/5/71, Portland, OR
Height: 6' 4" **Weight:** 180
Bats: Right **Throws:** Right
1994 OBP: .280 **SLG:** .292

Hunter posted the longest hitting streak in pro baseball last year, hitting safely in twenty-six consecutive games for Tucson in the Pacific Coast League. He led the PCL in batting average (.372), steals (49), and runs (113). He can handle major league pitching, and scouts report he could become the best Astros outfielder since Jose Cruz.

	G	AB	H	2B	3B	HR	RS	RBI	BB	SB	BA
1994	6	24	6	1	0	0	2	0	1	2	.250
Career	6	24	6	1	0	0	2	0	1	2	.250
Projected			No projection. Player was a rookie in 1994.								

Darryl Kile   No. 57/ P

Born: 12/2/68, Garden Grove, CA
Height: 6' 5"   **Weight:** 185
Bats: Right   **Throws:** Right
Opp. Batting Average: .275

If you want to see what a perfect curveball looks like, watch Darryl Kile's. Like a distortion in space, it's the most dramatic bender in the NL. Kile is also a great reminder of how walks will send a pitcher to the showers early. If he can harness his bouts of wildness, stardom awaits. If not, Kile will get plenty of chances to iron out the kinks because he's got tremendous stuff.

	G	GS	IP	ERA	H	BB	SO	W	L	SV
1994	24	24	147.2	4.57	153	82	105	9	6	0
Career	115	94	598.1	3.91	573	298	436	36	35	0
Projected	32	29	183.0	4.00	174	86	141	14	8	0

James Mouton   No. 18/ OF

Born: 12/29/68, Denver, CO
Height: 5' 9"   **Weight:** 175
Bats: Right   **Throws:** Right
1994 OBP: .315   **SLG:** .300

Mouton showed promise in the minors (126 runs scored in 134 games at Triple-A Tucson in 1993), but was not a very potent leadoff man last season, drawing twenty-seven walks while striking out sixty-nine times. Mouton did finish tenth in the NL in stolen bases. His speed serves him well in the expansive Astrodome outfield.

	G	AB	H	2B	3B	HR	RS	RBI	BB	SB	BA
1994	99	310	76	11	0	2	43	16	27	24	.245
Career	99	310	76	11	0	2	43	16	27	24	.245
Projected				No projection. Player was a rookie in 1994.							

Shane Reynolds   No. 37/ P

Born: 3/26/68, Bastrop, LA
Height: 6' 3"   **Weight:** 210
Bats: Right   **Throws:** Right
Opp. Batting Average: .263

Reynolds made the NL's top five in ERA, Ks per nine innings, and BB/IP ratio. He joined the rotation on May 11 versus the Dodgers, retiring the first fifteen batters while fanning eight. Reynolds' ERA in his fourteen starts was 2.54. He struck out five times as many batters as he walked, and scouts say he could soon be the ace of the Astros' excellent starting staff.

	G	GS	IP	ERA	H	BB	SO	W	L	SV
1994	33	14	124.0	3.05	128	21	110	8	5	0
Career	46	20	160.1	3.54	181	33	130	9	8	0
Projected			No projection. Player was a rookie in 1994.							

Greg Swindell   No. 21/ P

Born: 1/2/65, Fort Worth, TX
Height: 6' 3"   **Weight:** 225
Bats: Right   **Throws:** Left
Opp. Batting Average: .302

Breaking out to a 5–1 start, it looked as though Swindell was going to show his hometown fans that his sub-par '93 season was an aberration, but Swindell got hit hard from June till August 12. A quality professional pitcher, he gives up a lot of hits, but is very stingy with walks. Complaints about his durability have prompted trade speculation.

	G	GS	IP	ERA	H	BB	SO	W	L	SV
1994	24	24	148.1	4.37	175	26	74	8	9	0
Career	239	236	1595.1	3.74	1659	333	1092	92	85	0
Projected	32	31	194.0	4.26	223	38	113	11	13	0

Los Angeles
DODGERS

1995 Scouting Report

Outfielders: Like a battery-powered rabbit, Brett Butler just keeps going in center field. Rookie of the Year Raul Mondesi covers a lot of acreage in right field; he's also got a lively bat. Henry Rodriguez took over in left field and showed good speed and power at the plate.

Infielders: Tim Wallach (3B) saved his career with a rejuvenated bat in '94. Eric Karros has decent power if he gets a pitch to pull, but he's an average first baseman. Contact hitter Rafael Bournigal took over at shortstop when Jose Offerman was sent to the minors. Second baseman Delino DeShields is a catalyst when healthy, but he's made numerous trips to the DL in his career.

Catchers: Powerful Mike Piazza makes some mistakes with the glove, but he's the top offensive catcher in the big leagues. Carlos Hernandez is Piazza's backup.

Starting Pitchers: Crafty righty Tom Candiotti is the Dodgers' most consistent starter. Pedro Astacio is unhittable when he's ahead in the count, but too often he pitches from behind. Ramon Martinez has relearned to pitch effectively, having recovered from arm surgery in '93. Orel Hershiser was consistent throughout the season. The Dodgers could use some improvement in the starting rotation.

Relief Pitchers: The Dodgers' bullpen is well stocked. Todd Worrell led the team in saves. Omar Daal is a one-batter lefty specialist. Rudy Seanez and Ismael Valdes (the majors' youngest player) were sensational in '94.

Manager: Tommy Lasorda (1,480–1,338) is the winningest active manager in the major leagues.

1995 Outlook

The Dodgers were the only NL West club to finish the season above .500. They did it largely minus injured Delino DeShields, the All-Star second baseman acquired for Pedro J. Martinez. Despite a furious challenge to their first-place position by the rival Giants, sparked by ex-Dodger Darryl Strawberry, the Dodgers held fast to the top spot, finishing 3.5 games ahead of the pack. There's reason to expect another tight race in the NL's weakest division, and the Dodgers are likely to be in the thick of it once again.

The team at Chavez Ravine has one of baseball's deepest bullpens, but it's a bit thin at the top, lacking a reliable closer. The starting staff is adequate to compete, though the rotation as a whole was long in the teeth last season, with Hershiser, Candiotti, and Kevin Gross averaging 34.6 years of age. The organization is famous for developing quality young pitchers, and that's exactly what the team needs now.

The offense, too, counts heavily on veterans, the contributions of two thirty-seven-year-olds, Wallach and Butler, being crucial to the team's success last year. But there's a young heart to the batting order, with potent bats belonging to DeShields, Piazza, and Mondesi. A healthy DeShields could be the deciding factor in the Dodgers' race for the division crown. The batting order is a great deal more threatening when DeShields is wreaking havoc on the basepaths.

Sometimes the Dodgers seem to be winning on sheer organizational eminence. The team doesn't dominate in any facet of the game; they ranked ninth in fielding percentage, ninth in ERA (while playing in a park that heavily favors pitchers), and sixth or worse in most major offensive categories. But they do the little things well, their team chemistry is balanced, and the winning attitude that permeates the organization is a boon to the young players.

1995 Los Angeles Dodgers Roster

Manager: Tom Lasorda
Coaches: Joe Amalfitano, Mark Cresse, Bill Russell, Reggie Smith, Dave Wallace

No.	Pitchers	B	T	HT	WT	DOB	Birthplace
56	Astacio, Pedro	R	R	6–2	195	11/28/69	Hato Mayor, DR
49	Candiotti, Tom	R	R	6–2	228	8/31/57	Walnut Creek, CA
54	Daal, Omar	L	L	6–3	175	3/1/72	Maracaibo, Venezuela
37	Dreifort, Darren	R	R	6–2	205	5/18/72	Wichita, KS
35	Gott, Jim	R	R	6–4	229	8/3/59	Hollywood, CA
63	Hansell, Greg	R	R	6–5	213	3/12/71	Bellflower, CA
48	Martinez, Ramon	L	R	6–4	176	4/22/68	Santo Domingo, DR
45	Osuna, Al	L	L	6–3	200	8/10/65	Inglewood, CA
61	Park, Chan Ho	R	R	6–2	185	6/30/73	Kong Ju City, Korea
57	Seanez, Rudy	R	R	5–10	185	10/20/68	Brawley, CA
59	Valdes, Ismael	R	R	6–3	183	8/21/73	Victoria, Mexico
66	Williams, Todd	R	R	6–3	185	2/13/71	Syracuse, NY
38	Worrell, Todd	R	R	6–5	222	9/28/59	Arcadia, CA
	Catchers						
41	Hernandez, Carlos	R	R	5–11	218	5/24/67	Bolivar, Venezuela
31	Piazza, Mike	R	R	6–3	197	9/4/68	Norristown, PA
15	Prince, Tom	R	R	5–11	202	8/13/64	Kankakee, IL
	Infielders						
21	Bournigal, Rafael	R	R	5–11	165	5/12/66	Azusa, DR
70	Coomer, Ron	R	R	5–11	195	11/18/66	Crest Hill, IL
14	DeShields, Delino	L	R	6–1	175	1/15/69	Seaford, DE
5	Hansen, Dave	L	R	6–0	195	11/24/68	Long Beach, CA
33	Ingram, Garey	R	R	5–11	180	7/25/70	Columbus, GA
23	Karros, Eric	R	R	6–4	213	11/4/67	Hackensack, NJ
30	Offerman, Jose	B	R	6–0	165	11/8/68	San Pedro Macoris, DR
60	Pye, Eddie	R	R	5–10	175	2/13/67	Columbia, TN
12	Treadway, Jeff	L	R	6–0	185	1/22/63	Columbus, GA
25	Wallach, Tim	R	R	6–3	202	9/14/57	Huntington Park, CA
	Outfielders						
7	Ashley, Billy	R	R	6–7	227	7/11/70	Taylor, MI
43	Mondesi, Raul	R	R	5–11	202	3/12/71	San Cristobal, DR
26	Rodriguez, Henry	L	L	6–1	200	11/8/67	Santo Domingo, DR
28	Snyder, Cory	R	R	6–3	206	11/11/62	Inglewood, CA
41	Williams, Reggie	B	R	6–1	185	5/5/66	Laurens, SC

1995 Schedule

	April					
S	M	T	W	T	F	S
						1
2	FLO	FLO	FLO	HOU	HOU	HOU
9 HOU	10 FLO	11 FLO	12 FLO	13 HOU	14 HOU	15 HOU
16 HOU	17	18 CIN	19 CIN	20 CIN	21 ATL	22 ATL
23 ATL	24 CIN	25 CIN	26 CIN	27 ATL	28 ATL	29 ATL
30 ATL						

	May					
S	M	T	W	T	F	S
	1 SF	2 SF	3 SF	4	5 COL	6 COL
7 SF	8 SD	9 SD	10 SD	11	12 STL	13 STL
14 COL	15 PIT	16 PIT	17 PIT	18 PIT	19 CHI	20 CHI
21 STL	22	23 CHI	24 NY	25 NY	26 NY MON	27 MON
28 CHI	29 MON	30 PHI	31 PHI			

	June					
S	M	T	W	T	F	S
				1	2 NY	3 NY
4 NY	5 MON	6 MON	7 MON	8	9 PHI	10 PHI
11 PHI	12	13 PIT	14 PIT	15 PIT	16 CHI	17 CHI
18 CHI	19 STL	20 STL	21 STL	22 SF	23 SF	24 SF
25 SF	26 SD	27 SD	28 SD	29 COL	30 COL	

	July					
S	M	T	W	T	F	S
						1 COL
2 COL	3	4 ATL	5 ATL	6 ATL	7 CIN	8 CIN
9 CIN	10	11 ★	12	13 FLO	14 FLO	15 FLO
16 FLO	17 HOU	18 HOU	19 FLO	20 FLO	21 FLO	22 FLO
23 FLO	24 HOU	25 HOU	26 ATL	27 ATL	28 CIN	29 CIN
30 CIN	31					

	August					
S	M	T	W	T	F	S
		1 COL	2 COL	3 COL	4 SF	5 SF
6	7 SF	8 STL	9 STL	10 STL	11 PIT	12 PIT
13 PIT	14 CHI	15 CHI	16 CHI	17	18 NY	19 NY
20 PIT	21 CHI	22 MON	23 MON	24 PHI	25 PHI	26 PHI
27 NY	28 MON	29 NY	30 NY	31 NY		
PHI						

	Sept/Oct					
S	M	T	W	T	F	S
					1 MON	2 MON
3 MON	4 PHI	5 PHI	6 PHI	7	8 PIT	9 PIT
10 PIT	11 CHI	12 CHI	13 CHI	14	15 STL	16 STL
17 PIT	18	19 STL	20 SD	21 SD	22 SD	23 SD
24 SD	25 COL	26 COL	27 COL	28	29 SD	30 SD
1 SD	2					

 Home   ☐ Away   ★ All-Star Game

Dodger Stadium

Capacity: 56,000

Turf: Grass

Dimensions:
LF Line: 330'
RF Line: 330'
Center: 395'
Alleys: 385'

Tickets:
(213) 224-1400

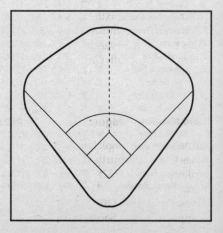

1994 Batting Order

1. Brett Butler (Center Field)
2. Delino DeShields (Second Base)
3. Mike Piazza (Catcher)
4. Tim Wallach (Third Base)
5. Henry Rodriguez (Left Field)
6. Eric Karros (First Base)
7. Raul Mondesi (Right Field)
8. Rafael Bournigal (Shortstop)
9. Pitcher

1994 Team Record
58–56 (.509); First in NL West

NL East	W	L	NL Central	W	L	NL West	W	L
Atlanta	0	6	Chicago	3	3	Colorado	6	4
Florida	3	3	Cincinnati	6	3	Los Angeles	—	—
Montreal	3	9	Houston	8	1	San Diego	6	4
New York	6	6	Pittsburgh	3	3	S. Francisco	5	5
Philadelphia	7	5	St. Louis	2	4			
Total	19	29		22	14		17	13

1994 National League Team Rank Batting

Batting Average: Sixth (.270)
Runs Scored: Seventh (532)
Runs Batted In: Seventh (505)
Stolen Bases: Eighth (74)
Slugging Percentage: Sixth (.414)
On-Base Percentage: Seventh (.333)

1994 National League Team Rank Pitching

Earned Run Average: Ninth (4.17)
Bases On Balls: Fourth (354)
Strikeouts: Sixth (732)
Wins: Fifth (58)
Saves: Fourteenth (20)
Complete Games: Second (14)

Los Angeles Dodgers MVP

Mike Piazza   No. 31/ C

Born: 9/4/68, Norristown, PA
Height: 6' 3"   **Weight:** 210
Bats: Right   **Throws:** Right
1994 OBP: .370   **SLG:** .541

Very productive in '94, the muscular Piazza continues to reset the offensive standards for himself and every catcher in the Show. He raised his walks total and frequency of RBIs, while continuing to crush fastballs to the opposite field, finishing tenth in the NL in home runs. Not too shabby for a sixty-second-round draft pick (1988) who many scouts thought would never make the majors.

Dodger Stadium has a choking effect on batting averages in general, and especially so on Piazza's average. He hit .358 with fifty-three RBIs on the road, including .386 on artificial turf, but a modest .275 with thirty-nine RBIs at home. His final stats should definitely be considered in the context of playing in a pitchers' park. Piazza is a clutch hitter extraordinaire, having hit .361 with ten homers when runners were in position to score, and .462 with the bases filled, including two grand slams last year. Fourteen of his home runs either tied the game or gave the Dodgers the lead. Piazza ranked fifth in RBIs in the NL.

The erratic aspects of Piazza's game are his glovework and throwing. He made an atrocious ten errors last year, though he's made strong progress as a handler of pitchers. Piazza has the work ethic and physical tools to be a great all-around catcher.

	G	AB	H	2B	3B	HR	RS	RBI	BB	SB	BA
1994	107	405	129	18	0	24	64	92	33	1	.319
Career	277	1021	319	45	2	60	150	211	83	4	.312
Projected	154	598	206	27	1	39	95	133	52	3	.331

Pedro Astacio   No. 56/ P

Born: 11/28/69, Hato Mayor, DR
Height: 6' 2"   **Weight:** 190
Bats: Both   **Throws:** Right
Opp. Batting Average: .252

The energetic Astacio had a severe case of Jekyll and Hyde syndrome in '94, suffering through streaks in which he either couldn't locate the strikezone or got hammered when he did. In between the dark periods, he was nearly unhittable. The formula is a common one: if Pedro gets ahead in the count, all is well. If he falls behind, it's going to be a long, scary evening.

	G	GS	IP	ERA	H	BB	SO	W	L	SV
1994	23	23	149.0	4.29	142	47	108	6	8	0
Career	65	65	417.1	3.52	387	135	273	25	22	0
Projected	31	31	191.0	3.89	175	66	131	11	10	0

Brett Butler   No. 22/ OF

Born: 6/15/59, Los Angeles, CA
Height: 5' 10"   **Weight:** 161
Bats: Left   **Throws:** Left
1994 OBP: .411   **SLG:** .446

Butler is the consummate pro, a veteran center fielder and a great leadoff batter who sweats the little things and makes the most of his skills. His nine triples tied for the NL lead, and he was sixth in the league in on-base percentage. Butler has made just three errors in his past 566 games. He's also the best bunter in the majors.

	G	AB	H	2B	3B	HR	RS	RBI	BB	SB	BA
1994	111	417	131	13	9	8	79	33	68	27	.314
Career	1945	7193	2089	250	118	53	1207	514	1011	503	.290
Projected	158	594	174	19	11	5	90	43	88	38	.299

Tom Candiotti   No. 49/ P

Born: 8/31/57, Walnut Creek, CA
Height: 6' 2"   **Weight:** 220
Bats: Right   **Throws:** Right
Opp. Batting Average: .259

An underrated veteran hurler, Candiotti once again pitched more effectively than his record indicates. His masterful knuckler rarely fails to flutter, and Candiotti can usually keep games close enough for his team to win. Candiotti pitched into the eighth inning in nine of his starts and ranked third in the NL with five complete games.

	G	GS	IP	ERA	H	BB	SO	W	L	SV
1994	23	22	153.0	4.12	149	54	102	7	7	0
Career	301	289	1975.0	3.46	1867	649	1287	110	110	0
Projected	32	31	209.0	3.54	194	71	146	9	10	0

Delino DeShields   No.14/ 2B

Born: 1/15/69, Seaford, DE
Height: 6' 1"   **Weight:** 175
Bats: Left   **Throws:** Right
1994 OBP: .357   **SLG:** .322

The speedy DeShields had a frustrating, injury-riddled season. There were murmurs that perhaps the Dodgers had erred in trading away promising Pedro J. Martinez for an infielder best suited to playing on artificial turf. DeShields can wreck a pitcher's concentration when he's leading off first base. Barring injuries, he should be entering his best years as a Dodgers.

	G	AB	H	2B	3B	HR	RS	RBI	BB	SB	BA
1994	89	320	80	11	3	2	51	33	54	27	.250
Career	627	2393	655	90	28	25	360	214	341	214	.274
Projected	130	511	153	19	7	3	84	41	84	46	.288

Kevin Gross   No. 46/ P

Born: 6/8/61, Downey, CA
Height: 6' 5"   **Weight:** 227
Bats: Right   **Throws:** Right
Opp. Batting Average: .263

Gross had the lowest ERA on the staff and led the team in strikeouts. The key to his success was control of the strikezone; he walked one batter or fewer in fifteen of his starts and allowed just two homers in his final eighty-four innings. Gross is helped immensely by pitcher-friendly Dodger Stadium, where his ERA was 3.07 in twelve games, but he may not be with LA in 1995.

	G	GS	IP	ERA	H	BB	SO	W	L	SV
1994	25	23	157.1	3.60	162	43	124	9	7	1
Career	403	316	2149.1	3.89	2138	827	1523	120	134	5
Projected	33	31	205.0	3.91	221	67	157	13	11	1

Orel Hershiser   No. 55/ P

Born: 9/16/58, Buffalo, NY
Height: 6' 3"   **Weight:** 195
Bats: Right   **Throws:** Right
Opp. Batting Average: .279

Hershiser's arm strength since 1990 shoulder surgery has been questioned. He made it into the sixth inning in eighteen of his starts, but his effectiveness diminishes after the third inning (4.48 ERA from the fourth inning on). He's obviously made intelligent adjustments, and he's still better than the league average in most categories.

	G	GS	IP	ERA	H	BB	SO	W	L	SV
1994	21	21	135.1	3.79	146	42	72	6	6	0
Career	343	303	2156.0	3.00	1934	653	1443	134	102	5
Projected	30	30	198.0	3.67	196	64	120	10	11	0

Eric Karros   No. 23/ 1B

Born: 11/4/67, Hackensack, NJ
Height: 6' 4"   **Weight:** 216
Bats: Right   **Throws:** Right
1994 OBP: .310   **SLG:** .426

Karros has knocked twenty doubles in each of his three seasons. He didn't get on base much in '94, nor did he drive in many runs, but he did have eleven sacrifice flies (second in the NL). Karros seems to have established a level of performance that will keep him in the majors, but not among the league's elite. He could have a better season in 1995.

	G	AB	H	2B	3B	HR	RS	RBI	BB	SB	BA
1994	111	409	108	21	1	14	51	46	29	2	.266
Career	432	1584	402	79	4	57	188	215	101	4	.254
Projected	159	630	174	31	2	24	80	81	40	1	.256

Ramon Martinez   No. 48/ P

Born: 3/22/68, Santo Domingo, DR
Height: 6' 4"   **Weight:** 176
Bats: Left   **Throws:** Right
Opp. Batting Average: .249

Four years ago, the older brother of the Expos' Pedro was progressing toward greatness, but injuries and control troubles have stunted his development. Ramon did cut down his frequency of walks allowed in '94, and he hurled four complete games, three of them shutouts. He ranked sixth in the league in victories (tie) and innings pitched.

	G	GS	IP	ERA	H	BB	SO	W	L	SV
1994	24	24	170.0	3.97	160	56	119	12	7	0
Career	171	168	1121.1	3.44	990	428	832	74	56	0
Projected	32	32	218	3.68	207	91	141	13	11	0

Raul Mondesi   No. 43/ OF

Born: 3/12/71, San Cristobal, DR
Height: 5' 11"   **Weight:** 210
Bats: Right   **Throws:** Right
1994 OBP: .333   **SLG:** .516

Mondesi exhibited his almost-unlimited star potential, living up to the expectations of league scouts by hitting consistently in a difficult park for righthanded hitters and coming through in the clutch (.363 with runners in scoring position). Mondesi's fielding isn't polished, but his arm is the proverbial cannon—he had sixteen outfield assists to lead the majors.

	G	AB	H	2B	3B	HR	RS	RBI	BB	SB	BA
1994	112	434	133	27	8	16	63	56	16	11	.306
Career	154	520	158	30	9	20	76	66	20	15	.304
Projected	160	567	190	34	10	23	87	76	23	17	.319

Jose Offerman   No. 30/ SS

Born: 11/8/68, San Pedro Macoris, DR
Height: 6' 0"   **Weight:** 185
Bats: Both   **Throws:** Right
1994 OBP: .314   **SLG:** .288

Offerman regressed badly at the plate in '94, eventually finding himself demoted to Triple-A Albuquerque on June 27. He stumbled out to a .154 start (through April 24) and never seemed to get comfortable from either side of the plate. Offerman did hit well in the clutch, and he's been a key part of the Dodgers' offense in recent seasons.

	G	AB	H	2B	3B	HR	RS	RBI	BB	SB	BA
1994	72	243	51	8	4	1	27	25	38	2	.210
Career	460	1538	380	51	18	4	188	127	195	59	.247
Projected	134	506	138	18	6	1	66	55	69	20	.262

Henry Rodriguez   No. 40/ OF

Born: 11/8/67, Santo Domingo, DR
Height: 6' 1"   **Weight:** 210
Bats: Left   **Throws:** Left
1994 OBP: .307   **SLG:** .405

Rodriguez has been a prospect for some time, but '94 was his first full season. The Dodgers are pleased that Rodriguez was able to keep his average above .260, something he'd failed to do in previous big league trials. He was a sure bet with runners in scoring position, hitting at a .380 clip with thirty-six RBIs in seventy-nine at-bats. He's a quick, strong-armed outfielder.

	G	AB	H	2B	3B	HR	RS	RBI	BB	SB	BA
1994	104	306	82	14	2	8	33	49	17	0	.268
Career	233	628	153	31	0	19	64	86	36	1	.244
Projected	160	446	121	23	2	15	51	69	27	1	.261

Rudy Seanez   No. 57/ P

Born: 10/20/68, Brawley, CA
Height: 5' 10"   **Weight:** 185
Bats: Right   **Throws:** Right
Opp. Batting Average: .273

Seanez was a revelation in the Dodgers' bullpen. A minor leaguer since 1986, he pitched primarily in short relief last year, allowing a run in only four of his seventeen games. He was untouchable at Dodger Stadium, compiling an at-home ERA of 0.82. He finished the year on a roll, and the Dodgers will undoubtedly feature Seanez prominently in '95

	G	GS	IP	ERA	H	BB	SO	W	L	SV
1994	17	0	23.2	2.66	24	9	18	1	1	0
Career	54	0	64.1	5.60	65	47	57	3	2	0
Projected			No projection. Player was a rookie in 1994.							

Ismael Valdes   No. 59/ P

Born: 8/21/73, Tamaulipas, Mexico
Height: 6' 3"   **Weight:** 183
Bats: Right   **Throws:** Right
Opp. Batting Average: .206

Valzes was called to the majors on June 8 and became the NL's youngest player at age twenty. Valdes presented an almost insurmountable obstacle to righthanders; they managed a .154 batting average against him. He throws hard, pitches aggressively, and his upward potential is enormous. The Dodgers will need to be careful with his untested arm.

	G	GS	IP	ERA	H	BB	SO	W	L	SV
1994	21	1	28.1	3.18	21	10	28	3	1	0
Career	21	1	28.1	3.18	21	10	28	3	1	0
Projected			No projection. Player was a rookie in 1994.							

Tim Wallach   No. 29/ 3B

Born: 9/14/57, Huntington Park, CA
Height: 6' 3"   **Weight:** 205
Bats: Right   **Throws:** Right
1994 OBP: .356   **SLG:** .502

The shock of the year was the return of "Eli" to his form of ten years ago. Wallach had pundits scratching their heads while he hit for both power and average throughout '94. So much for tracking trends; Wallach snatched his career from the scrap pile and may well have made adjustments that will keep him in the Dodger lineup for another season or two.

	G	AB	H	2B	3B	HR	RS	RBI	BB	SB	BA
1994	113	414	116	21	1	23	68	78	46	0	.280
Career	2013	7420	1916	400	33	239	847	1045	592	50	.258
Projected	146	520	124	23	1	20	63	80	45	0	.244

Montreal
EXPOS

1995 Scouting Report

Outfielders: The majors' best young outfield is led by Marquis Grissom in center field. He's a complete player in every aspect of the game. Canadian free agent Larry Walker is baseball's best right fielder and a dangerous longball hitter. Moises Alou (LF) was the most productive player in the Expos' lineup in '94. Rondell White is a fine prospect who will take over if free agent Walker doesn't re-sign. Lou Frazier is pure speed off the bench.

Infielders: Wil Cordero is decidedly unpolished as a shortstop, but he's rapidly developed into an elite offensive middle infielder. Second base is covered by versatile Mike Lansing. A rookie in '94, Cliff Floyd (1B) is still learning his position, but he didn't appear overmatched at the plate. Sean Berry is a decent major league third baseman in every respect.

Catchers: Darrin Fletcher gets much of the credit for the Expos' league-best team ERA, due to his deft handling of pitchers..

Starting Pitchers: The Expos compiled the lowest team ERA in the majors last year (3.56). Workhorse Ken Hill was in contention for Cy Young honors. Pedro J. Martinez, acquired for Delino DeShields, looks like a superstar in the making. Jeff Fassero might be considered the staff ace after two consecutive superb seasons. Butch Henry, a lefty who wasn't certain of making the team when spring training began, finished with the lowest ERA of any Expos starter.

Relief Pitchers: John Wetteland is the NL's top stopper, once he gets in a groove. Mel Rojas did a yeoman's job filling in when Wetteland wasn't available early in '94.

Manager: Felipe Alou's (238–163) teams haven't finished below second place since he took over the reins in 1992.

1995 Outlook

It was a phenomenal season in Monteal, as the Expos came from last place on April 19 to finish the short season with the majors' best record. The club reeled off twenty wins in their last twenty-three games to secure the division title.

There was no aspect of the game in which the team failed to perform brilliantly in '94. The starting pitching was balanced, with the rotation's top four all posting ERAs of less than 3.50. The staff could actually be improved this season. Butch Henry, Ken Hill, and Pedro J. Martinez are each younger than thirty. The Expos' relief crew is dominant, with Mel Rojas and John Wetteland combining to form one of the NL's stingiest bullpens. The Expos are arguably the only team in baseball whose pitching is as solid as that of the Braves. The difference in the two corps is control of the strikezone: Montreal allowed 288 walks last year, the NL's best. Atlanta pitchers handed out 378 free passes, the league's tenth-best total.

The Montreal hitters are a formidable group, mixing individual speed and power like no other lineup in baseball. Olympic Stadium isn't conducive to the longball, but the Expos finished second in the league in doubles and fourth in slugging. No team in the NL swiped more bases than the Expos. Overall, the team had four players who reached double figures in both homers and steals. No club in the Eastern Division can do offensive damage in as many ways as the Expos.

The division won't be a runaway, and the Expos could falter over a full season. Their rotation is very strong, but in a starter-for-starter comparison with the Braves (Maddux vs. Hill, etc.), Atlanta appears to be a slightly safer bet. Montreal's infield defense is porous, and les Expos were eleventh in the National League in overall fielding percentage. If All-Star right fielder Larry Walker doesn't re-sign, the Expos will obviously miss his bat and glove. Still, the Expos will almost certainly make the playoffs, at least as a wild card, and their chances of winning the division are excellent.

1995 Montreal Expos Roster

Manager: Felipe Alou
Coaches: Pierre Arsenault, Tommy Harper, Joe Kerrigan, Jerry Manuel, Luis Pujols, Jim Tracy

No.	Pitchers	B	T	HT	WT	DOB	Birthplace
13	Fassero, Jeff	L	L	6–1	195	1/5/63	Springfield, IL
27	Henry, Butch	L	L	6–1	200	10/7/68	El Paso, TX
34	Heredia, Gil	R	R	6–1	205	10/26/65	Nogales, AZ
44	Hill, Ken	R	R	6–2	200	12/14/65	Lynn, MA
45	Martinez, Pedro J.	R	R	5–11	164	7/25/71	Manoguyabo, DR
50	Perez, Carlos	L	L	6–2	168	1/4/71	Nigua, DR
51	Rojas, Mel	R	R	5–11	195	12/10/66	Hanford, CA
42	Rueter, Kirk	L	L	6–3	195	12/1/70	Centralia, IL
54	Scott, Tim	R	R	6–2	205	11/16/66	Hanford, CA
31	Shaw, Jeff	R	R	6–2	200	7/7/66	Wash. Court., OH
57	Wetteland, John	R	R	6–2	215	8/21/66	San Mateo, CA
47	White, Gabe	L	L	6–2	200	11/20/71	Sebring, FL
	Catchers						
24	Fletcher, Darrin	L	R	6–1	198	10/3/66	Elmhurst, IL
19	Laker, Tim	R	R	6–2	190	11/27/69	Encino, CA
2	Spehr, Tim	R	R	6–2	200	7/2/66	Excelsior Springs, MO
25	Webster, Lenny	R	R	5–9	195	2/10/65	New Orleans, LA
	Infielders						
56	Alcantara, Israel	R	R	6–2	175	5/6/73	Santo Domingo, DR
58	Andrews, Shane	R	R	6–1	215	8/28/71	Dallas, TX
15	Benavides, Freddie	R	R	6–2	185	4/7/66	Laredo, TX
5	Berry, Sean	R	R	5–11	200	3/22/66	Santa Monica, CA
12	Cordero, Wil	R	R	6–2	190	10/3/71	Mayaguez, PR
30	Floyd, Cliff	L	R	6–4	220	5/12/72	Chicago, IL
52	Grudzielanek, Mark	R	R	6–1	180	6/30/70	Milwaukee, WI
3	Lansing, Mike	R	R	5–11	180	4/3/68	Rawlins, WY
	Outfielders						
18	Alou, Moises	R	R	6–3	190	7/3/66	Atlanta, GA
53	Benitez, Yamil	R	R	6–2	190	10/5/72	San Juan, PR
7	Frazier, Lou	B	R	6–2	175	1/26/65	St. Louis, MO
9	Grissom, Marquis	R	R	5–11	190	4/17/67	Atlanta, GA
16	Pride, Curtis	L	R	5–11	200	12/17/68	Washington, DC
37	White, Rondell	R	R	6–1	205	2/23/72	Milledgeville, GA

1995 Schedule

April

S	M	T	W	T	F	S
						1
2	3 PIT	4	5 PIT	6 PIT	7 PIT	8 STL
9 STL	10 COL	11 COL	12	13 STL	14 STL	15 STL
16 STL	17 COL	18 COL	19	20 CHI	21 CHI	22 CHI
23 CHI	24 PIT	25 PIT	26 PIT	27 CHI	28 CHI	29 CHI
30 CHI						

May

S	M	T	W	T	F	S
	1	2 NY	3 NY	4 NY	5 FLO	6 FLO
7 FLO	8 FLO	9 PHI	10 PHI	11 PHI	12 NY	13 NY
14 NY	15 NY	16 CIN	17 CIN	18	19 HOU	20 HOU
21	22	23 SD	24 SD	25 SD	26 LA	27 LA
28 LA	29 SF	30 SF	31 SF			

June

S	M	T	W	T	F	S
				1	2 SD	3 SD
4 SD	5 LA	6 LA	7 LA	8	9 SF	10 SF
11 SF	12	13 ATL	14 ATL	15 ATL	16 CIN	17 CIN
18 CIN	19 HOU	20 HOU	21 HOU	22	23 PIT	24 PIT
25 PIT	26 ATL	27 ATL	28 ATL	29 FLO	30 FLO	

July

S	M	T	W	T	F	S
						1 FLO
2 FLO	3 STL	4 STL	5 STL	6 COL	7 COL	8 COL
9 COL	10 PHI	11	12	13 PHI	14 PHI	15 PHI
16 PHI	17 STL	18 STL	19 CHI	20 CHI	21 PIT	22 PIT
23 PIT	24 CHI	25 CHI	26 CHI	27	28 COL	29 COL
30 COL	31 COL					

August

S	M	T	W	T	F	S
		1 FLO	2 FLO	3	4 ATL	5 ATL
6 ATL	7 ATL	8 HOU	9 HOU	10 HOU	11 PHI	12 PHI
13 PHI	14 PHI	15 NY	16 NY	17	18 SD	19 SD
20 PHI	21 SD	22 LA	23 LA	24 LA	25 SF	26 SF
27 SF	28	29 SD	30 SD	31 SD		

Sept/Oct

S	M	T	W	T	F	S
					1 LA	2 LA
3 LA	4 SF	5 SF	6 SF	7	8 NY	9 NY
10 NY	11 NY	12 PHI	13 PHI	14	15 HOU	16 HOU
17 HOU	18 CIN	19 CIN	20 CIN	21	22 ATL	23 ATL
24 ATL	25 FLA	26 FLA	27 FLA	28 CIN	29 CIN	30 CIN
1 CIN	2					

☐ Home   ☐ Away   ★ All-Star Game

Olympic Stadium

Capacity: 43,739

Turf: Artificial

Dimensions:
LF Line: 325'
RF Line: 325'
Center: 404'
Alleys: 375'

Tickets:
(514) 253-3434

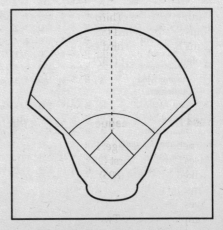

1994 Batting Order

1. Marquis Grissom (Center Field)
2. Cliff Floyd (First Base)
3. Moises Alou (Left Field)
4. Larry Walker (Right Field)
5. Darrin Fletcher (Catcher)
6. Wil Cordero (Shortstop)
7. Mike Lansing (Second Base)
8. Sean Berry (Third Base)
9. Pitcher

1994 Team Record
74–40 (.649); First in NL East

NL East	W	L	NL Central	W	L	NL West	W	L
Atlanta	5	4	Chicago	4	2	Colorado	2	4
Florida	7	2	Cincinnati	2	4	Los Angeles	9	3
Montreal	—	—	Houston	4	2	San Diego	12	0
New York	4	3	Pittsburgh	8	2	S. Francisco	5	7
Philadelphia	5	4	St. Louis	7	3			
Total	21	13		25	13		28	14

1994 National League Team Rank Batting

Batting Average: Third (.278)
Runs Scored: Third (585)
Runs Batted In: Third (542)
Stolen Bases: First (137)
Slugging Percentage: Fourth (.435)
On-Base Percentage: Third (.343)

1994 National League Team Rank Pitching

Earned Run Average: First (3.56)
Bases On Balls: First (288)
Strikeouts: Third (805)
Wins: First (74)
Saves: First (46)
Complete Games: Twelfth (4)

© Rich Pilling/MLB Photos

Montreal Expos MVP

Moises Alou   No.18/ OF

Born: 7/3/66, Atlanta, Georgia
Height: 6' 3"   **Weight:** 190
Bats: Right   **Throws:** Right
1994 OBP: .397   **SLG:** .592

Though he has been susceptible to streaks since his rookie season, Alou was very consistent in 1994. As well rounded as any ballplayer the Alou family has produced, his super-quick wrists and compact swing make him a very tough out. In an outfield full of young stars, Alou was the most steadily explosive offensive performer on the first-place Expos.

Alou finished third in the voting for National League MVP. He made the NL top ten in batting average (third), runs scored (sixth), slugging (sixth), on-base percentage (ninth), and extra-base hits (sixth).

It was a truly phenomenal season, especially considering that on September 16, 1993, Alou suffered a complete dislocation of his left ankle and a fractured fibula. Many who witnessed the horrific injury imagined that Alou would never play baseball again. His quick recovery, thanks to a grueling physical therapy regimen, was nothing less than miraculous.

Alou has incredibly quick reflexes. He can turn with authority on high fastballs that would tie most hitters in knots. Twice last season Alou blasted homers that traveled over 430 feet.

Just beginning to emerge as a star, Alou figures to be the most dynamic young outfielder in baseball this season.

	G	AB	H	2B	3B	HR	RS	RBI	BB	SB	BA
1994	107	442	143	31	5	22	81	78	42	7	.339
Career	374	1265	381	88	14	49	208	219	105	40	.301
Projected	148	573	193	40	7	26	99	107	53	16	.323

Sean Berry   No. 5/ 3B

Born: 3/22/66, Santa Monica, CA
Height: 5' 11"   **Weight:** 200
Bats: Right   **Throws:** Right
1994 OBP: .347   **SLG:** .453

Though he's neither an intimidating slugger nor an agile fielder, Berry is a steady everyday presence at third base. Berry is a very smart baserunner, as his remarkable 100% stolen-base-success rate last season attests. He hits well when behind in the count, and he cut down on his strikeout frequency compared to 1993. Berry had thirteen RBIs in his last fourteen games.

	G	AB	H	2B	3B	HR	RS	RBI	BB	SB	BA
1994	103	320	89	19	2	11	43	41	32	14	.278
Career	288	759	199	39	5	26	105	99	81	28	.262
Projected	140	401	117	23	3	17	63	61	49	18	.281

Wil Cordero   No. 12/ SS

Born: 10/3/71, Mayaguez, PR
Height: 6' 2"   **Weight:** 190
Bats: Right   **Throws:** Right
1994 OBP: .363   **SLG:** .489

Cordero tied for the league lead in errors last season, but that was the only glitch in an otherwise fantastic sophomore year. Showing an improved batting eye and making great strides on the basepaths (84% success rate), Cordero is developing a complete offensive package. He could crack twenty to twenty-five homers in '95.

	G	AB	H	2B	3B	HR	RS	RBI	BB	SB	BA
1994	110	415	122	30	3	15	65	63	41	16	.294
Career	293	1016	278	66	6	27	138	129	84	28	.274
Projected	149	561	167	41	3	17	80	80	66	19	.283

Jeff Fassero   No. 13/ P

Born: 1/5/63, Springfield, IL
Height: 6' 1"   **Weight:** 195
Bats: Left   **Throws:** Left
Opp. Batting Average: .229

Fassero was victimized by poor run support in his first full year as a starter, but the Expos have to be happy with his consistency (fifteen quality starts) and confidence. Possessing a large repertoire for an ex-reliever, Fassero presents a challenge to any batter, but is especially tough on lefties. He ranked fifth in the NL in opponents batting average.

	G	GS	IP	ERA	H	BB	SO	W	L	SV
1994	21	21	138.2	2.99	119	40	119	8	6	0
Career	198	36	429.1	2.64	358	145	364	30	23	10
Projected	29	29	191.0	2.62	164	59	161	11	6	0

Darrin Fletcher   No. 24/ C

Born: 10/3/66, Elmhurst, IL
Height: 6' 1"   **Weight:** 198
Bats: Left   **Throws:** Right
1994 OBP: .314   **SLG:** .435

The Expos are thrilled with Fletcher's progress at the plate, and his handling of the young starting staff gets a high grade as well. Fletcher has made adjustments in his swing to increase his power, and he goes with the pitch much better than he once did. He's great in the clutch; his RBI frequency is above average (.20 per at-bat). Fletcher's arm is a prominent weakness.

	G	AB	H	2B	3B	HR	RS	RBI	BB	SB	BA
1994	94	285	74	18	1	10	28	57	25	0	.260
Career	372	1070	267	57	4	23	83	158	80	0	.250
Projected	139	433	120	25	1	13	40	77	39	0	.267

Cliff Floyd   No. 30/ 1B

Born: 5/12/72, Chicago, IL
Height: 6' 4"   **Weight:** 220
Bats: Left   **Throws:** Right
1994 OBP: .332   **SLG:** .398

Floyd put up some eye-popping numbers in the minor leagues as an outfielder, but that production didn't carry over to the Show in 1994. Touted as a pre-season favorite for Rookie of the Year honors and a potential 20/20 man, Floyd showed good speed and some extra-base pop, but his home run total was disappointing.

	G	AB	H	2B	3B	HR	RS	RBI	BB	SB	BA
1994	100	334	94	19	4	4	43	41	24	10	.281
Career	110	365	101	19	4	5	46	43	24	10	.277
Projected	154	536	164	29	6	8	71	66	37	15	.291

Marquis Grissom No. 9/ OF

Born: 4/17/67, Atlanta, GA
Height: 5' 11"   **Weight:** 190
Bats: Right   **Throws:** Right
1994 OBP: .344   **SLG:** .427

One of the most complete players in the NL, Grissom is crucial to the Expos' success. A great percentage basestealer, a Gold Glove centerfielder, and a versatile hitter, Grissom is the anchor of the Expos. They'd be smart to insure that he spends his prime years in Montreal. He was second in the NL in runs scored and stolen bases.

	G	AB	H	2B	3B	HR	RS	RBI	BB	SB	BA
1994	110	475	137	25	4	11	96	45	41	36	.288
Career	698	2678	747	130	23	54	430	276	208	266	.279
Projected	158	682	217	33	4	19	128	90	60	57	.306

Butch Henry No. 27/ P

Born: 10/7/68, El Paso, TX
Height: 6' 1"   **Weight:** 200
Bats: Left   **Throws:** Left
Opp. Batting Average: .241

Lefthanded finesse specialist Henry was the Expos' brightest surprise in '94. He was able to maintain his pinpoint control while also becoming tougher to hit, especially for lefties, against whom he'd had trouble in '93. Henry will probably be in the league for another eight years on the basis of his performance last season and the virtue of being a lefthanded reliever.

	G	GS	IP	ERA	H	BB	SO	W	L	SV
1994	24	15	107.1	2.43	97	20	70	8	3	1
Career	82	59	376.0	4.14	417	89	213	17	21	1
Projected	31	18	121.0	4.24	133	28	67	6	7	1

Ken Hill No. 44/ P

Born: 12/14/65, Lynn, MA
Height: 6' 2"   **Weight:** 200
Bats: Right   **Throws:** Right
1994 Opp. Batting Average: .248

The Expos' ace and a superior athlete, Hill could be ready for national recognition this season. A perennial workhorse with a nasty forkball, Hill has been rock solid since coming over from St. Louis. Hill goes to the mound expecting to win, and his team often gives him plenty of offensive support. He finished second in the voting for NL Cy Young.

	G	GS	IP	ERA	H	BB	SO	W	L	SV
1994	23	23	154.2	3.32	145	44	85	16	5	0
Career	168	162	1027.0	3.50	923	398	622	64	53	0
Projected	29	29	195.0	3.27	177	68	101	14	7	0

Mike Lansing   No. 3/ 2B

Born: 4/3/68, Rawlins, WY
Height: 5' 11"   **Weight:** 180
Bats: Right   **Throws:** Right
1994 OBP: .328   **SLG:** .368

Lansing took over second base duties after popular Delino DeShields was dealt to the Dodgers. Lansing is a hard-nosed type of player; he does the little things well and is very aggressive. He's versatile enough to be competent at shortstop too. He was fifth in the league in fielding percentage among second basemen. His offensive prowess is solid for a middle infielder.

	G	AB	H	2B	3B	HR	RS	RBI	BB	SB	BA
1994	106	394	105	21	2	5	44	35	30	12	.266
Career	247	885	246	50	3	8	108	80	76	35	.278
Projected	150	561	169	33	2	5	71	53	50	23	.289

Pedro J. Martinez   No. 45/ P

Born: 7/25/71, Manoguyabo, DR
Height: 5' 11"   **Weight:** 164
Bats: Right   **Throws:** Right
Opp. Batting Average: .220

Martinez made an immediate impact on the Expos' rotation and confirmed what scouts already knew—if DeShields for Martinez was lopsided, it wasn't the Expos who got taken. Like his older brother, Ramon of the Dodgers, the younger Martinez appears fragile on the mound. His mechanics are very sound, but the Expos need to be careful not to overwork his skinny right arm.

	G	GS	IP	ERA	H	BB	SO	W	L	SV
1994	24	23	144.2	3.42	115	45	142	11	5	1
Career	91	26	259.2	3.05	197	103	269	21	11	3
Projected	30	27	214.0	3.07	190	66	199	18	6	1

Mel Rojas   No. 51/ P

Born: 12/10/66, Hanford, CA
Height: 5' 11"   **Weight:** 195
Bats: Right   **Throws:** Right
Opp. Batting Average: .227

Rojas replaced injured John Wetteland in the season's first months and gave the Expos the lift they needed. His effectiveness dropped toward mid-year, but Rojas is a solid setup man for ace Wetteland, and he could be a full-time closer for many teams. Rojas is especially tough on righthanders with his bat-freezing forkball.

	G	GS	IP	ERA	H	BB	SO	W	L	SV
1994	58	0	84.0	3.32	71	21	84	3	2	16
Career	252	0	361.0	2.79	298	122	265	21	15	43
Projected	72	0	99.0	3.13	87	29	76	5	6	15

Kirk Rueter   No. 42/ P

Born: 12/1/70, Centralia, IL
Height: 6' 3"   **Weight:** 195
Bats: Left   **Throws:** Left
Opp. Batting Average: .294

Rueter was the least challenging Expos hurler last year, the only full-time starter with an ERA over 4.00. He took a step back from his promising '93 performance (8-0, 2.73 ERA); his rate of home runs allowed was up, and he was very hittable, though his control remained excellent. Rueter's stuff isn't overpowering, and his lack of a strikeout pitch remains a concern.

	G	GS	IP	ERA	H	BB	SO	W	L	SV
1994	20	20	92.1	5.17	106	23	50	7	3	0
Career	34	34	178.1	3.99	191	41	81	15	3	0
Projected	20	20	106.0	4.00	114	25	48	9	2	0

Larry Walker　　No. 33/ OF

Born: 12/1/66, Maple Ridge, Canada
Height: 6' 3"　**Weight:** 215
Bats: Left　**Throws:** Right
1994 OBP: .394　**SLG:** .587

Canadian native Walker had the big year everyone expected of him. Probably the league's most exciting rightfielder, Walker brings a hard-nosed demeanor to the field. At the plate, he's capable of finishing an at-bat as quickly as any slugger around, when he gets his hips rotated. A unique mix of pure talent and all-out effort makes Walker a fan favorite.

	G	AB	H	2B	3B	HR	RS	RBI	BB	SB	BA
1994	103	395	127	44	2	19	76	86	47	15	.322
Career	674	2366	666	147	16	99	368	384	264	98	.281
Projected	148	566	178	45	5	27	107	114	84	29	.302

John Wetteland　·　No. 57/ P

Born: 8/21/66, San Mateo, CA
Height: 6' 2"　**Weight:** 215
Bats: Right　**Throws:** Right
Opp. Batting Average: .202

Entering '94 as baseball's top closer, Wetteland battled injury for the second straight year. He's at his best when locating his high-nineties fastball, not mixing pitches. The alarming stat was Wetteland's strikeouts-per-inning rate of 1.06, down from 1.33 in '93. When he's right, no one slams the door harder, but it remains to be seen if Wetteland can remain healthy.

	G	GS	IP	ERA	H	BB	SO	W	L	SV
1994	52	0	63.2	2.83	46	21	68	4	6	25
Career	248	17	387.0	2.93	298	139	421	25	25	106
Projected	70	0	85.0	1.99	59	28	103	7	5	39

New York
METS

1995 Scouting Report

Outfielders: The outfield picture is blurry. Ryan Thompson had a frustrating season that included more strikeouts than hits, but he's young and talented and will return in either center or left. The other two outfield positions are decidedly up in the air as of this writing. Joe Orsulak, a fine part-time player, was forced into virtual full-time action last year. The scuttlebutt is that Bobby Bonilla may move back to right field, with newcomer Carl Everett starting in center.

Infielders: Jeff Kent is a championship-caliber second baseman. Jose Vizcaino brought both stability and excitement to the Mets' shortstop slot, though he contributes little with the bat. Bobby Bonilla isn't much of a third baseman, but he's a switch-hitting nightmare for opposing pitchers. First base will belong to sensational newcomer Rico Brogna.

Catchers: Todd Hundley made the most of his hits by blasting almost 25% of them over the fence. Kelly Stinnett also sees significant playing time.

Starting Pitchers: Bret Saberhagen is a brilliant pitcher who showed his best stuff in '94. Pete Harnisch is the kind of power pitcher the team needs. Bobby Jones features an excellent change-up and showed great poise and maturity. Jason Jacome looked promising in eight starts. Eric Hillman is the fifth arm.

Relief Pitchers: The Mets acquired Jerry DiPoto from Cleveland and Doug Henry from Milwaukee. Josias Manzanillo pitched well in a setup role in '94. John Franco was an unsigned free agent as of this writing.

Manager: Dallas Green (326–331) is the strict disciplinarian the troubled Mets needed.

1995 Outlook

The Mets entered 1994 focused on enthusiasm and attention to detail, two qualities they had been sorely lacking in recent years. It paid off, as the team may have actually overachieved in relation to its talent level. The Mets will be in a rebuilding mode for the next few seasons. The rate of progress will be dependent on the development of potential stars Jeff Kent, Rico Brogna, and Ryan Thompson.

The beasts of the NL East, Atlanta and Montreal, are too talented to allow room at the top for the Mets. And Philadelphia will be much tougher minus the injuries that weakened them last season. That leaves the Mets and Florida on bottom, and both teams will be thinking more of progress than of pennants.

The Mets are still trying to rebuild their image after several ugly off-field incidents in 1993. Regrettably, it has been the high-priced veteran talent that has gotten into trouble with both the law and the media. Doc Gooden's drug-related suspension is the latest scandal. Of course, the Mets wouldn't win many games without Bret Saberhagen's arm or Bobby Bonilla's bat. But it's crucial for the Mets' potential new leaders, Thompson and Kent, to lead the team if it's going to return to a championship level in the future, after the current stars have departed.

There's certainly room for improvement in the pitching department. David Cone, Dwight Gooden, Jerry Koosman, Tom Seaver—the greatest pitchers in the organization's history have all been hard throwers, able to take advantage of the poor visibility at Shea. The Mets ranked thirteenth in the league in Ks last season. The Mets have never put together a winning campaign without amassing high strikeout totals; they need to begin grooming power pitchers. Pete Harnisch's arrival will help.

The Mets are four years away from challenging for a division crown. But thanks to Dallas Green, the team is no longer the league's most undisciplined.

1995 New York Mets Roster

Manager: Dallas Green
Coaches: Mike Cubbage, Frank Howard, Tom McCraw, Greg Pavlick, Steve Swisher, Bobby Wine

No.	Pitchers	B	T	HT	WT	DOB	Birthplace
50	Castillo, Juan	R	R	6–5	205	6/23/70	Caracas, Venezuela
—	DiPoto, Jerry	R	R	6–2	200	5/24/68	Jersey City, NJ
40	Gunderson, Eric	R	L	6–0	195	3/29/66	Portland, OR
47	Jacome, Jason	L	L	6–1	175	11/24/70	Tulsa, OK
28	Jones, Bobby	R	R	6–4	225	2/10/70	Fresno, CA
—	Henry, Doug	R	R	6–4	185	12/10/63	Sacramento, CA
39	Manzanillo, Josias	R	R	6–0	190	10/16/67	San Pedro Macoris, DR
—	Minor, Blas	R	R	6–3	195	3/20/66	Merced, CA
—	Mlicki, Dave	R	R	6–4	190	6/8/68	Cleveland, OH
43	Remlinger, Mike	L	L	6–0	195	3/26/66	Middletown, NY
17	Saberhagen, Bret	R	R	6–1	190	4/11/64	Chicago Heights, IL
71	Walker, Pete	R	R	6–2	195	4/8/69	Beverly, MA
	Catchers						
2	Castillo, Alberto	R	R	6–0	184	2/10/70	San Juan Maguana, DR
—	Fordyce, Brook	R	R	6–1	185	5/7/70	New London, CT
9	Hundley, Todd	B	R	5–11	185	5/27/69	Martinsville, VA
33	Stinnett, Kelly	R	R	5–11	195	2/14/70	Lawton, OK
	Infielders						
23	Bogar, Tim	R	R	6–2	198	10/28/66	Indianapolis, IN
25	Bonilla, Bobby	B	R	6–3	240	2/23/63	New York, NY
26	Brogna, Rico	L	L	6–2	200	11/10/71	Turner Falls, MA
42	Huskey, Butch	R	R	6–3	244	11/10/71	Anadarko, OK
12	Kent, Jeff	R	R	6–1	185	3/7/68	Bellflower, CA
61	Ledesma, Aaron	R	R	6–2	200	6/3/71	Union City, CA
21	Segui, David	B	L	6–1	202	7/19/66	Kansas City, KS
—	Spiers, Bill	L	R	6–2	190	6/5/66	Orangeburg, SC
62	Veras, Quilvio	B	R	5–9	166	4/3/71	Santo Domingo, DR
1	Vina, Fernando	L	R	5–9	170	4/16/69	Sacramento, CA
15	Vizcaino, Jose	B	R	6–1	180	3/26/68	Palenque Cristobal, DR
	Outfielders						
—	Everett, Carl	B	R	6–0	181	6/3/71	Tampa, FL
29	Lindeman, Jim	R	R	6–1	200	1/10/62	Evanston, IL
36	Navarro, Tito	B	R	5–10	155	9/12/70	Rio Piedras, PR
6	Orsulak, Joe	L	L	6–1	205	5/31/62	Glen Ridge, NJ
20	Thompson, Ryan	R	R	6–3	215	11/4/67	Chestertown, MD

1995 Schedule

April

S	M	T	W	T	F	S
						1
2 FLO	3	4 COL	5	6 COL	7 CHI	8 CHI
9 CHI	10	11 PIT	12 PIT	13 PIT	14 CHI	15 CHI
16 CHI	17	18 PIT	19	20 STL	21 STL	22 STL
23 STL	24 COL	25 COL	26 COL	27	28 STL	29 STL
30 STL						

May

S	M	T	W	T	F	S
	1	2 MON	3 MON	4 MON	5 CIN	6 CIN
7 CIN	8	9 ATL	10 ATL	11 ATL	12 MON	13 MON
14 MON	15	16 HOU	17 HOU	18 HOU	19 PHI	20 PHI
21 PHI	22	23 LA	24 LA	25 LA	26 SF	27 SF
28 SF	29 SD	30 SD	31 SD			

June

S	M	T	W	T	F	S
				1	2 LA	3 LA
4	5 SF	6 SF	7 SF	8 SF	9 SD	10 SD
11	12 FLO	13 FLO	14 FLO	15	16 HOU	17 HOU
18 HOU	19 PHI	20 PHI	21 PHI	22 PHI	23 ATL	24 ATL
25 ATL	26	27 FLO	28 FLO	29	30 CIN	

July

S	M	T	W	T	F	S
						1
2	3	4 CHI	5 CHI	6 CHI	7 PIT	8 PIT
9 PIT	10	11 ★	12	13 COL	14 COL	15 COL
16 COL	17 CHI	18 CHI	19 STL	20 STL	21 COL	22 COL
23 COL	24	25 STL	26 STL	27 STL	28 PIT	29 PIT
30 PIT	31 PIT					

August

S	M	T	W	T	F	S
		1 CIN	2 CIN	3 CIN	4 FLO	5 FLO
6 FLO	7 FLO	8 PHI	9 PHI	10 PHI	11 HOU	12 HOU
13 HOU	14	15 MON	16 MON	17	18 LA	19 LA
20 LA	21 SF	22 SF	23 SF	24 SD	25 SD	26 SD
27 SD	28	29 LA	30 LA	31 LA		

Sept/Oct

S	M	T	W	T	F	S
					1 SF	2 SF
3 SF	4 SD	5 SD	6 SD	7	8 MON	9 MON
10 MON	11 MON	12 HOU	13 HOU	14 HOU	15 PHI	16 PHI
17 PHI	18 ATL	19 ATL	20 ATL	21 ATL	22 FLO	23 FLO
24 FLO	25 CIN	26 CIN	27 CIN	28	29 ATL	30 ATL
1 ATL	2					

☐ Home   ☐ Away   ★ All-Star Game

Shea Stadium

Capacity: 55,601

Turf: Grass

Dimensions:
LF Line: 338'
RF Line: 338'
Center: 410'
Alleys: 371'

Tickets:
(718) 507-8499

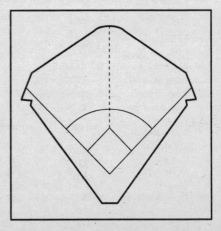

1994 Batting Order

1. Jose Vizcaino (Shortstop)
2. Todd Hundley (Catcher)
3. Jeromy Burnitz (Right Field)
4. Bobby Bonilla (Third Base)
5. Jeff Kent (Second Base)
6. Rico Brogna (First Base)
7. Joe Orsulak (Left Field)
8. Ryan Thompson (Center Field)
9. Pitcher

1994 Team Record
55–58 (.487); Third in NL East

NL East	W	L	NL Central	W	L	NL West	W	L
Atlanta	4	5	Chicago	4	1	Colorado	1	5
Florida	4	6	Cincinnati	4	2	Los Angeles	6	6
Montreal	3	4	Houston	3	3	San Diego	6	6
New York	—	—	Pittsburgh	4	5	S. Francisco	6	6
Philadelphia	4	6	St. Louis	6	3			
Total	15	21		21	14		19	23

1994 National League Team Rank Batting

Batting Average: Thirteenth (.250)
Runs Scored: Ninth (506)
Runs Batted In: Ninth (477)
Stolen Bases: Fourteenth (25)
Slugging Percentage: Twelfth (.394)
On-Base Percentage: Fourteenth (.316)

1994 National League Team Rank Pitching

Earned Run Average: Eighth (4.13)
Bases On Balls: Ninth (332)
Strikeouts: Thirteenth (640)
Wins: Sixth (55)
Saves: Second (35)
Complete Games: Sixth (7)

New York Mets MVP

Bret Saberhagen   No. 17/ P

Born: 4/11/64, Chicago Heights, IL
Height: 6' 1"   **Weight:** 190
Bats: Right   **Throws:** Right
Opp. Batting Average: .254

Saberhagen's career has had a touch of Bela Lugosi in it; equal parts bizzare and brilliant. Last year heralded the return of Sabes' Cy Young–type mastery, as he stayed healthy and started more games than he had in the previous, non-strike season.

Saberhagen has more variations on his fastball than most pitchers have pitches, and his control is almost freakish; thirteen walks in 177 innings is not a typo! In fact, it's a modern record (since 1900) for best walks-per-nine-innings ratio (0.7). He put together a club-record streak of 47.1 innings without allowing a base on balls. He finished the season on fire with a 7–0 record in nine starts, sculpting a 1.51 ERA with sixty-two Ks and just five walks.

Saberhagen is a pure power pitcher—perfect for Shea Stadium with its poor visibility. He struck out eleven batters for every base on balls allowed last year, the best ratio of the twentieth century. An exceptional athlete, Sabes fields his position like a shortstop and cuts off the running game well. Despite his past foibles, involving squirting bleach and the New York media, Saberhagen is a very likeable person. He's had tendencies toward alternatingly excellent and ineffective seasons, but there should be continued dominance for Saberhagen in 1995.

	G	GS	IP	ERA	H	BB	SO	W	L	SV
1994	24	24	177.1	2.74	169	13	143	14	4	0
Career	312	284	2074.2	3.19	1935	388	1410	134	94	1
Projected	26	26	187.0	2.99	178	18	140	12	7	0

Bobby Bonilla   No. 25/ 3B

Born: 2/23/63, New York, NY
Height: 6' 3"   **Weight:** 240
Bats: Both   **Throws:** Right
1994 OBP: .374   **SLG:** .504

Bonilla wasn't hitting in April, and the New York media were wailing, but by the end of May, Bobby Bo was his old self, hitting for power to all fields from both sides of the plate. Whatever the expectations, Bonilla had a productive offensive season, and figures to do so again in '95. Unfortunately, he's still not smooth at third (eighteen errors, most of any third baseman in the league).

	G	AB	H	2B	3B	HR	RS	RBI	BB	SB	BA
1994	108	403	117	24	1	20	60	67	55	1	.290
Career	1293	4637	1290	269	41	189	711	750	590	34	.278
Projected	150	553	156	28	2	33	87	95	78	2	.279

Rico Brogna   No. 26/ 1B

Born: 4/18/70, Turner Falls, MA
Height: 6' 2"   **Weight:** 200
Bats: Left   **Throws:** Left
1994 OBP: .380   **SLG:** .626

Acquired from Detroit, Brogna has Mets management beaming with joy. He showed better power than he had in the minors, even homering in three consecutive games. He also put together a fifteen-game hitting streak. Brogna cuffed around lefthanders at a .385 clip. He was no slouch with the glove, making just one miscue in 366 total chances (.997).

	G	AB	H	2B	3B	HR	RS	RBI	BB	SB	BA
1994	39	131	46	11	2	7	16	20	6	1	.351
Career	48	157	51	12	2	8	19	23	29	3	.325
Projected	No projection. Player was a rookie in 1994.										

Jeromy Burnitz   No. 5/ OF

Born: 4/15/69, Westminster, CA
Height: 6' 0"   **Weight:** 190
Bats: Left   **Throws:** Right
1994 OBP: .347   **SLG:** .329

Burnitz was a hot prospect for '94, having put up superior power/speed numbers in the minors. Scouts raved about his bat speed, but Burnitz struggled at the plate. Burnitz is a dead pull hitter, always looking for the longball, but he struck out once per game last season. The Mets gave up on Burnitz, sending him to the Indians during the off-season.

	G	AB	H	2B	3B	HR	RS	RBI	BB	SB	BA
1994	45	143	34	4	0	3	26	15	23	1	.238
Career	131	406	98	14	6	16	75	53	61	4	.241
Projected	78	250	65	9	4	10	48	34	39	3	.251

John Franco   No. 31/ P

Born: 9/17/60, Brooklyn, NY
Height: 5' 10"   **Weight:** 185
Bats: Left   **Throws:** Left
Opp. Batting Average: .244

A smart competitor, Franco may never be dominant again, but his screwball is still reliable when his arm is sound. Leading the league in saves with a team like the Mets is no small feat, and Franco is crafty enough to continue frustrating opposing batters for a couple of more seasons. Franco filed for free agency and was unsigned as of this writing.

	G	GS	IP	ERA	H	BB	SO	W	L	SV
1994	47	0	50.0	2.70	47	19	42	1	4	30
Career	613	0	770.1	2.62	704	298	559	63	51	256
Projected	49	0	51.0	3.75	55	23	42	3	4	24

Dwight Gooden   No. 16/ P

Born: 11/16/64, Tampa, FL
Height: 6' 3"   **Weight:** 210
Bats: Right   **Throws:** Right
Opp. Batting Average: .282

Doc Gooden spent time on the DL with a hairline fracture of his right big toe, then was suspended for sixty days for violation of his Aftercare Program. His season was essentially lost. He's currently suspended for 1995, though it's conceivable that he won't have to serve the entire suspension. One can only hope that Doc will be able to put his life on the right track.

	G	GS	IP	ERA	H	BB	SO	W	L	SV
1994	7	7	41.1	6.31	46	15	40	3	4	0
Career	298	296	2128.1	3.04	1852	636	1835	154	81	1
Projected			No projection. Player is suspended for 1995.							

Todd Hundley   No. 9/ C

Born: 5/27/69, Martinsville, VA
Height: 5' 11"   **Weight:** 185
Bats: Both   **Throws:** Right
1994 OBP: .303   **SLG:** .443

Another development in the majors' widening pool of slugging backstops, righthanders would do well to stop throwing Hundley inside fastballs. His game still has some big holes, batting average and throwing, to name two, but '95 should be an interesting year as Hundley takes over full-time duties. Hundley went deep from both sides of the plate June 18 at Florida.

	G	AB	H	2B	3B	HR	RS	RBI	BB	SB	BA
1994	91	291	69	10	1	16	45	42	25	2	.237
Career	401	1193	261	50	4	35	130	136	79	6	.219
Projected	135	450	113	18	2	18	56	63	32	2	.241

Jason Jacome   No. 47/ P

Born: 11/24/70, Tulsa, OK
Height: 6' 1"   **Weight:** 175
Bats: Left   **Throws:** Left
Opp. Batting Average: .269

Slender lefthander Jacome pitched well at AA-Binghamton in '93, and rose quickly to a Mets starting role last season, compiling an excellent ERA in his eight starts. He's an aggressive pitcher, though not dominant, and he's tough with men on base. His season highlights included a nineteen-inning scoreless streak. Look for Jacome's strikeouts rate to increase in '95.

	G	GS	IP	ERA	H	BB	SO	W	L	SV
1994	8	8	54.0	2.67	54	17	30	4	3	0
Career	8	8	54.0	2.67	54	17	30	4	3	0
Projected			No projection. Player was a rookie in 1994.							

Bobby Jones   No. 28/ P

Born: 2/10/70, Fresno, CA
Height: 6' 4"   **Weight:** 225
Bats: Right   **Throws:** Right
Opp. Batting Average: .257

A big, righthanded control pitcher, Jones put together the seventh-lowest ERA in the NL. The Mets love his pitching smarts. He can throw both his curve and fastball for strikes, setting up his money pitch, the change-up. Control pitchers are less valuable at Shea—Jones compiled a 1.77 ERA in ten road starts, but his fourteen home starts produced a 4.25 mark.

	G	GS	IP	ERA	H	BB	SO	W	L	SV
1994	24	24	160.0	3.15	157	56	80	12	7	0
Career	33	33	221.2	3.29	218	78	115	14	11	0
Projected	20	20	138.0	3.29	135	48	71	9	7	0

Jeff Kent   No. 12/ 2B

Born: 3/7/68, Bellflower, CA
Height: 6' 1"   **Weight:** 185
Bats: Right   **Throws:** Right
1994 OBP: .341   **SLG:** .475

The NL's hottest hitter in April, Kent amassed eleven HRs by the start of June and infused hope and enthusiasm into the entire organization, then jogged the bases just three more times the entire year. A very humble person, Kent is the kind of stable clubhouse leader the Mets need. Kent led all NL second basemen in errors and Ks; he struck out more times per at-bat than Matt Williams.

	G	AB	H	2B	3B	HR	RS	RBI	BB	SB	BA
1994	107	415	121	24	5	14	53	68	23	1	.292
Career	349	1216	328	69	7	46	170	198	80	7	.270
Proected	150	575	174	32	3	23	78	97	35	3	.291

Josias Manzanillo   No. 39/ P

Born: 10/16/67, San Pedro Macoris, PR
Height: 6' 0"   **Weight:** 190
Bats: Right   **Throws:** Right
Opp. Batting Average: .200

After giving up three homers in one inning on April 30, Manzanillo was terrific in a setup role, bringing his moving fastball and high strikeout totals from the farm systems of Boston and Milwaukee to the Mets' bullpen. He's very tough on hitters from both sides of the plate. On August 6 he was placed on the DL with tendinitis of his right shoulder.

	G	GS	IP	ERA	H	BB	SO	W	L	SV
1994	37	0	47.1	2.66	34	13	48	3	2	2
Career	54	1	77.1	4.42	66	35	70	5	3	3
Projected										

Joe Orsulak   No. 6/ OF

Born: 5/31/62, Glen Ridge, NJ
Height: 6' 1"   **Weight:** 205
Bats: Left   **Throws:** Left
1994 OBP: .299   **SLG:** .353

Orsulak is best utilized in a non-everyday capacity, but the thin-on-talent Mets were forced to call on his services often. Orsulak always contributes something, be it his solid defense at all three outfield spots, his consistently above-average situational hitting skills, or his intelligent base running. His eight outfield assists were good for fifth in the NL.

	G	AB	H	2B	3B	HR	RS	RBI	BB	SB	BA
1994	96	292	76	3	0	8	39	42	16	4	.260
Career	1160	3636	1009	149	33	53	482	342	265	91	.278
Projected	141	421	111	11	2	9	58	45	26	5	.268

Pete Smith   No. 32/ P

Born: 2/27/66, Weymouth, MA
Height: 6' 2"   **Weight:** 200
Bats: Right   **Throws:** Right
Opp. Batting Average: .285

The Mets were hoping ex-Brave Pete Smith could solidify the third or fourth spot in their rotation. He pitched seven strong innings for the win in his first start at cold Wrigley Field. Regrettably, that was the highlight of his season. The Mets stuck with Smith for the duration, but he filed for free agency and was unsigned as of this writing.

	G	GS	IP	ERA	H	BB	SO	W	L	SV
1994	21	21	131.1	5.55	145	42	62	4	10	0
Career	146	134	795.0	3.33	791	311	493	34	58	0
Projected	24	20	130.0	5.08	139	46	67	5	11	0

Ryan Thompson   No. 20/OF

Born: 11/4/67, Chestertown, MD
Height: 6' 3"   **Weight:** 215
Bats: Right   **Throws:** Right
1994 OBP: .301   **SLG:** .434

Ryan Thompson needs to keep his swing compact in order to avoid prolonged slumps and high whiff totals, but an early season home run outburst seemed to set him back to his wild-swinging ways. This will be a pivotal campaign for Thompson at the plate. He's got good range in center field, and has wisely stopped trying to steal bases.

	G	AB	H	2B	3B	HR	RS	RBI	BB	SB	BA
1994	98	334	75	14	1	18	39	59	28	1	.225
Career	208	730	171	40	4	32	88	95	55	5	.234
Projected	151	548	140	30	3	27	67	78	43	3	.246

Jose Vizcaino   No. 15/SS

Born: 3/26/68, Palenque San Cristobal, DR
Height: 6' 1"   **Weight:** 180
Bats: Both   **Throws:** Right
1994 OBP: .310   **SLG:** .324

Versatile infielder Vizcaino can play several positions, but the Mets made him their full-time shortstop, and he helped their up-the-middle defense immensely. He's got a knack for the spectacular defensive play. Vizcaino doesn't hit much, and he was an awful percentage basestealer last year, successful only once in twelve attempts.

	G	AB	H	2B	3B	HR	RS	RBI	BB	SB	BA
1994	103	410	105	13	3	3	47	33	33	1	.256
Career	477	1452	381	48	12	8	158	116	102	19	.262
Projected	155	609	180	21	5	5	80	57	52	9	.285

Philadelphia
PHILLIES

1995 Scouting Report

Outfielders: Lenny Dykstra gets it all started for the Phillies, both in center field and in the leadoff slot. Billy Hatcher came over in the Wes Chamberlain deal and did service in all three outfield positions. Veteran right fielder Jim Eisenreich contributes consistent hitting and solid defense. The Phils will probably make a deal to get more depth in the outfield.

Infielders: Mariano Duncan makes the routine plays at second base, and he has excellent doubles power with the bat. Kevin Stocker is nothing special at the plate, but he's a decent gloveman. John Kruk (1B) and Dave Hollins (3B) are both super-intense, somewhat injury prone due to the abandon with which they play, and always productive.

Catchers: Darren Daulton has been one of the most steadily great-hitting catchers of the '90s. He's extremely durable. Todd Pratt is the backup.

Starting Pitchers: Curt Schilling's injury-hampered performance was perhaps the biggest disappointment of the Phillies' difficult season. Big, hard-throwing Bobby Munoz came over from the Yankees and was tough on NL batters. David West made fourteen starts and stifled opposing bats while struggling with the strikezone. The team hopes Tommy Greene can return from injury and regain his '93 form.

Relief Pitching: Doug Jones finished third in the NL in saves, but the team opted not to re-sign him. Toby Borland posted a sparkling 2.36 ERA in twenty-four middle-relief appearances.

Manager: Jim Fregosi (725–767) did an exceptional job last year, considering the Phillies' injury troubles.

1995 Outlook

The Phillies' 1994 season was an unmitigated disaster, as the club was decimated by injuries. The Phils lost a total of 590 player-games on the disabled list, with many of the injuries sidelining key personnel. Among the damaged were ace hurler Curt Schilling (elbow and knee surgeries), All-Stars Darren Daulton (fractured clavicle) and John Kruk (testicular cancer and knee surgery), starting third baseman Dave Hollins (fractured hand—twice), All-Star spark plug Len Dykstra (appendicitis), and starting pitcher Tommy Greene (shoulder surgery). It's unreasonable to evaluate the Phillies' chances in 1995 based on their performance in 1994—it simply won't be the same team.

The National League East competition is brutal. Montreal and Atlanta finished the season with two of the three best records in the major leagues, and Philadelphia will be hard pressed to make the playoffs in '95, even if their players can stay off the DL.

Nevertheless, the batting order is potent when healthy. The Phillies present a balanced hitting attack. They are adept at getting on base—even in last season's debacle, the team finished second in the NL in walks. The Phils were 12–26 in one-run contests last year, a record they'll be likely to reverse in 1995.

Philadelphia pitching managed to compile the NL's fourth-best ERA overall, led by the now departed Danny Jackson, despite an injury-influenced 0–7, 5.40 first half from ace Curt Schilling. Schilling looked great after the All-Star break (2.63 ERA in four starts), and he can be expected to return to form this season. The emergence of Bobby Munoz—an outstanding young pitcher the Phils received from the Yankees in exchange for Terry Mulholland—gives Philadelphia a rotation that could be the competitive with the Expos' and Braves' starters.

1995 Philadelphia Phillies Roster

Manager: Jim Fregosi
Coaches: Larry Bowa, Denis Menke, Johnny Podres, Mel Roberts, Mike Ryan, John Vukovich

No.	Pitchers	B	T	HT	WT	DOB	Birthplace
42	Borland, Toby	R	R	6–6	182	5/29/69	Quitman, LA
31	Brink, Brad	R	R	6–2	203	1/20/65	Roseville, CA
28	Green, Tyler	R	R	6–5	185	2/18/70	Inglewood, CO
49	Greene, Tommy	R	R	6–5	219	4/6/67	Lumberton, NC
44	Juden, Jeff	R	R	6–7	245	1/19/71	Salem, MA
48	Mason, Roger	R	R	6–6	220	9/18/58	Bellaire, MI
35	Munoz, Bobby	R	R	6–7	237	3/3/68	Rio Piedras, PR
39	Pall, Donn	R	R	6–1	180	1/11/62	Chicago, IL
34	Rivera, Ben	R	R	6–6	230	1/11/68	San Pedro Macoris, DR
38	Schilling, Curt	R	R	6–4	215	11/14/66	Anchorage, AK
40	West, David	L	L	6–6	230	9/1/64	Memphis, TN
41	Williams, Mike	R	R	6–2	196	7/29/69	Redford, VA
	Catchers						
10	Daulton, Darren	L	R	6–2	201	1/3/62	Arkansas City, KS
23	Pratt, Todd	R	R	6–3	227	2/9/67	Bellevue, NE
	Infielders						
5	Batiste, Kim	R	R	6–0	193	3/15/68	New Orleans, LA
7	Duncan, Mariano	R	R	6–0	191	3/13/63	San Pedro Macoris, DR
15	Hollins, Dave	B	R	6–1	207	5/25/66	Buffalo, NY
17	Jordan, Ricky	R	R	6–3	205	5/26/65	Richmond, CA
29	Kruk, John	L	L	5–10	214	2/9/61	Charleston, WV
12	Morandini, Mickey	L	R	5–11	171	4/22/66	Kittanning, PA
19	Stocker, Kevin	B	R	6–1	178	2/13/70	Spokane, WA
	Outfielders						
4	Dykstra, Lenny	L	L	5–10	193	2/10/63	Santa Ana, CA
8	Eisenreich, Jim	L	L	5–11	200	4/18/59	St. Cloud, MN
3	Hatcher, Billy	R	R	5–10	190	10/4/60	Williams, AZ
59	Jackson, Jeff	R	R	6–2	185	1/2/72	Chicago, IL
16	Longmire, Tony	L	R	6–1	197	8/12/68	Vallejo, CA

1995 Schedule

April

S	M	T	W	T	F	S
						1
2	3 STL	4 STL	5 STL	6 STL	7 COL	8 COL
9 COL	10 STL	11 STL	12 STL	13 COL	14 COL	15 COL
16 COL	17 CHI	18 CHI	19 CHI	20	21 PIT	22 PIT
23 PIT	24 CHI	25 CHI	26 CHI	27 PIT	28 PIT	29 PIT
30 PIT						

May

S	M	T	W	T	F	S
	1	2 CIN	3 CIN	4 CIN	5 ATL	6 ATL
7 ATL	8 ATL	9 MON	10 MON	11 MON	12 HOU	13 HOU
14 HOU	15 FLA	16 FLA	17 FLA	18	19 NY	20 NY
21 NY	22	23 SF	24 SF	25 SD	26 SD	27 SD
28 SD	29 LA	30 LA	31 LA			

June

S	M	T	W	T	F	S
				1	2 SF	3 SF
4 SF	5 SD	6 SD	7 SD	8	9 LA	10 LA
11 LA	12	13 HOU	14 HOU	15 HOU	16 FLA	17 FLA
18 FLA	19 NY	20 NY	21 NY	22 NY	23 STL	24 STL
25 STL	26	27 CIN	28 CIN	29 CIN	30 ATL	

July

S	M	T	W	T	F	S
						1 ATL
2 ATL	3 ATL	4 PIT	5 PIT	6 PIT	7 CHI	8 CHI
9 CHI	10	11 ★	12	13 MON	14 MON	15 MON
16 MON	17 COL	18 COL	19 COL	20	21 STL	22 STL
23 STL	24 COL	25 COL	26 PIT	27 PIT	28 CHI	29 CHI
30 CHI	31					

August

S	M	T	W	T	F	S
		1 ATL	2 ATL	3 ATL	4 CIN	5 CIN
6 CIN	7	8 NY	9 NY	10 NY	11 MON	12 MON
13 MON	14 MON	15 HOU	16 HOU	17 HOU	18 SF	19 SF
20 SF	21 SD	22 SD	23 SD	24 LA	25 LA	26 LA
27 LA	28	29 SF	30 SF	31 SF		

Sept/Oct

S	M	T	W	T	F	S
					1 SD	2 SD
3 SD	4 LA	5 LA	6 LA	7	8 HOU	9 HOU
10 HOU	11	12 MON	13 MON	14	15 NY	16 NY
17 NY	18 FLA	19 FLA	20 FLA	21 FLA	22 CIN	23 CIN
24 CIN	25	26 ATL	27 ATL	28	29 FLA	30 FLA
1 FLA	2					

☐ Home   ☐ Away   ★ All-Star Game

Veterans Stadium

Capacity: 62,586

Turf: Artificial

Dimensions:
LF Line: 330'
RF Line: 330'
Center: 408'
Alleys: 371'

Tickets:
(215) 463-1000

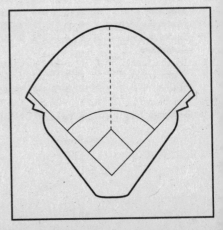

1994 Batting Order

1. Lenny Dykstra (Center Field)
2. Mariano Duncan (Second Base)
3. John Kruk (First Base)
4. Darren Daulton (Catcher)
5. Dave Hollins (Third Base)
6. Milt Thompson (Left Field)
7. Jim Eisenreich (Right Field)
8. Kevin Stocker (Shortstop)
9. Pitcher

1994 Team Record
54–61 (.470); Fourth in NL East

NL East	W	L	NL Central	W	L	NL West	W	L
Atlanta	3	6	Chicago	6	1	Colorado	4	2
Florida	6	4	Cincinnati	2	4	Los Angeles	5	7
Montreal	4	5	Houston	1	5	San Diego	4	8
New York	6	4	Pittsburgh	5	4	S. Francisco	4	8
Philadelphia	—	—	St. Louis	4	3			
Total	19	19		18	17		17	25

1994 National League Team Rank Batting

Batting Average: Tenth (.262)
Runs Scored: Eighth (521)
Runs Batted In: Eighth (484)
Stolen Bases: Tenth (67)
Slugging Percentage: Thirteenth (.390)
On-Base Percentage: Eighth (.332)

1994 National League Team Rank Pitching

Earned Run Average: Fourth (3.85)
Bases On Balls: Ninth (377)
Strikeouts: Ninth (699)
Wins: Eighth (54)
Saves: Fourth (30)
Complete Games: Sixth (7)

Philadelphia Phillies MVP

Danny Jackson   No. 27/ P

Born: 1/5/62, San Antonio, TX
Height: 6' 3"   **Weight:** 205
Bats: Right   **Throws:** Left
Opp. Batting Average: .266

Jackson was one of the game's top power pitchers for the Royals in the late '80s, and he still has a deadly slider and a hard fastball. In '94 he demonstrated that he's truly beyond his past injuries and can again be a true workhorse, taking games into the later innings on a regular basis.

The strongest starter on the Phillies' troubled starting staff last year, Jackson was second in the National League in innings pitched and tied for second in starts. He ranked third in the league in wins, fourth in complete games with four, seventh in strikeouts, ninth in ERA, and tenth in walks-per-nine-innings ratio (2.3). Jackson's fourteen wins were the most in the NL by a lefthander.

Armed with arguably the sharpest slider of any lefty in the National League, plus a fastball that tops out at ninety mph, Jackson is as tough on righthanders as he is on lefties.

Jackson's command of the strikezone has never been stronger. He put together a twenty-four inning walkless streak June 18 to July 9, and he didn't walk more than four batters in any outing. Jackson made six starts in which he didn't walk a single batter.

Jackson signed with St. Louis as a free agent over the winter.

	G	GS	IP	ERA	H	BB	SO	W	L	SV
1994	25	25	179.1	3.26	183	46	129	14	6	0
Career	304	288	1688.2	3.77	1859	724	1114	107	109	1
Projected	33	33	223.0	3.54	228	72	143	15	10	0

Larry Andersen　　No. 47/ P

Born: 5/6/53, Portland, OR
Height: 6' 3"　**Weight:** 205
Bats: Right　**Throws:** Right
Opp. Batting Average: .256

Andersen is forty-one years old, and his slender body is finally beginning to rebel. He endured three stints on the DL; including one for surgery on his left knee. Andersen's arm is still a death knell to righthanders; they managed a .193 batting average in fifty-seven at-bats versus Andersen. Opposing batters hit just .185 against him with runners in scoring position.

	G	GS	IP	ERA	H	BB	SO	W	L	SV
1994	29	0	32.2	4.41	33	15	27	1	2	0
Career	699	1	995.2	3.14	932	311	758	40	39	49
Projected	51	0	52.0	3.42	48	20	52	2	2	0

Toby Borland　　No. 42/ P

Born: 5/29/69, Quitman, LA
Height: 6' 6"　**Weight:** 182
Bats: Right　**Throws:** Right
Opp. Batting Average: .248

Borland has pitched well at every minor league level. Last year he brought his excellent stuff to the Show (when Tommy Greene was injured) and continued to handcuff professional hitters. Borland is just wild enough to keep hitters guessing, and his strikeout rates have been excellent throughout his career. He could be the Phillies' closer in waiting

	G	GS	IP	ERA	H	BB	SO	W	L	SV
1994	24	0	34.1	2.36	31	14	26	1	0	1
Career	24	0	34.1	2.36	31	14	26	1	0	1
Projected				No projection. Player was a rookie in 1994.						

Darren Daulton No. 10/ C

Born: 1/3/62, Arkansas City, KS
Height: 6' 2" **Weight:** 201
Bats: Left **Throws:** Right
1994 OBP: .380 **SLG:** .549

Daulton was on pace to set personal bests in several offensive categories, but he fractured his right clavicle and missed the final thirty-nine games. He hit .325 with runners in scoring position. Daulton has great power when he pulls the ball, but he's been prone to slumps. He's a skilled, experienced backstop with a great throwing arm.

	G	AB	H	2B	3B	HR	RS	RBI	BB	SB	BA
1994	69	257	77	17	1	15	43	56	33	4	.300
Career	922	2881	700	157	14	114	396	470	491	41	.243
Projected	127	440	115	29	3	22	75	91	84	5	.266

Mariano Duncan No. 7/ 2B

Born: 3/13/63, San Pedro Macoris, DR
Height: 6' 0" **Weight:** 191
Bats: Right **Throws:** Right
1994 OBP: .306 **SLG:** .406

Despite the pitiful on-base percentage, Duncan has become a very important member of the Phillies' offensive scheme. He's got good linedrive power, especially for a middle infielder, and he has a knack for the timely hit. Duncan is a fine percentage base stealer, and he doesn't make many bad plays at second base. He was the NL All-Star starting second baseman.

	G	AB	H	2B	3B	HR	RS	RBI	BB	SB	BA
1994	88	347	93	22	1	8	49	48	17	10	.268
Career	1000	3673	955	171	32	72	485	374	175	163	.260
Projected	130	521	147	30	3	12	73	76	18	10	.279

Lenny Dykstra   No. 4/ OF

Born: 2/10/63, Santa Ana, CA
Height: 5' 10"   **Weight:** 193
Bats: Left   **Throws:** Left
1994 OBP: .404   **SLG:** .435

Dykstra is more intelligent than his outward image suggests. He's got a deep understanding of what's required to win baseball games. He had the eighth-best on-base percentage in the NL and smashed three leadoff homers last season. Dykstra missed thirty days with appendicitis, but still finished third in the NL in walks. The bottom line is that Dykstra is a great competitor.

	G	AB	H	2B	3B	HR	RS	RBI	BB	SB	BA
1994	84	315	86	26	5	5	68	24	68	15	.273
Career	1176	4171	1196	260	39	76	744	373	581	272	.287
Projected	145	570	171	42	7	15	127	54	119	31	.297

Jim Eisenreich   No. 8/ OF

Born: 4/18/59, St. Cloud, MN
Height: 5' 11"   **Weight:** 200
Bats: Left   **Throws:** Left
1994 OBP: .371   **SLG:** .421

Eisenreich is a durable, consistent veteran who has hit .310 over a two-year span while providing excellent outfield defense. Eisenreich is aggressive at the plate, but he's not a wild swinger. He's at his best in a platoon situation in which he can stay well rested, but the outfielder-thin Phillies don't have the luxury of keeping Eisenreich's glove and bat on the bench.

	G	AB	H	2B	3B	HR	RS	RBI	BB	SB	BA
1994	104	290	87	15	4	4	42	43	33	6	.300
Career	955	2796	796	153	31	36	344	334	209	78	.285
Projected	156	389	116	19	5	6	54	57	35	6	.304

Tommy Greene   No. 49/ P

Born: 4/6/67, Lumberton, NC
Height: 6' 5"   **Weight:** 219
Bats: Right   **Throws:** Right
Opp. Batting Average: .272

Greene endured seven rocky starts in '94 before shoulder surgery. He's had a history of arm problems and inconsistency, but he's tough to hit when he pitches with confidence. The Phillies need for Greene to figure into their '94 starting rotation equation. He's currently working on a streak of fourteen winning decisions with no losses in twenty-seven starts at the Vet.

	G	GS	IP	ERA	H	BB	SO	W	L	SV
1994	7	7	35.2	4.54	37	22	28	2	0	0
Career	106	89	585.1	3.86	536	216	426	38	19	0
Projected			No projection. Player was injured in 1994.							

Dave Hollins   No. 15/ 3B

Born: 5/25/66, Buffalo. NY
Height: 6' 1"   **Weight:** 207
Bats: Both   **Throws:** Right
1994 OBP: .328   **SLG:** .352

Hollins's presence on the DL was a prime factor in the Phillies' downfall. Hollins has a linebacker's mentality: 100% aggressive. His intensity is infectious and helped set the team's all-out attitude in '93. He's a switch-hitter, but Hollins hits with more authority from the right side. In the field, he's unpolished, but his arm is strong and his glovework should improve.

	G	AB	H	2B	3B	HR	RS	RBI	BB	SB	BA
1994	44	162	36	7	1	4	28	26	23	1	.222
Career	471	1556	408	75	11	60	268	248	211	13	.262
Projected	68	265	75	14	2	9	52	47	42	1	.271

Doug Jones   No. 23/ P

Born: 6/24/57, Covina, CA
Height: 6' 2"   **Weight:** 195
Bats: Right   **Throws:** Right
Opp. Batting Average: .255

Jones made a complete turnaround from his poor '93 performance. He relies on pure touch and pinpoint control. If he's radically changing speeds, batters are utterly frustrated, as most were in '94. Jones's control of the strikezone was almost uncanny last season; he relinquished less than one walk per nine innings. He was unsigned as of this writing.

	G	GS	IP	ERA	H	BB	SO	W	L	SV
1994	47	0	54.0	2.17	55	6	38	2	4	27
Career	474	4	674.2	2.99	675	143	537	43	54	217
Projected	67	0	79.0	3.62	89	15	59	3	8	30

John Kruk   No. 29/ 1B

Born: 2/9/61, Charleston, WV
Height: 5' 10"   **Weight:** 214
Bats: Left   **Throws:** Left
1994 OBP: .395   **SLG:** .427

One of baseball's great characters and a superior talent, Kruk is a brilliant batsman. He's not young, and he's not in top physical shape, so injuries may become an annual setback. But when his timing is set, he's a phenomenal "mistake" hitter and as patient at the plate as anyone in the league. Kruk has quick hands around the bag, but not a lot of range.

	G	AB	H	2B	3B	HR	RS	RBI	BB	SB	BA
1994	75	255	77	17	0	5	35	38	42	4	.302
Career	1155	3738	1121	192	34	98	569	569	623	58	.300
Projected	133	457	137	28	3	11	76	70	87	6	.305

Bobby Munoz   No. 35/ P

Born: 3/3/68, Rio Piedras, PR
Height: 6' 7"   **Weight:** 237
Bats: Right   **Throws:** Right
Opp. Batting Average: .252

The Phillies more than made up for the loss of Terry Mulholland by replacing him with Bobby Munoz. Munoz is physically intimidating, and his fastball comes in at close to ninety-five mph. He has several pitches he can use to setup his heat, and he's still developing as a pitcher. Munoz could be a permanent fixture in the Phillies' future. Expect his strikeout rate to improve.

	G	GS	IP	ERA	H	BB	SO	W	L	SV
1994	24	14	104.1	2.67	101	35	59	7	5	1
Career	59	14	150.1	3.48	149	61	92	10	8	1
Projected	33	8	84.0	3.49	83	34	51	6	4	1

Curt Schilling   No. 38/ P

Born: 11/14/66, Anchorage, AK
Height: 6' 4"   **Weight:** 215
Bats: Right   **Throws:** Right
Opp. Batting Average: .270

Coming off his dominating '93 postseason performance, Schilling figured to challenge for Cy Young honors last season. It wasn't meant to be. Schilling fell flat, going 0–7 before various injuries to his elbow and knee finished his season. Make no mistake, he's a pitcher's pitcher, cut from the same cloth as Greg Maddux. If Schilling is healthy, he'll be a great one.

	G	GS	IP	ERA	H	BB	SO	W	L	SV
1994	13	13	82.1	4.48	87	28	58	2	8	0
Career	189	78	689.0	3.56	635	215	544	36	37	13
Projected	26	26	173.0	4.14	175	46	133	10	8	0

Kevin Stocker   No. 19/ SS

Born: 2/13/70, Spokane, WA
Height: 6' 1"   **Weight:** 178
Bats: Both   **Throws:** Right
1994 OBP: .383   **SLG:** .351

Stocker made a lasting impression on the Phillies' management in '93 during the pennant race when he batted .324 in seventy games. Stocker isn't really a potent hitter; he's an easy out for pitchers who throw hard. But he does draw some walks and exhibits a veteran's maturity in the field. Stocker underwent surgery on his right wrist early in the season.

	G	AB	H	2B	3B	HR	RS	RBI	BB	SB	BA
1994	82	271	74	11	2	2	38	28	44	2	.273
Career	152	530	158	23	5	4	84	59	74	7	.298
Projected	126	462	152	21	5	4	77	54	68	6	.313

David West   No. 40/ P

Born: 9/1/64, Memphis, TN
Height: 6' 6"   **Weight:** 230
Bats: Left   **Throws:** Left
Opp. Batting Average: .205

West's 4–10 season was actually something of a success. He handed out a stunning sixty-one walks in ninety-nine innings, but he thrived as a starter after sputtering in the bullpen. West kept opposing bats relatively silent, which helped keep his ERA at an acceptable level. Lefties hit just .156 against West. If his mechanics are sound, he could be a dark horse in 1995.

	G	GS	IP	ERA	H	BB	SO	W	L	SV
1994	31	14	99.0	3.55	74	61	83	4	10	0
Career	183	64	501.0	4.63	453	274	386	26	34	3
Projected	59	8	101.0	3.25	73	61	93	5	8	2

Pittsburgh
PIRATES

1995 Scouting Report

Outfielders: Andy Van Slyke knows the ropes in center field, but his run production is in decline, so the team let him go. Left field is set with speedy Al Martin committing just three errors in '94. Dave Clark will see part-time duty in right field. All are lefthanded, linedrive hitters. The Bucs' outfield mix includes prospects Midre Cummings, Jacob Brumfield, and Steve Pegues.

Infielders: The Bucs have stellar middle-infield defense. Jay Bell (SS) and Carlos Garcia (2B) are one of the NL's best doubleplay combos. Jeff King has a good glove at third, but he doesn't produce many runs. Orlando Merced will cover first base, but he earns his salary via his bat.

Catchers: Don Slaught returns for his fourteenth season in the majors. He contributes leadership to the Pirate pitchers. Solid fielder Mark Parent will play when Slaught rests.

Starting Pitchers: The Pirates' starting corps is thin; their only established starter is southpaw Zane Smith. Denny Neagle racked up the strikeouts in '94, and could develop into a fine pitcher. The rotation rounds out with young lefty Steve Cooke, John Lieber, and Paul Wagner. Rick White has shown promise as a starter.

Relief Pitchers: The Bucs under Jim Leyland have always utilized a bullpen-by-committee, with no true stopper. They'll draw from a crowd including Mike Dyer, Ravelo Manzanillo, and Rick White.

Manager: Jim Leyland (720–688) is a master at getting the most from his players, but the Pirates' mediocre talent level creates a daunting challenge. Only the Dodgers' Tom Lasorda has been with his team longer than Leyland has been with the Bucs.

1995 Outlook

The Pirates tried ninety-four different lineups during the 1994 season, which tells you all you need to know about the thin-on-talent Bucs. Their chances of staying out of the NL Central basement are largely dependent on the managerial genius of Jim Leyland.

Last year's Pirates suffered some deep lows, such as giving up thirty-five runs in a three-game series with Montreal in June, and a 19–2 loss versus the Dodgers April 17. The Bucs tied a dubious record versus St. Louis on June 16, hitting into seven doubleplays. At San Diego on May 31, Pirate hurlers allowed thirteen runs in one inning.

But it wasn't completely gloomy in '94, and the Bucs can take heart at having the also-weak Cubs in their division. The Pirates' strengths are flawless up-the-middle infield defense (138 DPs; first in the majors), good clubhouse chemistry, and plenty of openings for young talent to emerge. And of course, their brilliant skipper. Jim Leyland's crew finished with a winning percentage greater than or equal to five other NL clubs, yet they ranked last in the league in runs scored and twelfth in ERA. The Pirates overachieved in '94, and Leyland deserves much of the credit.

The Pirates bullpen needs bolstering in '95 if the team is to avoid a 100-loss campaign. The starting staff isn't equipped to finish fourth in complete games, as they did last season. Middle relief is one area in baseball in which there is something of a surplus, and the Bucs can't afford to make do with their current crop of arms.

There is good news from the Pirates' farm clubs, where several hot prospects are ready to contribute, the most exciting of the lot being outfielder Jacob Brumfield. But Andy Van Slyke filed for free agency, and the pitching is beyond suspect, so it's easy to envision another season of experimentation in Pittsburgh.

1995 Pittsburgh Pirates Roster

Manager: Jim Leyland
Coaches: Rich Donnelly, Milt May, Ray Miller, Tommy Sandt, Bill Verdon, Spin Williams

No.	Pitchers	B	T	HT	WT	DOB	Birthplace
26	Cooke, Steve	R	L	6–6	220	1/14/70	Kanai, HI
62	Dyer, Mike	R	R	6–3	200	9/8/66	Upland, CA
47	Lieber, John	L	R	6–3	220	4/2/70	Council Bluffs, IA
59	Manzanillo, Ravelo	L	L	5–10	190	10/17/63	San Pedro Macoris, DR
32	Miceli, Dan	R	R	6–0	207	9/9/70	Newark, NJ
15	Neagle, Denny	L	L	6–2	215	9/13/68	Gambrills, MD
19	Plesac, Dan	L	L	6–5	215	2/4/62	Gary, IN
38	Ramirez, Roberto	R	L	5–11	170	8/17/72	Varacruz, Mexico
41	Smith, Zane	L	L	6–1	205	12/28/60	Madison, WI
29	Tomlin, Randy	L	L	5–10	170	6/14/66	Bainbridge, MA
43	Wagner, Paul	R	R	6–1	185	11/14/67	Milwaukee, WI
49	Wakefield, Tim	R	R	6–2	195	8/2/66	Melbourne, FL
44	White, Rick	R	R	6–4	215	12/23/68	Springfield, OH
	Catchers						
14	Parent, Mark	R	R	6–5	240	9/16/61	Ashland, OR
11	Slaught, Don	R	R	6–1	190	9/11/58	Long Beach, CA
	Infielders						
48	Aude, Rich	R	R	6–5	209	7/13/71	Van Nuys, CA
3	Bell, Jay	R	R	6–0	185	12/11/65	Eglin AFB, FL
13	Garcia, Carlos	R	R	6–1	185	10/15/67	Tachira, Venezuela
7	King, Jeff	R	R	6–1	180	12/26/64	Marion, IN
16	Liriano, Nelson	B	R	5–10	178	6/3/64	Puerto Plata, DR
44	Shelton, Ben	R	L	6–3	210	9/21/69	Chicago, IL
51	Womack, Tony	L	R	5–9	153	9/25/69	Danville, VA
36	Young, Kevin	R	R	6–2	213	6/16/69	Alpena, MI
	Outfielders						
5	Brumfield, Jacob	R	R	6–10	195	5/27/65	Bogalusa, LA
35	Clark, Dave	L	R	6–2	210	9/3/62	Tupelo, MS
30	Cummings, Midre	L	R	6–0	196	10/14/71	St. Croix, VI
28	Martin, Al	L	L	6–2	220	11/24/67	West Covina, CA
6	Merced, Orlando	B	R	5–11	170	11/2/66	San Juan, PR
25	Pegues, Steve	R	R	6–2	190	5/21/69	Pontotac, MS

1995 Schedule

April

S	M	T	W	T	F	S
						1
2	3 MON	4	5 MON	6 MON	7 ATL	8 ATL
9 ATL	10 NY	11 NY	12 NY	13	14 ATL	15 ATL
16 ATL	17 ATL	18 NY	19 NY	20	21 PHI	22 PHI
23 PHI	24 MON	25 MON	26 MON	27 PHI	28 PHI	29 PHI
30 PHI						

May

S	M	T	W	T	F	S
	1 STL	2 STL	3 STL	4	5 CHI	6 CHI
7 CHI	8 HOU	9 HOU	10 HOU	11 HOU	12 SF	13 SF
14 SF	15 LA	16 LA	17 LA	18 LA	19 SD	20 SD
21 SD	22	23 FLO	24 FLO	25 FLO	26 COL	27 COL
28 COL	29 CIN	30 CIN	31 CIN			

June

S	M	T	W	T	F	S
				1 CIN	2 COL	3 COL
4 COL	5 CIN	6 CIN	7 CIN	8 FLO	9 FLO	10 FLO
11 FLO	12	13 LA	14 LA	15 LA	16 SD	17 SD
18 SD	19 SF	20 SF	21 SF	22	23 MON	24 MON
25 MON	26 CHI	27 CHI	28 CHI	29	30 HOU	

July

S	M	T	W	T	F	S
						1 HOU
2 HOU	3	4 PHI	5 PHI	6 PHI	7 NY	8 NY
9 NY	10	11 ★	12	13 STL	14 STL	15 STL
16 STL	17	18 ATL	19 ATL	20 ATL	21 MON	22 MON
23 MON	24 ATL	25 ATL	26 PHI	27 PHI	28 NY	29 NY
30 NY	31 NY					

August

S	M	T	W	T	F	S
		1 CHI	2 CHI	3 CHI	4 HOU	5 HOU
6 HOU	7	8 SF	9 SF	10 SF	11 LA	12 LA
13 LA	14 SD	15 SD	16 SD	17	18 FLO	19 FLO
20 FLO	21 FLO	22 COL	23 COL	24 COL	25 CIN	26 CIN
27 CIN	28 COL	29 COL	30 COL	31 CIN		

Sept/Oct

S	M	T	W	T	F	S
					1 CIN	2 CIN
3 CIN	4 FLO	5	6 FLO	7	8 LA	9 LA
10 LA	11 LA	12 SD	13 SD	14 SD	15 SF	16 SF
17 SF	18 STL	19 STL	20 STL	21 CHI	22 CHI	23 CHI
24 CHI	25 HOU	26 HOU	27 HOU	28	29 STL	30 STL
1 STL	2					

 Home   ☐ Away   ★ All-Star Game

Three Rivers Stadium

Capacity: 47,972

Turf: Artificial

Dimensions:
LF Line: 335'
RF Line: 335'
Center: 400'
Alleys: 375'

Tickets:
(412) 321-2827

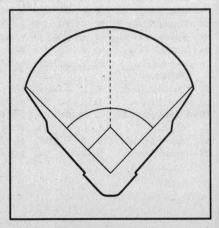

1994 Batting Order

1. Carlos Garcia (Second Base)
2. Jay Bell (Shortstop)
3. Andy Van Slyke (Center Field)
4. Brian Hunter (First Base)
5. Orlando Merced (Right Field)
6. Al Martin (Left Field)
7. Jeff King (Third Base)
8. Don Slaught (Catcher)
9. Pitcher

1994 Team Record
53–61 (.465); Third in NL Central

NL East	W	L	NL Central	W	L	NL West	W	L
Atlanta	9	3	Chicago	5	5	Colorado	3	2
Florida	6	1	Cincinnati	3	9	Los Angeles	3	3
Montreal	2	8	Houston	4	8	San Diego	3	3
New York	5	4	Pittsburgh	—	—	S. Francisco	1	5
Philadelphia	4	5	St. Louis	5	5			
Total	26	21		17	27		10	13

1994 National League Team Rank Batting

Batting Average: Twelfth (.259)
Runs Scored: Fourteenth (466)
Runs Batted In: Fourteenth (435)
Stolen Bases: Twelfth (53)
Slugging Percentage: Fourteenth (.384)
On-Base Percentage: Twelfth (.322)

1994 National League Team Rank Pitching

Earned Run Average: Twelfth (4.64)
Bases On Balls: Seventh (370)
Strikeouts: Eleventh (650)
Wins: Ninth (53)
Saves: Thirteenth (24)
Complete Games: Fourth (8)

Pittsburgh Pirates MVP

Jay Bell   No. 3/ SS

Born: 12/11/65, Eglin AFB, FL
Height: 6' 0"   **Weight:** 185
Bats: Right   **Throws:** Right
1994 OBP: .353   **SLG:** .441

Following a breakthrough '93 season, Bell started slowly last season, barely keeping his average above .200 into June. But warmer weather heated up Bell's bat; he hit .333 after June 5, including .357 in August. Bell has excellent extra-base pop (41% of his hits went for extra bases), and he was third in the NL in doubles. He's the Bucs' anchor on defense, and their most consistently productive threat with the bat.

Bell has rapped out thirty or more doubles in four consecutive seasons, a feat the club hasn't seen from a shortstop since Hall of Famer Honus Wagner (1903–1910). Bell led the Pirates in hits for the second straight year, batting primarily from the number-two hole. He used to be a prolific bunter, but the team can no longer afford to sacrifice Bell's hitting. Bell has as much long-ball ability as any Pirate batter.

A genius at positioning himself in the infield, Bell has led all major league shortstops in total chances (547) for two years in a row, and he was first in assists among big leaguers in '94. Few middle infielders can boast of having a throwing arm as strong as Bell's.

Bell's importance to the Pirates can't be overstated. He has become the club's most recognizable presence, as well as one of the NL's finest shortstops.

	G	AB	H	2B	3B	HR	RS	RBI	BB	SB	BA
1994	110	424	117	35	4	9	68	45	49	2	.276
Career	933	3472	931	192	39	57	519	335	348	56	.268
Projected	157	636	203	43	8	12	109	62	81	12	.308

Dave Clark   No. 35/ OF

Born: 9/3/62, Tupelo, MS
Height: 6' 2"   **Weight:** 210
Bats: Left   **Throws:** Right
1994 OBP: .355   **SLG:** .489

A useful role player, Clark was second in the majors in pinch-hit RBIs (11). Clark is a free swinger who doesn't fare well when behind in the count. He hits righthanders, against whom he bopped all ten of his home runs, much better than he hits lefties. Fielding isn't his strength, but his throwing arm is accurate. Clark was a first-round draft choice (Cleveland) in 1983.

	G	AB	H	2B	3B	HR	RS	RBI	BB	SB	BA
1994	86	223	66	11	1	10	37	46	22	2	.296
Career	526	1268	332	48	6	45	159	188	131	12	.262
Projected	121	312	90	14	2	13	50	58	38	2	.285

Steve Cooke   No. 26/ P

Born: 1/14/70, Kanai, HI
Height: 6' 6"   **Weight:** 220
Bats: Right   **Throws:** Left
Opp. Batting Average: .298

Cooke had a disastrous sophomore year, and his record reflects that fact. He pitched great at times (2.50 ERA in five June starts), but served up a disturbing twenty-one gopher balls, third most in the NL. He went 0–5 with an 8.57 ERA in his final five outings. Cooke's still a youngster, but if he learns to throw strikes he'll be a solid lefty starter.

	G	GS	IP	ERA	H	BB	SO	W	L	SV
1994	25	23	134.1	5.02	157	46	74	4	11	0
Career	68	55	368.0	4.28	386	109	216	16	21	1
Projected	33	32	198.0	4.34	209	60	118	8	12	0

Mark Dewey   No. 50/ P

Born: 1/1/65, Grand Rapids, MI
Height: 6' 0"   **Weight:** 216
Bats: Right   **Throws:** Right
Opp. Batting Average: .303

The Pirates use a sea chest of middle relief, and Dewey was called on often in '94. He has decent command of several pitches, though his stuff isn't overpowering. He needs to hit his spots or it's time for the white flag. He gave up one earned run in his first ten appearances in '94, but recorded an unsightly 5.85 ERA in his final twenty-three outings.

	G	GS	IP	ERA	H	BB	SO	W	L	SV
1994	45	0	51.1	3.68	61	19	30	2	1	1
Career	100	0	134.0	3.43	134	44	79	5	4	8
Projected	40	0	48.0	3.24	46	18	27	2	2	5

Carlos Garcia   No. 13/ 2B

Born: 10/15/67, Tachira, Venezuela
Height: 6' 1"   **Weight:** 185
Bats: Right   **Throws:** Right
1994 OBP: .309   **SLG:** .367

Streak-hitting Garcia led off seventy-seven games last season, despite a marginal on-base percentage. He's one of the more exciting second basemen in the NL, in fact Garcia made the All-Star team, but he doesn't draw enough walks to be leading off. Garcia has great range at second; he had ten assists at Colorado on June 5, two shy of tying a major league record.

	G	AB	H	2B	3B	HR	RS	RBI	BB	SB	BA
1994	98	412	114	15	2	6	49	28	16	18	.277
Career	277	1025	277	41	9	18	133	80	48	36	.270
Projected	146	608	179	26	5	12	83	50	31	24	.283

Jeff King   No. 7/ 3B

Born: 12/26/64, Marion, IN
Height: 6' 1"   **Weight:** 180
Bats: Right   **Throws:** Right
1994 OBP: .316   **SLG:** .375

The Bucs have been very patient with King since making him the number-one pick in the '86 draft, but his offensive production was much too low last year for a cornerman. King didn't homer till his 136th at-bat in '94, and his forty-two RBIs came batting in the heart of the order. He did lead the club in sacrifice flies with seven, good for sixth in the NL in that category.

	G	AB	H	2B	3B	HR	RS	RBI	BB	SB	BA
1994	94	339	89	23	0	5	36	42	30	3	.263
Career	617	2125	539	110	10	51	267	295	171	25	.254
Projected	151	576	166	36	2	9	72	86	55	7	.286

Jon Lieber   No. 47/ P

Born: 4/2/70, Council Bluffs, IA
Height: 6' 2"   **Weight:** 220
Bats: Left   **Throws:** Right
Opp. Batting Average: .271

Lieber's major league debut was bittersweet as he wound up on the short end of a 1–0 final score, but his performance boded well for the remainder of his first season. He tossed fourteen straight scoreless innings May 15–27, and allowed three earned runs or less (2.89 ERA) in each of his first ten starts. Expect Lieber's strikeout numbers to rise in '95.

	G	GS	IP	ERA	H	BB	SO	W	L	SV
1994	17	17	108.2	3.73	116	25	71	6	7	0
Career	17	17	108.2	3.73	116	25	71	6	7	0
Projected			No projection. Player was a rookie in 1994.							

Ravello Manzanillo No. 59/ P

Born: 10/17/63, San Pedro Macoris, DR
Height: 5' 10"   **Weight:** 190
Bats: Left   **Throws:** Left
Opp. Batting Average: .245

Not exactly a household name in Pittsburgh or anywhere else, the thirty-year-old Manzanillo ranked second in NL rookie appearances. He was knocked around in his first four outings, but by June 13 his ERA was down to 1.96. Manzanillo suffered a league-leading five balk calls, one of which led to an ejection for arguing. He also handed out more walks than strikeouts.

	G	GS	IP	ERA	H	BB	SO	W	L	SV
1994	46	0	50.0	4.14	45	42	39	4	2	1
Career	48	0	59.1	4.40	52	54	49	4	3	1
Projected			No projection. Player was a rookie in 1994.							

Al Martin   No. 28/ OF

Born: 11/24/67, West Covina, CA
Height: 6' 2"   **Weight:** 220
Bats: Left   **Throws:** Left
1994 OBP: .367   **SLG:** .457

An exciting player to watch, Martin has loads of raw talent, and he's developing quickly. His baserunning and outfield play were much improved since '93, and he was on a roll before a wrist injury ended his season. Martin hits for average against both righties and lefties, but eight of his homers were off righthanders.

	G	AB	H	2B	3B	HR	RS	RBI	BB	SB	BA
1994	82	276	79	12	4	9	48	33	34	15	.286
Career	237	768	216	38	13	27	134	99	76	31	.281
Projected	135	470	144	25	8	17	86	63	49	20	.294

Orlando Merced   No. 6/ OF

Born: 11/2/66, San Juan, PR
Height: 5' 11"   **Weight:** 170
Bats: Both   **Throws:** Right
1994 OBP: .343   **SLG:** .412

For the second straight year, Merced started hot, but slowed in the second half. He led the club in RBIs, batting primarily in the fifth spot. Merced split time at both first base and right field, though he's not a good fielder at either position. Merced grounded into seventeen doubleplays, second most in the league behind Tony Gwynn.

	G	AB	H	2B	3B	HR	RS	RBI	BB	SB	BA
1994	108	386	105	21	3	9	48	51	42	4	.272
Career	524	1673	463	93	14	33	252	231	236	20	.277
Projected	148	525	167	31	5	11	76	79	78	5	.306

Denny Neagle   No. 15/ P

Born: 9/13/68, Gambrills, MD
Height: 6' 2"   **Weight:** 215
Bats: Left   **Throws:** Left
Opp. Batting Average: .259

Used exclusively as a starter for the first time since '90, Neagle showed signs of coming into his own as a pitcher. Though his ERA was on the high side, he was fourth in the league in Ks per nine innings, a very strong indicator of future performance. Neagle's personality is unpredictable to say the least, and his velocity isn't dominant, but he should improve in '95.

	G	GS	IP	ERA	H	BB	SO	W	L	SV
1994	24	24	137.0	5.12	135	49	122	9	10	0
Career	136	40	324.2	4.93	326	136	286	16	22	3
Projected	41	17	121.0	5.19	75	30	69	7	8	1

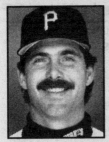

Don Slaught No. 11/ C

Born: 9/11/58, Long Beach, CA
Height: 6' 1" **Weight:** 190
Bats: Right **Throws:** Right
1994 OBP: .381 **SLG:** .342

Slaught has been a solid major league catcher, and a better-than-average hitter, but he's finally beginning to slow down. He's become vulnerable to the stolen base, though he's an expert at handling pitchers. He won't hit many longballs, but Slaught makes good contact at the plate, and he was the only Pirate's player who had more walks than strikeouts last year.

	G	AB	H	2B	3B	HR	RS	RBI	BB	SB	BA
1994	76	240	69	7	0	2	21	21	34	0	.288
Career	1196	3688	1041	219	28	71	375	427	282	18	.282
Projected	116	367	104	15	1	7	32	44	37	1	.289

Zane Smith No. 41/ P

Born: 12/28/60, Madison, WI
Height: 6' 1" **Weight:** 205
Bats: Left **Throws:** Left
Opp. Batting Average: .270

He presents a daunting challenge for left-handed batters, but Zane Smith has been perennially underrated by fans. Buy yourself a hot dog if you knew Smith's '94 ERA cracked the NL's top ten. Smith changes speeds well, and he never puts two pitches in the same spot, but he's had injury problems. The Pirates need Smith's skill and experience in their rotation.

	G	GS	IP	ERA	H	BB	SO	W	L	SV
1994	25	24	157.0	3.27	162	34	57	10	8	0
Career	320	254	1725.1	3.56	1732	539	917	88	101	3
Projected	24	23	146.0	3.71	157	34	54	8	9	0

Andy Van Slyke   No. 18/ OF

Born: 12/21/60, Utica, NY
Height: 6' 2"   **Weight:** 195
Bats: Left   **Throws:** Right
1994 OBP: .340   **SLG:** .358

Van Slyke has been slowed a little by age and injury, and '94 was a quiet year at the plate, so the Bucs didn't re-sign him. "Slick" has better range than most, and his arm is deadly accurate (nine outfield assists, fifth in the NL). He doesn't steal much anymore, but was safe in all seven of his attempts last year. An enthusiastic sense of humor makes him a fan favorite.

	G	AB	H	2B	3B	HR	RS	RBI	BB	SB	BA
1994	105	374	92	18	3	6	41	30	52	7	.246
Career	1578	5434	1500	282	89	158	803	768	634	238	.276
Projected	160	581	154	25	6	11	68	65	62	15	.270

Paul Wagner   No. 43/ P

Born: 11/14/67, Milwaukee, WI
Height: 6' 1"   **Weight:** 185
Bats: Right   **Throws:** Right
Opp. Batting Average: .293

Wagner began the year as a starter, but had a 4.84 ERA in seventeen starts. Coming out of the bullpen, his ERA was 3.12 in twelve appearances. Yet it still isn't clear that he has the make-up of a top-flight closer, so the question is: How should the Pirates utilize the best arm on their staff? The Pirates are hoping that Wagner won't be the next Stan Belinda.

	G	GS	IP	ERA	H	BB	SO	W	L	SV
1994	29	17	119.2	4.59	136	50	86	7	8	0
Career	79	35	274.0	4.24	288	97	205	17	16	2
Projected	41	19	148.0	4.41	158	52	113	8	9	1

St. Louis
CARDINALS

1995 Scouting Report

Outfielders: Cardinals outfielders are always blessed with speed to burn. It's a neccessity on the fast turf of Busch Stadium. This Cardinals outfield has something extra: power. When he's healthy, Mark Whiten (RF) has a tremendous arm and a big bat. Ray Lankford led the Cardinals on offense and in center field for the first half of '94. The Cards can play Brian Jordan, Bernard Gilkey, or Gerald Young in left field.

Infielders: The infield defense isn't what it once was. Ozzie Smith is still the man at shortstop, though his bat and glove are in decline. Second base can be occupied by either Geronimo Pena or Luis Alicea. At third base, Todd Zeile is error prone, but he's productive on offense. First baseman Gregg Jefferies is the best baseball player in St. Louis, unless he doesn't re-sign.

Catchers: Tom Pagnozzi won a Gold Glove for his stellar defense in 1994.

Starting Pitchers: Danny Jackson is the team's new ace. Free agent Bob Tewksbury is the leader of the staff, but Brian Barber could replace him. Twenty-four-year-old Allen Watson is the only Cardinals starter whose fastball tops ninety mph. The remainder of the rotation is unsettled. Rene Arocha, Vicente Palacios, and Tom Urbani were starters last season.

Relief Pitchers: Newly acquired Tom Henke will be the closer. Rich Rodriguez and Rene Arocha make appearances in the middle and late innings.

Manager: Joe Torre (874–976) won a National League MVP Award in 1971 as a slugging cornerman for St. Louis.

1995 Outlook

The Cardinals finished thirteen games out of first in 1994 because they simply didn't execute the kind of baseball that must be played by any club that calls Busch Stadium home. No St. Louis team has ever had a winning season without a huge advantage in its home park. Unfortunately for Cardinals fans, the hometown team was 23–33 in Busch, 30–28 on the road.

The keys to the Cards' demise at home were poor pitching and failure to capitalize on run-scoring opportunities.

Though the fences have been lowered and the alleys aren't as deep as they once were, Busch Stadium is still not a place where the home run usually flourishes. Yet Cardinals pitching allowed more big flies than any other staff in the National League, to go with the thirteenth-worst ERA. Troublesome circumstances for a team playing in a stadium that's supposed to be tough on power hitters. Veteran hurlers Jackson and Henke should stabilize the pitching situation.

The organization has certainly tried to develop young control pitchers, modeled after staff ace Bob Tewksbury. But the contributions of their recent prospects (Donovan Osborne, Rene Arocha, Mike Perez) have been limited. The next wave of prospective Cardinals' hurlers will be led by Allen Watson and Brian Barber.

The Cards' offense wasn't anemic last year. The team finished fourth in the NL in on-base percentage, including 434 walks. The Cardinals were the National League's only club to garner 400+ bases on balls. But St. Louis failed to capitalize on many of those potential runs. Though St. Louis does have some productive players in their batting order, they managed to leave 845 runners on base, the eleventh-worst total in the NL. Even more distressing, the Redbirds compiled a rally-killing 62% rate of success when attempting to steal.

1995 St. Louis Cardinals Roster

Manager: Joe Torre
Coaches: Jose Cardenal, Chris Chambliss, Bob Gibson, Gaylen Pitts, Mark Riggins, Red Schoendienst

No.	Pitchers	B	T	HT	WT	DOB	Birthplace
43	Arocha, Rene	R	R	6–0	180	2/24/66	Havana, Cuba
52	Barber, Brian	R	R	6–1	175	3/4/73	Hamilton, OH
52	Cormier, Rheal	L	L	5–10	185	4/23/67	Moncton, Canada
24	Eversgerd, Bryan	R	L	6–1	190	2/11/69	Centralia, IL
50	Frascatore, John	R	R	6–1	200	2/4/70	Queens, NY
32	Habyan, John	R	R	6–2	195	1/29/64	Bayshore, NY
—	Henke, Tom	R	R	6–5	225	12/21/57	Kansas City, MO
—	Jackson, Danny	R	L	6–3	205	1/5/62	San Antonio, TX
26	Olivares, Omar	R	R	6–1	193	7/6/67	Mayaguez, PR
31	Osborne, Donovan	L	L	6–2	195	6/21/69	Roseville, CA
58	Palacios, Vicente	R	R	6–3	175	7/19/63	Mataloma, Mexico
42	Perez, Mike	R	R	6–0	187	10/19/64	Yauco, PR
33	Rodriguez, Rich	R	L	6–0	200	3/1/63	Downey, CA
41	Urbani, Tom	L	L	6–1	190	1/21/68	Santa Cruz, CA
38	Watson, Allen	L	L	6–3	190	11/18/70	Jamaica, NY
	Catchers						
7	McGriff, Terry	R	R	6–2	195	9/23/63	Ft. Pierce, FL
19	Pagnozzi, Tom	R	R	6–1	190	7/30/62	Tucson, AZ
	Infielders						
44	Cromer, Tripp	R	R	6–2	165	11/21/67	Lake City, SC
68	Holbert, Aaron	R	R	6–0	160	1/9/73	Torrence, CA
11	Oquendo, Jose	B	R	5–10	171	7/4/63	Rio Piedras, PR
21	Pena, Geronimo	B	R	6–1	195	3/29/67	Distrito Nacional, DR
1	Smith, Ozzie	B	R	5–10	168	12/26/54	Mobile, AL
63	Young, Dmitri	B	R	6–2	210	10/11/73	Vicksburg, MS
27	Zeile, Todd	R	R	6–1	190	9/9/65	Van Nuys, CA
	Outfielders						
55	Bradshaw, Terry	L	R	6–0	180	2/3/69	Franklin, VA
23	Gilkey, Bernard	R	R	6–0	190	9/24/66	St. Louis, MO
3	Jordan, Brian	R	R	6–1	205	3/29/67	Baltimore, MD
16	Lankford, Ray	L	L	5–11	198	6/5/67	Modesto, CA
47	Mabry, John	L	R	6–4	195	10/17/70	Wilmington, DE
22	Whiten, Mark	B	R	6–3	215	11/25/66	Pensacola, FL
15	Young, Gerald	B	R	6–2	185	10/22/64	Tele, Honduras

1995 Schedule

April

S	M	T	W	T	F	S
						1
2	3	4	5	6	7	8
	PHI	PHI	PHI	PHI	MON	MON
9	10	11	12	13	14	15
MON	PHI	PHI	PHI	MON	MON	MON
16	17	18	19	20	21	22
MON		FLO	FLO	NY	NY	NY
23	24	25	26	27	28	29
NY		FLO	FLO		NY	NY
30						
NY						

May

S	M	T	W	T	F	S
	1	2	3	4	5	6
	PIT	PIT	HOU	HOU	HOU	HOU
7	8	9	10	11	12	13
HOU	CHI	CHI	CHI		LA	LA
14	15	16	17	18	19	20
LA	SD	SD	SD	SF	SF	SF
21	22	23	24	25	26	27
SF		ATL	ATL	ATL	CIN	CIN
28	29	30	31			
CIN	COL	COL	COL			

June

S	M	T	W	T	F	S
				1	2	3
					CIN	CIN
4	5	6	7	8	9	10
CIN	COL	COL	COL		ATL	ATL
11	12	13	14	15	16	17
ATL			SD	SD	SD	SF
18	19	20	21	22	23	24
SF	LA	LA	LA		PHI	PHI
25	26	27	28	29	30	
PHI	HOU	HOU	HOU	CHI	CHI	

July

S	M	T	W	T	F	S
						1
						CHI
2	3	4	5	6	7	8
CHI	MON	MON	MON	FLO	FLO	FLO
9	10	11	12	13	14	15
FLO		★		PIT	PIT	PIT
16	17	18	19	20	21	22
PIT	MON	MON	NY	NY	PHI	PHI
23	24	25	26	27	28	29
PHI		NY	NY	NY	FLO	FLO
30	31					
FLO	FLO					

August

S	M	T	W	T	F	S
		1	2	3	4	5
		HOU	HOU	HOU	CHI	CHI
6	7	8	9	10	11	12
CHI		LA	LA	LA	SD	SD
13	14	15	16	17	18	19
SD	SF	SF	SF	SF	ATL	ATL
20	21	22	23	24	25	26
ATL	CIN	CIN	CIN	CIN	CIN	COL
27	28	29	30	31		
COL	CIN	CIN	CIN			

Sept/Oct

S	M	T	W	T	F	S
					1	2
					COL	COL
3	4	5	6	7	8	9
COL	ATL	ATL	ATL		SD	SD
10	11	12	13	14	15	16
SD	SF	SF	SF		LA	LA
17	18	19	20	21	22	23
LA	PIT	PIT	PIT		HOU	HOU
24	25	26	27	28	29	30
HOU	CHI	CHI	CHI		PIT	PIT
1	2					
PIT						

☐ Home ☐ Away ★ All-Star Game

Busch Stadium

Capacity: 57,001

Turf: Artificial

Dimensions:
LF Line: 330'
RF Line: 330'
Center: 402'
Alleys: 378'

Tickets:
(314) 421-3060

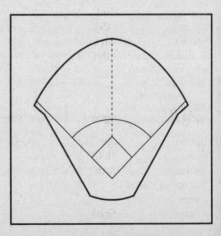

1994 Batting Order

1. Gerald Young (Left Field)
2. Ozzie Smith (Shortstop)
3. Gregg Jefferies (First Base)
4. Ray Lankford (Center Field)
5. Todd Zeile (Third Base)
6. Mark Whiten (Right Field)
7. Geronimo Pena (Second Base)
8. Tom Pagnozzi (Catcher)
9. Pitcher

1994 Team Record
53–61 (.465); Fourth in NL Central

NL East	W	L	NL Central	W	L	NL West	W	L
Atlanta	4	4	Chicago	5	5	Colorado	4	8
Florida	7	3	Cincinnati	5	3	Los Angeles	4	2
Montreal	3	7	Houston	4	8	San Diego	2	4
New York	3	6	Pittsburgh	5	5	S. Francisco	4	2
Philadelphia	3	4	St. Louis	—	—			
Total	20	24		19	21		14	16

1994 National League Team Rank Batting

Batting Average: Ninth (.263)
Runs Scored: Sixth (535)
Runs Batted In: Sixth (506)
Stolen Bases: Seventh (76)
Slugging Percentage: Seventh (.414)
On-Base Percentage: Fourth (.339)

1994 National League Team Rank Pitching

Earned Run Average: Thirteenth (5.14)
Bases On Balls: Fifth (355)
Strikeouts: Fourteenth (632)
Wins: Ninth (53)
Saves: Sixth (29)
Complete Games: Sixth (7)

St. Louis Cardinals MVP

Gregg Jefferies   No. 9/ 1B

Born: 8/1/67, Burlingame, CA
Height: 5' 10"   **Weight:** 185
Bats: Both   **Throws:** Right
1994 OBP: .391   **SLG:** .489

Jefferies is a superstar hitter who is in his prime. His quick, compact swing generates exceptional linedrive power from both sides of the plate, and he rarely wastes an at-bat. The number-one basestealer among league cornermen, and a competent fielder, there's nothing on a baseball diamond that Jefferies can't do.

In 1989, his first full season in the majors, Jefferies was the most touted New York Mets hitting prospect since Darryl Strawberry. He's always had incredible tools; it simply took a reasonable amount of time for his talents to fully develop. Neither the Mets nor the Kansas City Royals, to whom Jefferies was dealt in 1992, had the patience to wait for him to reach his prime.

Jefferies is an intense, never-quit type of athlete on the field. There aren't too many twenty-year-olds who could enter the New York limelight, then come out as stable and focused as Gregg Jefferies.

Last season, Jefferies compiled the NL's fourth-longest hitting streak (seventeen games) and finished the season sixth in batting average. Jefferies' level swing generates explosive longball power without sacrificing contact. His plate-appearances-per-strikeout rate was second best in the league (17.2). Now at the age of twenty-seven, Jefferies probably will win a batting title in the next three years.

	G	AB	H	2B	3B	HR	RS	RBI	BB	SB	BA
1994	103	397	129	27	1	12	52	55	45	12	.325
Career	862	3258	959	183	16	80	453	418	290	140	.294
Projected	147	565	189	30	3	17	92	89	70	31	.335

Luis Alicea   No. 18/ 2B

Born: 7/29/65, Santurce, PR
Height: 5' 9"   **Weight:** 177
Bats: Both   **Throws:** Right
1994 OBP: .373   **SLG:** .459

Of the two Cardinals second basemen, Alicea has less longball power, but he's slightly better at getting on base via hit or walk. He's a good artificial-turf infielder, quick turning the double-play and able to cover a lot of area. As we go to press, the Cardinals are close to dealing Alicea for Boston starter Nate Minchey.

	G	AB	H	2B	3B	HR	RS	RBI	BB	SB	BA
1994	88	205	57	12	5	5	32	29	30	4	.278
Career	437	1197	299	53	23	11	133	131	137	18	.250
Projected	125	364	110	21	5	5	55	50	51	10	.290

Rene Arocha   No. 43/ P

Born: 2/24/66, Havana, Cuba
Height: 6' 0"   **Weight:** 180
Bats: Right   **Throws:** Right
Opp. Batting Average: .287

Arocha didn't demonstrate the same command of his extensive array of pitches as he'd shown in his rookie season, but 1994 wasn't a bad year for him. He wound up being the Cardinals' main closer out of the bullpen, after having made twenty-nine starts the year before. Arocha did hurl one complete game last season. He finished second on the team in saves.

	G	GS	IP	ERA	H	BB	SO	W	L	SV
1994	45	7	83.0	4.01	94	21	62	4	4	11
Career	77	36	271.0	3.85	291	52	158	15	12	11
Projected	46	22	162.0	1.23	174	31	94	9	7	7

Bernard Gilkey   No. 23/ OF

Born: 9/24/66, St. Louis, MO
Height: 6' 0"   **Weight:** 190
Bats: Right   **Throws:** Right
1994 OBP: .336   **SLG:** .363

Gilkey's failure to build on his '93 offensive successes was a big part of the Cardinals' unraveling process. In the past, Gilkey has shown solid linedrive pop to all fields, but last year he seemed to be trying to pull the ball more. The result was more than his share of groundball outs to shortstop. Given another chance, Gilkey could make a strong comeback in '95.

	G	AB	H	2B	3B	HR	RS	RBI	BB	SB	BA
1994	105	380	96	22	1	6	52	45	39	15	.253
Career	472	1653	459	93	14	35	246	181	181	68	.278
Projected	148	598	184	41	4	15	100	76	63	20	.295

Ray Lankford   No. 16/ OF

Born: 6/5/67, Modesto, CA
Height: 5' 11"   **Weight:** 198
Bats: Left   **Throws:** Left
1994 OBP: .359   **SLG:** .488

Lankford christened the season with a line-shot homer on April 3, then continued to hit home runs all season. But he suffered numerous o-fers after the All-Star break. Lankford is fast, but he's not a good percentage basestealer, sliding in safe just once more than he was punched out last year. Lankford is an offensive force when he plays within himself.

	G	AB	H	2B	3B	HR	RS	RBI	BB	SB	BA
1994	109	416	111	25	5	19	89	57	58	11	.267
Career	579	2113	561	115	30	58	335	269	265	119	.265
Projected	144	520	142	28	5	17	101	67	91	16	.263

Tom Pagnozzi   No. 19/ C

Born: 7/30/62, Tucson, AZ
Height: 6' 1"   **Weight:** 190
Bats: Right   **Throws:** Right
1994 OBP: .327   **SLG:** .416

Pagnozzi had a solid year at the plate in 1994. He's got decent power to the gaps, and he hits well with runners on base. But he's most valued for his defense and his handling of pitchers. Pagnozzi has had stamina problems in the past; he can't carry the Cardinals on his back, but he can contribute to a championship run. He was awarded a Gold Glove in 1994.

	G	AB	H	2B	3B	HR	RS	RBI	BB	SB	BA
1994	70	243	66	12	1	7	21	40	21	0	.272
Career	670	2060	530	104	10	27	171	232	139	14	.257
Projected	100	346	88	16	1	8	31	48	24	1	.258

Geronimo Pena   No. 21/ 2B

Born: 3/29/67, Distrito Nacional, DR
Height: 6' 1"   **Weight:** 195
Bats: Both   **Throws:** Right
1994 OBP: .344   **SLG:** .479

A switch-hitter who is much more comfortable batting from the right side of the plate, Pena showed impressive power last year. Considered something of a defensive liability in the past, Pena has worked hard on his fielding. He made just three miscues in eighty-three games at second base in '94, after having made twelve errors in seventy-four games the previous season.

	G	AB	H	2B	3B	HR	RS	RBI	BB	SB	BA
1994	83	213	54	13	1	11	33	34	24	9	.254
Career	94	248	65	13	2	11	38	34	27	10	.262
Projected	128	395	109	28	3	14	59	56	43	15	.265

Mike Perez   No. 42/ P

Born: 10/19/64, Yauco, PR
Height: 6' 0"   **Weight:** 187
Bats: Right   **Throws:** Right
Opp. Batting Average: .391

On June 5, Perez had accumulated eleven
saves and a bloated 7.04 ERA, an unlikely
combination. Perez had been forced into
the closer role by Cardinals management in late '93, and he
struggled with the responsibility last season. Perez was hit so
hard and so frequently in '94 that his future as a major league
pitcher may be in jeopardy.

	G	GS	IP	ERA	H	BB	SO	W	L	SV
1994	36	0	31.0	8.71	52	10	20	2	3	12
Career	205	0	227.1	3.41	218	72	136	19	10	20
Projected	56	0	58.0	4.40	65	17	44	5	3	11

Ozzie Smith   No. 1/ SS

Born: 12/26/54, Mobile, AL
Height: 5' 10"   **Weight:** 168
Bats: Both   **Throws:** Right
1994 OBP: .326   **SLG:** .349

The greatest fielding shortstop since the
game was invented, "The Wizard" transformed himself into an offensive threat in
the late '80s, but last season saw a major drop in production.
Smith stopped trying to steal in '94, bringing an end to his string
of sixteen straight seasons with at least twenty thefts, a feat
equaled only by Honus "The Flying Dutchman" Wagner.

	G	AB	H	2B	3B	HR	RS	RBI	BB	SB	BA
1994	98	381	100	18	3	3	51	30	38	6	.262
Career	2447	9013	2365	387	66	26	1205	764	1030	569	.262
Projected	146	554	148	23	5	2	74	49	47	16	.272

Rick Sutcliffe   No. 40/ P

Born: 6/21/56, Independence, MO
Height: 6' 7"   **Weight:** 239
Bats: Left   **Throws:** Right
Opp. Batting Average: .331

Sutcliffe's won-lost record for the past three years is 32–29, not too shabby for a thirty-eight-year-old pitcher. Unfortunately, his ERAs in those same three seasons have been 4.47, 5.75, and 6.52. Sutcliffe was once a fine pitcher with a blazing fastball. In 1984, he went 16–1 for the Cubs. Free agent Sutcliffe won't be pitching for the Cardinals in 1995.

	G	GS	IP	ERA	H	BB	SO	W	L	SV
1994	16	14	67.2	6.52	93	32	26	6	4	0
Career	457	392	2998.0	4.08	2662	1081	1679	171	139	6
Projected	25	24	131.0	5.96	171	59	59	9	8	0

Bob Tewksbury   No. 39/ P

Born: 11/30/60, Concord, NH
Height: 6' 4"   **Weight:** 208
Bats: Right   **Throws:** Right
Opp. Batting Average: .304

Tewksbury is the Cardinals' ace and baseball's most recognized control pitcher. The highlight of his season was a string of seven straight wins, equal to the longest streak in the National League. Tewksbury finished second in the league in fewest walks per nine innings (1.3). His ERA ballooned from previous seasons, but Tewksbury is still a fine pitcher.

	G	GS	IP	ERA	H	BB	SO	W	L	SV
1994	24	24	155.2	5.32	190	22	79	12	10	0
Career	193	172	1153.2	3.62	1276	178	481	77	59	1
Projected	32	32	211.0	4.45	256	24	101	17	11	0

Tom Urbani   No. 34/ P

Born: 1/21/68, Santa Cruz, CA
Height: 6' 1"   **Weight:** 190
Bats: Left   **Throws:** Left
Opp. Batting Average: .302

Urbani moved fairly rapidly through the Cardinals' minor league system, and last year was his first full season in the majors. Like all Cardinals pitchers, Urbani doesn't overpower hitters. Instead, he relies on changing speeds and mixing pitches, while keeping walks to a mimimum. Urbani got hit hard in '94, giving up twelve homers in eighty innings.

	G	GS	IP	ERA	H	BB	SO	W	L	SV
1994	20	10	80.1	5.15	98	21	43	3	7	0
Career	38	19	142.1	4.93	171	47	76	4	10	0
Projected	22	11	83.0	4.95	100	28	45	2	6	0

Allen Watson   No. 38/ P

Born: 11/18/70, Jamaica, NY
Height: 6' 3"   **Weight:** 190
Bats: Left   **Throws:** Left
Opp. Batting Average: .286

Watson is the closest thing the Cardinals have to a power pitcher. His fastball reaches ninety on radar, and his slider has some bite. He's a confident young player, and the Cardinals felt sure enough of his talents to draft him in the first round of the 1991 June draft. Last season, Watson struggled with his control, sometimes trying to pitch too perfectly.

	G	GS	IP	ERA	H	BB	SO	W	L	SV
1994	22	22	115.2	5.52	130	53	74	6	5	0
Career	38	37	201.2	5.13	220	81	123	12	12	0
Projected	23	22	120.0	5.12	131	48	73	7	7	0

Mark Whiten   No. 22/ OF

Born: 11/25/66, Pensacola, FL
Height: 6' 3"   **Weight:** 215
Bats: Both   **Throws:** Right
1994 OBP: .364   **SLG:** .485

Baseball pundits have been critical of the imperfections in Whiten's game, but he looks like a potential Joe Carter to us. Though slowed by injuries in '94, Whiten was on base regularly when in the lineup, and he can hit the ball to the moon. He's twenty-eight years old, an age when many hitters have career years. Whiten's throwing arm is legendary.

	G	AB	H	2B	3B	HR	RS	RBI	BB	SB	BA
1994	92	334	98	18	2	14	57	53	37	10	.293
Career	541	1899	492	69	18	59	269	247	204	47	.259
Projected	147	561	162	20	4	25	90	99	62	16	.279

Todd Zeile   No. 27/ 3B

Born: 9/9/65, Van Nuys, CA
Height: 6' 1"   **Weight:** 190
Bats: Right   **Throws:** Right
1994 OBP: .348   **SLG:** .470

A power burst from late July boosted Zeile's numbers, but the converted catcher with the Steve Garveyesque batting stance struggled at the plate somewhat in '94. On the encouraging side, Zeile made progress at third base and is no longer a liability with the glove. A full season of baseball in '95 might crystallize Zeile's skills at an All-Star level.

	G	AB	H	2B	3B	HR	RS	RBI	BB	SB	BA
1994	113	415	111	25	1	19	62	75	52	1	.267
Career	723	2567	682	143	13	70	340	372	328	32	.266
Projected	158	602	178	39	1	23	91	113	77	4	.284

San Diego
PADRES

1995 Scouting Report

Outfielders: The Padres have a pair of future All-Stars in Derek Bell and Phil Plantier, not to mention future Hall of Famer Tony Gwynn. As a trio, their defense is solid, and their run production is prolific. The average numbers of the Padres' outfielders combined were a nifty .314 with fifteen HRs. Billy Bean and Phil Clark are serviceable backups.

Infielders: Up the middle, Bip Roberts (2B) and Luis Lopez (SS) cover a lot of ground. Roberts is the Padres' offensive spark plug. Ricky Gutierrez will sub at short and second, or start if Roberts isn't re-signed. Eddie Williams (1B) could hit thirty homers in '95. Scott Livingstone plays third.

Catchers: The Padres are banking on former Dartmouth College product Brad Ausmus to continue improving at, and behind, the plate. Ausmus' backup will be young Brian Johnson.

Starting Pitchers: The rotation is the Padres' deepest concern, but things should improve in '95. Andy Benes has been everything one looks for in an ace, except a consistent winner, and the improved offense should solve that problem. Joey Hamilton and Andy Ashby both made long strides forward last year, and Scott Sanders was sometimes dominant. Tim Worrell and former Braves prospect Donnie Elliott will both have a chance to join the rotation

Relief Pitchers: The Padres were 39–3 when leading after eight innings. Trevor Hoffman is already the team's stopper, but the Padres believe he could be as good as any closer in the league. Pedro A. Martinez is an ideal setup man and backup closer.

Manager: New manager Bruce Bochy signed a one-year contract, making him baseball's youngest manager.

1995 Outlook

Lost in the furor surrounding the organization's trading-off of most of its highly paid stars is the intriguing young talent that has developed in the absence of big names. After a 10–32 start through May 21 last season, the Padres went 37–38, the top mark in their division over that period of time. The Padres could be the league's most improved unit in 1995.

Good news abounds for the Padres' offense. After May 24, they were tops in the NL in batting average (.293). Two significant contributors were the scorching hot Tony Gwynn and June call-up Eddie Williams. The overall production should increase even more with the return of a healthy Phil Plantier, the team's top power source.

The Padres won only eighteen of their fifty-five contests that were decided by two runs or less. That may not sound like good news for 1995, but it actually indicates that the team kept a lot of games close and probably got more than their share of bad luck. Odds are that those narrow margins will turn in the Padres' favor this season.

San Diego pitching was also much better than the final won-lost record indicates. The staff allowed the fourth fewest home runs in the NL (99) and the third fewest hits. The starters are young, hard throwers, each with a great deal of upward potential. Staff ace Andy Benes is certain to win more often this season than in 1994. Joey Hamilton could be special.

Of course, this is a club that finished with the worst final winning percentage in the major leagues. But the NL West is one of the weakest divisions, and an improvement of eight or nine games would have put them in striking distance of first place last year. We aren't ready to predict a worst-to-first scenario for the Padres, but keep in mind that the Pittsburgh Pirates finished forty-four games out in 1986, then won eighty-five games just two years later. Look for the Padres to surprise in 1995.

1995 San Diego Padres Roster

Manager: Bruce Bochy
Coaches: Davey Lopes, Graig Nettles, Rob Picciolo, Merv Rettenmund,
Sonny Siebert, Tye Waller

No.	Pitchers	B	T	HT	WT	DOB	Birthplace
43	Ashby, Andy	R	R	6–5	180	7/11/67	Kansas City, MO
38	Beckett, Robbie	R	L	6–5	235	7/16/72	Austin, TX
40	Benes, Andy	R	R	6–6	240	8/20/67	Evansville, IN
45	Bochtler, Doug	R	R	6–3	185	7/5/70	W. Palm Beach, FL
49	Brocail, Doug	L	R	6–5	220	5/16/67	Clearfield, PA
38	Elliott, Donnie	R	R	6–4	190	9/20/68	Pasadena, TX
39	Florie, Bryce	R	R	6–0	170	5/21/70	Charleston, SC
50	Hamilton, Joey	R	R	6–4	230	9/9/70	Statesboro, GA
51	Hoffman, Trevor	R	R	6–1	200	10/13/67	Bellflower, CA
42	Martinez, Pedro A.	L	L	6–2	155	11/29/68	Villa Mella, DR
27	Sanders, Scott	R	R	6–4	210	3/25/69	Thibodaux, LA
46	Tabaka, Jeff	R	L	6–2	195	1/17/64	Barberton, OH
37	Taylor, Kerry	R	R	6–3	200	1/25/71	Bemidji, MN
58	Worrell, Tim	R	R	6–4	210	7/5/67	Arcadia, CA
	Catchers						
11	Ausmus, Brad	R	R	5–11	185	4/14/69	New Haven, CT
55	Johnson, Brian	R	R	6–2	195	1/8/68	Oakland, CA
	Infielders						
25	Bruno, Julio	R	R	5–10	160	10/15/72	Puerta Plata, DR
7	Gutierrez, Ricky	R	R	6–1	175	5/23/70	Miami, FL
53	Holbert, Ray	R	R	6–0	170	9/25/70	Torrance, CA
9	Livingstone, Scott	L	R	6–0	190	7/15/65	Dallas, TX
14	Lopez, Luis	B	R	5–11	175	9/4/70	Cidra, PR
18	Shipley, Craig	R	R	6–1	190	1/7/63	Sydney, Australia
23	Williams, Eddie	R	R	6–0	210	11/1/64	Shreveport, LA
	Outfielders						
21	Bean, Billy	L	L	6–0	195	5/11/64	Santa Ana, CA
14	Bell, Derek	R	R	6–2	205	12/11/68	Tampa, FL
40	Clark, Phil	R	R	6–0	180	5/6/68	Crockett, TX
19	Gwynn, Tony	L	L	5–11	215	5/9/60	Los Angeles, CA
20	McDavid, Ray	L	R	6–3	190	7/20/71	San Diego, CA
56	Moore, Vince	B	L	6–1	177	9/22/71	Houston, TX
10	Nieves, Melvin	B	R	6–2	186	12/28/71	San Juan, PR
24	Plantier, Phil	L	R	5–10	195	1/27/69	Manchester, NH

1995 Schedule

April

S	M	T	W	T	F	S
						1
2	3	4 ATL	5 ATL	6	7 CIN	8 CIN
9 CIN	10 CIN	11 ATL	12 ATL	13 ATL	14 FLO	15 FLO
16 FLO	17 HOU	18 HOU	19 HOU	20 FLO	21 FLO	22 FLO
23 FLO	24	25 HOU	26 HOU	27 CIN	28 CIN	29 CIN
30 CIN						

May

S	M	T	W	T	F	S
	1 COL	2 COL	3 COL	4 SF	5 SF	6 SF
7 SF	8 LA	9 LA	10 LA	11	12 CHI	13 CHI
14 CHI	15 STL	16 STL	17 STL	18	19 PIT	20 PIT
21 PIT	22	23 MON	24 MON	25 MON	26 PHI	27 PHI
28 PHI	29 NY	30 NY	31 NY			

June

S	M	T	W	T	F	S
				1	2 MON	3 MON
4 MON	5	6 PHI	7 PHI	8 PHI	9 NY	10 NY
11 NY	12	13 STL	14 STL	15 STL	16 PIT	17 PIT
18 PIT	19 CHI	20 CHI	21 CHI	22 COL	23 COL	24 COL
25 COL	26 LA	27 LA	28 LA	29	30 SF	

July

S	M	T	W	T	F	S
						1 SF
2 SF	3 FLO	4 FLO	5 FLO	6 HOU	7 HOU	8 HOU
9 HOU	10	11 ★	12	13 ATL	14 ATL	15 ATL
16 ATL	17 CIN	18 CIN	19 CIN	20	21 ATL	22 ATL
23 ATL	24 CIN	25 CIN	26 FLO	27 FLO	28 HOU	29 HOU
30 HOU	31 HOU					

August

S	M	T	W	T	F	S
		1 SF	2 SF	3 COL	4 COL	5 COL
6 COL	7	8 CHI	9 CHI	10 CHI	11 STL	12
13 STL	14 PIT	15 PIT	16 PIT	17	18 MON	19 MON
20 MON	21 PHI	22 PHI	23 PHI	24 NY	25 NY	26 NY
27 NY	28	29 MON	30 MON	31 MON		

Sept/Oct

S	M	T	W	T	F	S
					1 PHI	2 PHI
3 PHI	4 NY	5 NY	6 NY	7	8 STL	9 STL
10 STL	11 PIT	12 PIT	13 PIT	14	15 CHI	16 CHI
17 CHI	18 COL	19 COL	20 COL	21	22 LA	23 LA
24 LA	25 SF	26 SF	27 SF	28	29 LA	30 LA
1 LA	2					

☐ Home   ☐ Away   ★ All-Star Game

Jack Murphy Stadium

Capacity: 59,722

Turf: Grass

Dimensions:
LF Line: 327'
RF Line: 327'
Center: 405'
Alleys: 370'

Tickets:
(619) 283-4494

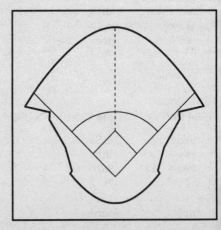

1994 Batting Order

1. Bip Roberts (Second Base)
2. Tony Gwynn (Right Field)
3. Derek Bell (Center Field)
4. Eddie Williams (First Base)
5. Phil Plantier (Left Field)
6. Scott Livingstone (Third Base)
7. Luis López (Shortstop)
8. Brad Ausmus (Catcher)
9. Pitcher

1994 Team Record
47–70 (.402); Fourth in NL West

NL East	W	L	NL Central	W	L	NL West	W	L
Atlanta	1	6	Chicago	3	6	Colorado	5	5
Florida	1	5	Cincinnati	2	8	Los Angeles	4	6
Montreal	0	12	Houston	5	5	San Diego	—	—
New York	6	6	Pittsburgh	3	3	S. Francisco	5	2
Philadelphia	8	4	St. Louis	4	2			
Total	16	33		17	24		14	13

1994 National League Team Rank Batting

Batting Average: Fourth (.275)
Runs Scored: Twelfth (479)
Runs Batted In: Thirteenth (445)
Stolen Bases: Sixth (79)
Slugging Percentage: Tenth (.401)
On-Base Percentage: Ninth (.330)

1994 National League Team Rank Pitching

Earned Run Average: Seventh (4.08)
Bases On Balls: Twelfth (393)
Strikeouts: Second (862)
Wins: Fourteenth (47)
Saves: Ninth (27)
Complete Games: Fourth (8)

© Rich Pilling/MLB Photos

San Diego Padres MVP

Tony Gwynn   No. 19/ OF

Born: 5/9/60, Los Angeles, CA
Height: 5' 11"   **Weight:** 215
Bats: Left   **Throws:** Left
1994 OBP: .454   **SLG:** .568

Few active major league hitters have per-formed at such a high level for as long as Tony Gwynn. It's likely that no player will ever again hit .400 for a season, and Gwynn's failure to accomplish that feat may be the proof.

The game's consummate student, Gwynn often knows more about an opposing pitcher's patterns than the pitcher's own coach. Gwynn creates a detailed analysis of every pitcher in the league, and he's arguably the most prepared hitter of all time.

A perfectly tuned hitting machine, Gwynn led the NL in on-base percentage and still increased his power output from '94, finishing tenth in slugging. He won his fifth batting title with the highest average of his career (.394). It was the highest mark in the majors since Ted Williams' .406 in 1941. Gwynn struck out just once in every twenty-five at-bats, the best rate in baseball.

Gwynn works hard in the field and is a valuable asset on defense. He will rarely make a mistake in judgement, and his throwing is smart-bomb accurate. His range has diminished a little with age.

When they hang Gwynn's plaque at Cooperstown, they'll undoubtedly speculate about the strike-spoiled possibility of a .400 season from Gwynn in 1994.

	G	AB	H	2B	3B	HR	RS	RBI	BB	SB	BA
1994	110	419	165	35	1	12	79	64	48	5	.394
Career	1695	6609	2204	351	79	78	991	714	590	268	.333
Projected	141	541	194	44	2	11	87	72	49	11	.367

Andy Ashby   No. 43/ P

Born: 7/11/67, Kansas City, MO
Height: 6' 5"   **Weight:** 180
Bats: Right   **Throws:** Right
Opp. Batting Average: .233

As assistant GM in Colorado, Padres GM Randy Smith helped the Rockies acquire Ashby. Smith then traded for Ashby in San Diego. Ashby got a lot of decisions last year, but little run support, hence the losing record. Still, his slider was biting more often than not; he was fourth in the league in complete games with four and sixth in opponents batting average.

	G	GS	IP	ERA	H	BB	SO	W	L	SV
1994	24	24	164.1	3.40	145	43	121	6	11	0
Career	74	61	366.1	5.26	396	139	248	11	29	1
Projected	32	26	164.0	4.86	179	57	113	5	12	1

Brad Ausmus   No. 11/ C

Born: 4/14/69, New Haven, CT
Height: 5' 11"   **Weight:** 185
Bats: Right   **Throws:** Right
1994 OBP: .314   **SLG:** .358

Ausmus' reputation for excellent defense notwithstanding, he made the second-most errors of any backstop in the NL. He's got great tools, they simply need polishing. His hitting steadily improved during the year; he raised his batting average about ten points per month from June till the strike. Ausmus hasn't got Piazza-level power, but he could hit fifteen homers in '95.

	G	AB	H	2B	3B	HR	RS	RBI	BB	SB	BA
1994	101	327	82	12	1	7	45	24	30	5	.251
Career	150	487	123	20	2	12	63	36	36	7	.253
Projected	155	525	143	22	2	13	40	71	40	8	.263

Derek Bell   No. 4/ OF

Born: 12/11/68, Tampa, FL
Height: 6' 2"   **Weight:** 205
Bats: Right   **Throws:** Right
1994 OBP: .354   **SLG:** .454

Bell unleashes tremendous power to the opposite field, and he's got the speed and judgement to steal forty bases a year. He showed vast improvement last season in his understanding of the strikezone, an important sign for a developing slugger. Bell isn't exactly Tris Speaker in the outfield (ten errors in '94), but he is an entertaining player and probably a future All-Star.

	G	AB	H	2B	3B	HR	RS	RBI	BB	SB	BA
1994	108	434	135	20	0	14	54	54	29	24	.311
Career	337	1165	320	45	4	37	155	142	73	60	.275
Projected	155	610	187	25	1	23	83	82	34	32	.295

Andy Benes   No. 40/ P

Born: 8/20/67, Evansville, IN
Height: 6' 6"   **Weight:** 240
Bats: Right   **Throws:** Right
Opp. Batting Average: .237

Benes seemed intent on raising his strike-out rate last year, and the result was a career high .91 Ks per inning. His ratio of (H+BB)/IP was also excellent at 1.19. And yet it's difficult to label '94 a success considering the .300 winning percentage. Benes is still an even-money bet to become a star, rather than just the staff ace of a last place team.

	G	GS	IP	ERA	H	BB	SO	W	L	SV
1994	25	25	172.1	3.86	155	51	189	6	14	0
Career	168	167	1116.1	3.51	1007	357	910	65	68	0
Projected	34	34	230.0	3.82	203	78	210	12	17	0

Joey Hamilton   No. 50/ P

Born: 9/9/70, Statesboro, GA
Height: 6'4"   **Weight:** 220
Bats: Right   **Throws:** Right
Opp. Batting Average: .241

Another promising Padres call-up, Hamilton led the team in wins (9). He surrendered one earned run or fewer in seven of his starts, and he got stronger as the season progressed. Hamilton doesn't have overpowering stuff, but he does have excellent command of his pitches; he tallied a 3/1 K/BB ratio in his last four starts of '94.

	G	GS	IP	ERA	H	BB	SO	W	L	SV
1994	16	16	108.2	2.98	98	29	61	9	6	0
Career	16	16	108.2	2.98	98	29	61	9	6	0
Projected			No projection. Player was a rookie in 1994.							

Trevor Hoffman   No. 51/ P

Born: 10/13/67, Bellflower, CA
Height: 6' 1"   **Weight:** 200
Bats: Right   **Throws:** Right
Opp. Batting Average: .193

The prime component for the Padres in the deal that sent Gary Sheffield to Florida, Hoffman has the makeup to be the next Rod Beck. Looking downright dangerous from the mound, the lanky Hoffman has allowed only eight homers in his eighty-six Padres appearances. His twenty saves last season came in just twenty-three opportunities.

	G	GS	IP	ERA	H	BB	SO	W	L	SV
1994	47	0	56.0	2.57	39	20	68	4	4	20
Career	114	0	146.0	3.39	119	59	147	8	10	25
Projected	65	0	83.0	2.99	68	34	84	5	6	14

Bill Krueger No. 33/ P

Born: 4/24/58, Waukegan, IL
Height: 6' 5" **Weight:** 205
Bats: Left **Throws:** Left
Opp. Batting Average: .259

Journeyman Krueger began the year in Detroit, but hooked up with the Padres and pitched well, especially on four days' rest (3-0 with a 2.83 ERA). His repertoire is basic and unspectacular, but he usually has decent control (K/BB ratio of 4/1 in '94). Krueger was a welcome addition to a starting staff that's starved for southpaws, but he wasn't re-signed as of this writing.

	G	GS	IP	ERA	H	BB	SO	W	L	SV
1994	24	9	41	4.83	68	24	47	3	4	0
Career	289	159	1166.2	4.30	1255	485	623	66	65	4
Projected	32	9	82.0	4.66	90	31	61	5	5	0

Luis Lopez No. 1/ SS

Born: 9/4/70, Cidra, PR
Height: 5' 11" **Weight:** 175
Bats: Both **Throws:** Right
1994 OBP: .325 **SLG:** .379

Lopez began '94 in the minors, but was called to the big club in late May. It took him just two games to collect his first homer in the majors, a game-winning grand slam off Mark Portugal. Lopez took over the starting job from Ricky Gutierrez after the All-Star break. He fared far better versus lefties (.333) than against righthanders (.263).

	G	AB	H	2B	3B	HR	RS	RBI	BB	SB	BA
1994	77	235	65	16	1	2	29	20	15	3	.277
Career	94	278	70	17	1	2	30	21	15	3	.252
Rookie	No projection. Player was a rookie in 1994.										

Pedro A. Martinez   No. 42/ P

Born: 11/29/68, Villa Mella, DR
Height: 6' 2"   **Weight:** 155
Bats: Left   **Throws:** Left
Opp. Batting Average: .210

Martinez has produced two straight seasons of excellent setup relief. He dramatically improved his ability to stop lefty hitters; they batted just .206 against him last year. Martinez throws a hard screwball, and his fastball is above average. He has the ability to reach for something extra with runners on base, allowing only eight of thirty-five inherited runners to score.

	G	GS	IP	ERA	H	BB	SO	W	L	SV
1994	48	1	68.1	2.90	52	49	52	3	2	3
Career	80	1	105.1	2.73	75	62	84	6	3	3
Projected	48	1	63.0	2.74	45	37	50	4	2	2

Phil Plantier   No. 24/ OF

Born: 1/27/69, Manchester, NH
Height: 5' 10"   **Weight:** 195
Bats: Left   **Throws:** Right
1994 OBP: .302   **SLG:** .440

The Padres made a shrewd trade in acquiring Plantier from Boston in exchange for Jose Melendez in '93. Plantier generates great power with his crouched stance and uppercut swing. He started '94 on a home run tear, collecting fourteen round-trippers by June. But he was slowed by injuries and wound up hitting just a buck seventy-eight from June 5 till the strike.

	G	AB	H	2B	3B	HR	RS	RBI	BB	SB	BA
1994	96	341	75	21	0	18	44	41	36	3	.220
Career	409	1315	323	68	2	70	185	209	168	10	.246
Projected	143	510	128	27	1	34	73	93	64	5	.241

Bip Roberts   No. 10/ 2B

Born: 10/27/63, Berkeley, CA
Height: 5' 7"   **Weight:** 160
Bats: Both   **Throws:** Right
1994 OBP: .383   **SLG:** .397

A versatile infielder and a fine leadoff man, Roberts came back strong after the Reds gave up on him. Roberts rewarded the Padres with the eighth-best batting average in the league, including the league's longest hitting streak (twenty-three games). Roberts is a good percentage basestealer, and an adequate second baseman. He was unsigned as of this writing.

	G	AB	H	2B	3B	HR	RS	RBI	BB	SB	BA
1994	105	403	129	15	5	2	52	31	39	21	.320
Career	824	2786	825	131	27	23	476	207	295	198	.296
Projected	160	597	174	24	4	3	85	43	67	41	.289

Scott Sanders   No. 27/ P

Born: 3/25/69, Thibodaux, LA
Height: 6' 4"   **Weight:** 210
Bats: Right   **Throws:** Right
Opp. Batting Average: .245

Sanders started the season in the majors for the first time in his career, and he immediately showed signs that he may help stabilize the Padres' rotation. Sanders demonstrated promising consistency, giving up just two earned runs or fewer in six of his last ten starts. He held righthanders to a .188 batting average, thanks to his most effective offering, a hard-biting slider.

	G	GS	IP	ERA	H	BB	SO	W	L	SV
1994	23	20	111.0	4.78	103	48	109	4	8	1
Career	32	29	163.1	4.57	157	71	146	7	11	1
Projected	20	18	101.0	4.58	97	44	90	7	7	1

Wally Whitehurst   No. 41/ P

Born: 4/11/64, Shreveport, LA
Height: 6' 3"   **Weight:** 185
Bats: Right   **Throws:** Right
Opp. Batting Average: .319

Whitehurst suffered another short season when he underwent arthroscopic surgery in mid-June. He's never made it through a complete season, but he's a serviceable third or fourth starter when healthy. Whitehurst hangs his hat on good control and a fine curveball, but if his control isn't sharp, he's vulnerable to the longball. The Padres released him during the winter.

	G	GS	IP	ERA	H	BB	SO	W	L	SV
1994	13	13	64.0	4.92	84	26	43	4	7	0
Career	161	64	479.2	3.98	514	128	312	19	36	3
Projected	19	18	96.0	4.24	109	32	56	5	8	0

Eddie Williams   No. 23/ 3B

Born: 11/1/64, Shreveport, LA
Height: 6' 0"   **Weight:** 175
Bats: Right   **Throws:** Right
1994 OBP: .392   **SLG:** .594

Williams has bounced around various minor league systems, but he put up major league numbers after being promoted from Las Vegas. In forty-five starts he batted .337 with forty-five RBIs. Williams will enter '95 as the Padres' number-one first baseman, and he could be the key to helping San Diego fans forget about Fred McGriff.

	G	AB	H	2B	3B	HR	RS	RBI	BB	SB	BA
1994	49	175	58	11	1	11	32	42	15	9	.331
Career	166	510	141	26	1	18	76	62	47	10	.276
Projected				No projection. Player was a rookie in 1994.							

San Francisco
GIANTS

1995 Scouting Report

Outfielders: The number-one offensive player in baseball and one of the greatest left fielders in history is Barry Bonds. In center field, Darren Lewis finally made an error last season after having played 392 consecutive flawless games. Darryl Strawberry made an immediate positive impact in the number-five hole behind Matt Williams and Bonds.

Infielders: Third base is the permanent residence of Matt Williams, who's making a strong bid as the new Mike Schmidt. Robby Thompson is the top second sacker in Giants history, but he had a miserable, injury-riddled '94 campaign. Royce Clayton contributes to the Giants' impressive team speed and defense. First base will be occupied by prospect J. R. Phillips.

Catchers: Kirt Manwaring was second on the team in doubles, but he hit just one homer in more than 300 at-bats. He regressed in the field from his Gold Glove '93 season.

Starting Pitchers: The Giants will miss Billy Swift if he doesn't re-sign. John Burkett came back to reality after a stellar twenty-two-win 1993 campaign. Mark Portugal was the team's winningest pitcher last season. William VanLandingham is a hot newcomer who led the Giants in winning percentage. Joe Rosselli was 7–2 with a 1.89 ERA at Triple-A Shreveport.

Relief Pitchers: Rod Beck is a stopper's stopper. Mike Jackson is a great backup closer and a top-notch setup man. Kevin Rogers and Dave Burba fill out one of baseball's best bullpens.

Manager: Ex-Dodgers All-Star Dusty Baker (158–119) followed his award-winning 1993 campaign with another competitive season.

1995 Outlook

The contemptuous rivalry between opposing fans in San Francisco and Los Angeles was enhanced last year by the July 7 arrival of ex-Dodger Darryl Strawberry, whose impact on the division race was immediate. The injury-hampered Giants had fallen behind in the NL West race, but by July 27, the Giants with Straw had cut nine games off their deficit to stand just a half game behind the Dodgers.

That scenario exemplifies the Giants' explosive capabilities. They're extremely well rounded—the National League's best defensive unit (.985 fielding percentage), speed on the basepaths (fourth in steals with 114), and two very big bats belonging to Matt Williams and a gentleman named Bonds. Manager Dusty Baker guides perhaps the league's most fundamentally sound lineup, and they never squander a lead late in the game (48–0 last season when leading after eight innings). The Giants have the talent to compete for a division title in the weak NL West.

But it might not be an easy road. The Giants have a couple of dead zones in their batting order, especially the first base slot, where Will Clark left behind some large shoes for J. R. Phillips to fill. Veteran second baseman Robby Thompson will be attempting to come back from an injury-marred season, Darryl Strawberry is one of baseball's least predictable individuals, and the starting pitching is suspect. If the Giants don't re-sign Billy Swift, they could be a middle-of-the-pack team.

The key to a winning season at Candlestick will be the production ability of the players batting around Bonds and Williams. San Francisco would be the weakest hitting team in the league without the dynamic duo. The Giants finished last in the NL in batting average, and they'll need to turn that around in 1995. But perhaps even more crucial will be the ability of the starting staff to keep the majority of games within striking distance of the team's offensive weapons. The Giants should be in the thick of the NL West title fight.

1995 San Francisco Giants Roster

Manager: Dusty Baker
Coaches: Bobby Bonds, Bob Brenly, Wendell Kim, Bob Lillis, Dick Pole, Denny Sommers

No.	Pitchers	B	T	HT	WT	DOB	Birthplace
47	Beck, Rod	R	R	6–1	236	8/3/68	Burbank, CA
—	Brink, Brad	R	R	6–2	200	1/20/65	Roseville, CA
34	Burba, Dave	R	R	6–4	240	7/7/66	Dayton, OH
33	Burkett, John	R	R	6–2	211	11/28/64	New Brighton, PA
57	Carlson, Dan	R	R	6–1	185	1/26/70	Portland, OR
—	Dewey, Mark	R	R	6–0	216	1/3/65	Grand Rapids, MI
46	Frey, Steve	L	L	5–9	170	7/29/63	Southhampton, PA
38	Gomez, Pat	L	L	5–11	185	3/17/68	Roseville, CA
—	Beckman, Andy	R	L	6–3	175	10/17/71	Flushing, NY
19	Portugal, Mark	R	R	6–0	190	10/30/62	Los Angeles, CA
28	Rogers, Kevin	B	L	6–1	198	8/20/68	Cleveland, MS
53	Rosselli, Joe	R	R	6–1	170	5/28/72	Burbank, CA
35	Torres, Salomon	R	R	5–11	165	3/11/72	San Pedro Macoris, DR
50	VanLandingham, Wm.	R	R	6–2	210	7/16/70	Columbia, TN
32	Wilson, Trevor	L	L	6–0	204	6/7/66	Torrance, CA
	Catchers						
54	Jensen, Marcus	B	R	6–4	195	12/14/72	Oakland, CA
8	Manwaring, Kurt	R	R	5–11	203	7/15/65	Scottsdale, AZ
52	Reed, Jeff	L	R	6–2	190	11/12/62	Elizabethton, TN
	Infielders						
18	Benjamin, Mike	R	R	6–0	169	11/22/65	Euclid, OH
10	Clayton, Royce	R	R	6–0	183	1/2/70	Burbank, CA
7	Patterson, John	B	R	5–9	168	2/11/67	Key West, FL
31	Phillips, J. R.	L	L	6–1	185	4/29/70	West Covina, CA
23	Scarsone, Steve	R	R	6–2	195	4/11/66	Anaheim, CA
6	Thompson, Robby	R	R	5–11	173	5/10/62	W. Palm Beach, FL
9	Williams, Matt	R	R	6–2	216	11/28/65	Bishop, CA
	Outfielders						
25	Bonds, Barry	L	L	6–1	185	7/24/64	Riverside, CA
45	Carreon, Mark	R	L	6–0	195	7/9/63	Chicago, IL
38	Faneyte, Rikkert	R	R	6–1	170	5/31/69	Amsterdam, Holland
56	Jones, Dax	R	R	5–9	180	8/4/70	Pittsburgh, PA
21	Leonard, Mark	L	R	6–1	195	8/14/64	Mountain View, CA
2	Lewis, Darren	R	R	6–0	189	8/28/67	Berkeley, CA
17	Strawberry, Darryl	L	L	6–6	215	3/12/62	Los Angeles, CA

1995 Schedule

April

S	M	T	W	T	F	S
					31 OAK	1 OAK
2 OAK	3	4 HOU	5 HOU	6 FLO	7 FLO	8 FLO
9 FLO	10	11 HOU	12 HOU	13 CIN	14 CIN	15 CIN
16 CIN	17	18 ATL	19 ATL	20 ATL	21 FLO	22 FLO
23 CIN	24 ATL	25 ATL	26 ATL	27 FLO	28 FLO	29 FLO
30 FLO						

May

S	M	T	W	T	F	S
	1 LA	2 LA	3 LA	4 SD	5 SD	6 SD
7 SD	8	9 COL	10 COL	11 COL	12 PIT	13 PIT
14 SD	15	16 CHI	17 CHI	18 CHI	19 STL	20 STL
21 PIT	22	23 CHI	24 PHI	25 PHI	26 NY	27 NY
28 NY	29 MON	30 MON	31 MON			

June

S	M	T	W	T	F	S
				1	2 PHI	3 PHI
4 PHI	5 NY	6 NY	7 NY	8 NY	9 MON	10 MON
11 MON	12	13 CHI	14 CHI	15 CHI	16 STL	17 STL
18 STL	19 PIT	20 PIT	21 PIT	22 LA	23 LA	24 LA
25 LA	26	27 COL	28 COL	29 SD	30 SD	

July

S	M	T	W	T	F	S
						1 SD
2 SD	3	4 CIN	5 CIN	6 CIN	7 ATL	8 ATL
9 ATL	10	11 ★	12	13 HOU	14 HOU	15 HOU
16 HOU	17 FLO	18 FLO	19	20 HOU	21 HOU	22 HOU
23 HOU	24 FLO	25 FLO	26 CIN	27 CIN	28 ATL	29 ATL
30 ATL	31					

August

S	M	T	W	T	F	S
		1 SD	2 SD	3 SD	4 LA	5 LA
6 LA	7	8 PIT	9 PIT	10 PIT	11 CHI	12 CHI
13 CHI	14 STL	15 STL	16 STL	17	18 PHI	19 PHI
20 PHI	21 NY	22 NY	23 NY	24 MON	25 MON	26 MON
27 MON	28	29 PHI	30 PHI	31 PHI		

Sept/Oct

S	M	T	W	T	F	S
					1 NY	2 NY
3 NY	4 MON	5 MON	6 MON	7	8 CHI	9 CHI
10 CHI	11 STL	12 STL	13 STL	14	15 PIT	16 PIT
17 PIT	18	19 LA	20 LA	21 COL	22 COL	23 COL
24 COL	25 SD	26 SD	27 SD	28 COL	29 COL	30 COL
1 COL	2					

☐ Home   ☐ Away   ★ All-Star Game

Candlestick Park

Capacity: 62,000

Turf: Grass

Dimensions:
LF Line: 335'
RF Line: 328'
Center: 400'
Alleys: 365'

Tickets:
(415) 467-8000

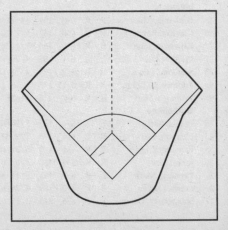

1994 Batting Order

1. Darren Lewis (Center Field)
2. Robby Thompson (Second Base)
3. Barry Bonds (Left Field)
4. Matt Williams (Third Base)
5. Darryl Strawberry (Right Field)
6. Todd Benzinger (First Base)
7. Royce Clayton (Shortstop)
8. Kirt Manwaring (Catcher)
9. Pitcher

1994 Team Record
55–60 (.478); Second in NL West

NL East	W	L	NL Central	W	L	NL West	W	L
Atlanta	1	5	Chicago	4	5	Colorado	7	3
Florida	4	2	Cincinnati	2	7	Los Angeles	5	5
Montreal	7	5	Houston	2	8	San Diego	2	5
New York	6	6	Pittsburgh	5	1	S. Francisco	—	—
Philadelphia	8	4	St. Louis	2	4			
Total	26	22		15	25		14	13

1994 National League Team Rank Batting

Batting Average: Fourteenth (.249)
Runs Scored: Tenth (504)
Runs Batted In: Tenth (472)
Stolen Bases: Fourth (114)
Slugging Percentage: Ninth (.402)
On-Base Percentage: Thirteenth (.318)

1994 National League Team Rank Pitching

Earned Run Average: Sixth (3.99)
Bases On Balls: Eighth (372)
Strikeouts: Tenth (655)
Wins: Sixth (55)
Saves: Third (33)
Complete Games: Fourteenth (2)

San Francisco Giants MVP

Barry Bonds No. 25/ OF

Born: 7/24/64, Riverside, CA
Height: 6'1"   **Weight:** 185
Bats: Left   **Throws:** Left
1994 OBP: .426   **SLG:** .647

Still the number-one all-around baseball player on the planet, Bonds was just hitting full stride when the season was cut short. Bonds is almost too great; anything less than a four-RBI day seems like a slump. Taking nothing from Matt Williams, the MVP voters can't possibly justify rating Bonds as the Giants' second-best player in 1994. He is one of only eight players in baseball history to win three MVP Awards. He's a Gold Glove left fielder, a fantastic basestealer, and a bona fide slugger. In short, he's Superman with batting gloves.

Bonds uses a relatively small bat and chokes up more than most sluggers, allowing him to rely on bat speed and timing to generate power, while still making plenty of contact. Bonds ranked in the top five in both slugging and on-base percentage. He fell one steal short of being the league's only 30/30 man.

His fielding is understandably overshadowed by his prolific offense, but Bonds tied for third among NL outfielders in assists with ten. He positions himself intelligently, has fine range, and gets rid of the ball quickly.

Bonds is quick to make adjustments on offense—if he's slumping in one area, he'll turn up the juice in another. And having his father as the team's hitting coach hasn't hurt. Bonds is one of the six greatest left fielders of all time.

	G	AB	H	2B	3B	HR	RS	RBI	BB	SB	BA
1994	112	391	122	18	1	37	89	81	74	29	.312
Career	1281	4514	1287	276	41	259	890	760	811	309	.285
Projected	160	553	184	34	3	50	131	122	120	35	.329

Rod Beck   No. 47/ P

Born: 8/3/68, Burbank, CA
Height: 6' 1"   **Weight:** 236
Bats: Right   **Throws:** Right
Opp. Batting Average: .261

Not as overpowering last year as he was in '93, Beck's foot was broken by a batted ball April 5. His rates of walks and strikeouts per inning both went the wrong direction in '94, and he allowed ten homers. But he still rang up an NL record twenty-eight consecutive saves. Beck's split-finger pitch is the definition of nasty, and he's as intense on the mound as any closer in baseball.

	G	GS	IP	ERA	H	BB	SO	W	L	SV
1994	48	0	48.2	2.77	49	13	39	2	4	28
Career	220	0	272.1	2.45	221	54	250	9	9	94
Projected	70	0	72.0	2.39	60	15	71	3	3	43

Todd Benzinger   No. 14/ 1B

Born: 2/11/63, Dayton, KY
Height: 6' 1"   **Weight:** 195
Bats: Both   **Throws:** Right
1994 OBP: .304   **SLG:** .399

Benzinger was an unsigned free agent as of this writing, and power-hitting newcomer J. R. Phillips has the starting job. Benzinger is a fine defensive first baseman; he made three errors in one game last season, but just two errors in his other ninety-three games, finishing the year with a .994 percentage (second in the league). Benzinger doesn't hit enough to play full-time.

	G	AB	H	2B	3B	HR	RS	RBI	BB	SB	BA
1994	107	328	87	13	2	9	32	31	17	2	.265
Career	558	1410	376	59	4	47	161	170	94	11	.267
Projected	160	423	118	17	3	13	48	48	25	2	.276

John Burkett No. 33/ P

Born: 7/7/66, Dayton, OH
Height: 6' 2"   **Weight:** 211
Bats: Right   **Throws:** Right
Opp. Batting Average: .286

Last season Burkett didn't get the run support the Giants provided for him in '93, when he won twenty-two games. Neither record is a clear reflection of his pitching skills. Burkett has pinpoint control; he was eighth in the NL in fewest walks per nine innings (2.0). But he also allowed the fourth most hits in the league. Burkett is a fine fielder, committing no errors in '94.

	G	GS	IP	ERA	H	BB	SO	W	L	SV
1994	25	25	159.1	3.62	176	36	85	6	8	0
Career	163	157	997.1	3.81	1025	245	591	67	42	1
Projected	34	34	223.0	3.64	228	43	131	16	9	0

Royce Clayton No. 10/ SS

Born: 1/2/70, Burbank, CA
Height: 6' 0"   **Weight:** 183
1994 OBP: .295   **SLG:** .327

Clayton has already played in 368 major league games at age twenty-five. He probably won't become a star, but his defense was vastly improved from the previous season, and he ranked sixth in the NL in steals and triples. Clayton is helpless against southpaws, batting just .176 versus lefties. He could steal sixty bases if he were to draw more walks.

	G	AB	H	2B	3B	HR	RS	RBI	BB	SB	BA
1994	108	385	91	14	6	3	38	30	30	23	.236
Career	368	1281	321	43	15	13	123	126	95	42	.251
Projected	156	588	171	23	7	6	61	66	45	22	.277

Mike Jackson   No. 42/ P

Born: 11/22/64, Houston, TX
Height: 6' 2"   **Weight:** 223
Bats: Right   **Throws:** Right
Opp. Batting Average: .164

Despite tendinitis in his right elbow, big Mike Jackson pitched the best ball of his career in '94. Jackson throws hard, but he complements his heat with a slider that's cruel to righties, who hit just .137 against him. Jackson is a workhorse, he keeps his walks totals down and his strikeouts up, and he fills in perfectly as a closer when Rod Beck isn't available.

	G	GS	IP	ERA	H	BB	SO	W	L	SV
1994	36	0	42.1	1.49	23	11	51	3	2	4
Career	510	7	689.0	3.37	540	303	610	40	49	36
Projected	64	0	66.0	2.49	45	19	67	5	4	3

Darren Lewis   No. 2/ OF

Born: 8/28/67, Berkeley, CA
Height: 6' 0"   **Weight:** 189
Bats: Right   **Throws:** Right
1994 OBP: .340   **SLG:** .357

Speed and defense are what Lewis brings to the Giants' lineup. He made the first error in center field of his career last season, and he led the team with thirty steals, though with only 69.7% success. Lewis also improved his on-base percentage by thirty-eight points from '93, a crucial improvement for a leadoff hitter, though he's still well below average in that capacity.

	G	AB	H	2B	3B	HR	RS	RBI	BB	SB	BA
1994	114	451	116	15	9	4	70	29	53	30	.257
Career	447	1550	385	45	20	8	237	111	155	119	.248
Projected	148	599	165	20	10	4	99	49	53	49	.265

Kirt Manwaring   No. 8/ C

Born: 7/15/65, Elmira, NY
Height: 5' 11"   **Weight:** 203
Bats: Right   **Throws:** Right
1994 OBP: .308   **SLG:** .320

An alarming decline in Manwaring's fielding performance is cause for concern. He won a Gold Glove in '93, but threw out just four of his last thirty would-be thieves last year, while ranking eighth among NL catchers in fielding percentage (.993). He continues to be a marginal hitter, going deep only once in '94, primarily earning his salary behind the plate.

	G	AB	H	2B	3B	HR	RS	RBI	BB	SB	BA
1994	97	316	79	17	1	1	30	29	25	1	.250
Career	542	1611	397	62	10	11	144	157	117	7	.246
Projected	140	465	125	20	1	4	49	49	41	1	.267

Mark Portugal   No. 19/ P

Born: 10/30/62, Los Angeles, CA
Height: 6' 0"   **Weight:** 190
Bats: Right   **Throws:** Right
Opp. Batting Average: .260

Though he isn't a star, Portugal is something better—a consistent winner (.620 winning percentage over the last six seasons). His fourteen-game winning streak over two seasons ended April 24 versus New York. Portugal is the majors' most dangerous hitting pitcher, slugging .500 in twenty-one games. He's got a vast repertoire, including a masterful change-up.

	G	GS	IP	ERA	H	BB	SO	W	L	SV
1994	21	21	137.1	3.93	135	45	87	10	8	0
Career	228	170	1158.1	3.78	1100	431	760	73	57	5
Projected	30	30	195.0	3.24	186	69	123	16	7	0

Darryl Strawberry   No. 17/OF

Born: 3/12/62, Los Angeles, CA
Height: 6' 6"   **Weight:** 215
Bats: Left   **Throws:** Left
1994 OBP: .363   **SLG:** .424

Questions will always swirl around Strawberry regarding his off-field troubles, yet he entered 1994 as the NL's home run leader (264) over the past ten years. He rejuvenated the Giants' offense, igniting a nine-game winning streak upon his arrival, but he finished the year in a skid. It's impossible to predict what he'll do at any given moment, much less over an entire season.

	G	AB	H	2B	3B	HR	RS	RBI	BB	SB	BA
1994	29	92	22	3	1	4	13	17	19	0	.239
Career	1352	4756	1232	222	35	294	793	886	709	205	.259
Projected			No projection. Player was injured in 1993.								

Bill Swift   No. 26/ P

Born: 10/27/61, South Portland, ME
Height: 6' 0"   **Weight:** 191
Bats: Right   **Throws:** Right
Opp. Batting Average: .262

With an ERA of 2.56 over his last 725 innings, Swift is as close to a sure thing as any NL starter. His '94 ERA was 2.89 going into his season-ending start, but he got rocked for seven earned runs in 3.1 innings, inflating his final tally. Swift's sinker creates groundballs by the dozen, and he's untouchable at Candlestick, generating a 1.98 ERA in nine starts at home.

	G	GS	IP	ERA	H	BB	SO	W	L	SV
1994	17	17	109.1	3.38	109	31	62	8	7	0
Career	334	159	1265.2	3.51	1275	382	588	69	59	25
Projected	28	28	190.0	3.00	169	48	122	16	8	0

Robby Thompson   No. 6/2B

Born: 5/10/62, West Palm Beach, FL
Height: 5' 11"   **Weight:** 173
Bats: Right   **Throws:** Right
1994 OBP: .290   **SLG:** .349

An inspiring player and the greatest second baseman in Giants history, Thompson is essential to his team's chances for success in 1995. Last season was lost to surgery on Thompson's rotator cuff. When healthy, he turns the DP as well as anyone, hits for surprising power in the clutch, and is the acknowledged on-field team leader.

	G	AB	H	2B	3B	HR	RS	RBI	BB	SB	BA
1994	35	129	27	8	2	2	13	7	15	3	.209
Career	1146	4049	1072	212	38	106	268	414	373	100	.265
Projected	54	208	62	13	1	7	33	24	20	4	.293

Wm. VanLandingham No.50/P

Born: 7/16/70, Columbia, TN
Height: 6' 2"   **Weight:** 210
Bats: Right   **Throws:** Right
Opp. Batting Average: .223

Owner of the longest full name in major league history, William VanLandingham is the Giants organization's brightest pitching prospect. He began his big league career 3–0 and won five of his last six decisions. He yielded two runs or less in ten of his fourteen starts. VanLandingham didn't always control the strikezone last year; he walked six July 31 versus Colorado .

	G	GS	IP	ERA	H	BB	SO	W	L	SV
1994	14	12	84.0	3.54	70	41	54	8	2	0
Career	14	12	84.0	3.54	70	41	54	8	2	0
Projected				No projection. Player was a rookie in 1994.						

Matt Williams   No. 9/ 3B

Born: 11/28/65, Bishop, CA
Height: 6' 2"   **Weight:** 216
Bats: Right   **Throws:** Right
1994 OBP: .319   **SLG:** .607

Wow. Williams came into the majors as a shortstop—if he'd stayed at that position, we might already be speculating about Cooperstown. Williams is a Gold Glover, led the majors in homers, and finished second in NL MVP voting. Williams was on the most prolific home run binge in NL history until the strike; his forty homers through July 31 set a league record.

	G	AB	H	2B	3B	HR	RS	RBI	BB	SB	BA
1994	112	445	119	16	3	43	74	96	33	1	.267
Career	939	3452	875	146	23	202	472	582	149	26	.253
Projected	152	632	193	31	4	52	115	132	39	1	.294

Trevor Wilson   No. 32/ P

Born: 6/7/66, Torrance, CA
Height: 6' 0"   **Weight:** 204
Bats: Left   **Throws:** Left
Opp. Batting Average: —

Wilson missed the entire '94 campaign, but he could be ready to go by spring. His health is especially important, as the team lacks a reliable lefty starter. Opposing managers usually rest their lefthanded batters when Wilson is scheduled to throw; he doesn't pose much of a mystery to righties, though. This will be a pivotal season for the injury-prone Wilson.

	G	GS	IP	ERA	H	BB	SO	W	L	SV
1994	0	0	0	0.00	0	0	0	0	0	0
Career	137	98	637.2	3.87	575	262	387	38	42	0
Projected					No projection. Player was injured in 1994.					

American League

1994 Recap

AL East

The Yankees gradually pulled away from Baltimore, leading by 4.5 games through June 30 and eight full games at the end of July. Led by ace Jimmy Key, who was almost unbeatable, and the most potent offense in the league, New York finished the year as the only AL club to win seventy games in 1994.

The Orioles hung tough through the summer and were gaining ground on New York when the season was called off. Baltimore free agents Rafael Palmeiro and Lee Smith joined Cal Ripken, Jr. to challenge the Bronx Bombers.

The East became a two-dog fight as the Blue Jays, 1993 World Series champs, fell apart in May. Toronto received a jolt when bullpen closer Duane Ward was lost for the season to shoulder surgery. The starting rotation was ineffective, and the offense wasn't able to carry the team.

The Red Sox were in a downward spiral from June till the season's premature end. A lack of men on base was the primary culprit, though an absence of depth in the starting rotation didn't make matters easier for Boston.

Detroit was out of contention by the end of April, but the Tigers scored enough runs to finish the season within striking distance of third-place Toronto.

AL Central

The league's most competitive division provided thrills and spills galore. Frank Thomas and the cream of American League starting rotations helped Chicago cling to first place through July and August.

The Indians would have qualified as the AL wild card team had the playoffs been held. Cleveland inaugurated Jacobs Field by leading the league in homers, while Tribe pitching yielded the majors' fewest longballs.

Kansas City weathered another subpar April. A fourteen-game winning streak after the All-Star break put them in contention for first place. If the 1994 campaign had been played to fruition, the Royals would have challenged for the division title.

The Twins organization is committed to cutting the team's payroll, and the dearth of frontline talent reflects that goal. Minnesota did succeed in staying out of last place, and excellent production from Chuck Knoblauch and Kirby Puckett gave fans at the Hubiedome something to cheer about.

Milwaukee was hit by costly injuries. The Brew Crew dropped from a first-place tie in late April to sole possession of the cellar in mid-May.

AL West
The West is easily the least potent division in baseball. Western Division winner Texas finished the season ten games below .500, just 5.5 games ahead of cellar dwelling California.

Oakland was twelve games out on June 8 and going south in a hurry, but the A's applied the brakes to their downward slide. When the season was cancelled, Oakland was ready to take over the top spot in the division.

Seattle won nine of their final ten games to join Oakland in the chase for the division penthouse. The Mariners were tough on their division foes, compiling a 19–7 record against the West.

California placed all hope in their lefty-dominated pitching corps, but Langston and Finley both struggled in 1994. The Angels' offense wasn't able to pick up the slack, and the team finished the season headed in the wrong direction.

American League Standings

AL CENTRAL	W	L	PCT	GB	HOME	ROAD	vs. EAST	vs. CENT.	vs. WEST
Chicago	67	46	.593	—	34–19	33–27	22–13	21–19	24–14
Cleveland	66	47	.584	1.0	35–16	31–31	27–22	20–16	19–9
Kansas City	64	51	.557	4.0	35–24	29–27	21–20	22–15	21–16
Minnesota	53	60	.469	14.0	32–27	21–33	24–21	17–23	12–16
Milwaukee	53	62	.461	15.0	24–32	29–30	21–28	18–25	14–9

AL EAST	W	L	PCT	GB	HOME	ROAD	vs. EAST	vs. CENT.	vs. WEST
New York	70	43	.619	—	33–24	37–19	19–14	25–14	26–15
Baltimore	63	49	.563	6.5	28–27	35–22	18–14	21–19	24–16
Toronto	55	60	.478	16.0	33–26	22–34	13–22	24–25	18–13
Boston	54	61	.470	17.0	31–33	23–28	16–16	15–26	23–19
Detroit	53	62	.461	18.0	34–24	19–38	14–14	19–31	20–17

AL WEST	W	L	PCT	GB	HOME	ROAD	vs. EAST	vs. CENT.	vs. WEST
Texas	52	62	.456	—	31–32	21–30	21–20	23–20	8–22
Oakland	51	63	.447	1.0	24–32	27–31	22–29	12–25	17–9
Seattle	49	63	.438	2.0	22–22	27–41	18–31	12–25	19–7
California	47	68	.409	5.5	23–40	24–28	19–31	17–20	11–17

1995 Preview

AL East	AL Central	AL West
1. New York	1. Kansas City	1. Oakland
2. Baltimore	2. Chicago	2. Seattle
3. Toronto	3. Cleveland	3. Texas
4. Boston	4. Milwaukee	4. California
5. Detroit	5. Minnesota	

Playoffs: New York over Chicago; Kansas City over Oakland
Pennant Winner: New York
World Series Winner: New York over Houston

New York has the most talented, experienced ballclub in the AL East. The Yankees' veterans know the time is now; Boggs, Mattingly, Key, and company will be focused on a championship. The Orioles will keep things compelling until August. The Blue Jays will make some deals to slow their decline; a frontline starter could keep Toronto closer to the top than to the bottom. Boston doesn't have enough firepower, while Detroit needs to trade some of their aging boppers for a quality arm.

Kansas City has strong pitching and defense to go with an improved offense. They'll be the surprise winners of the three-team battle for the AL Central crown. Chicago and Cleveland will go down swinging into the last week of the season, with the White Sox gaining a wild card berth on the strength of their starting corps. The lower two-fifths of the Central are the division's dark underbelly. The Twins and Brewers are rebuilding.

The AL West is infamously mediocre, but there's no denying the division's parity. Oakland will benefit from the return of Mark McGwire, Steve Karsay, and Brent Gates. Tony La Russa will figure out a way to pull a title out of his hat. Seattle can ride Ken Griffey, Jr.'s bat to second place. The Rangers won't be able to generate as many runs as their starting pitchers will relinquish. California isn't a very good team, but they are in the right division. Honestly, any one of these four clubs could finish in first, last, or in between.

Baltimore
ORIOLES

1995 Scouting Report

Outfielders: Brady Anderson had another great year in left and center fields and the leadoff slot. Jeffrey Hammonds should continue to make progress as a hitter. Dwight Smith hit well in his American League debut.

Infielders: The O's infield is explosive. Future Hall of Famer Cal Ripken, Jr. plays every inning at shortstop, and 1994 was his best campaign since 1991. The Orioles inked Rafael Palmeiro to a big contract, and the All-Star first baseman proved that he was worth every penny. Chris Sabo was signed to play third base, but Leo Gomez took over the job. Mark McLemore is a solid young second baseman.

Catchers: Chris Hoiles is an extremely dangerous hitter and an underrated backstop. Lefty Matt Nokes will platoon.

Starting Pitchers: The Orioles utilized a four-man rotation in '94, headed by ace Mike Mussina. Big Ben McDonald also has ace-quality stuff, though he hasn't had a breakthrough season yet. Sid Fernandez came over from the NL and had a rocky season, but he, too, has excellent stuff. Jamie Moyer followed his surprising '93 success with a serviceable performance last year.

Relief Pitchers: Lee Smith, baseball's all-time saves leader, continues to add to his record. Mark Eichhorn pitched brilliantly in a setup role.

Designated Hitters: Harold Baines still has a sweet lefthanded stroke. He's one of the game's greatest pure hitters.

Manager: Phil Regan was hired to replace Johnny Oates and take the Orioles to the next level.

1995 Outlook

The Orioles invested heavily in the 1994 season, spicing their lineup with free agents Chris Sabo and Sid Fernandez, both National League fixtures. The O's also signed Rafael Palmeiro, who paid big dividends, while Fernandez and Sabo provided mixed returns. The Orioles' hope is that Fernandez just needed a season of adjustment to the American League, while Sabo can contribute at the plate and in the clubhouse if he's healthy.

Pitching is the key for Baltimore, and they have a great one-two punch in aces Mike Mussina and Ben McDonald. Mussina was a Cy Young contender in 1994, and he hasn't peaked yet. McDonald has progressed slowly, but scouts say he's nearing top form and could be ready to win twenty games in '95. Unfortunately for Baltimore, someone else in the rotation will need to step up if the team is going to mount a serious challenge to the AL East favorite Yankees. Pitching is the area in which the Orioles can make up the difference between themselves and the Bronx Bombers.

Offensively, the Orioles bear some resemblance to the great Earl Weaver teams that featured plenty of bases on balls and three-run homers. The 1994 Orioles ranked fourth in the AL in both walks and home runs. The heart of the order is strong and experienced, with Ripken and Palmeiro hitting for power and average. The wild card in the lineup is catcher Chris Hoiles, whose offense slipped a bit in '94, but who's a good bet for a return to his status as the AL's most dominant slugging backstop. If Harold Baines doesn't re-sign, Baltimore will need to replace his potent lefty bat.

The American League East is a strong division, with the Yankees setting the pace, while Toronto and Boston pursue the Orioles from behind. Wins won't come easily in the long haul, and pitching figures to seperate the true contenders from the middle of the pack. Baltimore will once again look to "El Sid" Fernandez to stabilize the starting rotation, with Mussina and McDonald leading the way.

1995 Baltimore Orioles Roster

Manager: Phil Regan
Coaches: Steve Boros, Al Bumbry, Chuck Cottier, Mike Flanagan,
Elrod Hendricks, Lee May

No.	Pitchers	B	T	HT	WT	DOB	Birthplace
—	Benitez, Armando	R	R	6–4	180	11/3/72	Santo Domingo, DR
38	Eichhorn, Mark	R	R	6–3	210	11/21/60	San Jose, CA
50	Fernandez, Sid	L	L	6–1	225	10/12/62	Honolulu, HI
49	Frohwirth, Todd	R	R	6–4	211	9/28/62	Milwaukee, WI
—	Haynes, Jimmy	R	R	6–4	175	9/5/72	LaGrange, GA
19	McDonald, Ben	R	R	6–7	213	11/24/67	Baton Rouge, LA
75	Mills, Alan	B	R	6–1	192	10/18/66	Lakeland, FL
51	Moyer, Jamie	L	L	6–0	170	11/16/62	Sellersville, PA
35	Mussina, Mike	R	R	6–2	185	12/8/68	Williamsport, PA
46	O'Donoghue, John	L	L	6–6	198	5/26/69	Elkton, MD
56	Oquist, Mike	R	R	6–2	170	5/30/68	La Junta, CO
47	Pennington, Brad	L	L	6–5	205	4/14/69	Salem, IN
45	Poole, Jim	L	L	6–2	203	4/28/66	Rochester, NY
53	Rhodes, Arthur	L	L	6–2	206	10/24/69	Waco, TX
—	Sackinsky, Brian	R	R	6–4	220	6/22/71	Library, PA
	Catchers						
23	Hoiles, Chris	R	R	6–0	213	3/20/65	Bowling Green, OH
—	Nokes, Matt	L	R	6–1	210	10/31/63	San Diego, CA
41	Tackett, Jeff	R	R	6–2	205	12/1/65	Fresno, CA
—	Zaun, Greg	B	R	5–10	170	4/14/71	Glendale, CA
	Infielders						
48	Alexander, Manny	R	R	5–10	165	3/20/71	San Pedro Macoris, DR
—	Carey, Paul	R	L	6–4	215	1/8/68	Weymouth, MA
10	Gomez, Leo	R	R	6–0	208	3/2/67	Canovanas, PR
25	Palmeiro, Rafael	L	L	6–0	188	9/24/64	Havana, Cuba
8	Ripken Jr., Cal	R	R	6–4	220	8/24/60	Havre de Grace, MD
	Outfielders						
9	Anderson, Brady	L	L	6–1	190	1/18/64	Silver Spring, MD
18	Buford, Damon	R	R	5–10	170	6/12/70	Sherman Oaks, CA
11	Hammonds, Jeffrey	R	R	6–0	195	3/5/71	Plainfield, NJ
—	Ochoa, Alex	R	R	6–0	173	3/29/72	Miami Lakes, FL
30	Smith, Dwight	L	R	5–11	195	11/8/63	Tallahassee, FL
—	Smith, Mark	R	R	6–4	195	4/9/66	Houston, TX
28	Voigt, Jack	R	R	6–1	175	5/17/66	Sarasota, FL

1995 Schedule

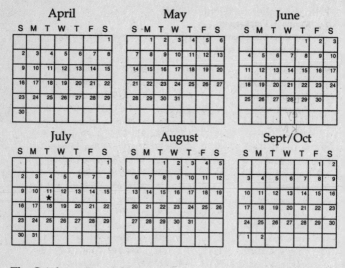

April

S	M	T	W	T	F	S
						1
2	3	4	5	6	7	8
9	10	11	12	13	14	15
16	17	18	19	20	21	22
23	24	25	26	27	28	29
30						

May

S	M	T	W	T	F	S
	1	2	3	4	5	6
7	8	9	10	11	12	13
14	15	16	17	18	19	20
21	22	23	24	25	26	27
28	29	30	31			

June

S	M	T	W	T	F	S
				1	2	3
4	5	6	7	8	9	10
11	12	13	14	15	16	17
18	19	20	21	22	23	24
25	26	27	28	29	30	

July

S	M	T	W	T	F	S
						1
2	3	4	5	6	7	8
9	10	11★	12	13	14	15
16	17	18	19	20	21	22
23	24	25	26	27	28	29
30	31					

August

S	M	T	W	T	F	S
		1	2	3	4	5
6	7	8	9	10	11	12
13	14	15	16	17	18	19
20	21	22	23	24	25	26
27	28	29	30	31		

Sept/Oct

S	M	T	W	T	F	S
					1	2
3	4	5	6	7	8	9
10	11	12	13	14	15	16
17	18	19	20	21	22	23
24	25	26	27	28	29	30
1	2					

The Orioles were unable to provide a schedule by press time.

Oriole Park at Camden Yards

Capacity: 48,079

Turf: Grass

Dimensions:
LF Line: 333'
RF Line: 318'
Center: 400'
Left CF: 410'
Right CF: 373'

Tickets:
(410) 685-9800

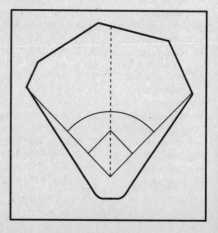

1994 Batting Order

1. Brady Anderson (Center Field)
2. Chris Sabo (Third Base)
3. Rafael Palmeiro (First Base)
4. Cal Ripken (Shortstop)
5. Harold Baines (Designated Hitter)
6. Dwight Smith (Left Field)
7. Chris Hoiles (Catcher)
8. Jeffrey Hammonds (Right Field)
9. Mark McLemore (Second Base)

1994 Team Record
63–49 (.563); Second in AL East

AL East	W	L	AL Central	W	L	AL West	W	L
Baltimore	—	—	Chicago	2	4	California	8	4
Boston	4	2	Cleveland	4	6	Oakland	7	5
Detroit	3	4	Kansas City	4	1	Seattle	6	4
New York	4	6	Milwaukee	7	3	Texas	3	3
Toronto	7	2	Minnesota	4	5			
Total	18	14		21	19		24	16

1994 American League Team Rank Batting

Batting Average: Sixth (.272)
Runs Scored: Seventh (589)
Runs Batted In: Sixth (557)
Stolen Bases: Ninth (69)
Slugging Percentage: Sixth (.438)
On-Base Percentage: Sixth (.349)

1994 American League Team Rank Pitching

Earned Run Average: Third (4.31)
Bases On Balls: First (351)
Strikeouts: Ninth (666)
Wins: Fifth (63)
Saves: Second (37)
Complete Games: Third (13)

Baltimore Orioles MVP

Mike Mussina   No. 35/ P

Born: 12/8/68, Williamsport, PA
Height: 6' 2"   **Weight:** 185
Bats: Right   **Throws:** Right
Opp. Batting Average: .248

Mussina is on the verge of becoming a household name. Coaches and scouts regularly mention him in the same breath with Roger Clemens, and last year Mussina took a giant stride toward justifying that praise with great numbers.

The missing ingredient in Mussina's recipe for stardom has been uncertainty about the health of his pitching arm. Last season he answered those questions by being the Orioles' workhorse. Mussina was the only AL starter to finish in the top five in innings pitched without making twenty-five starts. He averaged more than seven innings per start.

Mussina has one of the game's deepest repertoires. He has the confidence to throw his curve, slider, change-up, and fastball at any point in the count and to any hitter in the American League. He has pinpoint command; Mussina ranked sixth in the league in fewest walks per nine innings (2.1).

Mussina was arguably the league's second-best starter in 1994. He finished in the AL top ten among starters in earned run average (fourth, behind David Cone) and winning percentage (fourth, ahead of Cone). Mussina is the kind of pitcher who pitches a shutout in a championship situation. He's extremely intelligent and poised. Mussina seems almost certain to win a Cy Young Award in the near future.

	G	GS	IP	ERA	H	BB	SO	W	L	SV
1994	24	24	176.1	3.06	163	42	99	16	5	0
Career	93	93	672.2	3.20	615	155	398	52	21	0
Projected	28	28	200.0	2.95	190	50	126	17	6	0

Brady Anderson No. 9/ OF

Born: 1/8/64, Silver Spring, MD
Height: 6' 1" **Weight:** 190
Bats: Left **Throws:** Left
1994 OBP: .356 **SLG:** .419

It seems like not so long ago Anderson was a touted prospect struggling to fulfill his potential. Anderson isn't a kid anymore, and he has indeed become a very valuable contributor to the Orioles' offense. Anderson knows his job as a leadoff man; he was second on the club in walks and runs scored. He's an amazing percentage basestealer (96.9% success in '94).

	G	AB	H	2B	3B	HR	RS	RBI	BB	SB	BA
1994	111	453	119	25	5	12	78	48	57	31	.263
Career	802	2717	672	131	34	56	404	282	372	161	.247
Projected	151	611	164	37	8	15	100	69	85	33	.265

Harold Baines No. 3/ DH

Born: 3/15/59, Easton, MD
Height: 6' 2" **Weight:** 195
Bats: Left **Throws:** Left
1994 OBP: .356 **SLG:** .485

Baines entered the league with Chicago in 1980 as one of the game's most graceful athletes. Numerous knee surgeries have reduced him to DH status, but his swing is still a thing of beauty. Baines is an extreme pull hitter when he hits the ball on the ground, and his bat speed is as quick as it has ever been. Baines is a free agent as of this writing.

	G	AB	H	2B	3B	HR	RS	RBI	BB	SB	BA
1994	94	326	96	12	1	16	44	54	30	0	.294
Career	2056	7486	2156	368	47	277	973	1198	734	30	.288
Projected	131	450	132	20	1	21	64	79	52	0	.298

Mike Devereaux   No.12/ OF

Born: 4/10/63, Casper, WY
Height: 6' 0"   **Weight:** 195
Bats: Right   **Throws:** Right
1994 OBP: .256   **SLG:** .332

In 1992 Devereaux made a bid for MVP recognition, but since then his career has taken a trip south. He still possesses a unique knack for making spectacular catches in the outfield, but at the plate he often seems to be guessing. Devereaux collects his share of homers, but his impatience at the plate caused a 3/1 strikeout-to-walks ratio in '94.

	G	AB	H	2B	3B	HR	RS	RBI	BB	SB	BA
1994	84	301	61	8	2	9	35	33	22	1	.203
Career	799	2944	740	131	30	86	379	375	225	68	.251
Projected	130	506	120	24	3	14	66	67	40	2	.235

Sid Fernandez   No. 50/ P

Born: 10/12/62, Honolulu, HI
Height: 6' 1"   **Weight:** 225
Bats: Left   **Throws:** Left
Opp. Batting Average: .248

Fernandez is one of the baseball's most entertaining hurlers. He throws a rising fast-ball that induces opposing batters to climb the ladder. Consequently, Fernandez racks up high strikeout totals when his stuff is working well. His weight has been an annual cause for concern. Fernandez is a flyball pitcher; he served up twenty-seven gopher balls in '94.

	G	GS	IP	ERA	H	BB	SO	W	L	SV
1994	19	19	115.1	5.15	109	46	95	6	6	0
Career	276	270	1706.0	3.29	1283	649	1553	104	85	1
Projected	22	22	138.0	4.02	112	48	103	6	7	0

Leo Gomez   No. 10/ 3B

Born: 3/2/67, Canovanas, PR
Height: 6' 0"   **Weight:** 208
Bats: Right   **Throws:** Right
1994 OBP: .366   **SLG:** .502

The Orioles signed Chris Sabo last year because Gomez had failed to establish himself in '93. But when Sabo couldn't stay healthy, Gomez took over third base with authority. Gomez provides the longball threat that the O's desperately need to compete in the slugging AL East. He slumped toward year's end, and the Orioles are hoping that Gomez can be consistent.

	G	AB	H	2B	3B	HR	RS	RBI	BB	SB	BA
1994	84	285	78	20	0	15	46	56	41	0	.274
Career	422	1427	350	68	2	58	181	191	184	3	.245
Projected	129	459	118	24	0	23	69	73	66	0	.248

Jeffrey Hammonds   No. 11/ OF

Born: 3/5/71, Plainfield, NJ
Height: 6' 0"   **Weight:** 195
Bats: Right   **Throws:** Right
1994 OBP: .339   **SLG:** .480

Hammonds is a bright prospect who has hit well in the majors so far. His only flaw at the plate is a lack of patience, but he makes enough contact to eventually hit .300, and he's shown glimpses of decent power. Hammonds is very fast; he hasn't been caught stealing in two seasons, but he's only made nine attempts. He has the ability to steal thirty-plus bases.

	G	AB	H	2B	3B	HR	RS	RBI	BB	SB	BA
1994	68	250	74	18	2	8	45	31	17	5	.296
Career	101	355	106	26	2	11	55	50	19	9	.299
Projected	105	386	127	30	2	13	63	57	22	10	.314

Chris Hoiles   No. 23/ C

Born: 3/20/65, Bowling Green, OH
Height: 6' 0"   **Weight:** 213
Bats: Right   **Throws:** Right
1994 OBP: .371   **SLG:** .449

Hoiles slugged more home runs last season than any other AL catcher, yet he had a disappointing season at the plate in comparison to 1993, dropping sixty-three points in batting average. Hoiles is a flyball hitter in a great home run park, and he led the team in walks last year. If he avoids nagging injuries, expect a big year from Hoiles in 1995.

	G	AB	H	2B	3B	HR	RS	RBI	BB	SB	BA
1994	99	332	82	10	0	19	45	53	63	2	.247
Career	457	1474	393	67	1	80	217	213	222	3	.267
Projected	139	469	135	24	0	30	79	85	83	2	.285

Ben McDonald   No. 19/ P

Born: 11/24/67, Baton Rouge, LA
Height: 6' 7"   **Weight:** 213
Bats: Right   **Throws:** Right
Opp. Batting Average: .255

McDonald is entering his prime, and '95 could be a breakthrough season for the towering righthander from the Bayou. McDonald throws a hard, heavy fastball that induces grounders in droves. He's tough to hit, but his control was spotty in '94; his (H+BB)/IP ratio was over 1.3, which is higher than what's expected from a pitcher of McDonald's caliber.

	G	GS	IP	ERA	H	BB	SO	W	L	SV
1994	24	24	157.1	4.06	151	54	94	14	7	0
Career	141	129	857.0	3.86	771	296	576	55	47	0
Projected	33	33	214.0	3.67	191	80	151	15	12	0

Mark McLemore No. 2/ 2B

Born: 10/4/64, San Diego, CA
Height: 5' 11"   **Weight:** 207
Bats: Both   **Throws:** Right
1994 OBP: .354   **SLG:** .321

McLemore has been shifted from second base to the outfield, then back again. His fielding instincts are excellent, and he's sure-handed in the infield. McLemore has shown a good batting eye, drawing more than fifty walks in each of the past two seasons. He doesn't hit lefties at all, compiling a .167 BA when batting from the right side of the plate.

	G	AB	H	2B	3B	HR	RS	RBI	BB	SB	BA
1994	104	353	88	11	1	3	44	29	51	20	.257
Career	654	2046	510	75	14	12	288	203	227	97	.249
Projected	154	570	159	24	4	4	78	63	72	26	.277

Jamie Moyer   No. 51/ P

Born: 11/16/62, Sellersville, PA
Height: 6' 6"   **Weight:** 170
Bats: Left   **Throws:** Left
Opp. Batting Average: .271

The veteran ex-National Leaguer worked the entire '94 campaign in the Orioles' regular rotation. After starting out slowly (5.56 ERA through June 28) Moyer threw reasonably well into the second half of the season. Moyer's stuff is anything but overpowering—he needs to hit the right spots and mix his pitches in order to survive. If he's on, Moyer is an acceptable fourth starter.

	G	GS	IP	ERA	H	BB	SO	W	L	SV
1994	23	23	149.0	4.77	158	38	87	5	7	0
Career	189	159	1001.0	4.42	1078	358	612	51	70	0
Projected	28	28	175.0	4.09	181	44	103	10	9	0

Rafael Palmeiro   No. 25/ 1B

Born: 9/24/64, Havana, Cuba
Height: 6' 0"   **Weight:** 188
Bats: Left   **Throws:** Right
1994 OBP: .392   **SLG:** .550

Palmeiro is the Orioles' best hitter, and one of baseball's purest offensive threats. His timeless lefty stroke produced top ten totals in batting average (ninth), homers (tied for tenth), runs scored (ninth), and slugging (ninth). His twenty-four-game hitting streak was the longest in the majors last season. Palmeiro has also become a reliable fielder at first base.

	G	AB	H	2B	3B	HR	RS	RBI	BB	SB	BA
1994	111	436	139	32	0	23	82	76	54	7	.319
Career	1157	4303	1283	266	25	155	669	602	432	57	.298
Projected	160	616	192	43	1	36	124	109	76	17	.308

Cal Ripken, Jr.   No. 8/ SS

Born: 8/24/60, Havre de Grace, MD
Height: 6' 4"   **Weight:** 220
Bats: Right   **Throws:** Right
1994 OBP: .364   **SLG:** .459

A legendary iron man, Ripken is the most consistent slugging shortstop in the league. If there's a full season in '95, he should surpass Lou Gehrig's total of 2,130 consecutive games played. Ripken has gone from being an inept fielder to becoming one of the AL's steadiest with the glove. Subjectively, we think he'll have a better year than our statistical projections suggest.

	G	AB	H	2B	3B	HR	RS	RBI	BB	SB	BA
1994	112	444	140	19	3	13	71	75	32	1	.315
Career	2074	8027	2227	414	40	310	1201	1179	849	34	.277
Projected	162	625	169	25	3	21	89	93	55	1	.275

Chris Sabo   No. 17/ 3B

Born: 1/19/62, Detroit, MI
Height: 5' 11"   **Weight:** 185
Bats: Right   **Throws:** Right
1994 OBP: .320   **SLG:** .465

The Orioles signed Sabo as a free agent in hopes that he would add juice to their batting order, but he was bothered by back troubles and never got into a groove. Sabo plays as aggressively as anyone in the game, and he's productive when healthy. His body may not hold up to a full season of kamikaze baseball, but Sabo's bat could come back strong in 1995.

	G	AB	H	2B	3B	HR	RS	RBI	BB	SB	BA
1994	68	258	66	15	3	11	41	42	20	1	.256
Career	832	3145	846	201	16	112	469	399	252	115	.269
Projected	126	464	115	27	3	18	71	70	35	4	.253

Lee Smith   No. 47/ P

Born: 12/4/57, Shreveport, LA
Height: 6' 6"   **Weight:** 225
Bats: Right   **Throws:** Right
Opp. Batting Average: .239

Make no mistake, he isn't as overpowering as he once was, but that's like saying a tsunami has become just a tidal wave. Smith has the craftiness and repertoire of a seasoned veteran, to go with his ninety-plus heater. He led the majors in saves in '94, but his ERA rose from 1.61 on June 28 to his season-ending +3.00 mark.

	G	GS	IP	ERA	H	BB	SO	W	L	SV
1994	41	0	38.1	3.29	34	11	42	1	4	33
Career	891	6	1163.2	2.92	1006	427	1152	68	82	434
Projected	59	0	54.0	3.66	49	14	58	2	5	45

Boston
RED SOX

1995 Scouting Report

Outfielders: The Red Sox have had some Hall of Fame out-fields, but these are not the days of Yaz and Dewey. Boston may acquire Steve Finley to cover the expansive center field at Fenway. Mike Greenwell (LF) is a sweet-swinging lefty. Right field could belong to rookie Greg Blosser or perennial prospect Wes Chamberlain.

Infielders: Scott Cooper has a great arm at third base, and his hitting has improved. John Valentin is a fine hitting shortstop. The Bosox batting order boasts the big stick of Mo Vaughn (1B). At second base, Tim Naehring is solid.

Catchers: Boston has a question mark at catcher. The possibilities include rookie Scott Hatteberg and former Mariner backup Bill Haselman, who has some power but no glove.

Starting Pitchers: Roger Clemens is baseball's most recognizable staff ace. Young righty Aaron Sele has a laws-of-physics-defying curveball. The other slots in the rotation aren't set. Chris Nabholz will have an opportunity. The team made numerous off-season signings of prospects, so someone special may emerge from the chaos.

Relief Pitchers: The best arms belong to super-prospects Chris Howard and Ken Ryan, Jr.

Designated Hitters: Andre Dawson filed for free agency, so the Red Sox dealt for slugger Jose Canseco.

Manager: Smart, enthusiastic Kevin Kennedy (138–138) takes over the clubhouse leadership in Boston.

1995 Outlook

The Red Sox were in first place through April last season, but they weren't ready to contend over a full season, even a strike-shortened one. The Bosox offense didn't generate nearly enough runs for a team playing in a bandbox ballpark; the acquisition of Canseco will help.

Fenway Park is a powerful influence on the shape and character of all Red Sox teams. Three elements are crucial to the success of any club that plays in Beantown: hitters who get on base, pitchers who don't give up walks, and fresh infusions of talent. Problematically, the Bosox tied for the second-lowest on-base percentage in the American League, due largely to their having the twelfth-lowest AL batting average. On the pitching side of the equation, only three pitching staffs in the league handed out more free passes than Boston's. These are two areas the organization will need to address if the club is going to avoid the AL East cellar.

In regards to the need for new faces in the Red Sox clubhouse, there has been a change in management. Kevin Kennedy, one of the youngest skippers in the majors, will be looking to rejuvenate the lineup. Boston is near the beginning of a rebuilding process that could take three or four years to complete. But the materials are present in the form of some glowing rookie prospects. The bullpen in particular contains two talented young arms, belonging to Chris Howard and Ken Ryan, Jr. The Red Sox gave Ryan full-time closer duties, and he responded with thirteen saves in 1994.

The Red Sox don't currently field enough frontline talent to compete with Baltimore and New York, but there are some promising outfielders in the minor league system, and if Aaron Sele takes a step forward, Boston will have two aces the equal of the Orioles' Mussina and McDonald.

It's likely that the Bosox will be making more deals before the season gets underway.

1995 Boston Red Sox Roster

Manager: Kevin Kennedy
Coaches: Mike Easler, Tim Johnson, Dave Oliver, Herman Starrette,
Frank White

No.	Pitchers	B	T	HT	WT	DOB	Birthplace
—	Bailey, Cory	R	R	6–1	208	1/24/71	Herrin, IL
21	Clemens, Roger	R	R	6–4	220	8/4/62	Dayton, OH
—	Finnvold, Gar	R	R	6–5	195	3/11/68	Boynton Beach, FL
48	Fossas, Tony	L	L	6–0	197	9/23/67	Havana, Cuba
27	Harris, Greg	B	R	6–0	175	11/2/55	Lynwood, CA
31	Howard, Chris	R	L	6–0	185	11/18/65	Nahant, MA
—	Looney, Brian	L	L	5–10	185	9/26/69	New Haven, CT
49	Nabholz, Chris	L	L	6–5	210	1/5/67	Harrisburg, PA
50	Ryan Jr., Ken	R	R	6–3	215	10/24/68	Pawtucket, RI
34	Sele, Aaron	R	R	6–5	205	6/25/70	Golden Valley, MN
—	Trlicek, Ricky	R	R	6–2	200	4/26/69	Houston, TX
—	Vanegmond, Tim	R	R	6–2	175	5/31/69	Senoia, GA
	Catchers						
—	Haselman, Bill	R	R	6–3	215	5/25/66	Long Branch, NJ
—	Hatteberg, Scott	L	R	6–1	185	12/14/69	Salem, OR
—	Wedge, Eric	R	R	6–3	215	1/27/68	Fort Wayne, IN
	Infielders						
45	Cooper, Scott	L	R	6–3	205	10/13/67	St. Louis, MO
11	Naehring, Tim	R	R	6–2	205	2/1/67	Cincinnati, OH
51	Ortiz, Luis	R	R	6–0	185	5/25/70	Santo Domingo, DR
—	Rodriguez, Carlos	B	R	5–9	160	11/1/67	Mexico City, Mexico
13	Valentin, John	R	R	6–0	180	2/18/67	Mineola, NY
42	Vaughn, Mo	L	R	6–1	225	12/15/67	Norwalk, CT
	Outfielders						
38	Blosser, Greg	L	L	6–3	200	6/26/71	Bradenton, FL
—	Canseco, Jose	R	R	6–4	240	7/2/64	Havana, Cuba
26	Chamberlain, Wes	R	R	6–2	219	4/13/66	Chicago, IL
39	Greenwell, Mike	L	R	6–0	205	7/18/63	Louisville, KY
—	Malave, Jose	R	R	6–2	184	5/31/71	Cumana, Venezuela
—	McNeely, Jeff	R	R	6–2	190	10/18/69	Monroe, NC

1995 Schedule

April

S	M	T	W	T	F	S
						1
2	3	4 MIN	5 MIN	6	7 KC	8 KC
9 KC	10 TEX	11 TEX	12	13	14 KC	15 KC
16 KC	17 TEX	18 MIN	19 MIN	20	21 CHI	22 CHI
23 CHI	24 CHI	25 MIN	26 MIN	27	28 CHI	29 CHI
30 CHI						

May

S	M	T	W	T	F	S
	1 NY	2 NY	3 NY	4 NY	5 DET	6 DET
7 DET	8 BAL	9 BAL	10 BAL	11 BAL	12 NY	13 NY
14 NY	15	16 MIL	17 MIL	18 CLE	19 CLE	20 CLE
21 CLE	22	23 SEA	24 SEA	25 SEA	26 CAL	27 CAL
28 CAL	29 OAK	30 OAK	31 OAK			

June

S	M	T	W	T	F	S
				1	2 SEA	3 SEA
4 SEA	5 CAL	6 CAL	7 CAL	8 CAL	9 OAK	10 OAK
11 OAK	12 TOR	13 TOR	14 TOR	15	16 MIL	17 MIL
18 MIL	19 CLE	20 CLE	21 CLE	22	23 BAL	24 BAL
25 BAL	26 TOR	27 TOR	28 TOR	29 DET	30 DET	

July

S	M	T	W	T	F	S
						1 DET
2 DET	3 KC	4 KC	5 KC	6 MIN	7 MIN	8 MIN
9 MIN	10	11 ★	12	13 TEX	14 TEX	15 TEX
16 TEX	17 KC	18 KC	19 CHI	20 CHI	21 MIN	22 MIN
23 MIN	24 MIN	25 CHI	26 CHI	27 CHI	28 TEX	29 TEX
30 TEX	31					

August

S	M	T	W	T	F	S
		1 DET	2 DET	3 DET	4 TOR	5 TOR
6 TOR	7 TOR	8 CLE	9 CLE	10	11 BAL	12 BAL
13 BAL	14 NY	15 NY	16 NY	17	18 SEA	19 SEA
20 SEA	21 CAL	22 CAL	23 CAL	24 OAK	25 OAK	26 OAK
27 OAK	28	29 SEA	30 SEA	31 SEA		

Sept/Oct

S	M	T	W	T	F	S
					1 CAL	2 CAL
3 CAL	4 OAK	5 OAK	6 OAK	7	8 NY	9 NY
10 NY	11 BAL	12 BAL	13 BAL	14	15 CLE	16 CLE
17 CLE	18 MIL	19 MIL	20 MIL	21	22 TOR	23 TOR
24 TOR	25 DET	26 DET	27 DET	28 MIL	29 MIL	30 MIL
1 MIL	2					

☐ Home ☐ Away ★ All-Star Game

Fenway Park

Capacity: 34,142

Turf: Grass

Dimensions:
LF Line: 315'
RF Line: 302'
Center: 420'
Left CF: 379'
Right CF: 380'

Tickets:
(617) 267-8661

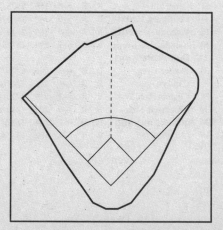

1994 Batting Order

1. Otis Nixon (Center Field)
2. Tim Naehring (Second Base)
3. John Valentin (Shortstop)
4. Mo Vaughn (First Base)
5. Mike Greenwell (Left Field)
6. Andre Dawson (Designated Hitter)
7. Scott Cooper (Third Base)
8. Wes Chamberlain (Right Field)
9. Damon Berryhill (Catcher)

1994 Team Record
54–61 (.470); Fourth in AL East

AL East	W	L	AL Central	W	L	AL West	W	L
Baltimore	2	4	Chicago	2	4	California	7	5
Boston	—	—	Cleveland	3	7	Oakland	9	3
Detroit	4	2	Kansas City	4	2	Seattle	6	6
New York	3	7	Milwaukee	5	5	Texas	1	5
Toronto	7	3	Minnesota	1	8			
Total	16	16		15	26		23	19

1994 American League Team Rank Batting

Batting Average: Twelfth (.263)
Runs Scored: Eleventh (552)
Runs Batted In: Eleventh (523)
Stolen Bases: Sixth (81)
Slugging Percentage: Tenth (.421)
On-Base Percentage: Thirteenth (.334)

1994 American League Team Rank Pitching

Earned Run Average: Ninth (4.93)
Bases On Balls: Eleventh (450)
Strikeouts: Fifth (729)
Wins: Seventh (54)
Saves: Fourth (30)
Complete Games: Twelfth (6)

© Dennis Brearlby

Boston Red Sox MVP

Roger Clemens   No. 21/ P

Born: 8/4/62, Dayton, OH
Height: 6' 4"   **Weight:** 220
Bats: Right   **Throws:** Right
Opp. Batting Average: .204

Clemens has led the league in ERA four times, a Red Sox team record matched only by Lefty Grove, who was arguably the greatest pitcher who ever played the game. The big Texas righthander was throwing extremely hard in '94, and he ranked first in the AL in opponents batting average.

His conspicuous absence from the top five in American League Cy Young Award voting is difficult to understand. Except for Clemens' won-lost record, which is primarily a reflection of the anemic Bosox offense, his numbers were as impressive as those of any AL hurler. "The Rocket" finished second in both ERA and strikeouts per nine innings. Clemens was the team's only consistent starter; he meant as much to Boston as Jimmy Key meant to New York.

The most complete pitcher in baseball, Clemens might not throw as hard as Randy Johnson or mix pitches as well as Greg Maddux, but he has more dominant pitching characteristics than any other starter in the majors. Clemens endured a down season in '93, but last season he was throwing as well as ever, and the extra rest his arm will get as a result of the work stoppage could make him deadly in 1995. The Boston Red Sox have retired only four numbers in the organization's history. None were worn by pitchers, but Clemens is well on his way to having his number, twenty-one, be the first.

	G	GS	IP	ERA	H	BB	SO	W	L	SV
1994	24	24	170.2	2.85	124	71	168	9	7	0
Career	326	325	2393.1	2.93	2002	690	2201	172	93	0
Projected	30	30	209.0	3.70	172	79	189	12	12	0

Wes Chamberlain   No. 26/OF

Born: 4/13/66, Chicago, IL
Height: 6' 2"   **Weight:** 219
Bats: Right   **Throws:** Right
1994 OBP: .307   **SLG:** .396

Chamberlain, so highly touted in 1991, never panned out in Philly. He could very well be the new Mel Hall, if hitter-friendly Fenway can jump start his bat. His problems have always been lack of discipline, both at the plate and in the field (though he's a much better fielder than he once was). A mid-career turnaround isn't out of the question.

	G	AB	H	2B	3B	HR	RS	RBI	BB	SB	BA
1994	75	233	61	14	1	6	20	26	15	0	.262
Career	366	1221	317	71	6	40	140	166	74	19	.260
Projected	106	320	91	22	2	10	35	46	21	1	.284

Scott Cooper   No. 45/3B

Born: 10/13/67, St. Louis, MO
Height: 6' 3"   **Weight:** 205
Bats: Left   **Throws:** Right
1994 OBP: .333   **SLG:** .453

Cooper isn't a bad player, and being a lefty linedrive hitter in Fenway Park helps his numbers. Cooper seems to be improving his stroke a little bit each year, and that's all the Red Sox are asking for right now. Cooper has an arm that's the equal of any third baseman in the league. He did make sixteen errors last year and has been the subject of trade talks.

	G	AB	H	2B	3B	HR	RS	RBI	BB	SB	BA
1994	104	369	104	16	4	13	49	53	30	0	.282
Career	399	1268	360	70	9	27	156	156	127	6	.284
Projected	158	566	172	30	5	14	76	76	58	3	.292

Danny Darwin   No. 44/ P

Born: 10/25/55, Bonham, TX
Height: 6' 3"   **Weight:** 195
Bats: Right   **Throws:** Right
Opp. Batting Average: .317

Darwin renewed the lease on his career in 1993, but he may have broken the terms of that lease last year. He still had pinpoint control, but his velocity was down a notch. Consequently, hitters were laying off his forkball and feasting on his fastball. Darwin continued to be prone to the longball. It's possible that Darwin can make a comeback, if there's nothing wrong with his arm.

	G	GS	IP	ERA	H	BB	SO	W	L	SV
1994	13	13	75.2	6.30	101	24	54	7	5	0
Career	598	282	2447.1	3.56	2303	722	1615	145	140	32
Projected	26	26	167.0	4.01	162	40	100	12	9	0

Andre Dawson   No. 10/ DH

Born: 7/10/54, Miami, FL
Height: 6' 3"   **Weight:** 197
Bats: Right   **Throws:** Right
1994 OBP: .271   **SLG:** .466

The Red Sox didn't offer Dawson salary arbitration, so he is a free agent as of this writing. "The Hawk" has perhaps the worst pair of knees in baseball, but the rest of his body is in fantastic shape. Until he hangs up his spikes voluntarily, it would be foolish to predict his exit from active play. He still has power when he gets his arms extended.

	G	AB	H	2B	3B	HR	RS	RBI	BB	SB	BA
1994	75	292	70	18	0	16	34	48	9	2	.240
Career	2506	9643	2700	491	95	428	1337	1540	578	314	.280
Projected	118	445	111	27	1	17	45	67	15	2	.255

Mike Greenwell   No. 39/ OF

Born: 7/18/63, Louisville, KY
Height: 6' 0"   **Weight:** 205
Bats: Left   **Throws:** Right
1994 SLG: .348   **OBA:** .453

"Gator" has raised expectations by having big years in the past, so it's hard to achieve a reasonable perspective on his performance. Greenwell is a solid hitter with linedrive pop, but junkballers can ruin his timing for days after he faces them. Greenwell knows the nooks and crannies of left field at Fenway, but he's a below-average outfielder.

	G	AB	H	2B	3B	HR	RS	RBI	BB	SB	BA
1994	95	327	88	25	1	11	60	45	38	2	.269
Career	1072	3847	1170	230	33	108	555	606	404	67	.304
Projected	146	531	161	39	4	15	85	72	57	4	.301

Joe Hesketh   No. 55/ P

Born: 2/15/59, Lackawanna, NY
Height: 6' 2"   **Weight:** 173
Bats: Left   **Throws:** Left
Opp. Batting Average: .267

The Bosox allowed Hesketh to file for free agency, largely because of his fat contract and history of injuries. Actually, Hesketh had a pretty good season for a lefty at Fenway. His ERA ranked twenty-second in the league, and his strikeout rates were above the norm. Hesketh has three things that will keep him in the league: lefthandedness, experience, and a nasty slider.

	G	GS	IP	ERA	H	BB	SO	W	L	SV
1994	25	20	114.0	4.26	117	46	83	8	5	0
Career	339	114	961.2	3.78	947	378	726	60	47	21
Projected	31	14	97.0	4.52	104	43	68	6	5	1

Chris Howard   No. 71/ P

Born: 11/18/65, Lynn, MA
Height: 6' 0"   **Weight:** 185
Bats: Right   **Throws:** Left
Opp. Batting Average: .233

Howard posted some nice numbers in the minors as a setup man, then brought his act to Boston last year. He's an intelligent, composed young pitcher, and he figures to help the Bosox bullpen. Howard does some crucial things well; he doesn't walk many batters, he keeps the ball in the park, and he can come up with a strikeout when one is needed.

	G	GS	IP	ERA	H	BB	SO	W	L	SV
1994	37	0	39.2	3.63	35	12	22	1	0	1
Career	40	0	41.2	3.46	37	15	23	2	0	1
Projected	26	0	67.0	3.43	24	10	15	1	0	1

Tim Naehring   No. 11/ 2B

Born: 2/1/67, Cincinnati, OH
Height: 6' 2"   **Weight:** 205
Bats: Right   **Throws:** Right
1994 OBP: .349   **SLG:** .414

Naehring made a name for himself as a top rookie prospect in 1991, but he hasn't lived up to the fanfare. At this stage of his career, Naehring is a solid regular in the Boston infield. He has good doubles power, and he does draw some walks, so his bat isn't a liability. Naehring's glovework has become very reliable, and he turns the doubleplay well.

	G	AB	H	2B	3B	HR	RS	RBI	BB	SB	BA
1994	80	297	82	18	1	7	41	42	30	1	.276
Career	235	750	196	43	1	13	78	88	72	2	.261
Projected	123	460	148	32	1	9	63	67	46	2	.307

Otis Nixon   No. 2/ OF

Born: 1/9/59, Evergreen, NC
Height: 6' 2"   **Weight:** 180
Bats: Both   **Throws:** Right
1994 OBP: .360   **SLG:** .317

Nixon brought stolen bases to Fenway Park. The Red Sox haven't seen such excitement in center field since Ellis Burks departed. Nixon is a very intelligent baserunner, not just a sprinter, and he knows how to draw walks. He's an asset in the leadoff slot and a slick center fielder as well, but the Bosox sent him to Texas for Jose Canseco.

	G	AB	H	2B	3B	HR	RS	RBI	BB	SB	BA
1994	103	398	109	15	1	0	60	25	55	42	.274
Career	1106	2855	746	80	14	7	518	172	324	394	.261
Projected	146	519	135	16	2	1	81	29	69	53	.266

Ken Ryan, Jr.   No. 50/ P

Born: 10/24/68, Pawtucket, RI
Height: 6' 3"   **Weight:** 215
Bats: Right   **Throws:** Right
Opp. Batting Average: .256

Keep an eye on Ryan—he's going to be a top stopper in 1995. He paid a lot of dues in the minors, and there have been doubts about his makeup, but his fastball is absolutely wicked—it almost lives up to its owner's last name. It seems like every year some reliever exceeds expectations and takes the league by storm. This season's leading candidate is Ryan.

	G	GS	IP	ERA	H	BB	SO	W	L	SV
1994	42	0	48.0	2.44	46	17	32	2	3	13
Career	96	0	105.0	3.26	93	51	86	9	5	15
Projected	52	0	57.0	3.03	52	27	47	5	3	8

Aaron Sele   No. 34/ P

Born: 6/25/70, Golden Valley, MN
Height: 6' 5"   **Weight:** 205
Bats: Right   **Throws:** Right
Opp. Batting Average: .261

The Red Sox could probably have gotten Marquis Grissom in '93 if they'd been willing to let go of Sele. As curveballers go, Sele could be the new Bert Blyleven. He's got two hooks—a sharp breaker and a long bender. Sele needs to pitch ahead in the count, and last year he was only partially successful. He looks almost as good as advertised, and that's pretty good.

	G	GS	IP	ERA	H	BB	SO	W	L	SV
1994	22	22	143.1	3.83	140	60	105	8	7	0
Career	40	40	255.1	3.35	240	108	198	15	9	0
Projected	24	24	151.0	3.36	142	64	117	9	5	0

John Valentin   No. 13/ SS

Born: 2/18/67, Mineola, NY
Height: 6' 0"   **Weight:** 170
Bats: Right   **Throws:** Right
1994 OBP: .400   **SLG:** .505

Valentin just keeps improving at the plate; he's become a fine hitter, one of the AL's most productive shortstops. He's become adept at jerking inside fastballs up against the Green Monster in left field. Valentin has responded to criticism about his lazy fielding syle by sharpening his skills and reducing his mental lapses. He turned a rare unassisted tripleplay last year.

	G	AB	H	2B	3B	HR	RS	RBI	BB	SB	BA
1994	84	301	95	26	2	9	53	49	42	3	.316
Career	286	954	276	79	5	25	124	140	111	7	.289
Projected	137	479	152	43	3	13	67	75	59	4	.304

Mo Vaughn   No. 42/ 1B

Born: 12/15/67, Norwalk, CT
Height: 6' 1"   **Weight:** 225
Bats: Left   **Throws:** Right
1994 OBA: .408   **SLG:** .576

Lovable Mo Vaughn is a becoming a great hitter, comparable if not equal to Frank Thomas. Vaughn has a good eye, willingness to hit the ball where it's pitched, and tremendous power. He finished sixth in the AL in slugging percentage. If "Hit Dog" gets his hips turned and the bat head in front of the plate, that's all she wrote. Vaughn is extremely popular in Beantown.

	G	AB	H	2B	3B	HR	RS	RBI	BB	SB	BA
1994	111	394	122	25	1	26	65	82	57	4	.310
Career	450	1507	422	87	4	72	214	272	209	13	.280
Projected	153	551	179	27	0	32	87	111	66	1	.324

Frank Viola   No. 16/ P

Born: 4/19/60, East Meadow, NY
Height: 6' 4"   **Weight:** 210
Bats: Left   **Throws:** Left
Opp. Batting Average: .296

Viola is a free agent as of this writing, which is what happens to a thirty-four-year-old pitcher with a questionable arm. If Viola's elbow is healthy, he can be a serviceable lefty starter. Viola is as smart as they come; his change-up is masterful, but it only works if there's enough velocity on his fastball. Watching Viola when he's throwing well is like a visit to a pitching clinic.

	G	GS	IP	ERA	H	BB	SO	W	L	SV
1994	6	6	31.0	4.65	34	17	9	1	1	0
Career	412	411	2791.2	3.67	2764	840	1822	175	146	0
Projected			No projection. Player was injured in 1994.							

California
ANGELS

1995 Scouting Report

Outfielders: Chad Curtis is fast and adept in center field; his offensive game is flawed but exciting. Tim Salmon (RF) is the Angels' rising star as a hitter. The left field platoon consists of comeback-minded Bo Jackson and young Jim Edmonds. Rookie Garret Anderson should contribute after his fine '94 performance at Triple-A Vancouver.

Infielders: The Angels' defense ranked second in the AL with a .983 fielding percentage. J. T. Snow recorded just one miscue in 456 total chances at first base. Spike Owen (3B) brought a shortstop's glove to his new position and hit well in the clutch. Gary DiSarcina flashes brilliant leather at shortstop, but he's a flyweight hitter. Second base will belong to last year's utility infielder Damion Easley.

Catchers: The Angels will be weighing their options. Veteran Greg Myers is probably the frontrunner, but youngsters Chris Turner and Jorge Fabregas will also have their shot at the job.

Starting Pitchers: The starting staff had a disappointing year. Star lefty duo Chuck Finley and Mark Langston both had off years. Another lefthander, young Brian Anderson, also was hit hard in '94. The righthanded hope was Phil Leftwich, who likewise was cuffed around all season. The fifth spot could go to Mark Leiter or Russ Springer.

Relief Pitchers: Mitch "Wild Thing" Williams was signed to take over the stopper role.

Designated Hitters: Chili Davis is a hitting machine.

Manager: Marcel Lachemann took over in mid-season and finished at 30–44. He's got a tough job ahead of him.

1995 Outlook

The Angels seem to have reached rock bottom, finishing with the worst record in the American League, good for last place in the AL West. The team was hit by injuries to the pitching corps, which it could ill afford. The Angels are structured on a base of pitching and defense; it's crucial that their big-money arms produce consistently.

California isn't an atrociously awful ballclub. The team has gotten the most out of some marginal talents, such as Spike Owen, by putting them in situations where their skills would be maximized and their deficiencies would stay partially hidden. The team defense is stellar, and the club is fundamentally sound. It's simply a problem of not enough frontline talent.

The Angels aren't predestined to bring up the rear in their division; remember that they ended the season just 5.5 games out of first, despite compiling baseball's second-worst overall record. California has two expensive lefty starters (Finley and Langston) who could come up big in '95, although either one could be traded if the right deal is offered. The overall hitting isn't strong, but there are a couple of dangerous bats in the lineup (Salmon and Davis). The further growth of Chad Curtis and the emergence of a rookie could make the offense more of a threat.

The team has legitimate reason to believe that at least two of their young prospects will pan out. Brian Anderson has great lefty stuff, Russ Springer could fit into the rotation or the bullpen, and Garret Anderson might contribute in the outfield. The Angels are wisely inclined to wait patiently for the next Tim Salmon or Jim Abbott to develop in the farm system. Unlike the situation in Detroit, for example, there is bright hope for the future in Anaheim.

1995 California Angels Roster

Manager: Marcel Lachemann
Coaches: Rick Burleson, Rod Carew, Chuck Hernandez, Bill Lachemann
Bobby Knopp, Joe Maddon

No.	Pitchers	B	T	HT	WT	DOB	Birthplace
56	Anderson, Brian	B	L	6–1	190	4/26/72	Geneva, OH
47	Bennett, Erik	R	R	6–2	205	9/13/68	Yreka, CA
23	Butcher, Mike	R	R	6–1	200	5/10/65	Davenport, IA
31	Finley, Chuck	L	L	6–6	214	11/26/62	Monroe, LA
42	Holzener, Mark	L	L	6–0	165	8/20/69	Littleton, CO
12	Langston, Mark	R	L	6–2	184	8/20/60	San Diego, CA
45	Leftwich, Phil	R	R	6–5	205	5/19/69	Lynchburg, VA
27	Leiter, Mark	R	R	6–3	210	4/13/63	Joliet, IL
35	Lorraine, Andrew	L	L	6–3	195	8/11/72	Los Angeles, CA
32	Magrane, Joe	R	L	6–6	230	7/2/64	Des Moines, IA
27	Percival, Troy	R	R	6–3	200	8/9/69	Fontana, CA
51	Schmidt, Jeff	R	R	6–5	190	2/21/71	Northfield, MN
38	Schwarz, Jeff	R	R	6–5	190	5/20/64	Ft. Pierce, FL
58	Simas, Bill	R	R	6–3	200	11/28/71	Hanford, CA
40	Springer, Russ	R	R	6–4	195	11/7/68	Alexandria, LA
34	Valera, Julio	R	R	6–2	215	10/13/68	San Sebastian, PR
99	Williams, Mitch	L	L	6–4	205	11/17/64	Santa Ana, CA
	Catchers						
7	Dalesandro, Mark	R	R	6–0	195	5/14/68	Chicago, IL
14	Fabregas, Jorge	L	R	6–3	205	3/13/70	Miami, FL
11	Myers, Greg	L	R	6–2	215	4/14/66	Riverside, CA
53	Turner, Chris	R	R	6–1	190	3/23/69	Bowling Green, KY
	Infielders						
5	Correia, Rod	R	R	5–11	180	9/13/67	Providence, RI
24	DiSarcina, Gary	R	R	6–1	178	11/19/67	Malden, MA
1	Easley, Damion	R	R	5–11	185	1/11/69	New York, NY
8	Flora, Kevin	R	R	6–0	185	6/10/69	Fontana, CA
7	Owen, Spike	B	R	5–10	170	4/19/61	Cleburne, TX
24	Perez, Eduardo	R	R	6–4	215	9/11/59	Cincinnati, OH
6	Snow, J. T.	B	L	6–2	202	2/28/68	Long Beach, CA
	Outfielders						
16	Anderson, Garret	R	R	6–3	190	6/30/72	Los Angeles, CA
9	Curtis, Chad	R	R	5–10	175	11/6/68	Marion, IN
44	Davis, Chili	B	R	6–3	217	1/17/60	Kingston, JM
46	Edmonds, Jim	L	L	6–1	190	6/2/70	Fullerton, CA
3	Riley, Marquis	R	R	5–11	170	12/27/70	Ashdown, AR
15	Salmon, Tim	R	R	6–3	220	8/24/68	Long Beach, CA

1995 Schedule

April

S	M	T	W	T	F	S
						1
2	3	4 MIL	5 MIL	6 MIL	7 CLE	8 CLE
9 CLE	10 MIL	11 MIL	12	13	14 CLE	15 CLE
16 CLE	17	18	19	20	21 TOR	22 TOR
23 TOR	24 DET	25 DET	26 DET	27	28 TOR	29 TOR
30 TOR						

May

S	M	T	W	T	F	S
	1 TOR	2 OAK	3 OAK	4 OAK	5 SEA	6 SEA
7 SEA	8	9 TEX	10 TEX	11 TEX	12 KC	13 KC
14 KC	15 MIN	16 MIN	17 MIN	18 MIN	19 CHI	20 CHI
21	22	23 NY	24 NY	25 NY	26 BOS	27 BOS
28 BOS	29 BAL	30 BAL	31 BAL			

June

S	M	T	W	T	F	S
				1	2 NY	3 NY
4	5 BOS	6 BOS	7 BOS	8 BOS	9 BAL	10 BAL
11 BAL	12 MIN	13 MIN	14 MIN	15 CHI	16 CHI	17 CHI
18 CHI	19 KC	20 KC	21 KC	22	23 SEA	24 SEA
25 SEA	26 SEA	27 TEX	28 TEX	29 TEX	30 OAK	

July

S	M	T	W	T	F	S
						1 OAK
2 OAK	3	4 TOR	5 TOR	6 TOR	7 MIL	8 MIL
9 MIL	10	11 ★	12	13 DET	14 DET	15 DET
16 DET	17 CLE	18 TOR	19 TOR	20 TOR	21 DET	22 DET
23 DET	24 CLE	25 CLE	26 CLE	27 MIL	28 MIL	29 MIL
30 MIL	31					

August

S	M	T	W	T	F	S
		1 SEA	2 SEA	3 SEA	4 TEX	5 TEX
6 TEX	7 TEX	8 KC	9 KC	10 KC	11 MIN	12 MIN
13 MIN	14 CHI	15 CHI	16 CHI	17	18 NY	19 NY
20 NY	21 BOS	22 BOS	23 BOS	24 BAL	25 BAL	26 BAL
27 BAL	28	29 NY	30 NY	31 NY		

Sept/Oct

S	M	T	W	T	F	S
					1 BOS	2 BOS
3 BOS	4 BAL	5 BAL	6 BAL	7	8 MIN	9 MIN
10 MIN	11	12 CHI	13 CHI	14	15 KC	16 KC
17 KC	18 OAK	19 OAK	20 OAK	21	22 TEX	23 TEX
24 TEX	25 SEA	26 SEA	27 SEA	28 OAK	29 OAK	30 OAK
1 OAK	2					

☐ Home   ☐ Away   ★ All-Star Game

Anaheim Stadium

Capacity: 64,593

Turf: Grass

Dimensions:
LF Line: 370'
RF Line: 370'
Center: 404'
Alleys: 386'

Tickets:
(714) 634-2000

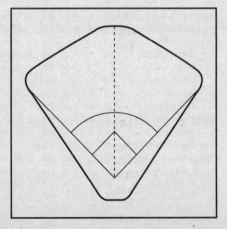

1994 Batting Order

1. Damion Easley (Second Base)
2. Spike Owen (Third Base)
3. Tim Salmon (Right Field)
4. Chili Davis (Designated Hitter)
5. Bo Jackson (Left Field)
6. Chad Curtis (Center Field)
7. J. T. Snow (First Base)
8. Chris Turner (Catcher)
9. Gary DiSarcina (Shortstop)

1994 Team Record
47–68 (.409); Fourth in AL West

AL East	W	L	AL Central	W	L	AL West	W	L
Baltimore	4	8	Chicago	5	5	California	—	—
Boston	5	7	Cleveland	5	5	Oakland	3	6
Detroit	3	4	Kansas City	6	4	Seattle	2	7
New York	4	8	Milwaukee	3	3	Texas	6	4
Toronto	3	4	Minnesota	3	3			
Total	19	31		22	20		11	17

1994 American League Team Rank Batting

Batting Average: Eleventh (.264)
Runs Scored: Fourteenth (543)
Runs Batted In: Twelfth (518)
Stolen Bases: Tenth (65)
Slugging Percentage: Twelfth (.409)
On-Base Percentage: Twelfth (.334)

1994 American League Team Rank Pitching

Earned Run Average: Twelfth (5.42)
Bases On Balls: Ninth (436)
Strikeouts: Eighth (682)
Wins: Fourteenth (47)
Saves: Tenth (21)
Complete Games: Eighth (11)

California Angels MVP

Chili Davis   No. 44/ DH

Born: 1/17/60, Kingston, Jamaica
Height: 6' 3"   **Weight:** 217
Bats: Both   **Throws:** Right
1994 OBP: .410   **SLG:** .561

He's been a productive professional hitter since 1983, but just when it seemed his career was out of breath, Davis found a second wind in Anaheim. The past two seasons have been the best back-to-back hitting performances of his career. He's currently the Angels' most dangerous offensive weapon, and his thirty-five-year-old body doesn't appear to be in decline.

Davis isn't helped much by his home park. The visibility in Anaheim Stadium has always been poor, and the team batting average was thirteen points higher away from home. Davis actually led the AL in BA on the road (.362, compared to his .270 mark in Anaheim). Davis loves to take his rips early in the count, when opposing hurlers are trying to get ahead by grooving the fastball. He ranked first in the league in batting average when putting the first pitch into play (.486 in seventy at-bats). Among designated hitters who appeared in thirty-five games or more, Davis ranked first in home runs and on-base percentage.

Davis joined some heady company July 23 when he became one of only eight switch hitters to gather 1,000 RBIs in MLB history. The list includes Hall of Famers Mickey Mantle and Frankie Frisch. Davis knocked in seven RBIs July 30 at Texas.

Davis is one of baseball's quietest stars, but he's been making big noise with the bat for thirteen full seasons.

	G	AB	H	2B	3B	HR	RS	RBI	BB	SB	BA
1994	108	392	122	18	1	26	72	84	69	3	.311
Career	1851	6663	1799	325	29	250	945	1014	847	124	.270
Projected	156	567	147	29	1	31	84	113	81	4	.265

Brian Anderson   No. 56/ P

Born: 4/26/72, Geneva, OH
Height: 6' 1"   **Weight:** 190
Bats: Both   **Throws:** Left
Opp. Batting Average: .300

Anderson showed a rookie's inconsistency in '94, but he also showed the potential to follow in the footsteps of recent Angels lefty stars. Anderson pitched into the seventh inning or later nine times, putting up fine numbers in those games (6–0, 2.99 ERA). His weakness is a lack of strikeouts, but perhaps those numbers will increase as he matures.

	G	GS	IP	ERA	H	BB	SO	W	L	SV
1994	18	18	101.2	5.22	120	27	47	7	5	0
Career	22	19	113.0	5.10	131	29	51	7	5	0
Projected	14	12	72.0	5.09	83	18	32	4	3	0

Chad Curtis   No. 9/ OF

Born: 11/6/68, Marion, IN
Height: 5' 10"   **Weight:** 175
Bats: Right   **Throws:** Right
1994 OBP: .317   **SLG:** .397

Curtis offers an intriguing package of skills and weaknesses. He's used his excellent speed to steal at least twenty-five bases in each of his three seasons, but his percentages aren't good; Curtis was caught eleven times in '94, the third-worst figure in the AL. He's got great range and an accurate arm, but he made the third-most errors among AL center fielders.

	G	AB	H	2B	3B	HR	RS	RBI	BB	SB	BA
1994	114	453	116	23	4	11	67	50	37	25	.256
Career	405	1477	396	64	9	27	220	155	158	116	.268
Projected	156	632	186	30	4	11	102	69	68	46	.283

Gary DiSarcina No. 24/ SS

Born: 11/19/67, Malden, MA
Height: 6' 1"   **Weight:** 178
Bats: Right   **Throws:** Right
1994 OBP: .294   **SLG:** .329

"All-field, no-hit" has rarely applied so perfectly. DiSarcina ranked first in the league in total chances (526) and assists (358). He tied for first in doubleplays with seventy-one. He was second among AL shortstops in putouts (159) and fielding percentage (.983). But he's also one of baseball's least productive regulars with the bat.

	G	AB	H	2B	3B	HR	RS	RBI	BB	SB	BA
1994	112	389	101	14	2	3	53	33	18	3	.260
Career	431	1437	348	56	4	9	158	123	59	18	.242
Projected	143	503	135	22	2	4	63	51	21	5	.258

Damion Easley No. 1/ 2B

Born: 1/11/69, New York, NY
Height: 5' 11"   **Weight:** 185
Bats: Right   **Throws:** Right
1994 OBP: .288   **SLG:** .329

Easley is another flashy gloveman who doesn't carry his weight with the bat. He'll probably be the Angels' starting second sacker now that Harold Reynolds has departed. Easley filled a utility role in '94, and his play at second yielded a stellar .994 percentage. His batting average versus lefthanders was an unsightly .189, matched with a .229 mark against righties.

	G	AB	H	2B	3B	HR	RS	RBI	BB	SB	BA
1994	88	316	68	16	1	6	41	30	29	4	.215
Career	208	697	179	34	3	9	88	64	65	19	.257
Projected	135	482	136	27	3	7	69	48	53	98	.269

Chuck Finley　　　No. 31/ P

Born: 11/26/62, Monroe, LA
Height: 6' 6"　　**Weight:** 214
Bats: Left　　**Throws:** Left
Opp. Batting Average: .260

The Angels were blanked or scored just one run in six of Finley's ten losses. Overall they gave him the third-lowest run support per nine innings of any AL hurler (4.22). Finley didn't have a good season by his standards, but he's a fine pitcher on a team that doesn't give him many chances to relax with a lead. Finley led the AL in innings pitched and ranked third in strikeouts.

	G	GS	IP	ERA	H	BB	SO	W	L	SV
1994	25	25	183.1	4.32	178	71	148	10	10	0
Career	277	220	1633.1	3.50	1552	663	1174	99	86	0
Projected	34	34	247.0	3.65	240	87	191	15	14	0

Joe Grahe　　　No. 19/ P

Born: 8/14/67, West Palm Beach, CA
Height: 6' 0"　　**Weight:** 200
Bats: Right　　**Throws:** Right
Opp. Batting Average: .362

The Angels' relief corps isn't quite up to par with the rest of the league, and Grahe was the designated closer. The unfortunate numbers include a .405 batting average allowed versus left-handers. The Angels let Bryan Harvey go in 1993, and Grahe was expected to replace him, but it looks as though Mitch Williams has replaced Grahe.

	G	GS	IP	ERA	H	BB	SO	W	L	SV
1994	40	0	43.1	6.65	68	18	26	2	5	13
Career	157	25	311.0	4.34	342	138	161	17	23	45
Projected	49	0	58.0	4.51	71	25	33	3	3	14

Bo Jackson   No. 22/ OF

Born: 11/30/62, Bessemer, AL
Height: 6' 1"   **Weight:** 225
Bats: Right   **Throws:** Right
1994 OBP: .344   **SLG:** .507

Jackson is more of an athlete than most players in the majors, but he's never been a refined baseball player. Last season, he added valuable punch to the singles-hitting Angels batting order, and proved that his comeback is for real. He's always a couple of adjustments, albeit major ones, from having a huge year at the plate. He was unsigned as of this writing.

	G	AB	H	2B	3B	HR	RS	RBI	BB	SB	BA
1994	75	201	56	7	0	13	23	43	20	1	.279
Career	694	2393	598	86	14	141	341	415	200	82	.250
Projected	100	307	79	10	0	19	35	56	27	1	.254

Mark Langston   No. 12/ P

Born: 8/20/60, San Diego, CA
Height: 6' 2"   **Weight:** 184
Bats: Both   **Throws:** Left
Opp. Batting Average: .268

Langston endured a year marred by elbow sugery, but he's in top physical condition and has been a workhorse, so it's likely he'll bounce back. Langston has a great pickoff move; he tied for the league lead with nine. He hasn't hit a batter since Opening Day 1993. He was fourth in the AL in Ks per nine innings, and he's had nine straight seasons with 100+ strikeouts.

	G	GS	IP	ER	H	BB	SO	W	L	SV
1994	18	18	119.1	4.68	121	54	109	7	8	0
Career	352	349	2448.1	3.74	1968	1081	2110	151	134	0
Projected	30	30	209.0	3.67	190	77	170	13	11	0

Phil Leftwich   No. 45/ P

Born: 5/19/69, Lynchburg, VA
Height: 6' 5"   **Weight:** 205
Bats: Right   **Throws:** Right
Opp. Batting Average: .283

Last year was Leftwich's first full major league season. He faltered in the early going, dropping his first four desicions, then was placed on the DL with an inflamed lower leg. Leftwich throws a heavy, diving fastball, and the Angels believe that he could still be a valuable part of their rotation. He ranked first in the league in pickoff throws (269).

	G	GS	IP	ERA	H	BB	SO	W	L	SV
1994	20	20	114.0	5.68	127	42	67	5	10	0
Career	32	32	194.2	4.90	208	69	98	9	16	0
Projected	19	19	118.0	4.90	126	42	59	5	10	0

Spike Owen   No. 17/ 3B

Born: 4/19/61, Cleburne, TX
Height: 5' 10"   **Weight:** 170
Bats: Both   **Throws:** Right
1994 OBP: .418   **SLG:** .422

Owen switched from shortstop to third base and completely reset his personal standards for offensive production. He tallied the highest average of his career. Surprisingly, he led the the AL in batting average with runners in scoring position (.454) and was fifth in the league in highest percentage of pitches taken (63.9). He had the league's best walks-to-strikeouts ratio (2.9/1).

	G	AB	H	2B	3B	HR	RS	RBI	BB	SB	BA
1994	82	268	83	17	2	3	30	37	49	2	.310
Career	1462	4712	1161	206	56	45	570	411	551	79	.246
Projected	115	365	94	20	2	3	42	34	46	3	.262

Tim Salmon   No. 15/ OF

Born: 8/24/68, Long Beach, CA
Height: 6' 3"   **Weight:** 220
Bats: Right   **Throws:** Right
1994 OBP: .382   **SLG:** .531

The brightest young star on the Angels roster, Salmon had a solid sophomore season. His homer and RBI rates improved from his Rookie of the Year campaign. His fielding percentage was the second lowest among AL right fielders, but he did register nine assists. Salmon strikes out a lot, but he also draws his share of walks. He's going to be a great one.

	G	AB	H	2B	3B	HR	RS	RBI	BB	SB	BA
1994	100	373	107	18	2	23	67	70	54	1	.287
Career	265	967	267	54	3	56	168	171	147	260	.276
Projected	148	565	174	35	2	36	106	109	90	4	.296

J. T. Snow   No. 6/ 1B

Born: 2/28/68, Long Beach, CA
Height: 6' 2"   **Weight:** 202
Bats: Both   **Throws:** Left
1994 OBP: .289   **SLG:** .345

Snow hasn't established consistency with the bat since joining the Angels, but he's got Gold Glove potential at first base. Snow shows occasional longball ability, but he doesn't draw many walks and rarely recovers when behind in the count. This will be a pivotal season for Snow; he'll need to do more hitting in order to justify a starting job.

	G	AB	H	2B	3B	HR	RS	RBI	BB	SB	BA
1994	61	223	49	4	0	8	22	30	19	0	.220
Career	147	696	152	23	42	24	83	89	79	3	.232
Projected	111	392	99	14	1	15	52	55	47	2	.243

Russ Springer   No. 40/ P

Born: 11/7/68, Alexandria, LA
Height: 6' 4"   **Weight:** 195
Bats: Right   **Throws:** Right
Opp. Batting Average: .291

Springer will make a strong bid to take control of the role of stopper in the Angels bullpen in 1995. His '94 ERA as a reliever was 2.11 in thirteen appearances, and he set down ten of thirteen first batters faced. Springer's velocity is in the low nineties, and a moving fastball is his primary weapon. He was acquired from the Yankees in the Jim Abbott trade.

	G	GS	IP	ERA	H	BB	SO	W	L	SV
1994	18	5	45.2	5.52	53	14	28	2	2	2
Career	46	14	121.2	6.44	144	56	71	3	8	2
Projected			No projection. Player was a rookie in 1994.							

Chris Turner   No. 53/ C

Born: 3/23/69, Bowling Green, KY
Height: 6' 1"   **Weight:** 190
Bats: Right   **Throws:** Right
1994 OBP: .290   **SLG:** .322

Turner hit .138 in his first thirty-eight games and was demoted to the minors. Once he readjusted his mechanics, Turner made a 180-degree turn upon being recalled, going five-for-five on July 5 and batting .418 in his final fifty-five at-bats. Turner committed only one error in 298 total chances, a .997 percentage. He'll have a strong shot at the starting job in 1995.

	G	AB	H	2B	3B	HR	RS	RBI	BB	SB	BA
1994	58	149	36	7	1	1	23	12	10	3	.242
Career	83	224	57	12	1	2	32	25	19	4	.254
Projected	89	250	69	14	1	2	37	29	22	5	.265

Chicago
WHITE SOX

1995 Scouting Report

Outfielders: The Chisox get great defense from center fielder Lance Johnson. Tim Raines (LF) is a prolific run scorer. Darrin Jackson (RF) had a breakthrough season at the plate.

Infielders: Third baseman Robin Ventura has great range and is a balanced hitter. Frank Thomas (1B) is the American League's most dominant hitter. The middle infield is anchored by shortstop Ozzie Guillen. Joey Cora plays second base and hits leadoff.

Starting Pitchers: The rotation is loaded with great arms. The consensus ace was Jack McDowell, but he was dealt to the Yankees over the winter. Alex Fernandez is young, confident, and often untouchable. Wilson Alvarez could be the ace of almost any team in the league. On a staff that slings heat, Jason Bere is the hardest thrower. Scott Sanderson was serviceable as the fifth starter last year.

Catchers: Ron Karkovice is tough on opposing basestealers. He's got good power with the bat. Mike "Spanky" LaValliere offers solid throwing and intelligent handling of pitchers as a backup.

Relief Pitchers: The bullpen was supposed to be a strength, but Roberto Hernandez struggled last season. Middle relief is handled by veterans Dennis Cook and Paul Assenmacher, with Jose DeLeon in a setup role.

Designated Hitters: The Chisox were amply rewarded for signing Julio Franco. He produced more RBIs than any other DH.

Manager: Gene Lamont (247–190) served as third base coach under Jim Leyland in Pittsburgh from 1986–1991.

1995 Outlook

The White Sox were locked in a tight race with Cleveland throughout the 1994 season, and finished the year in first place by one full game. The Indians will be competitive again, and the dark horse Royals will round out the three-way battle for '95. The Chisox will have a tough time defending their position as top dog in the American League Central.

The White Sox can boast of having the league's best starting rotation, with Alex Fernandez, Wilson Alvarez, and Jason Bere all having youth and talent to burn. The White Sox gave up the least hits and earned runs in the AL, as well as leading the loop in shutouts. Opposing clubs know that if they get past one quality arm, they'll be up against another the following night.

Offensively, batting coach Walt Hriniak can take much of the credit for formulating a batting philosophy based on getting men on base. Chicago hitters drew the third-most walks and compiled the third-highest batting average in the league, which translated into the AL's second-best on-base percentage. The White Sox could use another longball threat to balance out their batting order, but even if they don't make a deal, the offense will score enough runs to support the fantastic frontline pitching.

One of the characteristics of a championship ballclub is the expectation of winning, no matter what the circumstances. The Chisox have begun developing team confidence by putting together back-to-back division-winning campaigns. Veterans like Ozzie Guillen and Tim Raines provide the clubhouse intangibles that create a winning attitude. Chicago will undoubtedly be in the hunt for an AL Central title, but the task won't be easily accomplished. The performance of Wilson Alvarez will probably determine whether the team can repeat as division winners. The Chisox will also need to straighten out their bullpen situation. If the offense can once again finish fourth in the league in runs, fans at Comiskey will have plenty to cheer about in 1995.

1995 Chicago White Sox Roster

Manager: Gene Lamont

Coaches: Terry Bevington, Jackie Brown, Walt Hriniak, Doug Mansolino, Joe Nossek, Rick Peterson

No.	Pitchers	B	T	HT	WT	DOB	Birthplace
40	Alvarez, Wilson	L	L	6–1	235	3/24/70	Maracaibo, Venezuela
51	Bere, Jason	R	R	6–3	185	5/26/71	Cambridge, MA
42	Bolton, Rodney	R	R	6–2	190	9/23/68	Chattanooga, TN
48	DeLeon, Jose	R	R	6–3	226	12/20/60	Rancho Viejo, DR
48	Ellis, Robert	R	R	6–5	215	12/25/70	Baton Rouge, LA
32	Fernandez, Alex	R	R	6–1	215	8/13/69	Miami Beach, FL
39	Hernandez, Roberto	R	R	6–4	235	11/11/64	Santurce, PR
25	McCaskill, Kirk	R	R	6–1	205	4/9/61	Kapuskasing, Canada
31	Radinsky, Scott	L	L	6–3	204	3/3/68	Glendale, CA
45	Ruffcorn, Scott	R	R	6–4	210	12/21/69	New Braunfels, TX
49	Schwarz, Jeff	R	R	6–5	190	5/20/64	Ft. Pierce, FL
	Catchers						
20	Karkovice, Ron	R	R	6–1	219	8/8/63	Union, NJ
10	LaValliere, Mike	L	R	5–9	210	8/18/60	Charlotte, NC
68	Lindsey, Doug	R	R	6–2	232	9/22/67	Austin, TX
5	Merullo, Matt	L	R	6–2	200	8/4/65	Ridgefield, CT
	Infielders						
28	Cora, Joey	B	R	5–8	155	5/14/65	Caguas, PR
52	Denson, Drew	R	R	6–5	220	11/16/65	Cincinnati, OH
14	Grebeck, Craig	R	R	5–7	148	12/29/64	Johnstown, PA
13	Guillen, Ozzie	L	R	5–11	164	1/20/64	Oculare Tuy, Venezuela
53	Martin, Norberto	R	R	5–10	164	12/10/66	Santo Domingo, PR
35	Thomas, Frank	R	R	6–5	257	5/27/68	Columbus, GA
23	Ventura, Robin	L	R	6–1	198	7/14/67	Santa Maria, CA
57	Wilson, Brandon	R	R	6–1	170	2/26/69	Owensboro, KY
	Outfielders						
14	Franco, Julio	R	R	6–1	190	8/23/61	San Pedro Macoris, DR
22	Jackson, Darrin	R	R	6–0	185	8/22/63	Los Angeles, CA
1	Johnson, Lance	L	L	5–11	160	7/6/63	Cincinnati, OH
24	Newson, Warren	L	L	5–7	202	7/3/64	Newnan, GA
44	Pasqua, Dan	L	L	6–0	218	10/17/61	Yonkers, NY
30	Raines, Tim	B	R	5–8	186	9/16/59	Sanford, FL

1995 Schedule

April

S	M	T	W	T	F	S
						1
2 BAL	3 BAL	4	5 BAL	6 BAL	7 NY	8 NY
9 NY	10 BAL	11	12 BAL	13 NY	14 NY	15 NY
16 NY	17 MIL	18 MIL	19 MIL	20 MIL	21 BOS	22 BOS
23 BOS	24 BOS	25 MIL	26 MIL	27	28 BOS	29 BOS
30 BOS						

May

S	M	T	W	T	F	S
	1	2 TOR	3 TOR	4	5 KC	6 KC
7 KC	8 MIN	9 MIN	10	11	12 SEA	13 SEA
14 SEA	15	16 OAK	17 OAK	18 OAK	19 CAL	20 CAL
21 CAL	22	23 TEX	24 TEX	25	26 DET	27 DET
28 DET	29 CLE	30 CLE	31 CLE			

June

S	M	T	W	T	F	S
				1 CLE	2 DET	3 DET
4 DET	5 TOR	6 TOR	7 TOR	8	9 TEX	10 TEX
11 TEX	12 OAK	13 OAK	14 OAK	15 CAL	16 CAL	17 CAL
18 CAL	19 SEA	20 SEA	21 SEA	22 CAL	23 CLE	24 CLE
25 CLE	26 MIN	27 MIN	28 MIN	29	30 KC	

July

S	M	T	W	T	F	S
						1 KC
2 KC	3 NY	4 NY	5 NY	6 BAL	7 BAL	8 BAL
9 BAL	10	11 ★	12	13 MIL	14 MIL	15 MIL
16 MIL	17 NY	18 NY	19 BOS	20 BOS	21 MIL	22 MIL
23 MIL	24	25 BOS	26 BOS	27 BOS	28 BAL	29 BAL
30 BAL	31 KC					

August

S	M	T	W	T	F	S
		1 KC	2 KC	3 KC	4 CLE	5 CLE
6 CLE	7 SEA	8 SEA	9 SEA	10	11 OAK	12 OAK
13 OAK	14 CAL	15 CAL	16 CAL	17 TEX	18 TEX	19 TEX
20 TEX	21 DET	22 DET	23 DET	24 TOR	25 TOR	26 TOR
27 TOR	28	29 DET	30 DET	31 DET		

Sept/Oct

S	M	T	W	T	F	S
					1 TOR	2 TOR
3 TOR	4 TEX	5 TEX	6 TEX	7 TEX	8	9 OAK
10 OAK	11	12 CAL	13 CAL	14	15 SEA	16 SEA
17 SEA	18 CLE	19 CLE	20 CLE	21	22 MIN	23 MIN
24 MIN	25 MIN	26 KC	27 KC	28 KC	29 MIN	30 MIN
1 MIN	2					

 Home   Away   ★ All-Star Game

Comiskey Park

Capacity: 44,321

Turf: Grass

Dimensions:
LF Line: 347'
RF Line: 347'
Center: 400'
Alleys: 375'

Tickets:
(312) 924-1000

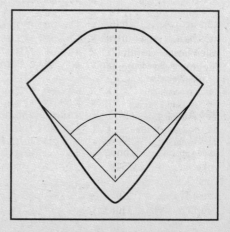

1994 Batting Order

1. Joey Cora (Second Base)
2. Tim Raines (Left Field)
3. Frank Thomas (First Base)
4. Julio Franco (Designated Hitter)
5. Robin Ventura (Third Base)
6. Darrin Jackson (Right Field)
7. Lance Johnson (Center Field)
8. Ron Karkovice (Catcher)
9. Ozzie Guillen (Shortstop)

1994 Team Record
67–46 (.593); First in AL Central

AL East	W	L	AL Central	W	L	AL West	W	L
Baltimore	4	2	Chicago	—	—	California	5	5
Boston	4	2	Cleveland	7	5	Oakland	6	3
Detroit	8	4	Kansas City	3	7	Seattle	9	1
New York	4	2	Milwaukee	9	3	Texas	4	5
Toronto	2	3	Minnesota	2	4			
Total	22	13		21	19		24	14

1994 American League Team Rank Batting

Batting Average: Third (.287)
Runs Scored: Fourth (633)
Runs Batted In: Fourth (602)
Stolen Bases: Eighth (77)
Slugging Percentage: Fifth (.444)
On-Base Percentage: Second (.366)

1994 American League Team Rank Pitching

Earned Run Average: First (3.96)
Bases On Balls: Second (377)
Strikeouts: Third (754)
Wins: Second (67)
Saves: Thirteenth (20)
Complete Games: Third (13)

© Rich Pilling/MLB Photos

Chicago White Sox MVP

Frank Thomas   No. 35/ 1B

Born: 5/27/68, Columbus, GA
Height: 6' 5"   **Weight:** 257
Bats: Right   **Throws:** Right
1994 OBP: .487   **SLG:** .729

Clearly the number-one offensive player in the American League, Thomas is a right-handed version of Ted Williams. Timing, vision, reflexes, bat speed—Thomas has all the tools, and he's still learning the pitching patterns of AL hurlers. It's scary to think that we may not have seen Thomas at his best in 1994.

Last year Thomas finished the season ranked first in the two most meaningful offensive statistical categories, on-base percentage and slugging percentage, a feat which "The Splendid Splinter" (Williams) accomplished nine times in his Hall of Fame career. Thomas increased his slugging percentage 122 points from his 1993 MVP campaign.

Categories in which Thomas led the American League in 1994 include walks, extra-base hits (73), runs scored, and home run ratio (10.5).

The only weakness in Thomas' game has been his glovework at first base, but he seems to be improving in that area. He's very quick, especially considering his large frame, and he has become more adept at scooping errant throws.

Thomas entered the majors as a complete force with the bat, and his output is increasing each season. Of the top sluggers in the game, Thomas has the best shot at winning a Triple Crown.

	G	AB	H	2B	3B	HR	RS	RBI	BB	SB	BA
1994	113	399	141	34	1	38	106	101	109	2	.353
Career	644	2271	741	158	8	142	463	484	525	13	.326
Projected	156	580	208	45	1	50	135	146	141	4	.346

Wilson Alvarez   No. 40/ P

Born: 3/24/70, Maracaibo, Venezuela
Height: 6' 1"   **Weight:** 235
Bats: Left   **Throws:** Left
Opp. Batting Average: .241

Alvarez began the year attacking hitters aggressively, and the results were an 8–0 record and a 2.55 ERA through June 5. But he struggled with his control, as he has in the past, and was inconsistent for the rest of the season. Alvarez throws an excellent curve to go with a mid-nineties heater. Few hitters in the league can handle Alvarez when he's on.

	G	GS	IP	ERA	H	BB	SO	W	L	SV
1994	24	24	161.2	3.45	147	62	108	12	8	0
Career	100	74	526.0	3.64	468	280	361	35	22	1
Projected	32	32	212.0	3.17	180	105	151	15	9	0

Jason Bere   No. 51/ P

Born: 5/26/71, Cambridge, MA
Height: 6' 3"   **Weight:** 185
Bats: Right   **Throws:** Right
Opp. Batting Average: .229

Picked in the thirty-sixth round of the 1990 draft, it's still too early to say that Bere is the next Roger Clemens. We will say this— if Bere can cut down on the number of free passes he issued in '94, he'll be the best pitcher on the formidable White Sox staff. Last year Bere led the AL in winning percentage and finished fifth in opponents batting average.

	G	GS	IP	ERA	H	BB	SO	W	L	SV
1994	24	24	141.2	3.81	119	80	127	12	2	0
Career	48	48	284.2	3.64	228	161	256	24	7	0
Projected	28	28	166.0	3.64	133	94	149	14	4	0

Joey Cora   No. 28/ 2B

Born: 5/14/65, Caguas, PR
Height: 5' 8"   **Weight:** 155
Bats: Both   **Throws:** Right
1994 OBP: .353   **SLG:** .362

Cora is a singles hitter who spent time in the leadoff spot of the batting order last year. In 1993, Cora made the most errors at second base in the American League, but he seemed to be more settled last year. He has good speed, but he wasn't looking to steal as often last year as he had in the previous campaign. He could steal thirty bases in 1995.

	G	AB	H	2B	3B	HR	RS	RBI	BB	SB	BA
1994	90	312	86	13	4	2	55	30	38	8	.276
Career	551	1601	416	48	23	4	254	124	182	73	.260
Projected	146	540	149	17	10	2	92	50	64	17	.273

Jose DeLeon   No. 48/ P

Born: 12/20/60, Rancho Viejo, DR
Height: 6' 03"   **Weight:** 226
Bats: Right   **Throws:** Right
Opp. Batting Average: .200

Oh, the elusive quality of greatness...As a starter in St. Louis in 1989, DeLeon led the National League in strikeouts (201) and opponents batting average (.197). His forkball was deadly, and his arm was strong. The next season, DeLeon's record was 7–19. He's a middle reliever these days, and a good one at that, but he's as far from stardom as a pitcher can be.

	G	GS	IP	ERA	H	BB	SO	W	L	SV
1994	42	0	67.0	3.36	48	31	67	3	2	2
Career	370	264	1821.1	3.69	1489	806	1529	81	115	6
Projected	46	2	73.0	3.18	54	36	63	4	1	1

Alex Fernandez   No. 32/ P

Born: 8/13/69, Miami Beach, FL
Height: 6' 1"   **Weight:** 215
Bats: Right   **Throws:** Right
Opp. Batting Average: .250

Fernandez is currently the most reliable pitcher in Chicago. It's sometimes worrisome when a young hurler develops too quickly, but Fernandez has gone through an arduous learning process since joining the majors at twenty years of age. Fernandez threw three shutouts last season, tied for second most in the American League.

	G	GS	IP	ERA	H	BB	SO	W	L	SV
1994	24	24	170.1	3.86	163	50	122	11	7	0
Career	132	132	884.2	3.88	858	289	592	51	45	0
Projected	33	33	237.0	3.43	218	67	166	16	9	0

Julio Franco   No. 14/ DH

Born: 8/23/61, San Pedro Macoris, DR
Height: 6' 1"   **Weight:** 188
Bats: Right   **Throws:** Right
1994 OBP: .406   **SLG:** .510

It was a remarkable season for the veteran Franco, who drove in the fifth most runs in the AL. Knee problems had threatened his career, but his hitting stroke hasn't suffered at all. Franco has a very quick bat; he can turn around any fastball thrown. He's especially focused in the clutch. Franco is a championship ballplayer and a great signing by the Chisox.

	G	AB	H	2B	3B	HR	RS	RBI	BB	SB	BA
1994	112	433	138	19	2	20	72	98	62	8	.319
Career	1658	6381	1922	299	45	120	964	861	623	237	.301
Projected	152	562	163	29	3	19	90	104	71	10	.297

Ozzie Guillen   No. 13/ SS

Born: 1/20/64, Oculare Tuy, Venezuela
Height: 5' 11"   **Weight:** 164
Bats: Left   **Throws:** Right
1994 OBP: .311   **SLG:** .348

Guillen's value to the Chisox is like oxygen; it isn't easy to measure, but there's no denying its importance. Knee surgery has sapped his basestealing abilities, and he's never been an effective hitter because his batting average represents 90% of his contribution with the bat. But Guillen is still a fine defensive shortstop and the motivational leader of the team.

	G	AB	H	2B	3B	HR	RS	RBI	BB	SB	BA
1994	100	365	105	9	5	1	46	39	14	5	.288
Career	1329	4663	1254	175	51	15	522	427	148	146	.269
Projected	144	511	148	20	6	3	56	56	15	6	.286

Roberto Hernandez No. 39/ P

Born: 11/11/64, Santurce, PR
Height: 6' 4"   **Weight:** 235
Bats: Right   **Throws:** Right
Opp. Batting Average .238

What happened? Hernandez had been consistently unreachable in 1993, relying on a Lee Smith–type fastball, but last year he got rocked on a regular basis. Hernandez didn't lose velocity; if anything, he was throwing harder in '94 than in the year before. But his control wasn't as sharp, and that's the key. No pitcher can be effective when he's behind in the count.

	G	GS	IP	ERA	H	BB	SO	W	L	SV
1994	45	0	47.2	4.91	44	19	50	4	4	14
Career	167	3	212.1	3.05	173	66	195	15	11	64
Projected	65	0	72.0	3.27	62	22	68	4	5	29

Darrin Jackson   No. 22/ OF

Born: 8/22/63, Los Angeles, CA
Height: 6' 0"   **Weight:** 185
Bats: Right   **Throws:** Right
1994 OBP: .362   **SLG:** .455

Jackson got lost in 1993 in a shuffle of trades. He also suffered a thyroid problem. But the White Sox picked him up and reaped the rewards. Jackson isn't a young prospect—he has been in the league since 1988—but he might be one of the rare players who has a career year after the age of thirty. He's an above-average left fielder.

	G	AB	H	2B	3B	HR	RS	RBI	BB	SB	BA
1994	104	369	115	17	3	10	43	51	27	7	.312
Career	698	2065	531	83	12	67	243	245	113	34	.257
Projected	160	564	155	23	3	14	56	69	33	6	.272

Lance Johnson   No. 1/ OF

Born: 7/6/63, Cincinnati, OH
Height: 5' 11"   **Weight:** 160
Bats: Left   **Throws:** Left
1994 OBP: .321   **SLG:** .393

Johnson has developed his talents into top-notch skills, making himself into a very valuable player. His great range in center field is the glue of the Chisox defense. He doesn't draw many walks, but Johnson is the most difficult player to strikeout in the AL. He excels as a base stealer—studying pitchers' moves and getting great jumps.

	G	AB	H	2B	3B	HR	RS	RBI	BB	SB	BA
1994	106	412	114	11	14	3	56	54	26	26	.277
Career	837	3011	845	90	66	7	389	277	182	192	.281
Projected	154	583	176	18	17	2	81	63	38	38	.299

Ron Karkovice   No. 20/ C

Born: 8/8/63, Union, NJ
Height: 6' 1"   **Weight:** 219
Bats: Right   **Throws:** Right
1994 OBP: .325   **SLG:** .425

Karkovice is an excellent defensive catcher who can hit for power. He waited on the Chicago bench through his prime years as Carlton Fisk held the starting job, but Karkovice has always been a quality player. His batting average will probably never see .240 again, but he'll smack some longballs and handle the pitching staff beautifully.

	G	AB	H	2B	3B	HR	RS	RBI	BB	SB	BA
1994	77	207	44	9	1	11	33	29	36	0	.213
Career	664	1781	401	81	5	67	238	228	159	22	.225
Projected	123	370	84	16	1	19	57	51	40	1	.225

Jack McDowell   No. 29/ P

Born: 1/16/66, Van Nuys, CA
Height: 6' 5"   **Weight:** 188
Bats: Right   **Throws:** Right
Opp. Batting Average: .266

McDowell is a fine pitcher who is in the unusual position of being hailed as his team's ace, while in reality he's arguably their fourth-best starter. McDowell throws a wicked split-finger fastball that is especially tough on lefties. He obviously knows how to win, but the Chisox were willing to deal him to the Yanks over the winter.

	G	GS	IP	ERA	H	BB	SO	W	L	SV
1994	25	25	181.0	3.73	186	42	127	10	9	0
Career	191	191	1343.2	3.50	1258	419	918	91	58	0
Projected	34	34	250.0	3.52	255	63	163	18	11	0

Tim Raines   No. 30/ OF

Born: 9/16/59, Sanford, FL
Height: 5' 8"   **Weight:** 186
Bats: Both   **Throws:** Right
1994 OBP: .365   **SLG:** .409

Tim Raines' 1994 batting average wasn't impressive, but he actually put together a fine season. His thirteen stolen bases came without one caught stealing, and his total of eighty runs just missed the league's top ten. Except for a slight decline due to age, "Rock" is essentially the same great player he has always been, getting on base and scoring runs.

	G	AB	H	2B	3B	HR	RS	RBI	BB	SB	BA
1994	101	384	102	15	5	10	80	52	61	13	.266
Career	1920	7264	2152	346	105	134	1293	762	1064	764	.296
Projected	135	490	135	19	5	16	93	64	75	20	.281

Robin Ventura   No. 23/ 3B

Born: 7/14/67, Santa Maria, CA
Height: 6' 1"   **Weight:** 198
Bats: Left   **Throws:** Right
1994 OBP: .373   **SLG:** .459

Ventura is one of the AL's most balanced hitters. He's at his most productive when driving hard liners to all fields, but he can turn on the power when needed. In the field, Ventura is known for his range, but he made twenty errors last season, second most in the league. The most prolific hitter in Oklahoma State University history, Ventura's best years are still to come.

	G	AB	H	2B	3B	HR	RS	RBI	BB	SB	BA
1994	109	401	113	15	1	18	57	78	61	3	.282
Career	746	2691	726	125	5	84	372	426	402	9	.271
Projected	158	592	173	27	1	26	92	111	107	3	.281

Cleveland
INDIANS

1995 Scouting Report

Outfielders: It all begins with franchise player Kenny Lofton in center field. The Indians can live with Albert Belle's flaws in right field because he's hugely productive at the plate. Manny Ramirez (LF) was the AL's second-best rookie. The Indians picked up Jeromy Burnitz from the Mets.

Infielders: The Tribe's cornermen aren't spectacular, but Jim Thome (3B) and Paul Sorrento (1B) are both capable of hitting twenty-five homers. Second base is nailed down by All-Star Carlos Baerga and his doubleplay partner, electrifying shortstop Omar Vizquel.

Catchers: Sandy Alomar may be ready to put together a season worthy of his prime-time talent, if he can remain healthy.

Starting Pitchers: The Indians' rotation is uncertain at best. Charles Nagy is the team's top hurler. They'll need for Nicaraguan national hero Dennis Martinez to stay sharp in his twentieth season. Mark Clark must show that he can repeat his impressive '94 winning percentage. Jason Grimsley and Albie Lopez are question marks.

Relief Pitchers: Jeff Russell was acquired from Boston to be the closer, a job he's qualified for when his mind is set. Middle relief is the job of rubber-armed Jose Mesa, underrated Eric Plunk.

Designated Hitters: Eddie Murray continues adding to his Hall of Fame credentials.

Manager: Former Tribe first baseman Mike Hargrove (250–272) enters his fourth full season as the Indians' manager.

1995 Outlook

The Indians inaugurated Jacobs Field with the franchise's highest winning percentage since 1955, good for second place in the competitive AL Central. The fans in Cleveland were rockin' by Lake Erie. The club was assured of setting a new attendance record if not for the strike. The Tribe did it with moderately effective starting pitching and a ton of offensive firepower.

The Indians were the AL's longball kings in '94, and the power thread ran throughout the lineup. Eight of the team's nine regulars finished with double-figure homer totals. The slugfest's primary instigator was awesome Albert Belle, who hit more than a third as many homers as the entire Milwaukee Brewers team. Most members of the Indians batting order are in their prime. Plus, last year's rookie sensation Manny Ramirez figures to increase his production as a sophomore. Cleveland can expect even more round-trippers in '95.

The Indians have structured their lineup toward extremes, electing to build strength upon strength. It's an effective strategy. Indians hitters devoured righthanded pitching, going 52–28 against righties. Jim Thome and Sandy Alomar combined to smash thirty-two of their thirty-four homers against righties.

Cleveland's starting pitching isn't loaded with big names, but in the pitching-poor American League, their rotation is at least adequate. The Indians' starters completed more games than any other AL staff, led by Dennis Martinez's seven. Still, the Indians' arms aren't completely golden. Both the White Sox and the Royals, the Indians' chief competition, are better armed than the Tribe. "El Presidente" (Martinez) may be reaching the end of his term. Mark Clark will need to prove that he's as good as his '94 winning percentage (.786).

The Indians are for real, especially at the plate, but they'll need to develop more pitching and defense if they're going to make the playoffs. It should be an interesting season in Cleveland.

1995 Cleveland Indians Roster

Manager: Mike Hargrove
Coaches: Buddy Bell, Luis Isaac, Charlie Manuel, Dave Nelson,
Jeff Newman, Mark Wiley

No.	Pitchers	B	T	HT	WT	DOB	Birthplace
54	Clark, Mark	R	R	6–5	225	5/12/68	Bath, IL
27	Cook, Dennis	L	L	6–3	185	10/4/62	LaMarque, TX
—	Embree, Alan	L	L	6–2	190	1/23/70	Brush Prairie, WA
48	Grimsley, Jason	R	R	6–3	182	8/7/67	Cleveland, TX
—	Lopez, Albie	R	R	6–1	205	8/18/71	Mesa, AZ
32	Martinez, Dennis	R	R	6–1	180	5/14/55	Granada, Nicaragua
49	Mesa, Jose	R	R	6–3	225	5/22/66	Winter Park, FL
41	Nagy, Charles	L	R	6–3	200	5/5/67	Fairfield, CT
—	Ogea, Chad	R	R	6–2	200	11/9/70	Lake Charles, LA
38	Plunk, Eric	R	R	6–6	220	9/3/63	Wilmington, CA
—	Shuey, Paul	R	R	6–3	215	9/16/70	Raleigh, NC
—	Tavarez, Julian	R	R	6–2	165	5/22/73	Santiago, DR
	Catchers						
15	Alomar, Jr., Sandy	R	R	6–5	215	6/18/66	Salinas, PR
—	Levis, Jesse	L	R	5–9	180	4/14/68	Philadelphia, PA
—	Wrona, Rick	R	R	6–1	185	12/10/63	Tulsa, OK
	Infielders						
9	Baerga, Carlos	B	R	5–11	200	11/4/68	San Juan, PR
10	Espinoza, Alvaro	R	R	6–0	190	2/19/62	Valencia, Venezuela
—	Lewis, Mark	R	R	6–1	190	11/30/69	Hamilton, OH
33	Murray, Eddie	B	R	6–2	222	2/24/56	Los Angeles, CA
—	Perry, Herbert	R	R	6–2	210	9/15/69	Mayo, FL
11	Sorrento, Paul	L	R	6–2	220	11/17/65	Somerville, MA
25	Thome, Jim	L	R	6–4	220	8/27/70	Peoria, IL
13	Vizquel, Omar	B	R	5–9	165	4/24/67	Caracas, Venezuela
	Outfielders						
30	Amaro, Ruben	B	R	5–10	175	2/12/65	Philadelphia, PA
8	Belle, Albert	R	R	6–2	210	8/25/66	Shreveport, LA
—	Burnitz, Jeromy	L	R	6–0	190	4/15/69	Westminster, CA
35	Kirby, Wayne	L	R	5–10	185	1/22/64	Williamsburg, VA
7	Lofton, Kenny	L	L	6–0	180	5/31/67	East Chicago, IN
24	Ramirez, Manny	R	R	6–0	190	5/30/72	Santo Domingo, DR
—	Ramirez, Omar	R	R	5–9	170	9/2/70	Santiago, DR

1995 Schedule

April

S	M	T	W	T	F	S
						1
2 OAK	3 OAK	4 OAK	5	6	7 CAL	8 CAL
9 CAL	10	11 OAK	12 OAK	13	14 CAL	15 CAL
16 CAL	17	18	19	20	21 TEX	22 TEX
23 TEX	24 TEX	25 SEA	26 SEA	27	28 TEX	29 TEX
30 TEX						

May

S	M	T	W	T	F	S
	1 DET	2 DET	3 DET	4 MIN	5 MIN	6
7 MIN	8 KC	9 KC	10 KC	11	12 BAL	13 BAL
14 BAL	15	16 NY	17 NY	18 BOS	19 BOS	20 BOS
21 BOS	22 MIL	23 MIL	24 MIL	25	26 TOR	27 TOR
28 TOR	29 CHI	30 CHI	31 CHI			

June

S	M	T	W	T	F	S
				1 CHI	2 TOR	3 TOR
4 TOR	5 DET	6 DET	7 DET	8 MIL	9 MIL	10 MIL
11 DET	12 BAL	13 BAL	14 BAL	15	16 NY	17 NY
18 NY	19 BOS	20 BOS	21 BOS	22	23 CHI	24 CHI
25 CHI	26 KC	27 KC	28 KC	29 MIN	30 MIN	

July

S	M	T	W	T	F	S
						1 MIN
2 MIN	3	4 TEX	5 TEX	6 SEA	7 SEA	8 SEA
9 SEA	10	11 ★	12	13 OAK	14 OAK	15 OAK
16 OAK	17 CAL	18 CAL	19 TEX	20 TEX	21 OAK	22 OAK
23 OAK	24 CAL	25 CAL	26 CAL	27 SEA	28 SEA	29 SEA
30 SEA	31					

August

S	M	T	W	T	F	S
		1 MIN	2 MIN	3 MIN	4 CHI	5 CHI
6 CHI	7	8 BOS	9 BOS	10 NY	11 NY	12 NY
13 NY	14 BAL	15 BAL	16 BAL	17 MIL	18 MIL	19 MIL
20 MIL	21 TOR	22 TOR	23 TOR	24	25 DET	26 DET
27 DET	28 TOR	29 TOR	30 TOR	31 TOR		

Sept/Oct

S	M	T	W	T	F	S
					1 DET	2 DET
3 DET	4 DET	5 MIL	6 MIL	7	8 BAL	9 BAL
10 BAL	11 NY	12 NY	13 NY	14	15 BOS	16 BOS
17 BOS	18 CHI	19 CHI	20 CHI	21	22 KC	23 KC
24 KC	25 KC	26 MIN	27 MIN	28 MIN	29 KC	30 KC
1 KC	2					

☐ Home   ☐ Away   ★ All-Star Game

Jacobs Field

Capacity: 42,400

Turf: Grass

Dimensions:
LF Line: 325'
RF Line: 325'
Center: 405'
Left CF: 370'
Right CF: 375'

Tickets:
(216) 241-8888

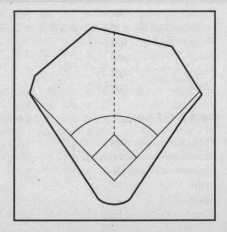

1994 Batting Order

1. Kenny Lofton (Center Field)
2. Omar Vizquel (Shortstop)
3. Carlos Baerga (Second Base)
4. Jim Thome (Third Base)
5. Albert Belle (Left Field)
6. Eddie Murray (Designated Hitter)
7. Manny Ramirez (Right Field)
8. Paul Sorrento (First Base)
9. Sandy Alomar, Jr. (Catcher)

1994 Team Record
66–47 (.584); Second in AL Central

AL East	W	L	AL Central	W	L	AL West	W	L
Baltimore	6	4	Chicago	5	7	California	5	0
Boston	7	3	Cleveland	—	—	Oakland	6	0
Detroit	8	2	Kansas City	1	4	Seattle	3	2
New York	0	9	Milwaukee	5	2	Texas	5	7
Toronto	6	4	Minnesota	9	3			
Total	27	22		20	16		19	9

1994 American League Team Rank Batting

Batting Average: Second (.290)
Runs Scored: First (679)
Runs Batted In: First (647)
Stolen Bases: Second (131)
Slugging Percentage: First (.484)
On-Base Percentage: Fifth (.351)

1994 American League Team Rank Pitching

Earned Run Average: Fifth (4.36)
Bases On Balls: Seventh (404)
Strikeouts: Ninth (666)
Wins: Third (66)
Saves: Tenth (21)
Complete Games: First (17)

Cleveland Indians MVP

Kenny Lofton   No. 7/ OF

Born: 5/31/67, East Chicago, IN
Height: 6' 0"   **Weight:** 180
Bats: Left   **Throws:** Left
1994 OBP: .412   **SLG:** .536

A complete offensive force, Lofton's value to the Indians can't be overstated. His numbers, though impressive, aren't as gaudy as those of teammate Albert Belle. But Lofton is the key that starts the Indians' engine, and they wouldn't be division contenders without him.

Acquired by the Tribe in 1991 in a lopsided exchange with Houston (the Astros received Willie Blair and Eddie Taubensee), Lofton has quickly become the premier leadoff man in the American League, following in Rickey Henderson's formidable footsteps. Last year saw a dramatic rise in longball prowess for Lofton, to go with his tremendous speed. If he can hit twenty homers a year, he'll be one of the majors' top three power/speed men. He's led the big leagues in steals over the past three years with 196. Lofton is anything but a one-dimensional sprinter. He ranked in the AL's top ten in eleven offensive categories, including batting average, on-base percentage, doubles, triples, extra-base hits, total bases, and runs scored. Lofton hit .322 with runners in scoring position.

Lofton is a Gold Glove centerfielder. His range, of course, is phenomenal, and so is his arm—he tied for the league lead with thirteen outfield assists, while committing just two miscues in 291 total chances. As spectacular as Lofton is on offense, his glovework makes him doubly valuable.

	G	AB	H	2B	3B	HR	RS	RBI	BB	SB	BA
1994	112	459	160	32	9	12	105	57	52	60	.349
Career	428	1678	524	76	25	18	326	141	206	198	.312
Projected	154	633	230	38	11	13	142	63	85	83	.349

Sandy Alomar, Jr.   No.15/ C

Born: 6/18/66, Salinas, PR
Height: 6' 5"   **Weight:** 215
Bats: Right   **Throws:** Right
1994 OBP: .347   **SLG:** .490

Alomar's progress has been stunted by injuries, but '94 was his best season so far. He had the second-best fielding percentage among AL backstops (.996), and tossed out 35% of would-be basestealers. Alomar finally generated longball power in proportion to his potential, due to a stance adjustment, and he could hit twenty homers this season.

	G	AB	H	2B	3B	HR	RS	RBI	BB	SB	BA
1994	80	292	84	15	1	14	44	43	25	8	.288
Career	424	1455	390	74	4	32	161	180	85	18	.268
Projected	123	451	137	20	2	18	63	69	33	10	.291

Carlos Baerga   No. 9/ 2B

Born: 11/4/68, San Juan, PR
Height: 5' 11"   **Weight:** 200
Bats: Both   **Throws:** Right
1994 OBP: .333   **SLG:** .525

Baerga made the AL's top ten in multi-hit games, total bases, hits, doubles, and extra-base hits. He turned on the juice after the All-Star break, hitting .346 with fifteen RBIs in twenty games. He led AL second basemen in total chances, but he made fifteen errors for a .973 percentage. He's not patient at the plate, but he makes plenty of intelligent situational adjustments.

	G	AB	H	2B	3B	HR	RS	RBI	BB	SB	BA
1994	103	442	139	32	2	19	81	80	10	8	.314
Career	685	2628	796	137	13	75	404	415	143	36	.303
Projected	156	674	232	39	5	26	122	128	29	15	.331

Albert Belle   No. 8/ OF

Born: 8/25/66, Shreveport, LA
Height: 6' 2"   **Weight:** 210
Bats: Right   **Throws:** Right
1994 OBP: .438   **SLG:** .714

Belle served a seven-game suspension for "suspicion of using a corked bat," but loaded bat or no, Belle is a devastating power hitter. Following the suspension, Belle uncorked ten big-flies in Cleveland's final twenty games. He finished in the AL's top three in ten offensive categories. Belle is one of the league's least adept outfielders, making six errors in only 219 chances.

	G	AB	H	2B	3B	HR	RS	RBI	BB	SB	BA
1994	106	412	147	35	2	36	90	101	58	9	.357
Career	612	2293	654	133	12	144	347	477	224	45	.286
Projected	160	630	216	46	3	48	119	150	87	21	.330

Mark Clark   No. 54/ P

Born: 5/12/68, Bath, IL
Height: 6' 5"   **Weight:** 225
Bats: Right   **Throws:** Right
Opp. Batting Average: .273

A change in mechanics gave Clark new confidence and helped him to a .786 winning percentage, fourth in the league. In May he threw three consecutive complete-game victories at home. A broken wrist ended his season on July 21. Clark isn't ace material, but he's young and will make a solid third or fourth starter on a contending team.

	G	GS	IP	ERA	H	BB	SO	W	L	SV
1994	20	20	127.1	3.82	133	40	60	11	3	0
Career	73	57	372.1	4.16	386	112	174	22	19	0
Projected	26	20	135.0	4.04	144	37	67	10	5	0

Derek Lilliquist No. 28/ P

Born: 2/20/66, Winter Park, FL
Height: 5' 10" **Weight:** 195
Bats: Left **Throws:** Left
Opp. Batting Average: .304

A difficult challenge for lefty hitters, Lilly held lefthanders to a combined .205 BA. Lilliquist is a finesse pitcher with a great amount of savvy. He wasn't as effective last season as he was in the past two, but he's a quality lefty setup man. The Indians placed Lilliquist on waivers during the off-season, and the Atlanta Braves picked him up.

	G	GS	IP	ERA	H	BB	SO	W	L	SV
1994	36	0	29.1	4.91	34	8	15	1	3	1
Career	229	52	457.0	4.00	500	125	251	23	33	17
Projected	52	1	53.0	3.10	55	15	31	3	4	6

Dennis Martinez No. 32/ P

Born: 5/14/55, Granada, Nicaragua
Height: 6' 1" **Weight:** 180
Bats: Right **Throws:** Right
Opp. Batting Average: .247

Martinez is a workhorse (fourth in the AL in innings pitched), a wily veteran, and master of a legendary curveball. Unlike most who rely on the curve, Martinez isn't vulnerable to the home run; he gave up just .71 homers per nine innings pitched, fifth best in the league. Martinez's stuff is still excellent, and he seems to have a tireless arm.

	G	GS	IP	ERA	H	BB	SO	W	L	SV
1994	24	24	176.2	3.52	166	44	92	11	6	0
Career	582	490	3561.0	3.63	3427	1034	1923	219	171	6
Projected	34	33	228.0	3.70	214	61	131	15	9	0

Jose Mesa   No. 49/ P

Born: 5/22/66, Winter Park, FL
Height: 6' 3"   **Weight:** 225
Bats: Right   **Throws:** Right
Opp. Batting Average: .254

Mesa had been a poor starting pitcher for his entire career prior to '94, but the Tribe used him strictly in relief last season, and he gave them a serviceable performance. From June 13 through July 9, Mesa's ERA was 1.02. He throws hard, and his arm is very resilient. He'll never be a star, but the Indians believe he can contribute if used wisely.

	G	GS	IP	ERA	H	BB	SO	W	L	SV
1994	51	0	73.0	3.82	71	26	63	7	5	2
Career	149	95	644.0	4.89	698	262	348	34	45	2
Projected	51	20	169.0	4.64	182	53	109	10	10	1

Eddie Murray   No. 33/ DH

Born: 2/24/56, Los Angeles, CA
Height: 6' 2"   **Weight:** 222
Bats: Both   **Throws:** Right
1994 OBP: .302   **SLG:** .425

Murray has driven in at least seventy-five RBIs for every season of his eighteen-year career, and he's played more games at first base than anyone in history. Though he has to slow down eventually, Murray's genius for hitting just increases with age. He ranks twentieth in history in games played and twenty-seventh in doubles. He'll attain hit number 3,000 in 1995.

	G	AB	H	2B	3B	HR	RS	RBI	BB	SB	BA
1994	108	433	110	21	1	17	57	76	31	8	.254
Career	2706	10167	2930	511	34	458	1477	1738	1218	100	.288
Projected	157	613	160	28	1	25	77	101	41	6	.267

Charles Nagy   No. 41/ P

Born: 5/5/67, Fairfield, CT
Height: 6' 3"   **Weight:** 200
Bats: Left   **Throws:** Right
Opp. Batting Average: .265

Nagy rebounded from an injury-marred '93 to pitch very well last season. Nagy throws a lot of innings (ninth most in the AL in '94), and he induces a ton of groundballs (fourth highest percentage in the league). The Indians gave Nagy great run support (9.0 RPG) in his wins, but abysmal support (2.6 RPG) in his losses. He could take a giant step forward this season.

	G	GS	IP	ERA	H	BB	SO	W	L	SV
1994	23	23	169.1	3.45	175	48	108	10	8	0
Career	107	106	727.0	3.83	772	205	442	41	43	0
Projected	20	20	135.0	4.10	149	38	86	7	9	0

Manny Ramirez   No. 24/ OF

Born: 5/30/72, Santo Domingo, DR
Height: 6' 0"   **Weight:** 190
Bats: Right   **Throws:** Right
1994 OBP: .357   **SLG:** .521

A pure hitter, Ramirez fulfilled his billing as a top prospect. Despite a six-for-fifty-two skid in May, he finished second among AL rookies in almost all categories. Not a particularly skilled out-fielder, Ramirez is still learning the fine points of major league play, but his upward potential is excellent. His power numbers in particular are likely to increase in '95.

	G	AB	H	2B	3B	HR	RS	RBI	BB	SB	BA
1994	91	290	78	22	0	17	51	60	42	4	.269
Career	113	343	87	23	0	19	56	65	36	0	.254
Projected	140	446	125	31	0	26	76	89	60	5	.266

Jeff Russell   No. 40/ P

Born: 9/2/61, Cincinnati, OH
Height: 6' 3"   **Weight:** 210
Bats: Right   **Throws:** Right
Opp. Batting Average: .265

Watching the movement on Russell's fastball, it's hard to understand why he's so inconsistent. The explanation rests partially in his tendency to lose focus because of non-game distractions. Russell is still capable of being dominant, but it's anyone's guess as to whether he can ever again sustain it for a full season. He was tenth in the AL in save percentage (.739).

	G	GS	IP	ERA	H	BB	SO	W	L	SV
1994	42	0	40.2	4.97	43	16	28	1	6	17
Career	497	79	1011.0	3.79	971	391	629	52	70	163
Projected	54	0	51.0	3.82	47	17	42	1	6	29

Paul Sorrento   No. 11/ 1B

Born: 11/17/65, Somerville, MA
Height: 6' 2"   **Weight:** 220
Bats: Left   **Throws:** Right
1994 OBP: .345   **SLG:** .453

Sorrento's game isn't star quality, but that's not to say he doesn't contribute. He's got a fine work ethic and has improved his glovework immensely (.995 fielding percentage). He's got good opposite-field power, and his '94 batting average was the highest of his career. Sorrento had more RBIs versus southpaws last year than in all his previous seasons combined.

	G	AB	H	2B	3B	HR	RS	RBI	BB	SB	BA
1994	95	322	90	14	0	14	43	62	34	0	.280
Career	464	1432	374	70	3	59	189	514	164	4	.261
Projected	147	494	142	26	1	21	77	83	60	2	.277

Jim Thome   No. 25/ 3B

Born: 8/27/70, Peoria, IL
Height: 6' 4"   **Weight:** 220
Bats: Left   **Throws:** Right
1994 OBP: .359   **SLG:** .523

Thome was a thirteenth-round selection in '89. He led all AL third basemen in home runs in '94, including a three-HR performance versus Chicago on July 22. Thome can't hit lefties; he hit .167 against them with two HRs in eighty-four at-bats, and he may have to be platooned. He's currently one of the AL's worst-fielding third basemen.

	G	AB	H	2B	3B	HR	RS	RBI	BB	SB	BA
1994	98	321	86	20	1	20	58	52	46	3	.268
Career	212	690	176	38	4	30	101	95	90	8	.255
Projected	151	519	153	36	1	31	99	85	86	6	.281

Omar Vizquel   No. 13/ SS

Born: 4/24/67, Caracas, Venezuela
Height: 5' 9"   **Weight:** 165
Bats: Both   **Throws:** Right
1994 OBP: .325   **SLG:** .325

Vizquel missed more than a month with a knee injury, but he played well when healthy. His .982 fielding percentage was third among AL shortstops. Vizquel has no power, but he puts the ball in play and hits in the clutch (.369 BA with runners in scoring position). Vizquel, like most Tribe hitters, fares far better versus righthanders than lefties.

	G	AB	H	2B	3B	HR	RS	RBI	BB	SB	BA
1994	69	286	78	10	1	1	39	33	23	13	.273
Career	729	2397	609	70	16	7	262	164	196	52	.254
Projected	106	411	116	12	2	2	54	32	37	13	.272

Detroit
TIGERS

1995 Scouting Report

Outfielders: The Tigers' outfield is a question mark for 1995. Junior Felix made the team as a non-roster invitee, then put together a decent season as the starting right fielder. Versatile leadoff man Tony Phillips slugged a career high in homers at the age of thirty-five. Oft-injured Eric Davis started the year in center field, but Milt Cuyler took over in late July.

Infielders: The corners are set with All-Stars Cecil Fielder (1B) and Travis Fryman (3B). Lou Whitaker will go to the Hall of Fame, but for now he's patrolling second base. Chris Gomez should see more time at shortstop this year, with the infield's other all-time All-Star, Alan Trammell, possibly leaving Detroit.

Catchers: Mickey Tettleton is consistently explosive with the bat. Chad Kreuter subs when Tettleton plays DH.

Starting Pitchers: Fans in Detroit roll their eyes at the mention of the words "quality start." The Tigers don't have one reliable starter, much less an ace. Mike Moore led the team in wins, but his ERA was 5.42. David Wells managed to keep his ERA under 4.00 after returning from elbow surgery. Veteran hurlers Bill Gullickson and Tim Belcher have both seen their best days. Second-year pitcher John Doherty's 6.48 ERA was a disappointment.

Relief Pitchers: The bullpen is even shakier than the starting rotation, with veteran ace Mike Henneman's career winding down. Gene Harris could help in '95.

Designated Hitters: Kirk Gibson continues to produce strong numbers at age thirty-seven.

Manager: Sparky Anderson (2134–1835) is fourth on the all-time wins list. He's always been popular with his players.

1995 Outlook

Why does this happen? The Tigers are a bad ballclub, and the future isn't bright. The best player their minor league system has produced in a long time, Rico Brogna, looked great in a Mets uniform last season after the Tigers traded him. They haven't developed quality prospects, in part due to the illusive attraction of past-prime veterans—it's too easy for an organization to get comfortable with the idea that it only has to sign an expensive free agent to shore up its weaknesses.

The Tigers have some powerful hitters in their lineup, which makes sense for a team that plays in a hitters' nirvana like Tiger Stadium. Their batting order is packed with heavy hitters such as Kirk Gibson, Mickey Tettleton (who claims to be 100% Froot Loops fueled), and the state of the art in slow-footed sluggers, Cecil Fielder. Detroit can score runs in a hurry, and there aren't many pitching duels at Tiger Stadium. But the lineup is baseball's oldest by far, so a decline is almost certain. Still, the Tigers averaged 5.67 runs per contest, enough to win 100 games with a good pitching staff.

Unfortunately, Tiger pitching is an oxymoron. It's a staff built on no strengths. There isn't a quality arm in the rotation, which is also the oldest in the majors, the bullpen is both thin and ineffective, and there are virtually no prospects. The organization desperately needs a hard-throwing young hurler—if Jack Morris were still in Detroit, he would have led the team in strikeouts last year at the age of thirty-nine.

It's a dismal situation for fans in the Motor City, who are some of baseball's most loyal. The Tigers are the lone American League club to draw over a million fans for thirty consecutive seasons, a remarkable tribute to Tigers rooters.

At least the team isn't dull. There are some big names in Detroit, and the potential for an over-the-roof shot exists in nearly every inning. But there won't be a contender at Tiger Stadium in 1995, or in 1996 for that matter.

1995 Detroit Tigers Roster

Manager: Sparky Anderson
Coaches: Billy Consolo, Larry Herndon, Jeff Jones, Gene Roof,
Dick Tracewski, Ralph Treuel

No.	Pitchers	B	T	HT	WT	DOB	Birthplace
—	Bergman, Sean	R	R	6–4	205	4/11/70	Joliet, IL
—	Boever, Joe	R	R	6–1	200	10/4/60	St. Louis, MO
49	Bolton, Tom	L	L	6–3	185	5/6/62	Nashville, TN
15	Davis, Storm	R	R	6–4	225	12/26/61	Dallas, TX
44	Doherty, John	R	R	6–4	210	6/11/67	Bronx, NY
—	Gardiner, Michael	B	R	6–0	200	10/19/65	Sarnia, Canada
34	Gohr, Greg	R	R	6–3	205	10/29/67	Santa Clara, CA
42	Groom, Buddy	L	L	6–2	200	7/10/65	Dallas, TX
36	Gullickson, Bill	R	R	6–3	225	2/20/59	Marshall, MN
33	Harris, Gene	R	R	5–11	190	12/5/64	Sebring, FL
39	Henneman, Mike	R	R	6–4	205	12/11/61	St. Charles, MO
27	Knudsen, Kurt	R	R	6–3	200	2/20/67	Arlington Hts., IL
21	Moore, Mike	R	R	6–4	205	11/26/59	Early, OK
16	Wells, David	L	L	6–4	225	5/20/63	Torrance, CA
	Catchers						
—	Flaherty, John	R	R	6–1	195	10/21/67	New York, NY
19	Kreuter, Chad	R	R	6–2	195	8/26/64	Greenbrae, CA
12	Rowland, Rich	R	R	6–1	215	2/25/67	Cloverdale, CA
20	Tettleton, Mickey	B	R	6–2	212	9/16/60	Oklahoma City, OK
	Infielders						
9	Barnes, Skeeter	R	R	5–10	180	3/7/57	Cincinnati, OH
45	Fielder, Cecil	R	R	6–3	250	9/21/63	Los Angeles, CA
24	Fryman, Travis	R	R	6–1	194	3/25/69	Lexington, KY
35	Gomez, Chris	R	R	6–1	183	6/16/71	Los Angeles, CA
7	Livingstone, Scott	L	R	6–0	198	7/15/65	Dallas, TX
3	Trammell, Alan	R	R	6–0	185	2/21/58	Garden Grove, CA
1	Whitaker, Lou	L	R	5–11	180	5/12/57	New York, NY
	Outfielders						
29	Bautista, Danny	R	R	5–11	170	5/24/72	Santo Domingo, DR
22	Cuyler, Milt	B	R	5–10	185	10/7/68	Macon, GA
33	Davis, Eric	R	R	6–3	185	5/29/62	Los Angeles, CA
49	Felix, Junior	B	R	6–0	170	10/3/67	Laguna Salada, DR
25	Hare, Shawn	L	L	6–1	200	3/26/67	St. Louis, MO
23	Gibson, Kirk	L	L	6–3	215	5/28/57	Pontiac, MI
4	Phillips, Tony	B	R	5–10	175	4/25/59	Atlanta, GA

1995 Schedule

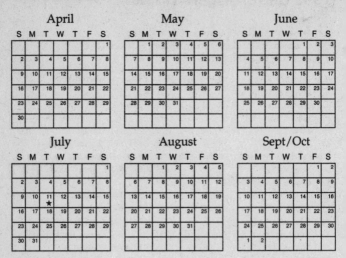

April

S	M	T	W	T	F	S
						1
2	3	4	5	6	7	8
9	10	11	12	13	14	15
16	17	18	19	20	21	22
23	24	25	26	27	28	29
30						

May

S	M	T	W	T	F	S
	1	2	3	4	5	6
7	8	9	10	11	12	13
14	15	16	17	18	19	20
21	22	23	24	25	26	27
28	29	30	31			

June

S	M	T	W	T	F	S
				1	2	3
4	5	6	7	8	9	10
11	12	13	14	15	16	17
18	19	20	21	22	23	24
25	26	27	28	29	30	

July

S	M	T	W	T	F	S
						1
2	3	4	5	6	7	8
9	10	11★	12	13	14	15
16	17	18	19	20	21	22
23	24	25	26	27	28	29
30	31					

August

S	M	T	W	T	F	S
		1	2	3	4	5
6	7	8	9	10	11	12
13	14	15	16	17	18	19
20	21	22	23	24	25	26
27	28	29	30	31		

Sept/Oct

S	M	T	W	T	F	S
					1	2
3	4	5	6	7	8	9
10	11	12	13	14	15	16
17	18	19	20	21	22	23
24	25	26	27	28	29	30
1	2					

The Tigers were unable to provide a schedule by press time.

Tiger Stadium

Capacity: 52,416

Turf: Grass

Dimensions:
LF Line: 340'
RF Line: 325'
Center: 440'
Left CF: 365'
Right CF: 370'

Tickets:
(313) 962-4000

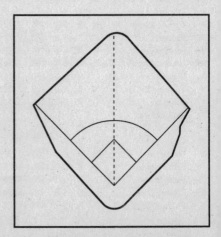

1994 Batting Order

1. Tony Phillips (Left Field)
2. Lou Whitaker (Second Base)
3. Travis Fryman (Third Base)
4. Cecil Fielder (First Base)
5. Kirk Gibson (Designated Hitter)
6. Mickey Tettleton (Catcher)
7. Junior Felix (Right Field)
8. Alan Trammell (Shortstop)
9. Milt Cuyler (Center Field)

1994 Team Record
53–62 (.461); Fifth in AL East

AL East	W	L	AL Central	W	L	AL West	W	L
Baltimore	4	3	Chicago	4	8	California	4	3
Boston	2	4	Cleveland	2	8	Oakland	5	4
Detroit	—	—	Kansas City	4	8	Seattle	6	3
New York	3	3	Milwaukee	6	4	Texas	5	7
Toronto	5	4	Minnesota	3	3			
Total	14	14		19	31		20	17

1994 American League Team Rank Batting

Batting Average: Tenth (.265)
Runs Scored: Third (652)
Runs Batted In: Third (622)
Stolen Bases: Fourteenth (46)
Slugging Percentage: Third (.454)
On-Base Percentage: Fourth (.352)

1994 American League Team Rank Pitching

Earned Run Average: Eleventh (5.38)
Bases On Balls: Tenth (449)
Strikeouts: Fourteenth (560)
Wins: Eighth (53)
Saves: Thirteenth (20)
Complete Games: Second (15)

Detroit Tigers MVP

Cecil Fielder   No. 45/ 1B

Born: 9/21/63, Los Angeles, CA
Height: 6' 3"   **Weight:** 250
Bats: Right   **Throws:** Right
1994 OBP: .337   **SLG:** .504

One of the majors' most recognizable stars, Fielder is an extremely large individual who gives enormous headaches to opposing pitchers. He uses his mass beautifully by making a perfectly timed forward weight shift that generates incredible bat speed. The result is power-plus—Fielder has clubbed 188 HRs since joining the Tigers in 1990.

When he entered the big leagues with Toronto in 1985, Fielder lost the Blue Jays first base job to a young slugger named Fred McGriff. Fielder responded by taking his bat to Japan in 1989, but he returned a year later to make life miserable for American League pitchers.

Fielder made the AL top ten in home runs and RBIs. His season highlights included an eleven-game hitting streak, two four-for-four outings, three multi-homer contests, and a game-winning homer in the bottom of the thirteenth inning on June 3 to beat Minnesota.

Fielder isn't a complete player—his fielding range is poor, and he makes too many errors at first base. It's a wonder he isn't a full-time DH by now. But he gets paid to hit, and few AL batters are as productive as Fielder. He also has that special quality, like the Twins' Kirby Puckett, of instant likability by the fans in every American League city.

	G	AB	H	2B	3B	HR	RS	RBI	BB	SB	BA
1994	109	425	110	16	2	28	67	90	50	0	.259
Career	959	3295	853	130	5	219	500	680	427	0	.259
Projected	157	602	162	24	1	35	90	126	85	0	.266

Tim Belcher   No. 41/ P

Born: 10/19/61, Mount Gilead, OH
Height: 6' 3"   **Weight:** 210
Bats: Right   **Throws:** Right
Opp. Batting Average: .290

Belcher made as many starts as any AL hurler last year, but his on-mound performance was inconsistent in the extreme. He lost his first seven decisions, proceeded to win seven of his next nine starts, then lost six to finish the campaign. Belcher has always relied on his outstanding fastball, and he was once one of the league's most dominant starters.

	G	GS	IP	ERA	H	BB	SO	W	L	SV
1994	25	25	162.0	5.89	192	78	76	7	15	0
Career	232	211	1404.1	3.69	1271	493	993	84	78	5
Projected	34	34	212.0	5.07	223	87	120	11	15	0

Eric Davis   No. 33/ OF

Born: 5/29/62, Los Angeles, CA
Height: 6' 3"   **Weight:** 185
Bats: Right   **Throws:** Right
1994 OBP: .290   **SLG:** .292

When a player enters the Show touted as the next Willie Mays, it's easy for him to end up branded a disappointment. Davis is built like a whippet, and his body has been his gift and his curse. In his finest moments, he's a stunning mixture of quick-wristed power and graceful speed. But injuries to Davis's fragile frame have chipped away the foundation of his career.

	G	AB	H	2B	3B	HR	RS	RBI	BB	SB	BA
1994	37	120	22	4	0	3	19	13	18	5	.183
Career	1100	3695	957	149	20	205	665	645	533	306	.259
Projected	57	190	41	7	0	7	29	26	24	13	.221

John Doherty   No. 44/ P

Born: 6/11/67, Bronx, NY
Height: 6' 4"   **Weight:** 210
Bats: Right   **Throws:** Right
Opp. Batting Average: .337

Strikeout ratio is one of the best indicators of a young pitcher's potential for longevity in the majors, and Doherty's rate of 2.49 Ks per nine innings is not a positive sign. He has shown flashes of ability, such as a 6–2 complete game victory versus Oakland on May 11. Doherty has precise control, and his sinking fastball induces a pile of grounders.

	G	GS	IP	ERA	H	BB	SO	W	L	SV
1994	18	17	101.1	6.48	139	26	28	6	7	0
Career	97	59	402.0	4.79	475	99	128	27	22	3
Projected	28	27	160.0	5.17	193	41	51	11	10	0

Junior Felix   No. 49/ OF

Born: 10/3/67, Laguna Salada, DR
Height: 6' 0"   **Weight:** 170
Bats: Both   **Throws:** Right
1994 OBP: .372   **SLG:** .525

Perhaps it had something to do with the league's expansion, but whatever the reason, 1994 featured some surprising career-revivals. Felix seemed to be on his way out of baseball for good, but he came to Detroit as a non-roster invitee and flourished at Tiger Stadium. He socked all thirteen of his homers in a short span between May 26 and July 8.

	G	AB	H	2B	3B	HR	RS	RBI	BB	SB	BA
1994	86	301	92	25	1	13	54	49	26	1	.306
Career	585	2132	562	105	24	55	309	280	158	49	.264
Projected	132	496	149	36	2	20	79	71	36	3	.289

Travis Fryman   No. 24/ 3B

Born: 3/25/69, Lexington, KY
Height: 6' 1"   **Weight:** 194
Bats: Right   **Throws:** Right
1994 OBP: .326   **SLG:** .474

A legitimate superstar, Fryman is the only Tiger currently in his prime. He was fourth in the AL with fifty-seven extra-base hits, and he's put together four straight seasons with at least thirty doubles. Fryman gathers whiffs like a slugger, but he's not a wild swinger, and he often sustains blazing hot streaks. He'll be the Tigers' third baseman for years to come.

	G	AB	H	2B	3B	HR	RS	RBI	BB	SB	BA
1994	114	464	122	34	5	18	66	85	45	2	.263
Career	641	2519	692	149	18	90	348	396	224	34	.275
Projected	156	654	201	45	6	25	104	116	77	7	.295

Kirk Gibson   No. 23/ DH

Born: 5/28/57, Pontiac, MI
Height: 6' 3"   **Weight:** 215
Bats: Left   **Throws:** Left
1994 OBP: .358   **SLG:** .548

Too bad he retired in mid-1992. Too bad for AL hurlers he didn't stay that way. Gibson's second baseball life has been nothing short of astonishing. He had the eighth-highest slugging percentage in the American League. He had six RBIs against Kansas City on April 19. He cleared the right field roof for the third time in his career. Gibson has become a baseball treasure at age thirty-seven.

	G	AB	H	2B	3B	HR	RS	RBI	BB	SB	BA
1994	98	330	91	17	2	23	71	72	42	4	.276
Career	1565	5571	1494	248	52	246	948	835	685	275	.268
Projected	133	448	115	21	5	22	80	80	51	11	.262

Chris Gomez   No. 35/ SS

Born: 6/16/71, Los Angeles, CA
Height: 6' 1"   **Weight:** 183
Bats: Right   **Throws:** Right
1994 OBP: .336   **SLG:** .402

Gomez should take over full-time duty from
the legendary Alan Trammell. Gomez is an
accomplished fielder, and his '94 offensive
production was excellent; he drove in a run every 5.6 at-bats.
Twenty-seven of his seventy-six hits went for extra bases.
Gomez is an exciting young player, and the Tigers will be thrilled
if he's the next Jay Bell.

	G	AB	H	2B	3B	HR	RS	RBI	BB	SB	BA
1994	84	285	78	20	0	15	46	56	41	0	.274
Career	130	424	108	26	1	8	43	64	42	7	.255
Projected	84	285	78	20	0	15	46	56	41	0	.274

Gene Harris   No. 38/ P

Born: 12/5/64, Sebring, FL
Height: 5' 11"   **Weight:** 190
Bats: Right   **Throws:** Right
Opp. Batting Average: .271

Detroit was bitten by hard luck when newly
acquired reliever Harris spent two months
on the DL with a sore elbow. Harris has an
exceptional slider and a hard fastball, and there's an outside
chance that he could develop into a closer. Harris is usually
very stingy about giving up the longball. If his strikeouts-to-walks
ratio is strong, and his arm is healthy, he's a dark horse.

	G	GS	IP	ERA	H	BB	SO	W	L	SV
1994	24	0	23.2	7.15	34	12	19	1	1	1
Career	159	7	218.0	4.75	223	129	157	10	16	26
Projected	46	0	46.0	4.32	50	27	32	4	4	13

Mike Henneman   No. 39/ P

Born: 12/11/61, St. Charles, MO
Height: 6' 4"   **Weight:** 205
Bats: Right   **Throws:** Right
Opp. Batting Average: .297

Henneman is the Tigers' all-time saves champion and a classy individual, but '94 was his most frustrating season. His rates of hits allowed and homers were up, and scouts say his velocity slipped as the season wore on. Detroit has never used him as a one-inning, go-to stopper, but 1994's eight saves matched his career low for a season.

	G	GS	IP	ERA	H	BB	SO	W	L	SV
1994	30	0	35	5.19	43	17	27	1	3	8
Career	462	0	640.1	3.12	600	241	456	57	33	136
Projected	52	0	59	3.46	62	27	47	3	3	18

Mike Moore   No. 21/ P

Born: 11/26/59, Early, OK
Height: 6' 4"   **Weight:** 205
Bats: Right   **Throws:** Right
Opp. Batting Average: .263

If only the Tigers' starting staff were in its prime, the aces would abound. Moore has been a consistent winner, and last year he led the Tigers in victories. But his ERA was the highest of his career, and he relinquished home runs at an alarming rate. Moore allowed the most walks in the AL, and scouts say inconsistent mechanics were to blame.

	G	GS	IP	ERA	H	BB	SO	W	L	SV
1994	25	25	154.1	5.42	152	89	62	11	10	0
Career	425	415	2699.0	4.23	2679	1088	1603	156	161	2
Projected	35	35	209.0	5.31	215	101	86	14	11	0

Tony Phillips　　No. 4/ OF

Born: 4/25/59, Atlanta, GA
Height: 5' 10"　　**Weight:** 175
Bats: Both　　**Throws:** Right
1994 OBP: .409　　**SLG:** .468

An amazing player, Phillips was having arguably his best season before the work stoppage. He's a super leadoff man—drawing walks, stealing successfully, and last year adding the third-best home run total in the slugging Tigers' lineup. Phillips has completely reinvented himself since his days as a utility player. He's one of the three best leadoff hitters in the AL.

	G	AB	H	2B	3B	HR	RS	RBI	BB	SB	BA
1994	114	438	123	19	3	19	91	61	95	13	.281
Career	1557	5335	1420	236	40	94	856	568	861	126	.266
Projected	156	577	166	26	2	15	115	66	128	16	.293

Mickey Tettleton　　No. 20/ C

Born: 9/16/60, Oklahoma City, OK
Height: 6' 2"　　**Weight:** 212
Bats: Both　　**Throws:** Right
1994 OBP: .419　　**SLG:** .463

Last year Tettleton wasn't hitting his daily homer the way he did in '93, but he's essentially the same hitter, and he figures to be very consistent through the remainder of his career. Other than his ability to uncoil on a fastball, Tettleton's most prominent characteristic as a hitter is his propensity for drawing walks. He drew the second most in the AL in '94.

	G	AB	H	2B	3B	HR	RS	RBI	BB	SB	BA
1994	107	339	84	18	2	17	57	51	97	0	.248
Career	1191	3734	905	164	14	186	552	567	744	21	.242
Projected	156	508	120	25	3	28	79	93	119	2	.241

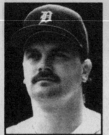

David Wells   No. 16/ P

Born: 5/20/63, Torrance, CA
Height: 6' 4"   **Weight:** 225
Bats: Left   **Throws:** Left
Opp. Batting Average: .260

Wells, the Tigers' top starter, had elbow surgery in April. It's not really clear that he isn't more effective as a reliever, but Detroit's weak rotation makes the question moot. Wells has fantastic control; he compiled a string of 156 batters faced without yielding a free pass. Wells's out-pitch is a vicious slider—he fanned eight Milwaukee batters in his last start of '94.

	G	GS	IP	ERA	H	BB	SO	W	L	SV
1994	16	16	111.1	3.96	113	24	71	5	7	0
Career	285	115	985.2	3.88	955	267	659	63	53	13
Projected	27	26	166.0	4.11	164	37	117	9	9	0

Lou Whitaker   No. 1/ 2B

Born: 5/12/57, New York, NY
Height: 5' 11"   **Weight:** 180
Bats: Left   **Throws:** Right
1994 OBP: .377   **SLG:** .491

Sweet Lou and Joe Morgan are the only second basemen in history with 2,000 games, 2,000 hits, and 200 home runs. Whitaker is one of the best athletes the game has ever seen, and he continues to post good numbers into his late thirties. He knocked in a career-high seven RBIs against Texas on May 4 and finished the year with a sixteen-game hitting streak.

	G	AB	H	2B	3B	HR	RS	RBI	BB	SB	BA
1994	92	322	97	21	2	12	67	43	41	2	.301
Career	2306	8320	2296	406	65	230	1350	1040	1166	139	.276
Projected	130	427	121	31	2	12	82	65	71	3	.289

Kansas City
ROYALS

1995 Scouting Report

Outfielders: Kauffman Stadium's expansive outfield demands that Royals outfielders possess great range. Felix Jose (RF), rookie Dwayne Hosey (LF), and Brian McRae (CF) all qualify. All three play strong defense and contribute decent run scoring abilities.

Infielders: The Royals have a pair of vacuum cleaners up the middle in Greg Gagne (SS) and Jose Lind (2B). Gagne drives in more runs than most of the league's other shortstops, while Lind chipped in some timely hits in '94. The corners are well defended by veterans Gary Gaetti (3B) and Wally Joyner (1B).

Catchers: Mike Macfarlane is the team's full-time backstop, but Brent Mayne is a capable backup. Macfarlane does most of his damage with the bat, while Mayne sported a .996 fielding percentage.

Starting Pitchers: The Royals organization has always been loaded with great starters. David Cone was in Cy Young form for '94, but Kevin Appier is the ace of the staff. Curveballer Tom Gordon is often brilliant, but generally inconsistent. The fourth and fifth spots will likely fall to veteran comeback-hopeful Jose DeJesus and rookie Brian Bevil.

Relief Pitchers: Billy Brewer is a prototype lefty setup man, while Jeff Montgomery is one of the game's top closers.

Designated Hitters: American League Rookie of the Year Bob Hamelin is the Royals number-one longball threat.

Manager: Former iron-man catcher Bob Boone will get his first taste of major league managing in 1995.

1995 Outlook

The Royals are confident that they can finish ahead of the pack in the AL Central's three-dog race, if only they can get out of the gate smoothly this season. A string of three straight years of bad starts has the team focused on April. Kansas City fell four games back in the 1994 season's first week, and finished four games out.

The Royals made month-by-month improvement, including eighteen wins in July. They put together a better record versus their division rivals (22–15) than against the East (21–20) or West (21–16), including an 11–4 mark when facing the Central's top two teams, Chicago and Cleveland. The Royals have reason for optimism in 1995.

Great pitching is a tradition in K.C., partly due to the home park, which is decidedly unfriendly to sluggers. The '94 staff ranked second in the league in ERA, but it was the worst mark for Royals pitching since 1983. The Royals welcomed David Cone back to where his career began, and he thanked them with a Cy Young season. He looked comfortable on the mound for the entire year, and he could be entering the best phase of his career. Kevin Appier looked anything but comfortable in the early going. He'll be looking to put together a complete season on the level of his '93 campaign (18–8; 2.56 ERA). Tom Gordon perennially seems to be on the verge of excellence.

The other half of the pitching-and-defense cliche was also a Royals strength, as the team went 91.1 innings July 9–22 without making an error. In total, the club played fifty-nine errorless games in '94. The Royals' fine fielding gives their pitchers confidence to throw strikes, which keeps big innings to a minimum. Down on the farm, the Royals system is baseball's best. Dwayne Hosey (not to be confused with the Brewers' Wayne Housie) hit .333 with twenty-seven homers at Triple-A Omaha and was named MVP of the American Association. If he can make an impact on the Royals' offense in '95, it could be the key ingredient to a recipe for first place.

1995 Kansas City Royals Roster

Manager: Bob Boone
Coaches: Jeff Cox, Bruce Kison, Greg Luzinski, Mitchell Page,
Jamie Quirk

No.	Pitchers	B	T	HT	WT	DOB	Birthplace
55	Appier, Kevin	R	R	6–2	200	12/6/67	Lancaster, CA
50	Belinda, Stan	R	R	6–3	187	8/6/66	Huntingdon, PA
—	Bevil, Brian	R	R	6–3	190	9/5/71	Houston, TX
29	Brewer, Billy	L	L	6–1	175	4/15/68	Ft. Worth, TX
—	Bunch, Melvin	R	R	6–1	165	11/4/71	Texarkana, TX
51	Burgos, Enrique	L	L	6–4	230	10/7/65	Chomera, Panama
17	Cone, David	L	R	6–1	190	1/2/63	Kansas City, MO
53	DeJesus, Jose	R	R	6–5	225	1/6/65	Brooklyn, NY
—	Evans, Bart	R	R	6–1	190	12/30/70	Springfield, MO
36	Gordon, Tom	R	R	5–9	180	11/18/67	Sebring, FL
27	Granger, Jeff	R	L	6–4	200	12/16/71	San Pedro, CA
33	Haney, Chris	L	L	6–3	185	11/16/68	Baltimore, MD
57	Magnante, Mike	L	L	6–1	180	6/17/65	Glendale, CA
28	Meacham, Rusty	R	R	6–2	165	1/27/68	Stuart, FL
21	Montgomery, Jeff	R	R	5–11	180	1/7/62	Wellston, OH
58	Pichardo, Hipolito	R	R	6–1	160	8/22/69	Esperanza, DR
	Catchers						
24	Mayne, Brent	L	R	6–1	190	4/19/68	Loma Linda, CA
66	Strickland, Chad	R	R	6–1	185	3/16/72	Oklahoma City, OK
	Infielders						
7	Gagne, Greg	R	R	5–11	175	11/12/61	Fall River, MA
63	Halter, Shane	R	R	5–10	160	11/8/69	LaPlata, MD
48	Hamelin, Bob	L	L	6–0	230	11/29/67	Elizabeth, NJ
6	Howard, David	B	R	6–0	165	2/26/67	Sarasota, FL
12	Joyner, Wally	L	L	6–2	205	6/16/62	Atlanta, GA
13	Lind, Jose	R	R	5–11	175	5/1/64	Toabaja, PR
65	Randa, Joe	R	R	5–11	190	12/18/69	Milwaukee, WI
3	Shumpert, Terry	R	R	5–11	190	8/16/66	Paducah, KY
67	Vitiello, Joe	R	R	6–2	215	4/11/70	Cambridge, MA
	Outfielders						
60	Burton, Darren	B	R	6–1	185	9/16/72	Somerset, KY
47	Goodwin, Tom	L	R	6–1	170	7/27/68	Fresno, CA
25	Hiatt, Phil	R	R	6–3	200	5/1/69	Pensacola, FL
52	Hosey, Dwayne	B	R	5–10	175	3/11/67	Sharon, PA
34	Jose, Felix	B	R	6–1	220	5/8/65	Santo Domingo, DR
40	Koslofski, Kevin	L	R	5–8	165	9/24/66	Decatur, IL
56	McRae, Brian	B	R	6–0	185	8/27/67	Bradenton, FL

1995 Schedule

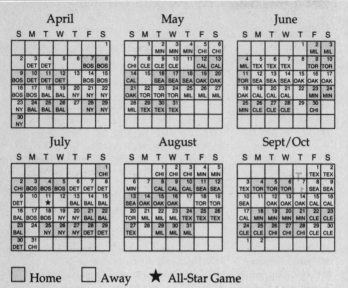

April

S	M	T	W	T	F	S
						1
2	3 DET	4 DET	5	6	7 BOS	8 BOS
9 BOS	10 DET	11 DET	12 DET	13	14 BOS	15 BOS
16 BOS	17 BOS	18 BAL	19 BAL	20 NY	21 NY	22 NY
23 NY	24 BAL	25 BAL	26 BAL	27	28 NY	29 NY
30 NY						

May

S	M	T	W	T	F	S
		1	2 MIN	3 MIN	4 MIN	5 CHI
						6 CHI
7 CHI	8 CLE	9 CLE	10 CLE	11	12 CAL	13 CAL
14 CAL	15	16 SEA	17 SEA	18 SEA	19 OAK	20 OAK
21 OAK	22 TOR	23 TOR	24 TOR	25 MIL	26 MIL	27 MIL
28 MIL	29 TEX	30 TEX	31 TEX			

June

S	M	T	W	T	F	S
				1	2 MIL	3 MIL
4 MIL	5 TEX	6 TEX	7 TEX	8	9 TOR	10 TOR
11 TOR	12 SEA	13 SEA	14 SEA	15 OAK	16 OAK	17 OAK
18 OAK	19 CAL	20 CAL	21 CAL	22	23 MIN	24 MIN
25 MIN	26 CLE	27 CLE	28 CLE	29	30 CHI	

July

S	M	T	W	T	F	S
						1 CHI
2 CHI	3 BOS	4 BOS	5 BOS	6 DET	7 DET	8 DET
9 DET	10	11 ★	12	13 BAL	14 BAL	15 BAL
16 BAL	17 BOS	18 BOS	19 NY	20 NY	21 NY	22 BAL
23 BAL	24	25 NY	26 NY	27 NY	28 DET	29 DET
30 DET	31 CHI					

August

S	M	T	W	T	F	S
		1 CHI	2 CHI	3 CHI	4 MIN	5 MIN
6 MIN	7	8 CAL	9 CAL	10 CAL	11 SEA	12 SEA
13 SEA	14 OAK	15 OAK	16 OAK	17	18 TOR	19 TOR
20 TOR	21 MIL	22 MIL	23 MIL	24 TEX	25 TEX	26 TEX
27	28 TEX	29 MIL	30 MIL	31 MIL		

Sept/Oct

S	M	T	W	T	F	S
					1 TEX	2 TEX
3	4 TOR	5 TOR	6 TOR	7	8 SEA	9 SEA
10	11 OAK	12 OAK	13 OAK	14 CAL	15 CAL	16 CAL
17 CAL	18 MIN	19 MIN	20 MIN	21 MIN	22 CLE	23 CLE
24 CLE	25 CLE	26 CHI	27 CHI	28 CHI	29 CLE	30 CLE
1	2					

☐ Home   ☐ Away   ★ All-Star Game

Kauffman Stadium

Capacity: 40,625

Turf: Grass

Dimensions:
LF Line: 330'
RF Line: 330'
Center: 410'
Alleys: 385'

Tickets:
(816) 921-8000

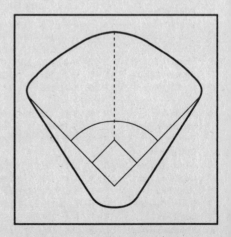

1994 Batting Order

1. Vince Coleman (Left Field)
2. Brian McRae (Center Field)
3. Wally Joyner (First Base)
4. Mike Macfarlane (Catcher)
5. Bob Hamelin (Designated Hitter)
6. Gary Gaetti (Third Base)
7. Felix Jose (Right Field)
8. Greg Gagne (Shortstop)
9. Jose Lind (Second Base)

1994 Team Record
64–51 (.557); Third in AL Central

AL East	W	L	AL Central	W	L	AL West	W	L
Baltimore	1	4	Chicago	7	3	California	4	6
Boston	2	4	Cleveland	4	1	Oakland	7	3
Detroit	8	4	Kansas City	—	—	Seattle	6	4
New York	4	2	Milwaukee	5	7	Texas	4	3
Toronto	6	6	Minnesota	6	4			
Total	21	20		22	15		21	16

1994 American League Team Rank Batting

Batting Average: Eighth (.269)
Runs Scored: Eighth (574)
Runs Batted In: Ninth (538)
Stolen Bases: First (140)
Slugging Percentage: Eleventh (.419)
On-Base Percentage: Ninth (.335)

1994 American League Team Rank Pitching

Earned Run Average: Second (4.23)
Bases On Balls: Fourth (392)
Strikeouts: Sixth (717)
Wins: Fourth (64)
Saves: First (38)
Complete Games: Fourteenth (5)

Kansas City Royals MVP

David Cone   No. 22/ P

Born: 1/2/63, Kansas City, MO
Height: 6' 1"   **Weight:** 190
Bats: Left   **Throws:** Right
Opp. Batting Average: .209

Cone pitched brilliantly in '94, holding batters to a .209 batting average, the AL's second-best mark, including .173 versus righties. He reeled off three straight shutouts in May, surrendering only eight hits during the streak. The league honored Cone with its 1994 Cy Young Award, and deservedly so.

Cone has a basic four-pitch repertoire, but when he's on, it seems more like twenty. He mixes his pitches well and is the owner of one of baseball's best sliders. A true "stopper," Cone tallied nine of his wins immediately following a Royals loss. He's also a workhorse, having gone six straight seasons with 200+ innings pitched before the '94 strike cut the streak short.

Cone is in the perfect home park for his flyball-inducing pitching style, but he still gave up fifteen home runs on the year. He actually pitched more effectively on the road than in his hometown. Allowing the longball isn't the only glitch in Cone's game; he does a poor job of holding runners on first base.

It's conceivable that Cone is coming into his own at a later age than most pitchers. He looked more consistently in control in '94 than in past seasons, and he may be gearing up for the most dominant stage of his career. A full year of decent run support should send Cone back to the twenty-win plateau for the first time since 1988 (20–3 with the Mets).

	G	GS	IP	ERA	H	BB	SO	W	L	SV
1994	23	23	171.2	2.94	130	54	132	16	5	0
Career	258	229	1692.2	3.12	1393	628	1650	111	70	1
Projected	32	32	242.0	3.17	190	95	183	15	11	0

Kevin Appier   No. 55/ P

Born: 12/6/67, Lancaster, CA
Height: 6' 2"   **Weight:** 200
Bats: Right   **Throws:** Right
Opp. Batting Average: .240

One of the majors' best starting pitchers, Appier got off to a slow start in '94 (6.22 ERA in his first eight starts), just as he did in '93. But he returned to his true form once the weather warmed, logging a 2.57 ERA in his final fifteen starts. Appier throws a hard, overhand split-finger fastball that is extremely tough on righties. Expect a dominant season from Appier.

	G	GS	IP	ERA	H	BB	SO	W	L	SV
1994	23	23	155.0	3.83	137	63	145	7	6	0
Career	159	147	1017.0	3.09	905	339	776	66	44	0
Projected	28	28	193.0	3.08	157	71	162	12	7	0

Billy Brewer   No. 41/ P

Born: 4/15/68, Fort Worth, TX
Height: 6' 1"   **Weight:** 175
Bats: Left   **Throws:** Left
Opp. Batting Average: .207

The lefty middle relief ace for the Royals last year, Brewer limited righthanded batters to a .179 batting average and no home runs. He sustained several streaks of virtual unhittability; his ERA stood at 0.48 through his first fifteen appearances. The Royals are very high on Brewer. He's made dramatic progress, and could be the AL's top setup man in '95.

	G	GS	IP	ERA	H	BB	SO	W	L	SV
1994	50	0	38.2	2.56	28	16	25	4	1	3
Career	96	0	77.2	3.01	59	36	53	6	3	3
Projected	56	0	46.0	3.00	35	21	31	4	2	2

Vince Coleman   No. 29/ OF

Born: 9/22/61, Jacksonville, FL
Height: 6' 1"   **Weight:** 185
Bats: Both   **Throws:** Right
1994 OBP: .285   **SLG:** .340

Despite the steals (excellent 86% success rate), Coleman is not a good leadoff hitter, due to his lack of ability to get on base. He doesn't hit for high average, nor does he draw many walks. Playing in expansive Kauffman Stadium helped Coleman finish second in the majors in triples with twelve. He'll probably be replaced by Dwayne Hosey this season.

	G	AB	H	2B	3B	HR	RS	RBI	BB	SB	BA
1994	104	438	105	14	12	2	61	33	29	50	.240
Career	1217	4853	1280	152	82	22	773	313	430	698	.264
Projected	160	649	161	22	16	3	98	45	39	69	.253

Gary Gaetti   No. 8/ 3B

Born: 8/19/58, Centralia, IL
Height: 6' 0"   **Weight:** 200
Bats: Right   **Throws:** Right
1994 OBP: .328   **SLG:** .462

Gaetti continues to baffle pundits by extending his career with solid offensive production. He's very good with runners on base because he can look for the fastball; he hit .455 with the bases loaded. Gaetti is still a fine fielder; he led AL third basemen with a .982 fielding percentage. Joe Randa, a slick-fielding rookie, may take over at third if Gaetti doesn't re-sign.

	G	AB	H	2B	3B	HR	RS	RBI	BB	SB	BA
1994	90	327	94	15	3	12	53	57	19	0	.287
Career	1835	6689	1698	322	32	257	838	979	452	83	.254
Projected	120	404	103	21	2	16	56	64	24	1	.261

Greg Gagne   No. 7/ SS

Born: 11/12/61, Fall River, MA
Height: 5' 11"   **Weight:** 175
Bats: Right   **Throws:** Right
1994 OBP: .314   **SLG:** .392

If individual defense were as valuable as individual offense (it isn't), Gagne would be an MVP candidate. He combines remarkable range, consistency, and arm strength. He's also productive with the bat, hitting .313 with runners in scoring position in '94. Gagne needs to stop attempting to steal bases; he was caught seventeen times in twenty-seven attempts.

	G	AB	H	2B	3B	HR	RS	RBI	BB	SB	BA
1994	107	375	97	23	3	7	39	51	27	10	.259
Career	1406	4301	1092	238	41	86	557	443	248	99	.254
Projected	160	538	140	32	3	10	60	62	35	12	.266

Tom Gordon   No. 36/ P

Born: 11/18/67, Sebring, FL
Height: 5' 9"   **Weight:** 180
Bats: Right   **Throws:** Right
Opp. Batting Average: .237

Gordon is still searching for control and consistency. His eighty-seven walks (the AL's third highest total) and fifteen home runs allowed were the reasons for his +4.00 ERA. He needs to mix his pitches to get maximum effect from his curveball (one of the best in the league). Gordon is still young, still striking batters out, and still potentially a great pitcher.

	G	GS	IP	ERA	H	BB	SO	W	L	SV
1994	24	24	155.1	4.35	136	87	126	11	7	0
Career	243	113	960.2	3.95	836	498	880	67	59	3
Projected	21	21	173.0	3.97	145	91	149	13	7	0

Mark Gubicza No. 23/ P

Born: 8/14/62, Philadelphia, PA
Height: 5' 9"   **Weight:** 180
Bats: Right   **Throws:** Right
Opp. Batting Average: .301

Back in 1988, Gubicza won twenty games for the Royals, but surgery to repair a torn rotator cuff has turned him into a different pitcher. No longer a power pitcher, Gubicza led the AL in fewest walks allowed per nine innings (1.8), but opposing batters hit him at a .301 clip. This season will be his eleventh consecutive with the Royals.

	G	GS	IP	ERA	H	BB	SO	W	L	SV
1994	22	22	130.0	4.50	158	26	59	7	9	0
Career	330	275	1886.0	3.86	1872	687	1230	116	109	2
Projected	39	15	129.0	4.57	158	38	77	7	9	1

Bob Hamelin No. 3/ DH

Born: 11/29/67, Elizabeth, NJ
Height: 6' 0"   **Weight:** 230
Bats: Left   **Throws:** Left
1994 OBP: .388   **SLG:** .599

"Hammer" is not the new Steve Balboni. Actually, he hits like Kent Hrbek. Hamelin had a Rookie of the Year season at the plate, finishing in the league's top ten in several categories, including home runs (ninth), slugging (fifth), and home run ratio (fourth). He's the team's best slugger since Danny Tartabull went to New York in 1991.

	G	AB	H	2B	3B	HR	RS	RBI	BB	SB	BA
1994	101	312	88	25	1	24	64	65	56	4	.282
Career	117	361	99	28	1	26	66	70	62	4	.274
Projected	155	499	148	40	1	37	95	101	89	6	.285

Felix Jose   No. 34/ OF

Born: 5/8/65, Santo Domingo, DR
Height: 6' 1"   **Weight:** 220
Bats: Both   **Throws:** Right
1994 OBP: .362   **SLG:** .475

After an injury-riddled '93, Jose bounced back nicely last season. A streak hitter capable of occasionally uncorking immense power, but more likely to hit linedrives into the gaps (club-leading twenty-eight doubles), Jose hits best from the right side. He's got a strong arm and good range in right field. Twelve caught stealings indicate an end to his effective-running days.

	G	AB	H	2B	3B	HR	RS	RBI	BB	SB	BA
1994	99	366	111	28	1	11	56	55	35	10	.303
Career	687	2431	686	133	14	50	310	308	189	102	.282
Projected	151	531	148	32	2	11	74	61	44	25	.277

Wally Joyner   No. 12/ 1B

Born: 6/16/62, Atlanta, GA
Height: 6' 2"   **Weight:** 205
Bats: Left   **Throws:** Left
1994 OBP: .386   **SLG:** .449

Joyner's power stats aren't helped by Kauffman Stadium, but he did hit .359 at home. Joyner's lefty swing is mechanically gorgeous, and he's one of the few Royals with patience at the plate. A consistent hitter and a smooth fielder (.991 fielding percentage), Joyner is a fan favorite in KC. Joyner could be ready for a Tim Wallach–style breakout season.

	G	AB	H	2B	3B	HR	RS	RBI	BB	SB	BA
1994	97	363	113	20	3	8	52	57	47	3	.311
Career	1233	4640	1337	262	19	146	656	706	491	47	.288
Projected	145	514	148	33	4	13	79	71	66	5	.294

Jose Lind   No. 13/ 2B

Born: 5/1/64, Tiabaja, PR
Height: 5' 11"   **Weight:** 175
Bats: Right   **Throws:** Right
1994 OBP: .306   **SLG:** .348

Lind contributed sparkling glovework and some timely hitting (.293 with runners in scoring position) last season. Lind probably has the best range of any second baseman in the game, and he made just five miscues in 406 chances last year. Anything positive he does at the plate is considered a bonus. Lind led the team with eight sacrifice bunts.

	G	AB	H	2B	3B	HR	RS	RBI	BB	SB	BA
1994	85	290	78	16	2	1	34	31	16	9	.269
Career	1000	3537	902	140	27	9	359	317	209	62	.255
Projected	133	440	115	18	2	1	41	42	18	7	.259

Mike Macfarlane   No. 15/ C

Born: 4/12/64, Stockton, CA
Height: 6' 1"   **Weight:** 205
Bats: Right   **Throws:** Right
1994 OBP: .359   **SLG:** .462

Macfarlane continues to contribute solid power numbers, though he hit just .222 with runners in scoring position last year. Macfarlane was hit by pitches a major league leading eighteen times. He's not a great defensive catcher; he threw out just 22% of runners attempting to steal. He's unsigned as of this writing, but he's the all-time leader in games caught for the Royals.

	G	AB	H	2B	3B	HR	RS	RBI	BB	SB	BA
1994	92	314	80	17	3	14	53	47	35	1	.255
Career	693	2158	551	136	12	76	268	309	177	6	.255
Projected	129	439	119	28	2	21	68	72	47	2	.268

Brian McRae   No. 56/ OF

Born: 8/27/67, Bradenton, FL
Height: 6' 0"   **Weight:** 185
Bats: Both   **Throws:** Right
1994 OBP: .359   **SLG:** .378

McRae has blossomed into a valuable offensive component, catching almost every ball hit his way, while generating offense from the number-two spot in the batting order. He finished seventh in the AL in steals and led the Royals in runs scored. He grounded into just one DP per 145 at-bats. McRae tied for second in the league in games played last year.

	G	AB	H	2B	3B	HR	RS	RBI	BB	SB	BA
1994	114	436	119	22	6	4	71	40	54	28	.273
Career	614	2393	627	109	32	30	319	248	166	93	.262
Projected	156	648	195	32	10	10	94	69	58	32	.290

Jeff Montgomery   No. 21/ P

Born: 1/7/62, Wellston, OH
Height: 5' 11"   **Weight:** 180
Bats: Right   **Throws:** Right
Opp. Batting Average: .276

Montgomery opened the season with shoulder soreness and recorded only one save in six April appearances. But from July 8 on, after receiving a cortisone shot, Montgomery converted saves in all of his fourteen appearances. Montgomery is one of the premier closers in baseball. He has averaged 33.6 saves per year since 1990.

	G	GS	IP	ERA	H	BB	SO	W	L	SV
1994	42	0	44.2	4.03	48	15	50	2	3	27
Career	438	1	573.0	2.64	483	191	510	36	30	187
Projected	62	0	74.0	2.86	64	21	65	5	5	41

Milwaukee
BREWERS

1995 Scouting Report

Outfielders: The Brewers' outfield scenario was muddled by injuries last season. Center fielder and leadoff man Darryl Hamilton is the Brewers' catalyst. Turner Ward had a good season in left field. Speedster Alex Diaz played all three outfield positions. Greg Vaughn, Brian Harper, and B. J. Surhoff also did time in right and left.

Infielders: Instability rules the Brewers' infield. This will be a pivotal campaign for struggling Pat Listach (SS). Jody Reed plays flawless second base. The backup middle infield consists of a mix of error-prone Jose Valentine and utility-infielder Bill Spiers. Kevin Seitzer (3B) plays hard but is limited as a hitter and fielder. John Jaha will get another crack as the first baseman.

Catchers: Dave Nilsson had a fine year at the plate, and he's penciled in as the everyday catcher. Brian Harper and B. J. Surhoff are both former full-time backstops.

Starting Pitchers: The Brewers' rotation is no worse off than many teams, but the pitching still needs help. Cal Eldred could develop into an ace, and Ricky Bones was the team's lone All-Star in '94. The next three spots are up for grabs, but they could belong to Bill Wegman, Angel Miranda, and Bob Scanlan.

Relief Pitchers: Mike Fetters took over the duties of closer from Doug Henry last season. Graeme Lloyd led the Brewers in relief appearances. Jesse Orosco held righties to a .195 batting average.

Designated Hitters: Greg Vaughn is the Brew Crew's best run producer.

Manager: Phil Garner (214–225) watched his team be decimated by injuries in 1994.

1995 Outlook

Perhaps no team in the big leagues could claim to have suffered as many serious injuries to key players as the Brewers in '94. It's difficult to evaluate their prospects for 1995, but if one assumes better health for Darryl Hamilton, Pat Listach, and Brian Harper, then the outlook has to be for an improved record.

The Brewers lack any quality which would clearly distinguish their strengths and weaknesses. They don't hit for power or average, and their team speed is minimal. The Brewers don't field badly or well, and their pitching, while not an unworkable disaster, isn't strong. The team is essentially devoid of stars, though it features some well-known veterans. In short, the Brewers are as middle-of-the-pack as a team can be.

The chance for an escape from sustained mediocrity will lie in the team's ability to begin replacing their stopgap veterans with promising young prospects. Kevin Seitzer, Brian Harper, B. J. Surhoff, and Jody Reed are serviceable major leaguers, but having a lineup filled with past-prime veterans isn't the way to build a contender.

But hope is eternal. The Brewer organization isn't unaware of what it takes to win. Their farm system has produced some quality young players, such as Greg Vaughn and Cal Eldred. Darryl Hamilton's return from elbow problems would mean instant offensive progress, and Pat Listach could still fulfill the promise of his rookie season. Ricky Bones, the team's lone All-Star, is only twenty-six years old.

The Brewers were out of contention by June in the tough AL Central, but their final '94 winning percentage would have been good for first place in the AL West. The Brewers will be far more potent if healthy, but they need to begin the process of replacing older players, defining roles, and building toward the future.

1995 Milwaukee Brewers Roster

Manager: Phil Garner
Coaches: Bill Castro, Duffy Dyer, Tim Foli, Don Rowe

No.	Pitchers	B	T	HT	WT	DOB	Birthplace
25	Bones, Ricky	R	R	6–0	190	4/7/69	Salinas, PR
57	Boze, Marshall	R	R	6–1	214	5/23/71	San Manuel, AZ
29	Bronkey, Jeff	R	R	6–3	211	9/18/65	Kabul, Afghanistan
59	Browne, Byron	R	R	6–7	200	8/8/70	Camden, NJ
21	Eldred, Cal	R	R	6–4	235	11/24/67	Cedar Rapids, IA
36	Fetters, Mike	R	R	6–4	215	12/19/64	Van Nuys, CA
58	Gamez, Francisco	R	R	6–2	196	4/2/70	Hemosillo, Mexico
55	Hill, Tyrone	L	L	6–6	195	3/7/72	Yucaipa, CA
40	Ignasiak, Michael	B	R	5–11	190	3/12/66	Anchorville, MI
69	Karl, Scott	L	L	6–2	195	8/9/71	Fontana, CA
43	Kiefer, Mark	R	R	6–4	184	11/13/68	Orange, CA
37	Lloyd, Graeme	L	L	6–7	230	4/9/67	Victoria, Australia
41	Mercedes, Jose	R	R	6–1	199	3/5/71	El Seibo, DR
38	Miranda, Angel	L	L	6–1	195	11/9/69	Arecibo, PR
31	Navarro, Jaime	R	R	6–4	225	3/27/67	Bayamon, PR
39	Scanlan, Bob	R	R	6–8	215	8/9/66	Los Angeles, CA
50	Sparks, Steve	R	R	6–0	187	7/2/65	Tulsa, OK
46	Wegman, Bill	R	R	6–5	235	12/19/62	Cincinnati, OH
	Catchers						
65	Matheny, Mike	R	R	6–3	205	9/22/70	Columbus, OH
11	Nilsson, Dave	L	R	6–3	215	12/14/69	Brisbane, Australia
64	Stefanski, Mike	R	R	6–2	190	9/12/69	Flint, MI
	Infielders						
27	Cirillo, Jeff	R	R	6–2	190	9/23/69	Pasadena, CA
32	Jaha, John	R	R	6–1	205	5/27/66	Portland, OR
16	Listach, Pat	B	R	5–9	170	9/12/67	Natchitoches, LA
20	Seitzer, Kevin	R	R	5–11	193	3/26/62	Springfield, IL
2	Valentin, Jose	B	R	5–10	175	10/12/69	Manati, PR
71	Weger, Wes	R	R	6–0	176	10/3/70	Madison, FL
	Outfielders						
—	Felder, Ken	R	R	6–3	220	2/9/71	Harrisburg, PA
24	Hamilton, Darryl	L	R	6–1	180	12/3/64	Baton Rouge, LA
30	Mieske, Matt	R	R	6–0	185	2/13/68	Midland, MI
33	O'Leary, Troy	L	L	6–0	190	8/4/69	Compton, CA
51	Singleton, Duane	L	R	6–1	170	8/6/72	Staten Island, NY
23	Vaughn, Greg	R	R	6–0	202	7/3/65	Sacramento, CA
24	Ward, Turner	B	R	6–2	200	4/11/65	Orlando, FL

1995 Schedule

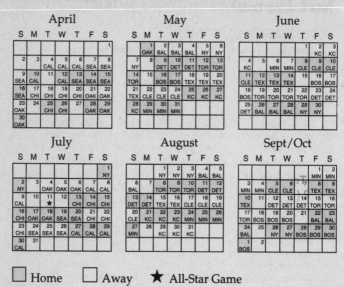

April

S	M	T	W	T	F	S
						1
2	3	4 CAL	5 CAL	6 CAL	7 SEA	8 SEA
9 SEA	10 CAL	11	12 CHI	13 CHI	14 CHI	15 SEA
16 SEA	17 CHI	18 CHI	19 CHI	20	21 OAK	22 OAK
23 OAK	24	25 CHI	26 CHI	27	28 OAK	29 OAK
30 OAK						

May

S	M	T	W	T	F	S
	1 OAK	2 BAL	3 BAL	4 BAL	5 NY	6 NY
7 NY	8	9 DET	10 DET	11 TOR	12 TOR	13 TOR
14 TOR	15	16 BOS	17 BOS	18 TEX	19 TEX	20 TEX
21 TEX	22 CLE	23 CLE	24 CLE	25 KC	26 KC	27 KC
28 KC	29 MIN	30 MIN	31 MIN			

June

S	M	T	W	T	F	S
				1	2 KC	3 KC
4 KC	5	6 MIN	7 MIN	8 CLE	9 CLE	10 CLE
11 CLE	12 TEX	13 TEX	14 TEX	15	16 BOS	17 BOS
18 BOS	19 TOR	20 TOR	21 TOR	22 TOR	23 DET	24 DET
25 DET	26 BAL	27 BAL	28 BAL	29 NY	30 NY	

July

S	M	T	W	T	F	S
						1 NY
2 NY	3	4 OAK	5 OAK	6 OAK	7 CAL	8 CAL
9 CAL	10	11 ★	12	13 CHI	14 CHI	15 CHI
16 CHI	17 OAK	18 OAK	19 SEA	20 SEA	21 CHI	22 CHI
23 CHI	24 SEA	25 SEA	26 CAL	27 CAL	28 CAL	29 CAL
30 CAL	31					

August

S	M	T	W	T	F	S
		1 NY	2 NY	3 NY	4 BAL	5 BAL
6 BAL	7	8 TOR	9 TOR	10 TOR	11 DET	12 DET
13 DET	14 DET	15 TEX	16 TEX	17 CLE	18 CLE	19 CLE
20 CLE	21 KC	22 KC	23 KC	24 MIN	25 MIN	26 MIN
27 MIN	28	29 KC	30 KC	31 KC		

Sept/Oct

S	M	T	W	T	F	S
					1 MIN	2 MIN
3 MIN	4 MIN	5 CLE	6 CLE	7	8 TEX	9 TEX
10 TEX	11	12 DET	13 DET	14 DET	15 TOR	16 TOR
17 TOR	18 BOS	19 BOS	20 BOS	21	22 BAL	23 BAL
24 BAL	25	26 NY	27 NY	28 BOS	29 BOS	30 BOS
1 BOS	2					

☐ Home   ☐ Away   ★ All-Star Game

Milwaukee County Stadium

Capacity: 53,192

Turf: Grass

Dimensions:
LF Line: 315'
RF Line: 315'
Center: 402'
Alleys: 392'

Tickets:
(414) 933-1818

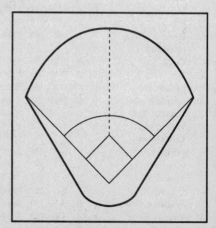

1994 Batting Order

1. Darryl Hamilton (Center Field)
2. Jody Reed (Second Base)
3. Kevin Seitzer (Third Base)
4. Greg Vaughn (Designated Hitter)
5. Dave Nilsson (Catcher)
6. John Jaha (First Base)
7. Turner Ward (Left Field)
8. Alex Diaz (Right Field)
9. Pat Listach (Shortstop)

1994 Team Record
53–62 (.461); Fifth in AL Central

AL East	W	L	AL Central	W	L	AL West	W	L
Baltimore	3	7	Chicago	3	9	California	3	3
Boston	5	5	Cleveland	2	5	Oakland	4	1
Detroit	4	6	Kansas City	7	5	Seattle	4	2
New York	2	7	Milwaukee	—	—	Texas	3	3
Toronto	7	3	Minnesota	6	6			
Total	21	28		18	25		14	9

1994 American League Team Rank Batting

Batting Average: Thirteenth (.263)
Runs Scored: Thirteenth (547)
Runs Batted In: Fourteenth (510)
Stolen Bases: Eleventh (59)
Slugging Percentage: Thirteenth (.408)
On-Base Percentage: Tenth (.335)

1994 American League Team Rank Pitching

Earned Run Average: Sixth (4.62)
Bases On Balls: Eighth (421)
Strikeouts: Thirteenth (577)
Wins: Eighth (53)
Saves: Eighth (23)
Complete Games: Eighth (11)

Milwaukee Brewers MVP

Ricky Bones   No. 25/ P

Born: 4/7/69, Salinas, PR
Height: 6' 0"   **Weight:** 190
Bats: Right   **Throws:** Right
Opp. Batting Average: .255

Bones (pronounced like "bonus") started the season as the AL's hottest pitcher, leading the league in ERA for April with a 1.11 mark, including two complete games and a shutout. He was elected to the All-Star team for the first time in his career, becoming only the ninth starter in Brewer history to accomplish that feat.

Bones' final ERA ranked eighth in the AL, and he finished tied for ninth in innings pitched. Bones throws a wide variety of pitches, none of which are dominant, relying on a mixture of speeds and spins to keep batters guessing. He has pinpoint control (2.4 walks per nine innings, tenth best in the league). He's always been consistently in the strikezone, but in past years his offerings were very hittable. Last year his hits-to-innings ratio was 0.97, compared to 1.09 in '93, a significant difference. Bones kept righthanders, who had previously hit him hard, well in hand in '94, slicing .43 points off the '93 BA of opposing righties.

Most baseball people were ready to give up on Bones before last season's breakthrough. Perhaps 1994 was a fluke based on one hot month—Bones has looked pretty unpromising in his first couple of campaigns. But considering the offensive fireworks that were generated by AL hitters in the early going, it's unlikely that his success was just sleight of hand. The Brewers desperately need a repeat performance from Bones.

	G	GS	IP	ERA	H	BB	SO	W	L	SV
1994	24	24	170.2	3.43	166	45	57	10	9	0
Career	98	94	591.2	4.37	614	174	216	34	36	0
Projected	32	31	214.0	4.20	222	62	69	12	11	0

Cal Eldred   No. 21/ P

Born: 11/24/67, Cedar Rapids, IA
Height: 6' 4"   **Weight:** 235
Bats: Right   **Throws:** Right
Opp. Batting Average: .236

Eldred actually pitched brilliantly in several starts, but he was prone to giving up big first innings (8.64 ERA in the opening frame), which inflated his ERA. Eldred threw four complete games in six June starts, good for AL Pitcher of the Month honors. He was sixth in the league in opponents batting average (.236). Eldred could be ready for a career year in 1995.

	G	GS	IP	ERA	H	BB	SO	W	L	SV
1994	25	25	179.0	4.68	158	84	98	11	11	0
Career	78	78	553.1	3.84	486	204	350	40	29	0
Projected	35	35	248.0	4.28	222	99	158	15	15	0

Mike Fetters   No. 36/ P

Born: 12/19/64, Van Nuys, CA
Height: 6' 4"   **Weight:** 215
Bats: Right   **Throws:** Right
Opp. Batting Average: .243

Not an overpowering closer, Fetters nevertheless was effective finishing games for the Brewers in '94. Fetters hasn't given up a home run in 63.1 innings, and he induces groundballs in bunches when his stuff is working. In his final thirty appearances, Fetters' ERA was 2.05. He tied for fifth in the American League in saves.

	G	GS	IP	ERA	H	BB	SO	W	L	SV
1994	42	0	46.0	2.54	41	27	31	1	4	17
Career	183	6	283.2	3.36	273	122	160	12	14	20
Projected	50	0	61.0	2.99	58	28	31	2	4	14

Darryl Hamilton   No. 24/ OF

Born: 12/3/64, Baton Rouge, LA
Height: 6' 1"   **Weight:** 180
Bats: Left   **Throws:** Right
1994 OBP: .331   **SLG:** .369

Hamilton suffered an injury-filled campaign. Tommy John surgery was performed on his non-throwing elbow in late June, and he should be fully recovered by April '95. Hamilton is a steady, line-drive hitter who can get on base consistently, and he's an accomplished center fielder. He's one of the league's most underrated players.

	G	AB	H	2B	3B	HR	RS	RBI	BB	SB	BA
1994	36	141	37	10	1	1	23	13	15	3	.262
Career	554	1795	529	74	15	18	269	209	159	98	.295
Projected	55	216	66	10	1	3	32	20	20	8	.303

Brian Harper   No. 12/ OF

Born: 10/16/59, Los Angeles, CA
Height: 6' 2"   **Weight:** 195
Bats: Right   **Throws:** Right
1994 OBP: .318   **SLG:** .398

Harper lost some of his best years trapped in the minors, but he has been a superlative professional hitter. Last season, his first in Milwaukee, he was hampered by various injuries and a poor April performance, but he eventually came around, hitting .325 (53–163) after May 11. Harper is used at catcher, outfield, and designated hitter.

	G	AB	H	2B	3B	HR	RS	RBI	BB	SB	BA
1994	64	251	73	15	0	4	23	32	9	0	.291
Career	1001	3144	931	186	7	63	339	428	133	8	.296
Projected	123	445	128	23	1	9	42	59	21	1	.294

John Jaha　No. 32/ 1B

Born: 5/27/66, Portland, OR
Height: 6' 1"　**Weight:** 205
Bats: Right　**Throws:** Right
1994 OBP: .332　**SLG:** .412

Jaha's third major league season had its ups and downs. He improved his performance against lefthanders (.283 BA in '94; .233 in '93), but hit just .229 versus righties. Jaha was sent to the minors in July, but he hit consistently in thirteen games after being recalled. He has decent speed for a first baseman, and he's a reliable fielder.

	G	AB	H	2B	3B	HR	RS	RBI	BB	SB	BA
1994	84	291	70	14	0	12	45	39	32	3	.241
Career	284	939	236	38	1	33	140	119	95	26	.251
Projected	141	499	138	23	0	20	79	70	53	10	.266

Pat Listach　No. 16/ SS

Born: 9/12/67, Natchitoches, LA
Height: 5' 9"　**Weight:** 170
Bats: Both　**Throws:** Right
1994 OBP: .333　**SLG:** .352

Rookie of the Year in '92, Listach's stock has dropped precipitously. Last season was lost to injuries that were linked to off-season knee surgery. A talented singles hitter with good speed, Listach still could have a future with the Brew Crew, but it's difficult to evaluate his prospects through the dark cloud of injuries. This will be the defining year in Listach's pro career.

	G	AB	H	2B	3B	HR	RS	RBI	BB	SB	BA
1994	16	54	16	3	0	0	8	2	3	2	.296
Career	263	989	271	37	7	4	151	79	95	74	.274
Projected		No projection. Player was injured in 1994.									

Dave Nilsson   No. 11/ C

Born: 12/14/69, Brisbane, Australia
Height: 6' 3"   **Weight:** 215
Bats: Left   **Throws:** Right
1994 OBP: .326   **SLG:** .451

The young Australian Nilsson was one of the Brewers' few longball threats last season, leading the team in RBIs and doubles. No one questions his hitting ability, and he could develop into a star, but his K/BB ratio regressed last year. Nilsson's play behind the plate needs work; he threw out just nine of sixty-two runners attempting to steal (15%).

	G	AB	H	2B	3B	HR	RS	RBI	BB	SB	BA
1994	109	397	109	28	3	12	51	69	34	1	.275
Career	260	857	223	46	5	23	101	134	88	6	.260
Projected	160	557	164	32	4	16	73	92	60	3	.280

Jody Reed   No. 8/ 2B

Born: 7/26/62, Tampa, FL
Height: 5' 9"   **Weight:** 170
Bats: Right   **Throws:** Right
1994 OBP: .362   **SLG:** .341

Reed is a rock-solid second baseman, the cornerstone of the Brewers' infield. He led all major league second sackers in fielding percentage (.995) and total chances (587), while leading the AL in doubleplays. At the plate, Reed cracked the twenty-doubles barrier for the seventh straight year. He also led the team in bases on balls.

	G	AB	H	2B	3B	HR	RS	RBI	BB	SB	BA
1994	108	399	108	22	0	2	48	37	57	5	.271
Career	955	3502	974	223	9	21	457	295	414	29	.278
Projected	146	503	132	25	1	2	56	40	56	4	.268

Kevin Seitzer   No. 20/ 3B

Born: 3/26/62, Springfield, IL
Height: 5' 11"   **Weight:** 180
Bats: Right   **Throws:** Right
1994 OBP: .375   **SLG:** .453

Seitzer's career was in decline until last season. He's given to phenomenal hot streaks; he hit .346 in April, .327 in June, and .333 in August. But he has as little home run power as any cornerman in baseball, and his glovework is erratic. Seitzer has guts; he suffered multiple facial fractures when hit by a Melido Perez pitch in August, but only missed one game.

	G	AB	H	2B	3B	HR	RS	RBI	BB	SB	BA
1994	80	309	97	24	2	5	44	49	30	2	.314
Career	1089	4015	1164	203	29	54	571	442	500	72	.290
Projected	122	432	120	23	2	9	52	62	43	5	.282

B. J. Surhoff   No. 5/ OF

Born: 8/4/64, Bronx, NY
Height: 6' 1"   **Weight:** 200
Bats: Left   **Throws:** Right
1994 OBP: .336   **SLG:** .485

Unsigned as of this writing, Surhoff has been dogged by streaky hitting, lack of a permanent defensive position, and injuries. He's a warm-weather hitter when healthy, so he's prone to cold starts. Surhoff did have a productive '93 season, but he needs to establish some consistency. He's played first base, third base, catcher, and outfield.

	G	AB	H	2B	3B	HR	RS	RBI	BB	SB	BA
1994	40	134	35	11	2	5	20	22	16	0	.261
Career	985	3469	931	168	21	44	400	451	257	95	.268
Projected				No projection. Player was injured in 1994.							

Dave Valle   No. 7/ C

Born: 10/30/60, Bayside, NY
Height: 6' 2"   **Weight:** 200
Bats: Right   **Throws:** Right
1994 OBP: .344   **SLG:** .375

The veteran Valle hit well after joining the Brewers from Seattle in a trade for Tom Brunansky. Considered a defensive specialist (meaning he couldn't hit), Valle has made stance adjustments to increase his plate coverage, which has helped his batting average somewhat. Valle possesses a strong arm and is an intelligent handler of pitchers.

	G	AB	H	2B	3B	HR	RS	RBI	BB	SB	BA
1994	46	112	26	8	1	2	14	10	18	0	.232
Career	892	2614	614	112	11	74	293	328	243	4	.235
Projected	71	205	50	10	0	6	23	27	25	0	.247

Greg Vaughn   No. 23/ OF

Born: 7/3/65, Sacramento,CA
Height: 6' 0"   **Weight:** 205
Bats: Right   **Throws:** Right
1994 OBP: .345   **SLG:** .478

Vaughn is the Brewers' most potent offensive threat, a free-swinging slugger (ninety-three Ks last year) who has thirty-homer power. He takes enough pitches to keep hurlers honest (fifty-one walks in '94), and he led the Brewers in runs scored and home runs. Vaughn plays a decent left field, but he gets a lot of at-bats as a DH, too.

	G	AB	H	2B	3B	HR	RS	RBI	BB	SB	BA
1994	95	370	94	24	1	19	59	55	51	9	.254
Career	693	2477	606	123	12	121	383	412	308	47	.245
Projected	150	572	153	32	2	30	96	93	86	12	.265

Turner Ward　　　No. 24/ OF

Born: 4/11/65, Orlando, FL
Height: 6' 2"　**Weight:** 200
Bats: Both　**Throws:** Right
1994 OBP: .328　**SLG:** .357

Ward languished in the minors through much of his prime, but he played adequately as the Brewers' starting left fielder last season. Ward had nineteen RBIs in April and had two nine-game hitting streaks. He's a decent professional ballplayer, drawing walks and driving in runs. Ward led the Brewers in outfield assists with eight.

	G	AB	H	2B	3B	HR	RS	RBI	BB	SB	BA
1994	102	367	85	15	2	9	55	45	52	6	.232
Career	254	722	170	31	5	15	104	93	93	12	.235
Projected	157	486	109	17	4	12	69	67	69	8	.221

Bill Wegman　　　No. 46/ P

Born: 12/19/62, Cincinnati, OH
Height: 6' 5"　**Weight:** 235
Bats: Right　**Throws:** Right
Opp. Batting Average: .303

An extreme control pitcher (2.0 walks per nine innings, tied for second in the AL), Wegman may be the most injury-hampered hurler in the majors. Wegman was 6–0 through June, but his season gradually fell apart in a wash of injuries. He hasn't been the same since the Brewers squeezed 261.2 innings from his fragile arm in 1992.

	G	GS	IP	ERA	H	BB	SO	W	L	SV
1994	19	19	115.2	4.51	140	26	59	8	4	0
Career	225	212	1412.0	4.10	1478	331	646	76	83	0
Projected	23	22	138.0	4.49	160	35	63	7	10	0

Minnesota
TWINS

1995 Scouting Report

Outfielders: The Twins receive much of their offense from All-Star outfielders Kirby Puckett (RF) and Shane Mack (LF). They increased their overall fielding range by acquiring speedster Alex Cole to run down balls in center field. Pedro Munoz will start if Mack isn't re-signed.

Infielders: Here is one of the team's deepest concerns. The retirement of perennially productive Kent Hrbek leaves a question mark at first base. Intriguing prospect Dave McCarty could be the answer to that query. Shortstop duties are handled by young Pat Meares. Converted shorstop Scott Leius is the Twinkies' third baseman. Second base is set in stone, with hard-hitting Chuck Knoblach posting All-Star numbers.

Catchers: Matt Walbeck flashed a strong throwing arm, but a weak bat, after coming over from the Chicago Cubs. Rookie hopeful Derek Parks could take the job in the spring.

Starting Pitchers: Uh-oh. The team's clear number-one pitcher is Kevin Tapani, whose 1994 individual ERA of 4.62 would have put him in the middle of the pack for American League team ERAs. Tapani is capable of performing on a higher level. Scott Erickson, Mike Trombley, and Pat Mahomes each have a lot to learn about how to fool major league hitters.

Relief Pitchers: Rick Aguilera is coming off a down year. Mark Guthrie and Kevin Campbell handle setup.

Designated Hitters: Dave Winfield hasn't re-signed, so there's a gap in the DH spot at the moment.

Manager: Tom Kelly (651–619) makes the most of his club's limited talent base.

1995 Outlook

The Twins are undeniably in a rebuilding mode. It's likely that this season will be one of great experimentation as manager Tom Kelly attempts to evaluate his young prospects. The organization doesn't generally make a habit of delving significantly into the free agent market, so we'll see a great many fresh faces in Minnesota in 1995.

Minnesota has the distinction of being one of only three clubs in the American League whose home games are played on artificial turf, now that Kauffman Stadium in Kansas City has been converted to grass. Yet the playing surface is perhaps the least obvious of the Hubiedome's defining characteristics. The park presents pitchers with a troublesome dilemma: groundballs are prone to scooting through the fast infield, yet the Metrodome gives a stated advantage to the longball. The kinds of hurlers who fare best in the Homerdome are strikeout pitchers with excellent control (e.g. Frank Viola circa 1987)—a rare breed indeed.

Clearly, the simplest route to winning baseball games in Minneapolis is to stock your batting order with sluggers, and this is where the Twinkies have fallen short in recent times. No team playing in a run-scoring factory like the HHH Metrodome can afford to finish in the lower half of the league in on-base percentage and slugging percentage. The Twins have the least amount of patience at the plate of any team in baseball. The batting order is rife with wild swingers, but few are as skilled at making contact as the team's leader, Kirby Puckett.

Whether because of stinginess or an earnest interest in player development, the Twins are committed to building from within. Any number of new names who received extended tryouts last season will grace the lineup in 1995. Chief among them are Rich Becker, Derek Parks, and David McCarty. The starting pitching is youthful enough as well, but the rotation appears destined for a 5.00+ team ERA for at least a couple of more years.

1995 Minnesota Twins Roster

Manager: Tom Kelly
Coaches: Terry Crowley, Ron Gardenhire, Rick Stelmaszek, Dick Such, Scott Ullger

No.	Pitchers	B	T	HT	WT	DOB	Birthplace
38	Aguilera, Rick	R	R	6–5	203	12/31/61	San Gabriel, CA
52	Campbell, Kevin	R	R	6–2	225	12/6/64	Marianna, AR
19	Erickson, Scott	R	R	6–4	224	2/2/68	Long Beach, CA
18	Guardado, Eddie	R	L	6–0	193	10/2/70	Stockton, CA
53	Guthrie, Mark	R	L	6–4	206	9/22/65	Buffalo, NY
20	Mahomes, Pat	R	R	6–4	210	8/9/70	Bryan, TX
—	Moten, Scott	R	R	6–1	198	4/12/72	Sun Valley, CA
55	Munoz, Oscar	R	R	6–3	210	9/25/69	Hialeah, FL
22	Pulido, Carlos	L	L	6–0	194	8/5/71	Caracas, Venezuela
30	Ritchie, Todd	R	R	6–3	190	11/7/71	Portsmouth, VA
58	Sanford, Mo	R	R	6–6	225	12/24/66	Americus, GA
41	Stevens, Dave	R	R	6–3	210	3/4/70	Fullerton, CA
36	Tapani, Kevin	R	R	6–0	187	2/18/64	Des Moines, IA
	Catchers						
27	Durant, Mike	R	R	6–2	200	9/14/69	Columbus, OH
16	Parks, Derek	R	R	6–0	217	9/29/68	Covina, CA
23	Walbeck, Matt	B	R	5–11	190	10/2/69	Sacramento, CA
	Infielders						
39	Dunn, Steve	L	L	6–4	225	4/18/70	Champaign, IL
4	Hale, Chip	L	R	5–11	191	12/2/64	Santa Clara, CA
11	Knoblauch, Chuck	R	R	5–9	180	7/7/68	Houston, TX
31	Leius, Scott	R	R	6–3	195	9/24/65	Yonkers, NY
2	Meares, Pat	R	R	5–11	180	9/6/68	Salina, KS
17	Reboulet, Jeff	R	R	6–0	169	4/30/64	Dayton, OH
37	Stahoviak, Scott	L	R	6–5	208	3/6/70	Waukegan, IL
	Outfielders						
25	Becker, Rich	B	L	5–10	180	2/1/72	Aurora, IL
1	Cole, Alex	L	L	6–0	170	8/17/65	Fayetteville, NC
40	Cordova, Marty	R	R	6–0	200	7/10/69	Las Vegas, NV
—	Lawton, Matt	L	R	5–10	180	11/3/71	Gulfport, MS
8	McCarty, David	R	L	6–5	207	11/23/69	Houston, TX
5	Munoz, Pedro	R	R	5–10	207	9/19/68	Ponce, PR
34	Puckett, Kirby	R	R	5–9	220	3/14/61	Chicago, IL

1995 Schedule

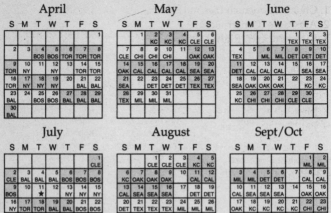

April

S	M	T	W	T	F	S
	.					1
2	3	4 BOS	5 BOS	6 TOR	7 TOR	8 TOR
9 TOR	10 NY	11 NY	12 NY	13	14 TOR	15 TOR
16 TOR	17 NY	18 NY	19 NY	20	21 BAL	22 BAL
23 BAL	24	25 BOS	26 BOS	27 BAL	28 BAL	29 BAL
30 BAL						

May

S	M	T	W	T	F	S
	1	2 KC	3 KC	4 KC	5 CLE	6 CLE
7 CLE	8 CHI	9 CHI	10 CHI	11	12 OAK	13 OAK
14 OAK	15 CAL	16 CAL	17 CAL	18 CAL	19 SEA	20 SEA
21 SEA	22 DET	23 DET	24 DET	25 TEX	26 TEX	27 TEX
28 TEX	29 MIL	30 MIL	31 MIL			

June

S	M	T	W	T	F	S
				1 TEX	2 TEX	3 TEX
4 TEX	5	6 MIL	7 MIL	8 DET	9 DET	10 DET
11 DET	12 CAL	13 CAL	14 CAL	15	16 SEA	17 SEA
18 SEA	19 OAK	20 OAK	21 OAK	22	23 KC	24 KC
25 KC	26 CHI	27 CHI	28 CHI	29 CLE	30 CLE	

July

S	M	T	W	T	F	S
						1 CLE
2 CLE	3 BAL	4 BAL	5 BAL	6 BOS	7 BOS	8 BOS
9 BOS	10	11 ★	12	13 NY	14 NY	15 NY
16 NY	17 TOR	18 TOR	19 BAL	20 BAL	21 BOS	22 BOS
23 BOS	24 BOS	25 TOR	26 TOR	27 TOR	28 NY	29 NY
30 NY	31					

August

S	M	T	W	T	F	S
		1 CLE	2 CLE	3 CLE	4 KC	5 KC
6	7 KC	8 OAK	9 OAK	10 OAK	11 CAL	12 CAL
13 CAL	14 SEA	15 SEA	16 SEA	17	18 DET	19 DET
20 DET	21 TEX	22 TEX	23 TEX	24	25 MIL	26 MIL
27 MIL	28 TEX	29 TEX	30 TEX	31		

Sept/Oct

S	M	T	W	T	F	S
					1 MIL	2 MIL
3 MIL	4 MIL	5 DET	6 DET	7	8 CAL	9 CAL
10 CAL	11 SEA	12 SEA	13 SEA	14	15 OAK	16 OAK
17 OAK	18 KC	19 KC	20 KC	21 KC	22 CHI	23 CHI
24 CHI	25 CLE	26 CLE	27 CLE	28 CHI	29 CHI	30 CHI
1 CHI	2					

☐ Home   ☐ Away   ★ All-Star Game

Hubert H. Humphrey Metrodome

Capacity: 55,883

Turf: Artificial

Dimensions:
LF Line: 343'
RF Line: 327'
Center: 408'
Left CF: 385'
Right CF: 367'

Tickets:
(612) 375-7444

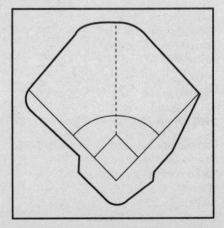

1994 Batting Order

1. Chuck Knoblauch (Second Base)
2. Alex Cole (Center Field)
3. Kirby Puckett (Right Field)
4. Kent Hrbek (First Base)
5. Shane Mack (Left Field)
6. Dave Winfield (Designated Hitter)
7. Scott Leius (Third Base)
8. Matt Walbeck (Catcher)
9. Pat Meares (Shortstop)

1994 Team Record
53–60 (.469); Fourth in AL Central

AL East	W	L	AL Central	W	L	AL West	W	L
Baltimore	5	4	Chicago	4	2	California	3	3
Boston	8	1	Cleveland	3	9	Oakland	2	5
Detroit	3	3	Kansas City	4	6	Seattle	3	3
New York	4	5	Milwaukee	6	6	Texas	4	5
Toronto	4	8	Minnesota	—	—			
Total	24	21		17	23		12	16

1994 American League Team Rank Batting

Batting Average: Fifth (.276)
Runs Scored: Sixth (594)
Runs Batted In: Seventh (556)
Stolen Bases: Third (94)
Slugging Percentage: Eighth (.427)
On-Base Percentage: Seventh (.340)

1994 American League Team Rank Pitching

Earned Run Average: Fourteenth (5.68)
Bases On Balls: Third (388)
Strikeouts: Thirteenth (602)
Wins: Eighth (53)
Saves: Fifth (29)
Complete Games: Twelfth (6)

Minnesota Twins MVP

Kirby Puckett   No. 34/ OF

Born: 3/14/61, Chicago, IL
Height: 5' 9"   **Weight:** 220
Bats: Right   **Throws:** Right
1994 OBP: .362   **SLG:** .540

The game's most beloved player, Puckett reversed his 1993 trend of difficulties with runners in scoring position. He led the American League in runs batted in, driving in twenty-three more runners last year than in the previous season, in 183 fewer at-bats.

Puckett isn't in top physical condition, though he's still a great athlete, and the extra pounds and years have precipitated a permanent move from center field to right field. The move is paying huge dividends, as Puckett has been able to flash his strong throwing arm more frequently. He tied for first in assists among American League outfielders.

Scouts say Puckett is swinging with as much pop as he did at age twenty-seven. Puckett would have shattered his personal best in RBIs had it not been for the work stoppage. His total of fifty-five extra-base hits was good for fifth (tie) in the league.The puckish one hammered thirty-two doubles, tied for fifth most in the AL. Puckett is a fabled bad-ball hitter, using his great batting eye to hit balls that are out of the strikezone, rather than using it to draw walks.

In a time when the fans' love of major league baseball players has been somewhat sullied by the strike, a player like Puckett is as important to the league as he is to the Twins.

	G	AB	H	2B	3B	HR	RS	RBI	BB	SB	BA
1994	108	439	139	32	3	20	79	112	28	6	.317
Career	1646	6706	2135	375	57	184	988	986	394	131	.318
Projected	158	622	182	41	3	24	97	116	43	8	.298

Rick Aguilera   No. 38/ P

Born: 12/31/61, San Gabriel, CA
Height: 6' 5"   **Weight:** 203
Bats: Right   **Throws:** Right
Opp. Batting Average: .306

One of the AL's most consistent closers for the past five years, last season Aguilera was tagged with the highest ERA of his Twins career. The problem wasn't his control; he walked less than one player per appearance. He also struck out more than one batter for every inning pitched. Unfortunately for Aguilera, his fastball didn't seem to be moving like it once did.

	G	GS	IP	ERA	H	BB	SO	W	L	SV
1994	44	0	44.2	3.63	57	10	46	1	4	23
Career	417	70	866.2	3.29	822	244	687	56	53	179
Projected	62	0	66.0	3.30	66	14	60	3	4	32

Rich Becker   No. 25/ OF

Born: 2/1/72, Aurora, IL
Height: 5' 10"   **Weight:** 180
Bats: Both   **Throws:** Left
1994 OBP: .351   **SLG:** .327

Becker is a young center fielder who tore cartilage in his knee in '93 in just his third major league game, after posting solid numbers at Double-A Nashville. Before the injury, the Twins had touted Becker as the next Lenny Dykstra. Last year he came back to play as a part-time outfielder and didn't look over-matched, though he slumped somewhat in the second half.

	G	AB	H	2B	3B	HR	RS	RBI	BB	SB	BA
1994	28	98	26	3	0	1	12	8	13	6	.265
Career	31	105	28	5	0	1	15	8	18	7	.267
Projection				No projection. Player was a rookie in 1994.							

Alex Cole   No. 1/ OF

Born: 8/17/65, Fayetteville, NC
Height: 6' 0"   **Weight:** 170
Bats: Left   **Throws:** Left
1994 OBP: .375   **SLG:** .403

Cole is a burner on the basepaths, and unlike many of his counterparts, such as Chuck Carr and Vince Coleman, Cole got on base enough last year to use his speed to its maximum value. Cole also showed better judgement on the basepaths than he had demonstrated when playing in Colorado for the Rockies.

	G	AB	H	2B	3B	HR	RS	RBI	BB	SB	BA
1994	105	345	102	15	5	4	68	23	44	29	.296
Career	521	1609	450	50	23	4	263	96	201	142	.280
Projected	143	446	133	16	6	3	79	31	58	40	.287

Jim Deshaies   No. 44/ P

Born: 6/23/60, Massena, NY
Height: 6' 5"   **Weight:** 220
Bats: Left   **Throws:** Left
Opp. Batting Average: .321

Deshaies has always been an enigma, even when he was successful (15–10, 2.91 ERA in 1989 for Houston). While with the Astros, Deshaies lived by the high strike, despite mediocre velocity—a rare and precarious situation. He's become a lefty journeyman, and last season's 7.00+ ERA is going to make it hard for him to stay in the league.

	G	GS	IP	ERA	H	BB	SO	W	L	SV
1994	25	25	130.1	7.39	170	54	78	6	12	0
Career	255	251	1519.2	4.09	1419	574	945	84	94	0
Projected	33	32	180.0	5.64	202	64	93	11	15	0

Scott Erickson   No. 19/ P

Born: 2/2/68, Long Beach, CA
Height: 6' 4"   **Weight:** 224
Bats: Right   **Throws:** Right
Opp. Batting Average: .299

Erickson won twenty games in 1991, but he hasn't been truly effective since the first half of that year. In the past two seasons combined, Erickson has lost thirty games. He doesn't appear to be having arm problems, but his fastball obviously isn't fooling most hitters, and Erickson doesn't have an extensive repertoire with which to bail himself out.

	G	GS	IP	ERA	H	BB	SO	W	L	SV
1994	23	23	144.0	5.44	173	59	104	8	11	0
Career	140	138	891.2	4.05	933	335	482	57	54	0
Projected	32	32	206.0	5.29	249	74	125	9	17	0

Chuck Knoblauch   No. 11/ 2B

Born: 7/7/68, Houston, TX
Height: 5' 9"   **Weight:** 180
Bats: Right   **Throws:** Right
1994 OBP: .381   **SLG:** .461

It was quite a season for Knoblauch, who led the majors in doubles with forty-five, which is a stunning statistic considering that he reached that plateau in just 445 at-bats. By comparison, Wade Boggs, who was a virtual doubles factory at Fenway in the 1980s, tallied forty-five doubles only thrice in his career, but never in a season of less than 580 at-bats.

	G	AB	H	2B	3B	HR	RS	RBI	BB	SB	BA
1994	109	445	139	45	3	5	85	51	41	35	.312
Career	568	2212	643	115	19	10	349	198	253	123	.291
Projected	156	650	206	47	5	5	108	59	68	41	.304

Scott Leius   No. 31/ 3B

Born: 9/24/65, Yonkers, NY
Height: 6' 3"   **Weight:** 195
Bats: Right   **Throws:** Right
1994 OBP: .318   **SLG:** .417

Leius was moved from shortstop to third base, after undergoing shoulder surgery in '93. He provided much-needed power in the Twins' batting order, bopping more homers in the strike-shortened '94 season than he had hit in 651 previous major league at-bats. The Twins believe that Leius can continue to be an everyday third baseman.

	G	AB	H	2B	3B	HR	RS	RBI	BB	SB	BA
1994	97	350	86	16	1	14	57	49	37	2	.246
Career	359	1001	254	42	5	22	150	110	105	13	.254
Projected	149	534	140	24	2	21	92	77	59	3	.252

Shane Mack   No. 24/ OF

Born: 12/7/63, Los Angeles, CA
Height: 6' 0"   **Weight:** 188
Bats: Right   **Throws:** Right
1994 OBP: .402   **SLG:** .564

A vastly underappreciated hitter, Mack would be a superstar if he played in a major media center. Like most Twins, he doesn't go to the plate looking for a base on balls. Mack is a free swinger with power to the gaps. Expect him to continue performing at a very high level with the bat next year. Mack is a solid left fielder, though his arm isn't very strong.

	G	AB	H	2B	3B	HR	RS	RBI	BB	SB	BA
1994	81	303	101	21	2	15	55	61	32	4	.333
Career	794	2518	754	133	27	71	392	352	232	80	.299
Projected	126	492	149	31	4	15	75	75	45	12	.301

Pat Mahomes　　No. 20/ P

Born: 8/9/70, Bryan, TX
Height: 6' 4"　**Weight:** 210
Bats: Right　**Throws:** Right
Opp. Batting Average: .269

The Twins organization was growing frustrated with Mahomes, who was coming off a 1993 season in which his ERA was 7.71. Mahomes is a young, hard-throwing fastball/slider pitcher who has trouble locating the strikezone. His control woes continued last season, but Mahomes was a lot tougher to hit in '94, and he finished as the team's number-two starter.

	G	GS	IP	ERA	H	BB	SO	W	L	SV
1994	21	21	120.0	4.73	121	62	53	9	5	0
Career	47	39	227.0	5.31	241	115	120	13	14	0
Projected	20	16	95	3.67	102	47	46	8	3	5

Pat Meares　　No. 2/ SS

Born: 9/6/68, Salina, KS
Height: 5' 11"　**Weight:** 180
Bats: Right　**Throws:** Right
1994 OBP: .310　**SLG:** .354

Mears took control of the starting shortstop job in '93 when Scott Leius was injured, and last year was his first full season as a regular. Though he isn't an impact player, Mears has a very strong arm and decent range in the field. At the plate, Mears is capable of driving the ball to the gaps, but he has accepted only twenty-one walks in his last 575 at-bats.

	G	AB	H	2B	3B	HR	RS	RBI	BB	SB	BA
1994	80	229	61	12	1	2	29	24	14	5	.266
Career	191	575	148	26	4	2	62	57	21	9	.257
Projected	117	366	102	17	3	1	41	38	14	6	.268

Pedro Munoz   No. 5/ OF

Born: 9/19/68, Ponce, PR
Height: 5' 10"   **Weight:** 207
Bats: Right   **Throws:** Right
1994 OBP: .348   **SLG:** .508

Munoz had a fine year at the plate in 1994, re-establishing himself as a quality hitter. Attempting to recover from knee surgery had wreaked havoc with Munoz's timing in '93, but his power and batting average were much improved last season. Like most Twins, walks aren't high on Munoz's list of priorities, but he could hit twenty home runs in a full season.

	G	AB	H	2B	3B	HR	RS	RBI	BB	SB	BA
1994	75	244	72	15	2	11	35	36	19	0	.295
Career	379	1211	323	53	8	43	141	176	72	11	.267
Projected	110	363	102	17	2	16	46	49	29	1	.270

Kevin Tapani   No. 36/ P

Born: 2/18/64, Des Moines, IA
Height: 6' 0"   **Weight:** 187
Bats: Right   **Throws:** Right
Opp. Batting Average: .291

Tapani is in the unenviable position of being the ace of an abysmal staff. He would be a solid third or fourth starter on many clubs, but he's the go-to guy in Minnesota. Tapani has good command of his four pitches, but good often isn't enough for a pitcher whose stuff isn't overpowering. Tapani is one of baseball's most interesting hurlers to watch.

	G	GS	IP	ERA	H	BB	SO	W	L	SV
1994	24	24	156.0	4.62	181	39	91	11	7	0
Career	164	160	1045.0	3.95	1078	255	638	69	52	0
Projected	34	33	216.0	4.51	240	54	137	13	12	0

Matt Walbeck   No. 9/ C

Born: 10/2/69, Sacramento, CA
Height: 5' 11"   **Weight:** 190
Bats: Both   **Throws:** Right
1994 OBP: .246   **SLG:** .284

The switch-hitting catcher who came over from the Cubs in exchange for pitcher Willie Banks, Walbeck was given the Twins' starting job from Opening Day. His arm proved to be excellent (he threw out 32.3% of runners attempting to steal), but Walbeck never got comfortable at the plate. His minor league offensive numbers weren't too bad, so perhaps last season was a fluke.

	G	AB	H	2B	3B	HR	RS	RBI	BB	SB	BA
1994	97	338	69	12	0	5	31	35	17	1	.204
Career	108	368	75	14	0	6	33	41	18	1	.204
Projected	149	534	120	21	0	9	50	62	27	2	.214

Dave Winfield   No. 32/ OF

Born: 10/3/51, St. Paul, MN
Height: 6' 6"   **Weight:** 245
Bats: Right   **Throws:** Right
1994 OBP: .321   **SLG:** .425

At the age of forty-two, Winfield had about as productive a season as could be expected. He's in the top twenty of all time in hits, home runs, RBIs, and total bases. Winfield is the career hits leader among active players. Winfield was one of the few Twins to reach double figures in home runs. He was traded to Cleveland in August, but he was a free agent as of this writing.

	G	AB	H	2B	3B	HR	RS	RBI	BB	SB	BA
1994	77	294	74	15	3	10	35	43	31	2	.252
Career	2927	10888	3088	535	88	463	1658	1829	1202	222	.284
Projected	131	490	124	24	3	18	61	68	43	2	.259

New York
YANKEES

1995 Scouting Report

Outfielders: The Yankees' outfield is well stocked. Paul O'Neill put up phenomenal offensive numbers and played solid defense in right field. Bernie Williams's (CF) performance is beginning to equal his exciting talent. Luis Polonia returned to the Bronx and had his best year in Yankees pinstripes. Others who see time in the outfield include Gerald Williams and Jim Leyritz.

Infielders: The corners are patrolled by two veteran professional hitters, Wade Boggs (3B) and Don Mattingly (1B). Both play airtight infield defense. Pat Kelly makes sparkling plays at second base, and he isn't an easy out with the bat. Utility infielder Randy Velarde will see more time at shortstop this season if Mike Gallego isn't resigned. Derek Jeeter may need more seasoning, but he could win the shortstop job in the spring.

Catchers: Mike Stanley gives the Yanks a longball threat and a veteran backstop. Jim Leyritz is the backup.

Starting Pitchers: Jimmy Key is the steadiest member of the starting staff. Jim Abbott has struggled often since his arrival from California. Melido Perez has nasty stuff, but he's still searching for consistency. Scott Kamieniecki made strides toward being a reliable fourth starter. New York traded for Jack McDowell in December.

Relief Pitchers: Steve Howe collected the bulk of the saves. Sterling Hitchcock and Bob Wickman both pitched well.

Designated Hitters: Danny Tartabull is a mammoth slugger.

Manager: 1994 American League Manager of the Year Buck Showalter (234–203) is extremely well liked by his players.

1995 Outlook

The Bronx Bombers emphatically lived up to their nickname in 1994, outputting league-dominating offensive totals. The Yankees were the only club to rank in the top two in baseball's two most important offensive categories—on-base percentage (first) and slugging percentage (second).

New York is a veteran unit, with the team's best hitters (O'Neill, Boggs, Mattingly, Stanley, and Tartabull) all older than thirty. The offense doesn't figure to show dramatic improvement in 1995, but then again, it's already the AL's most potent. The Yanks had two hitters in the top five in on-base percentage, a feat no other club could match. The team finished first in both walks and batting average, an impressive accomplishment. And the Bombers didn't waste those men on base; they drove in the second most runs in the AL.

The Yankees' starting rotation was built on free agency. Current management has never believed in developing young arms, and the pattern continued when the Yanks traded Bobby Munoz (2.67 ERA with Philadelphia) last year. One huge free agent acquisition (in 1993) was Jimmy Key, who was nearly unbeatable last year. The rest of the rotation is questionable but interesting. Will big Jack McDowell stabilize the rotation? Can unpredictable Melido Perez maintain his confidence and convert his electrifying arsenal into eighteen-plus wins? An affirmative answer to either of these uncertainties could mean a World Series berth for the Yankees, the first since 1981. Last season the Yankees maintained first place from May till the work stoppage, holding the Orioles at bay while distancing themselves from the remainder of the AL East pack. Perhaps no group of fans in baseball (with the exception of Indians rooters) were as disappointed at the abrupt end to the season as the New York faithful. The Yankees have a strong collection of talents, a fine manager, and at least some hope that the starting pitchers can carry their weight. It should be another intense summer in the Bronx.

1995 New York Yankees Roster

Manager: Buck Showalter
Coaches: Clete Boyer, Brian Butterfield, Tony Cloninger, Billy Connors, Rick Down, Willie Randolph

No.	Pitchers	B	T	HT	WT	DOB	Birthplace
25	Abbott, Jim	L	L	6–3	210	9/19/67	Flint, MI
—	Bankhead, Scott	R	R	5–10	185	7/31/63	Raleigh, NC
34	Hitchcock, Sterling	L	L	6–1	192	4/29/71	Fayetteville, NC
57	Howe, Steve	L	L	6–2	198	3/10/58	Pontiac, MI
52	Hutton, Mark	R	R	6–6	240	2/6/70	S. Adelaide, SA
28	Kamieniecki, Scott	R	R	6–0	195	4/19/64	Mt. Clemens, MI
22	Key, Jimmy	R	L	6–1	185	4/22/61	Huntsville, AL
—	McDowell, Jack	R	R	6–5	188	1/16/66	Van Nuys, CA
—	Murphy, Rob	L	L	6–2	215	5/26/60	Miami, FL
33	Perez, Melido	R	R	6–4	210	2/15/66	San Cristoban, DR
58	Rivera, Mariano	R	R	6–4	168	11/29/69	Panama City, Panama
64	Taylor, Brien	L	L	6–3	195	12/26/71	Beaufort, NC
27	Wickman, Bob	R	R	6–1	212	2/6/69	Green Bay, WI
	Catchers						
13	Leyritz, Jim	R	R	6–0	195	12/27/63	Lakewood, OH
76	Posada, Jorge	B	R	6–2	184	8/17/71	Santurce, PR
20	Stanley, Mike	R	R	6–0	192	6/25/63	Ft. Lauderdale, FL
	Infielders						
12	Boggs, Wade	L	R	6–2	197	6/15/58	Omaha, NE
24	Davis, Russell	R	R	6–0	170	9/13/69	Birmingham, AL
56	Fox, Andy	L	R	6–4	205	1/12/71	Sacramento, CA
2	Gallego, Mike	R	R	5–8	175	10/31/60	Whittier, CA
4	Kelly, Pat	R	R	6–0	182	10/14/67	Philadelphia, PA
23	Mattingly, Don	L	L	6–0	200	4/20/61	Evansville, IN
66	Seefried, Tate	L	R	6–4	205	4/22/72	Seattle, WA
47	Silvestri, Dave	R	R	6–0	196	9/29/67	St. Louis, MO
18	Velarde, Randy	R	R	6–0	192	11/24/62	Midland, TX
	Outfielders						
61	Leach, Jay	L	L	6–2	220	3/14/69	San Francisco, CA
21	O'Neill, Paul	L	L	6–4	215	2/25/63	Columbus, OH
17	Polonia, Luis	L	L	5–8	160	12/10/64	Santiago City, DR
59	Rivera, Ruben	R	R	6–3	170	8/3/71	Chorrera, Panama
62	Robertson, Jason	L	L	6–2	210	3/24/71	Chicago, IL
45	Tartabull, Danny	R	R	6–1	204	10/30/62	Miami, FL
51	Williams, Bernie	B	R	6–2	200	9/13/68	San Juan, PR
36	Williams, Gerald	R	R	6–2	190	8/10/66	New Orleans, LA

1995 Schedule

April

S	M	T	W	T	F	S
						1
2	3 TEX	4	5 TEX	6 TEX	7 CHI	8 CHI
9 CHI	10 MIN	11	12 MIN	13 CHI	14 CHI	15 CHI
16 CHI	17 MIN	18 MIN	19 MIN	20 KC	21 KC	22 KC
23 KC	24	25 TEX	26 TEX	27	28 KC	29 KC
30 KC						

May

S	M	T	W	T	F	S
	1 BOS	2 BOS	3 BOS	4 BOS	5 MIL	6 MIL
7 MIL	8	9 TOR	10 TOR	11 TOR	12 BOS	13 BOS
14 BOS	15	16 CLE	17 CLE	18	19 BAL	20 BAL
21	22	23 CAL	24 CAL	25 CAL	26 OAK	27 OAK
28 OAK	29 SEA	30 SEA	31 SEA			

June

S	M	T	W	T	F	S
				1	2 CAL	3 CAL
4 CAL	5 OAK	6 OAK	7 OAK	8 OAK	9 SEA	10 SEA
11 SEA	12 DET	13 DET	14 DET	15 DET	16 CLE	17 CLE
18 CLE	19 BAL	20 BAL	21 BAL	22	23 TOR	24 TOR
25 TOR	26 DET	27 DET	28 DET	29 MIL	30 MIL	

July

S	M	T	W	T	F	S
						1 MIL
2 MIL	3 CHI	4 CHI	5 TEX	6	7 TEX	8 TEX
9 TEX	10	11 ★	12	13 MIN	14 MIN	15 MIN
16 MIN	17 CHI	18 CHI	19 KC	20 KC	21 TEX	22 TEX
23 TEX	24 TEX	25 KC	26 KC	27 KC	28 MIN	29 MIN
30 MIN	31					

August

S	M	T	W	T	F	S
		1 MIL	2 MIL	3 MIL	4 DET	5 DET
6 DET	7 BAL	8 BAL	9 BAL	10 CLE	11 CLE	12 CLE
13 CLE	14 BOS	15 BOS	16 BOS	17	18 CAL	19 CAL
20 CAL	21 OAK	22 OAK	23 OAK	24 SEA	25 SEA	26 SEA
27 SEA	28	29 CAL	30 CAL	31 CAL		

Sept/Oct

S	M	T	W	T	F	S
					1 OAK	2 OAK
3 OAK	4 SEA	5 SEA	6 SEA	7	8 BOS	9 BOS
10	11 CLE	12 CLE	13 CLE	14 BAL	15 BAL	16 BAL
17 BAL	18 TOR	19 TOR	20 TOR	21 DET	22 DET	23 DET
24 DET	25	26 MIL	27 MIL	28	29 TOR	30 TOR
1 TOR	2					

☐ Home   ☐ Away   ★ All-Star Game

Yankee Stadium

Capacity: 57,545

Turf: Grass

Dimensions:
LF Line: 318'
RF Line: 314'
Center: 408'
Left CF: 399'
Right CF: 385'

Tickets:
(718) 293-6000

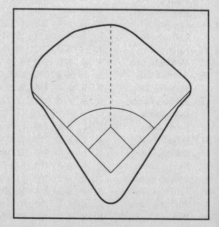

1994 Batting Order

1. Luis Polonia (Left Field)
2. Wade Boggs (Third Base)
3. Paul O'Neill (Right Field)
4. Danny Tartabull (Designated Hitter)
5. Don Mattingly (First Base)
6. Mike Stanley (Catcher)
7. Bernie Williams (Center Field)
8. Mike Gallego (Shortstop)
9. Pat Kelly (Second Base)

1994 Team Record
70–43 (.619); First in AL East

AL East	W	L	AL Central	W	L	AL West	W	L
Baltimore	6	4	Chicago	2	4	California	8	4
Boston	7	3	Cleveland	9	0	Oakland	7	5
Detroit	3	3	Kansas City	2	4	Seattle	8	4
New York	—	—	Milwaukee	7	2	Texas	3	2
Toronto	3	4	Minnesota	5	4			
Total	19	14		25	14		26	15

1994 American League Team Rank Batting

Batting Average: First (.290)
Runs Scored: Second (670)
Runs Batted In: Second (632)
Stolen Bases: Twelfth (55)
Slugging Percentage: Second (.462)
On-Base Percentage: First (.374)

1994 American League Team Rank Pitching

Earned Run Average: Fourth (4.34)
Bases On Balls: Sixth (398)
Strikeouts: Eleventh (656)
Wins: First (70)
Saves: Third (31)
Complete Games: Eleventh (8)

New York Yankees MVP

Paul O'Neill   No. 21/ OF

Born: 2/25/63, Columbus, OH
Height: 6' 4"   **Weight:** 215
Bats: Left   **Throws:** Left
1994 OBP: .460   **SLG:** .603

O'Neill has found a permanent home in Yankee Stadium. "The House that Ruth Built" has always been especially kind to lefthanded sluggers, and the Yankees have never had a winning lineup that wasn't centered around lefty pull hitters. O'Neill not only had a career season in 1994, he was one of the four hottest hitters in the American League.

O'Neill had never batted above .276 for a full season until he came to New York, but in two years with the Yankees he's compiled a .331 batting average. Last year he led the league with a .359 mark, a remarkable ninety-one points higher than his career average through the '93 season. Such a radical leap in performance by a veteran is extremely rare. By comparison, if Wade Boggs had experienced an identical increase, Boggs would have led the majors with a .426 batting average.

O'Neill keeps a healthy perspective on his performance, and he's one of the more level-headed players in the big leagues. He's made intelligent adjustments in several aspects—as a fast-ball hitter who was transplanted to a predominantly breaking-ball league, as an Ohio native interacting with the wolfish New York media, and as a lefty hitter who in the past has struggled against opposing southpaw hurlers. O'Neill may not finish fourth in the league in slugging again, but he's clearly become one of the best all-around hitters in the American League.

	G	AB	H	2B	3B	HR	RS	RBI	BB	SB	BA
1994	103	368	132	25	1	21	68	83	72	5	.359
Career	1043	3484	966	206	9	137	460	569	422	68	.277
Projected	150	537	181	37	1	26	87	99	73	4	.335

Jim Abbott   No. 25/ P

Born: 9/19/67, Flint, MI
Height: 6' 3"   **Weight:** 210
Bats: Left   **Throws:** Left
Opp. Batting Average: .273

Abbott hasn't been the pitcher the Yankees thought they were getting, but he hasn't been as bad as his numbers imply. He's still young, and he can be almost untouchable when he's moving the ball around the strikezone. Unfortunately, if he can't throw his curve for strikes, he gets hit hard. Abbott didn't look very sure of himself in '94. He'll need a fast start in 1995.

	G	GS	IP	ERA	H	BB	SO	W	L	SV
1994	24	24	160.1	4.55	167	64	90	9	8	0
Career	181	181	1221.1	3.78	1254	424	693	67	84	0
Projected	32	32	214.0	4.45	222	78	106	12	13	0

Wade Boggs   No. 12/ 3B

Born: 6/15/58, Omaha, NE
Height: 6' 2"   **Weight:** 197
Bats: Left   **Throws:** Right
1994 OBP: .433   **SLG:** .489

Boggs is one of baseball history's finest batsmen. A natural hitter with a smooth, quick swing and an uncanny eye for the strikezone, Boggs was fourth in the AL in on-base percentage. After hitting just two home runs in '93, Boggs had success pulling balls down the short line in right field at Yankee Stadium. Boggs has also become a Gold Glove winner at third base.

	G	AB	H	2B	3B	HR	RS	RBI	BB	SB	BA
1994	97	366	125	19	1	11	61	55	61	2	.342
Career	1865	7139	2392	467	49	98	1211	801	1139	18	.335
Projected	146	552	168	26	1	8	84	67	79	1	.311

Sterling Hitchcock   No. 34/ P

Born: 4/29/71, Fayetteville, NC
Height: 6' 1"   **Weight:** 192
Bats: Left   **Throws:** Left
Opp. Batting Average: .265

The Yankees have been patiently waiting for Hitchcock to blossom, and 1995 could be the year that he does just that. Hitchcock's fastball clocks out in the low nineties, and opposing batters report that his rotation is difficult to pick up. The key for Hitchcock, as with many young fireballers, is command of the strikezone.

	G	GS	IP	ERA	H	BB	SO	W	L	SV
1994	23	5	49.1	4.20	48	29	39	4	1	2
Career	32	14	93.1	4.92	103	49	71	5	5	2
Projected	18	7	51.0	4.39	51	27	41	3	2	1

Steve Howe   No. 57/ P

Born: 3/10/58, Pontiac, MI
Height: 6' 2"   **Weight:** 198
Bats: Left   **Throws:** Left
Opp. Batting Average: .194

Howe has a well-documented history of drug-related problems, but his arm appears to be in stunningly good shape for a thirty-seven-year-old relief pitcher. His (H+BB)/IP ratio was an impossibly stingy 0.88 (any number under 1.2 is excellent). Howe's fastball velocity still tops ninety-plus, and if his control is as sharp as it was in '94, he can mow down any hitter in baseball.

	G	GS	IP	ERA	H	BB	SO	W	L	SV
1994	40	0	40.0	1.80	28	7	18	3	0	15
Career	416	0	540.1	2.74	501	116	295	41	37	88
Projected	52	0	52.0	3.58	49	10	21	3	3	11

Scott Kamieniecki   No. 28/ P

Born: 4/19/64, Mount Clemens, MI
Height: 6' 0"   **Weight:** 195
Bats: Right   **Throws:** Right
Opp. Batting Average: .261

Kamieniecki is a solid member of the Yankees rotation. He doesn't get shelled very often, and the Yankees' offense is strong enough to make up the runs Kamieniecki does allow. Last year was his best so far; his frequency of walks was way up, but he relinquished fewer hits than innings pitched for the first time since his rookie year.

	G	GS	IP	ERA	H	BB	SO	W	L	SV
1994	22	16	117.1	3.76	115	59	71	8	6	0
Career	89	73	515.0	4.09	525	214	265	28	31	1
Projected	30	21	155.0	3.95	159	67	82	10	7	0

Pat Kelly   No. 14/ 2B

Born: 10/14/67, Philadelphia, PA
Height: 6' 0"   **Weight:** 182
Bats: Right   **Throws:** Right
1994 OBP: .330   **SLG:** .399

Kelly gives the Yankees a combination of solid fielding at second base and consistent hitting they haven't seen since Willie Randolph. Kelly makes some eye-popping grabs, especially ranging to his left, and his arm strength is the equal of any second baseman in the majors. At the plate, Kelly uses the entire field and has above-average doubles power to the gaps.

	G	AB	H	2B	3B	HR	RS	RBI	BB	SB	BA
1994	93	286	80	21	2	3	35	41	19	6	.280
Career	422	1308	335	79	9	20	157	142	83	40	.256
Projected	135	442	132	30	2	7	56	61	29	13	.287

Jimmy Key No. 22/ P

Born: 4/22/61, Huntsville, AL
Height: 6' 1" **Weight:** 185
Bats: Right **Throws:** Left
Opp. Batting Average: .273

Key is a maestro among AL starters. His teammates expect to win whenever he takes the mound, and he rarely disappoints. Key doesn't have a blazing fastball or a wicked curve, but he mixes his offerings brilliantly, keeping batters guessing from their first at-bat to their last. He won eleven straight decisions from mid-April through June. Key was sixth in the AL in ERA.

	G	GS	IP	ERA	H	BB	SO	W	L	SV
1994	25	25	168.0	3.27	177	52	97	17	4	0
Career	376	309	2100.1	3.36	2020	499	1214	151	91	10
Projected	34	34	231.0	3.11	226	54	154	20	6	0

Don Mattingly No. 23/ 1B

Born: 4/60/61, Evansville, IN
Height: 6' 0" **Weight:** 200
Bats: Left **Throws:** Left
1994 OBP: .397 **SLG:** .411

Mattingly remains the Yankees' captain, a leader-by-example who defines baseball professionalism. He's still got the error-saving glove and the surgically precise hitting stroke. What has abandoned Mattingly is his power, but fortunately the Yanks have plenty of slugging in their batting order. If his back is healthy, Mattingly will always be a productive player.

	G	AB	H	2B	3B	HR	RS	RBI	BB	SB	BA
1994	97	372	113	20	1	6	62	51	60	0	.304
Career	1657	6545	2021	410	18	215	948	1050	548	14	.309
Projected	142	542	154	28	2	14	82	81	71	0	.290

Melido Perez   No. 33/ P

Born: 2/15/66, San Cristobal, DR
Height: 6' 4"   **Weight:** 210
Bats: Right   **Throws:** Right
Opp. Batting Average: .238

The Yankees are baffled by the consistent inconsistency Perez has exhibited since coming to New York. There's no doubt that Perez has the potential to be unhittable, but control is especially crucial to his effectiveness, and it's been lacking at times. Perez must throw his fastball for strikes in order to set up his wicked forkball.

	G	GS	IP	ERA	H	BB	SO	W	L	SV
1994	22	22	151.1	4.10	134	58	109	9	4	0
Career	230	189	1285.1	4.09	1198	520	1048	73	80	1
Projected	27	27	181.0	4.67	177	71	149	9	10	0

Mike Stanley   No. 20/ C

Born: 6/25/63, Fort Lauderdale, FL
Height: 6' 0"   **Weight:** 192
Bats: Right   **Throws:** Right
1994 OBP: .384   **SLG:** .545

If there were any lingering doubts that Stanley had established a new level of offensive performance for himself, those doubts were quieted by his '94 output. Stanley is a dead fastball hitter, but if pitchers throw him junk outside the strikezone, he'll wait for his pitch or accept a base on balls. Stanley is an experienced handler of pitchers and a seasoned backstop.

	G	AB	H	2B	3B	HR	RS	RBI	BB	SB	BA
1994	82	290	87	20	0	17	54	57	39	0	.300
Career	732	1873	507	87	5	67	262	288	276	7	.271
Projected	128	435	134	23	1	27	76	87	59	1	.306

Danny Tartabull No. 45/ DH

Born: 10/30/62, Miami, FL
Height: 6' 1" **Weight:** 204
Bats: Right **Throws:** Right
1994 OBP: .360 **SLG:** .464

In 1987, Tartabull was arguably the game's most dangerous slugger. His skills have definitely dropped a notch, but he can still crush any fastball that's left out over the plate. Tartabull made the AL top ten in walks and strikeouts. Scouts say he's more likely to swing at a bad pitch than he once was, and Yankee Stadium's deep alleys tend to choke a righthander's power.

	G	AB	H	2B	3B	HR	RS	RBI	BB	SB	BA
1994	104	399	102	24	1	19	68	67	66	1	.256
Career	1188	4252	1180	250	19	227	662	789	657	36	.278
Projected	149	567	146	36	2	31	97	106	99	1	.255

Randy Velarde No. 18/ SS

Born: 11/24/62, Midland, TX
Height: 6' 0" **Weight:** 192
Bats: Right **Throws:** Right
1994 OBP: .338 **SLG:** .439

Velarde provides all things to the Yankees; as a utility player he's a manager's dream and has few peers. Velarde figures to garner most of his playing time at shortstop in '95. Velarde isn't a patient hitter, but he stepped up his power stroke last year, though hitting toward the bottom of the batting order. Velarde will never be a star, but he's a valuable player nevertheless.

	G	AB	H	2B	3B	HR	RS	RBI	BB	SB	BA
1994	77	280	78	16	1	9	47	34	22	4	.279
Career	547	1568	409	80	9	36	203	162	131	17	.261
Projected	102	321	94	19	2	10	48	37	26	4	.291

Bob Wickman   No. 27/ P

Born: 2/6/69, Green Bay, WI
Height: 6' 1"   **Weight:** 212
Bats: Right   **Throws:** Right
Opp. Batting Average: .213

The Yankees entered spring training in search of bullpen stability, and Wickman helped provide it. Being utilized strictly as a setup man gave Wickman the focus he'd been lacking prior to last season, and he responded by attacking opposing batters aggressively with his cut-fastball. Wickman's (H+BB)/IP ratio was a deadly 1.16.

	G	GS	IP	ERA	H	BB	SO	W	L	SV
1994	53	0	70.0	3.09	54	27	56	5	4	6
Career	102	27	260.1	4.11	261	116	147	25	9	10
Projected	56	11	125.0	4.12	125	57	75	11	5	6

Bernie Williams No. 51/ OF

Born: 9/13/68, San Juan, PR
Height: 6' 2"   **Weight:** 200
Bats: Both   **Throws:** Right
1994 OBP: .384   **SLG:** .453

Bernie Williams's bag of talents is filled to overflowing, and last year his natural gifts began to manifest themselves as clutch hits and spectacular catches. Williams has demonstrated a fine eye for the strikezone, power from both sides of the plate, and amazing instincts in center field. Williams is about to enter his prime years, and that means plenty of thrills for Yankees fans.

	G	AB	H	2B	3B	HR	RS	RBI	BB	SB	BA
1994	108	408	118	29	1	12	80	57	61	16	.289
Career	394	1556	419	93	11	32	229	185	191	42	.269
Projected	150	614	170	39	3	16	96	82	75	16	.267

Oakland
ATHLETICS

1995 Scouting Report

Outfielders: Ruben Sierra (RF) is Oakland's best run producer. Rickey Henderson (LF) will go to the Hall of Fame as baseball's greatest leadoff hitter, but 1994 was the least productive campaign of his career. Stan Javier (CF) had his career year in '94.

Infielders: Brent Gates returns from injury to anchor the middle infield. Light-hitting Mike Bordick completes the doubleplay tandem. Mark McGwire is a pure power hitter and an adept first baseman, but he's made fewer starts than Mike Aldrete the last two years, due to injuries. The hot corner is currently occupied by Scott Brosius.

Catchers: Terry Steinbach is one of the AL's best all-around catchers. Scott Hemond is Steinbach's backup.

Starting Pitchers: The A's rotation is iffy. Steve Karsay seems to have the makeup of an ace, but he's coming off elbow surgery. Ron Darling revived his career when it seemed to be on its last breath. Bobby Witt has always had dominant stuff, but he's never found consistency. Steve Ontiveros returned from oblivion to lead the AL in ERA. Touted rookie Todd Van Poppel struggled with the strikezone in his first full season.

Relief Pitchers: Ninth-inning specialist Dennis Eckersley is in decline, but that merely means he's no longer untouchable. The A's bullpen has led the league in appearances for four consecutive seasons.

Designated Hitters: Lefthanded slugger Troy Neel and righty Geronimo Berroa are both dangerous hitters.

Manager: Tony La Russa (1,253–1,106) is a thinking-man's manager. He's a genius at coaxing wins from difficult circumstances.

1995 Outlook

The remarkable story of the Athletics' 1994 season exemplifies the reason why they can never be written off as division contenders. The same team that lost twelve straight games in April to fall seemingly out of the race stormed back to win twenty of twenty-five contests between June 14 and the All-Star break.

The A's have an amazing history of reviving apparently dead arms, including Dave Stewart, Dennis Eckersley, and last year's miracle—Steve Ontiveros. Having not been on an opening day major league roster since 1989, Ontiveros's surge to the top of the league's ERA list was almost impossible to believe. Manager Tony La Russa and pitching coach Dave Duncan seem to come up with a similarly unlikely ace almost every year.

The core of the offense remains geared toward big innings. La Russa packs his batting order with sluggers (Sierra, Neel, McGwire) who draw a ton of walks and can drive each other home with the longball. It's a proven formula, and if McGwire's bad heels will let him stay off the DL, the A's will have more firepower in '95.

The Athletics' hard-throwing starting staff could be more formidable this season if young Steve Karsay returns from injury at full strength. But it doesn't seem natural to call Steve Ontiveros and Ron Darling sure bets to pitch consistently. The A's led the AL in shutouts last season, but their relievers threw more innings than any other bullpen in the league. It's an enigmatic group, one that only Tony La Russa knows how to guide.

Certainly the primary factor determining Oakland's chances for a division title is the inadequacy of the AL West competiton. The combined record of the division was fifty-seven games under .500, and the A's match up well against their AL West foes (17–9 in '94). The Athletics will be healthier this year, and the return of Karsay, McGwire, and potential All-Star second baseman Brent Gates means an over-.500 finish for Oakland and trouble for the Western Division.

1995 Oakland Athletics Roster

Manager: Tony La Russa
Coaches: Dave Duncan, Art Kusnyer, Carney Lansford, Jim Lefebvre, Dave McKay, Tommie Reynolds

No.	Pitchers	B	T	HT	WT	DOB	Birthplace
55	Acre, Mark	R	R	6–8	235	9/16/68	Concord, CA
62	Baker, Scott	L	L	6–2	175	5/18/70	San Jose, CA
17	Darling, Ron	R	R	6–3	195	8/19/60	Honolulu, HI
43	Eckersley, Dennis	R	R	6–2	195	10/3/54	Oakland, CA
20	Karsay, Steve	R	R	6–3	205	3/24/72	College Point, NY
47	Jiminez, Miguel	R	R	6–2	205	8/19/69	New York, NY
58	Mohler, Mike	R	L	6–2	195	7/26/68	Dayton, OH
50	Ontiveros, Steve	R	R	6–0	190	3/5/61	Tularosa, NM
38	Phoenix, Steve	R	R	6–2	175	1/31/68	Phoenix, AZ
40	Reyes, Carlos	B	R	6–1	190	4/4/69	Miami, FL
59	Van Poppel, Todd	R	R	6–5	210	12/9/71	Hinsdale, IL
32	Witt, Bobby	R	R	6–2	205	5/11/64	Arlington, VA
	Catchers						
48	Helfand, Eric	L	R	6–0	195	3/25/69	Erie, PA
2	Hemond, Scott	R	R	6–0	215	11/18/65	Taunton, MA
45	Molina, Izzy	R	R	6–1	200	6/3/71	New York, NY
36	Steinbach, Terry	R	R	6–1	195	3/2/62	New Ulm, MN
	Infielders						
23	Aldrete, Mike	L	L	5–11	185	1/29/61	Carmel, CA
14	Bordick, Mike	R	R	5–11	175	7/21/65	Marquette, MI
19	Bowie, Jim	L	L	6–0	205	2/17/65	Tokyo, Japan
7	Brosius, Scott	R	R	6–1	185	8/15/66	Hillsboro, OR
41	Cruz, Fausto	R	R	5–10	165	5/1/72	Monte Cristy, DR
13	Gates, Brent	B	R	6–1	180	3/14/70	Grand Rapids, MI
37	Matos, Francisco	R	R	6–1	160	7/23/69	Santo Domingo, DR
25	McGwire, Mark	R	R	6–5	225	10/1/63	Pomona, CA
16	Neel, Troy	L	R	6–4	215	9/14/65	Freeport, TX
3	Paquette, Craig	R	R	6–0	190	3/28/69	Long Beach, CA
	Outfielders						
29	Berroa, Geronimo	R	R	6–0	195	3/18/65	Santo Domingo, DR
24	Henderson, Rickey	R	L	5–10	190	12/25/58	Chicago, IL
28	Javier, Stan	B	R	6–0	185	1/9/64	San Pedro Macoris, DR
49	Lydy, Scott	R	R	6–5	195	10/26/68	Mesa, AZ
21	Sierra, Ruben	B	R	6–1	200	10/6/65	Rio Piedras, PR

1995 Schedule

April

S	M	T	W	T	F	S
						1 SF
2 SF	3 CLE	4 CLE	5 CLE	6 DET	7 DET	8 DET
9 DET	10	11 CLE	12 CLE	13	14 DET	15 DET
16 DET	17	18 TOR	19 TOR	20 TOR	21 MIL	22 MIL
23 MIL	24	25 TOR	26 TOR	27 TOR	28 MIL	29 MIL
30 MIL						

May

S	M	T	W	T	F	S
	1 MIL	2 CAL	3 CAL	4 CAL	5 TEX	6 TEX
7 TEX	8 TEX	9 SEA	10 SEA	11 SEA	12 MIN	13 MIN
14 MIN	15	16 CHI	17 CHI	18 CHI	19 KC	20 KC
21 KC	22	23 BAL	24 BAL	25 BAL	26 NY	27 NY
28 NY	29 BOS	30 BOS	31 BOS			

June

S	M	T	W	T	F	S
				1	2 BAL	3 BAL
4 BAL	5 NY	6 NY	7 NY	8 NY	9 BOS	10 BOS
11 BOS	12 CHI	13 CHI	14 CHI	15 KC	16 KC	17 KC
18 KC	19 MIN	20 MIN	21 MIN	22	23 TEX	24 TEX
25 TEX	26 TEX	27 SEA	28 SEA	29 SEA	30 CAL	

July

S	M	T	W	T	F	S
						1 CAL
2 CAL	3	4 MIL	5 MIL	6 MIL	7 TOR	8 TOR
9 TOR	10	11 ★	12	13 CLE	14 CLE	15 CLE
16 CLE	17 MIL	18 MIL	19 DET	20 DET	21 CLE	22 CLE
23 CLE	24	25 DET	26 DET	27 DET	28 TOR	29 TOR
30 TOR	31					

August

S	M	T	W	T	F	S
		1 TEX	2 TEX	3 TEX	4 SEA	5 SEA
6 SEA	7 MIN	8 MIN	9 MIN	10	11 CHI	12 CHI
13 CHI	14 KC	15 KC	16 KC	17	18 BAL	19 BAL
20 BAL	21 NY	22 NY	23 NY	24 BOS	25 BOS	26 BOS
27 BOS	28	29 BAL	30 BAL	31 BAL		

Sept/Oct

S	M	T	W	T	F	S
					1 NY	2 NY
3 NY	4 BOS	5 BOS	6 BOS	7	8 CHI	9 CHI
10 CHI	11	12 KC	13 KC	14 KC	15 MIN	16 MIN
17 MIN	18 CAL	19 CAL	20 CAL	21 SEA	22 SEA	23 SEA
24 SEA	25	26 TEX	27 TEX	28 CAL	29 CAL	30 CAL
1 CAL	2					

 Home   Away   ★ All-Star Game

Oakland–Alameda County Coliseum

Capacity: 46,942

Turf: Grass

Dimensions:
LF Line: 330'
RF Line: 330'
Center: 400'
Alleys: 372'

Tickets:
(519) 638-4900

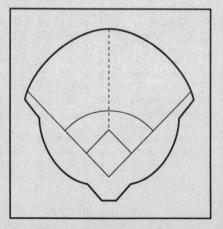

1994 Batting Order

1. Rickey Henderson (Left Field)
2. Stan Javier (Center Field)
3. Geronimo Berroa (Designated Hitter)
4. Ruben Sierra (Right Field)
5. Mark McGwire (First Base)
6. Terry Steinbach (Catcher)
7. Brent Gates (Second Base)
8. Scott Brosius (Third Base)
9. Mike Bordick (Shortstop)

1994 Team Record
51–63 (.447); Second in AL West

AL East	W	L	AL Central	W	L	AL West	W	L
Baltimore	5	7	Chicago	3	6	California	6	3
Boston	3	9	Cleveland	0	6	Oakland	—	—
Detroit	4	5	Kansas City	3	7	Seattle	4	3
New York	5	7	Milwaukee	1	4	Texas	7	3
Toronto	5	1	Minnesota	5	2			
Total	22	29		12	25		17	9

1994 American League Team Rank Batting

Batting Average: Fourteenth (.260)
Runs Scored: Twelfth (549)
Runs Batted In: Thirteenth (515)
Stolen Bases: Fourth (91)
Slugging Percentage: Fourteenth (.399)
On-Base Percentage: Fourteenth (.330)

1994 American League Team Rank Pitching

Earned Run Average: Eighth (4.80)
Bases On Balls: Fourteenth (510)
Strikeouts: Fourth (732)
Wins: Twelfth (51)
Saves: Eighth (23)
Complete Games: Seventh (12)

© John Klein/MLB Photos

Oakland Athletics MVP

Ruben Sierra   No. 21/ OF

Born: 10/6/65, Rio Piedras, PR
Height: 6' 1"   **Weight:** 200
Bats: Both   **Throws:** Right
1994 OBP: .298   **SLG:** .484

When Sierra was twenty years old, baseball people were calling him the majors' most valuable property and the next Roberto Clemente. Sierra is in the prime of a fine career, albeit not a Hall of Fame one. With Rickey Henderson having a down year and Mark McGwire on the DL, Sierra was Oakland's top offensive threat in 1994.

Sierra was on pace to drive in the most runs of his career when the strike began; he hit .342 with runners in scoring position, leading the team in that department. He's had trouble adjusting to breaking pitches off the plate, and his batting average woes carried over from '93. Sierra was hitting .197 on May 13, but he hit .305 for the remainder of the season to finish at an acceptable .268. On June 8 he homered from both sides of the plate for the fourth time in his career.

In right field, Sierra has been heavily criticized for occasional failures of concentration that look like laziness, and last year's nine errors only served to worsen his reputation. But he's actually got a strong and accurate arm, plus good range and instincts.

Sierra is productive with the bat, a proud competitor, and a four-time All-Star. Talk of his being the next Roberto Clemente may have created unreasonable expectations, but Sierra is still one of the majors' most productive hitters.

	G	AB	H	2B	3B	HR	RS	RBI	BB	SB	BA
1994	110	426	114	21	1	23	71	92	23	8	.268
Career	1328	5200	1421	274	50	201	736	866	373	121	.273
Projected	159	652	174	28	4	29	95	124	48	21	.257

Mike Bordick   No. 14/ SS

Born: 7/21/65, Marquette, MI
Height: 5' 11"   **Weight:** 175
Bats: Right   **Throws:** Right
1994 OBP: .320   **SLG:** .335

Bordick is the anchor of the A's infield and the only Athletics player to appear in every game in '94. He doesn't have much extra-base pop in his bat, but he's good in the clutch, and he isn't prone to slumps. Bordick's .974 fielding percentage was fifth among AL shortstops. His defensive contribution is so critical to the A's that any hitting he does is gravy.

	G	AB	H	2B	3B	HR	RS	RBI	BB	SB	BA
1994	114	391	99	18	4	2	38	37	38	7	.253
Career	542	1690	443	63	11	8	181	154	153	32	.262
Projected	160	553	141	23	4	3	58	51	58	10	.253

Scott Brosius   No. 7/ 3B

Born: 8/15/66, Hillsboro, OR
Height: 6' 1"   **Weight:** 185
Bats: Right   **Throws:** Right
1994 OBP: .289   **SLG:** .417

Except for a sixteen game stint on the DL in June, Brosius was the A's starter at third in '94. He turned on the power following his return from the DL, belting nine HRs in his last forty games. He's no longer a prospect after almost 700 career ABs, but he's a serviceable player. Brosius batted .299 from the seventh inning on, .207 from the first inning through the sixth.

	G	AB	H	2B	3B	HR	RS	RBI	BB	SB	BA
1994	96	324	77	14	1	14	31	49	24	2	.238
Career	240	692	165	31	2	26	79	91	44	14	.238
Projected	148	497	130	23	2	19	55	71	37	8	.252

Ron Darling No. 17/ P

Born: 8/19/60, Honolulu, HI
Height: 6' 3" **Weight:** 195
Bats: Right **Throws:** Right
Opp. Batting Average: .267

Darling rescued his career and Oakland's season by getting hot after starting out 4–9 with a 5.01 ERA. He was fanning batters, unlike in '93, and he induced twenty-one doubleplays (third in the league). Darling tied for the league lead in starts (25), and he solidified the staff as the team recovered from a disastrous April performance.

	G	GS	IP	ERA	H	BB	SO	W	L	SV
1994	25	25	160.0	4.50	162	59	108	10	11	0
Career	361	343	2256.1	3.77	2120	860	1521	132	109	0
Projected	33	25	164.0	4.50	170	59	118	10	11	0

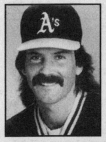

Dennis Eckersley No. 43/ P

Born: 10/3/54, Oakland, CA
Height: 6' 2" **Weight:** 195
Bats: Right **Throws:** Right
Opp. Batting Average: .275

Eck blew three save opportunities to start the year, but as with the entire team, he performed better as the season went along. He saved sixteen of his last eighteen chances. Eckersley had trouble with lefthanders in '94; they hit .322 against him. He has more saves (275) than any other active pitcher and ranks sixth in career saves.

	G	GS	IP	ERA	H	BB	SO	W	L	SV
1994	45	0	44.1	4.26	49	13	47	5	4	19
Career	849	361	3082.2	3.46	2863	705	2245	188	153	294
Projected	62	0	63.0	4.21	66	15	72	4	5	31

Brent Gates   No. 13/ 2B

Born: 3/14/70, Grand Rapids, MI
Height: 6' 1"   **Weight:** 180
Bats: Both   **Throws:** Right
1994 OBP: .337   **SLG:** .365

Gates's season was essentially lost to two serious injuries, but he remains a potential All-Star. He's got excellent pop in his bat, and he could eventually hit fifteen home runs in a season. Gates had eight consecutive hits versus Seattle on May 23 and 24 in the midst of a twelve-game hitting streak. He possesses excellent range at second and turns the DP very well.

	G	AB	H	2B	3B	HR	RS	RBI	BB	SB	BA
1994	64	233	66	11	1	2	29	24	21	3	.283
Career	203	768	221	40	3	9	93	93	77	10	.288
Projected				No projection. Player was injured in 1994.							

Rickey Henderson No. 24/ OF

Born: 12/25/58, Chicago, IL
Height: 5' 10"   **Weight:** 190
Bats: Right   **Throws:** Right
1994 OBP: .411   **SLG:** .365

The greatest leadoff hitter of all time, Henderson posted the lowest batting average of his career, but was still eighth in the AL in on-base percentage (.411). He reached base via hit or walk in seventy-four of his eighty-seven games. Henderson doesn't steal bases or hit the longball like he did in his prime, but he still does a leadoff hitter's job better than almost anyone.

	G	AB	H	2B	3B	HR	RS	RBI	BB	SB	BA
1994	87	296	77	13	0	6	66	20	72	22	.260
Career	2080	7656	2216	364	56	226	1652	804	1478	1117	.289
Projected	134	461	123	20	1	16	105	46	112	44	.272

Stan Javier   No. 28/ OF

Born: 1/9/64, San Pedro Macoris, DR
Height: 6' 0"   **Weight:** 185
Bats: Both   **Throws:** Right
1994 OBP: .349   **SLG:** .399

Javier has been a fine backup outfielder, but last season he made a splash as a starting center fielder. He set career highs in almost every category, while leading the A's in runs, doubles, and steals. Javier opened the year with a seventeen-game hitting streak. He's got great range in the field and is a good percentage basestealer.

	G	AB	H	2B	3B	HR	RS	RBI	BB	SB	BA
1994	109	419	114	23	0	10	75	44	49	24	.272
Career	959	2454	625	100	21	23	358	219	267	119	.255
Projected	160	527	150	27	3	11	88	58	62	29	.282

Steve Karsay   No. 20/ P

Born: 3/24/72, College Point, NY
Height: 6' 3"   **Weight:** 180
Bats: Right   **Throws:** Right
Opp. Batting Average: .252

The prospect the Blue Jays traded for Rickey Henderson during their '93 playoff run, Karsay looked fantastic early in '94 before elbow damage ended his season. Karsay has an explosive fastball, a hard slider, and outstanding poise. If his arm is sound, he's still one of the AL's most promising young hurlers. Lefthanders managed a .191 average versus Karsay.

	G	GS	IP	ERA	H	BB	SO	W	L	SV
1994	4	4	28.0	2.57	26	8	15	1	1	0
Career	12	12	77.0	3.51	75	24	48	4	4	0
Projected				No projection. Player was injured in 1994.						

Mark McGwire   No. 25/ 1B

Born: 10/1/63, Pomona, CA
Height: 6' 5"   **Weight:** 225
Bats: Right   **Throws:** Right
1994 OBP: .413   **SLG:** .474

Heel injuries have limited McGwire to playing in only seventy-six of the Oakland's last 276 games. When healthy, McGwire's size and strength give him tremendous power through the strike-zone. Since changing his batting stance in '93, he's had better plate coverage, and his batting eye is excellent. McGwire fields his position at a Gold Glove level.

	G	AB	H	2B	3B	HR	RS	RBI	BB	SB	BA
1994	47	135	34	3	0	9	26	25	37	0	.252
Career	990	3342	834	137	5	238	546	657	585	6	.250
Projected				No projection. Player was injured in 1994.							

Troy Neel   No. 16/ DH

Born: 9/14/65, Freeport, TX
Height: 6' 4"   **Weight:** 214
Bats: Left   **Throws:** Right
1994 OBP: .357   **SLG:** .475

A lefty hitter who absolutely kills southpaws (.350 in '94; .356 lifetime), Neel saw plenty of action at first base due to McGwire's injuries. Though his average dropped from the previous season, Neel is a dangerous hitter who punishes pitchers' mistakes. Surprisingly, Neel hit better last season in the Coliseum (.301), a difficult park for hitters, than on the road (.234).

	G	AB	H	2B	3B	HR	RS	RBI	BB	SB	BA
1994	83	278	74	13	0	15	43	48	38	2	.266
Career	230	758	212	37	0	37	110	120	92	5	.280
Projected	125	446	136	22	0	22	67	73	57	3	.292

Steve Ontiveros   No. 50/ P

Born: 3/5/61, Tularosa, NM
Height: 6' 0"   **Weight:** 190
Bats: Right   **Throws:** Right
Opp. Batting Average: .217

A former Athletics' castoff and ex-Mariner, swingman Ontiveros joined the starting rotation on May 30 and went on to lead the AL in ERA. The key was control of his deceptive stuff; he walked one batter or fewer in ten of his starts. In the second half, the league hit an anemic .180 off Ontiveros. His two losses in the second half were both complete games, 1–0 and 2–1.

	G	GS	IP	ERA	H	BB	SO	W	L	SV
1994	27	13	115.1	2.65	93	26	56	6	4	0
Career	182	50	526.2	3.43	469	165	304	24	22	19
Projected	25	25	184.0	2.44	181	37	71	10	9	0

Terry Steinbach   No. 36/ C

Born: 3/2/62, New Ulm, MN
Height: 6' 1"   **Weight:** 195
Bats: Right   **Throws:** Right
1994 OBP: .327   **SLG:** .442

Steinbach was having the best season of his career before the work stoppage. He made only one error in 628 chances to lead AL catchers in fielding percentage, and threw out 44% of runners attempting to steal, also the AL's best rate. Steinbach clobbered lefthanders at a .343 clip, and he hit .375 with two outs and runners in scoring position.

	G	AB	H	2B	3B	HR	RS	RBI	BB	SB	BA
1994	103	368	105	21	2	11	51	57	26	2	.285
Career	940	3242	891	154	12	82	376	430	233	14	.275
Projected	131	470	129	24	2	13	60	61	31	3	.280

Todd Van Poppel   No. 59/ P

Born: 12/9/71, Hinsdale, IL
Height: 6' 5"   **Weight:** 210
Bats: Right   **Throws:** Right
Opp. Batting Average: .250

Though Van Poppel seems like old news at twenty-two, don't write him off too early. His fastball has amazing movement, and he's yet to harness it (last year he allowed almost seven walks per nine innings), but in his seven winning starts, Van Poppel's ERA was just 2.98. He's a hard worker, a quick learner, and he's still got Cy Young stuff.

	G	GS	IP	ERA	H	BB	SO	W	L	SV
1994	23	23	116.2	6.09	108	89	83	7	10	0
Career	40	40	205.1	5.74	191	153	136	13	16	0
Projected	23	23	120.0	5.64	110	90	78	8	10	0

Bobby Witt   No. 32/ P

Born: 5/11/64, Arlington, MA
Height: 6' 2"   **Weight:** 205
Bats: Right   **Throws:** Right
Opp. Batting Average: .283

Though he's never developed into Sandy Koufax, Witt still shows flashes of staggering ability. In a three-game stretch from June 23 to July 3, Witt hurled three consecutive shutouts, allowing just one extra-base hit, and coming within a disputed bunt single of spinning a perfect game versus the Royals. When Witt is on a wild streak, things can get ugly in a hurry.

	G	GS	IP	ERA	H	BB	SO	W	L	SV
1994	24	24	135.2	5.04	151	70	111	8	10	0
Career	250	245	1528.2	4.56	1401	957	1318	91	96	0
Projected	34	32	202.0	4.52	214	91	137	12	13	0

Seattle
MARINERS

1995 Scouting Report

Outfielders: The Mariners have a slugging corps of outfielders. Ken Griffey, Jr. (CF) has Triple Crown potential and a 1994 Gold Glove. Jay Buhner (RF) crushes fastballs and has a potent throwing arm. Left fielder Eric Anthony is a streaky power hitter.

Infielders: Tino Martinez plays great defense at first base and has power at the plate. Edgar Martinez (3B) is a fine professional hitter. Mike Blowers is the backup cornerman. The middle infielders are light-hitting Luis Sojo (2B) and Felix Fermin (2B). Both are capable with the glove. Backup is provided by Rich Amaral.

Catchers: Dan Wilson, the starter in '94, will compete with rookie Chris Howard. Wilson throws well, but he ranked fourteenth in the AL in fielding percentage among catchers.

Starting Pitchers: Randy Johnson could be the righthanded Sandy Koufax. Chris Bosio suffered an injury-filled season, but he's got excellent stuff when he's healthy. Greg Hibbard is a solid lefty, but he was hurt in '94. The other spots in the rotation are open to experimentation. The options are youngsters John Cummings, Roger Salkeld, and Jim Converse. Dave Fleming, the ninth-winningest hurler in club history, had a rocky 1994.

Relief Pitchers: Bobby Ayala came up big for the M's last season, anchoring the bullpen with eighteen saves. Bill Risely and Jeff Nelson will be the setup men in '95.

Designated Hitters: Seattle uses a multi-player platoon in the DH slot.

Manager: Lou Piniella (610–567) has shown patience with his young players.

1995 Outlook

The trend of Japanese companies investing in American interests that turn out to be losing ventures is exemplified in Seattle. The team's financial backers at Nintendo are not happy with the situation at the Kingdome, where on June 19 the ceiling partially fell in. The Mariners organization is reporting an expected 1994 loss of $20 million dollars, and there has been talk of a potential move by the team away from Seattle in 1996.

On the field, the Mariners can be thankful for being in the AL West, where a .438 winning percentage can leave a team just two games out of first place. The M's have as legitimate a shot at winning the West as any other team in the division. Seattle could conceivably be home to 1995's Cy Young and MVP winners. This year's Mariners squad can boast of having both the greatest hitter and most dominant pitcher in club history. None of the other Western Division hopefuls can claim to have a position player the equal of Griffey, Jr. or a starter who can match Randy Johnson's stuff.

It was fashionable among baseball pundits to pick the Mariners as 1994's division-title frontrunners, and it probably will be again this season. Seattle has some interesting untested players, especially in the starting rotation. If someone develops, the Mariners might have the West's best corps of arms. On the other hand, the M's seem to be in a perpetual expansion mode, particularly in regards to pitching. They've produced numerous hot prospects, but few who've starred in a Mariners uniform.

The heart of the batting order contains some big bats, and the offense should be slightly improved in 1995. Edgar and Tino Martinez (no relation) should both perform more consistently this season, while Junior and Buhner keep on bopping. The Mariners have a large gap in talent between their top players and their replacement players. They get below-average production at catcher, shortstop, second base, and left field. We think that the M's still have some refinements to make before they can be a division champion, but in the West, anything is possible.

1995 Seattle Mariners Roster

Manager: Lou Piniella
Coaches: Bobby Cuellar, Lee Elia, John McLaren, Sam Mejias,
Sam Perlozzo, Matt Sinatro

No.	Pitchers	B	T	HT	WT	DOB	Birthplace
13	Ayala, Bobby	R	R	6–3	200	7/8/69	Ventura, CA
29	Bosio, Chris	R	R	6–3	225	4/3/63	Carmichael, CA
57	Converse, Jim	L	R	5–9	180	8/17/71	San Francisco, CA
44	Cummings, John	L	L	6–3	200	5/10/69	Torrance, CA
47	Davis, Tim	L	L	5–11	165	7/14/70	Marianna, FL
—	Davison, Scott	R	R	6–0	190	10/16/70	Inglewood, CA
—	Estes, Shawn	R	L	6–2	185	2/28/73	San Bernardino, CA
35	Fleming, Dave	L	L	6–3	200	11/7/69	Queens, NY
37	Hibbard, Greg	L	L	6–0	185	9/13/64	New Orleans, LA
51	Johnson, Randy	R	L	6–10	225	9/10/63	Walnut Creek, CA
50	King, Kevin	L	L	6–4	200	2/11/69	Atwater, CA
40	Nelson, Jeff	R	R	6–8	235	11/17/66	Baltimore, MD
55	Risley, Bill	R	R	6–2	215	5/29/67	Chicago, IL
41	Salkeld, Roger	R	R	6–5	215	3/6/71	Burbank, CA
96	Suzuki, Makoto	R	R	6–3	195	5/31/75	Kobe, Japan
	Catchers						
45	Howard, Chris	R	R	6–2	220	2/27/66	San Diego, CA
—	Widger, Chris	R	R	6–2	195	5/21/71	Wilmington, DE
6	Wilson, Dan	R	R	6–3	190	3/25/69	Arlington Heights, IL
	Infielders						
8	Amaral, Rich	R	R	6–0	175	4/1/62	Visalia, CA
16	Blowers, Mike	R	R	6–2	210	4/24/65	Wurzburg, Germany
18	Jefferson, Reggie	S	L	6–4	215	9/25/68	Tallahassee, FL
11	Martinez, Edgar	R	R	5–11	190	1/2/63	New York, NY
23	Martinez, Tino	L	R	6–2	210	12/7/67	Tampa, FL
20	Pirkl, Greg	R	R	6–5	225	8/7/70	Long Beach, CA
9	Sojo, Luis	R	R	5–11	174	1/3/66	Barquisimeto, Venezuela
	Outfielders						
5	Anthony, Eric	L	L	6–2	195	11/8/67	San Diego, CA
40	Bragg, Darren	L	R	5–9	180	9/7/69	Waterbury, CT
19	Buhner, Jay	R	R	6–3	210	8/13/64	Louisville, KY
—	Diaz, Alex	B	R	5–11	180	10/5/68	Brooklyn, NY
—	Griffey, Craig	R	R	5–11	175	6/3/71	Donora, PA
24	Griffey Jr., Ken	L	L	6–3	205	11/21/69	Donora, PA
28	Newfield, Marc	R	R	6–4	205	10/19/72	Sacramento, CA

1995 Schedule

April

S	M	T	W	T	F	S
						1
2	3 TOR	4 TOR	5 TOR	6	7 MIL	8 MIL
9 MIL	10	11 TOR	12 TOR	13 MIL	14 MIL	15 MIL
16 MIL	17 CLE	18 CLE	19	20 DET	21 DET	22 DET
23 DET	24	25 CLE	26 CLE	27 DET	28 DET	29 DET
30 DET						

May

S	M	T	W	T	F	S
	1 TEX	2 TEX	3 TEX	4	5 CAL	6 CAL
7 CAL	8 TEX	9 OAK	10 OAK	11 OAK	12 CHI	13 CHI
14 CHI	15 KC	16 KC	17 KC	18 KC	19 MIN	20 MIN
21 MIN	22	23 BOS	24 BOS	25 BOS	26 BAL	27 BAL
28 BAL	29 NY	30 NY	31 NY			

June

S	M	T	W	T	F	S
				1	2 BOS	3 BOS
4	5 BAL	6 BAL	7 BAL	8 BAL	9 NY	10 NY
11 NY	12 KC	13 KC	14 KC	15	16 MIN	17 MIN
18 MIN	19 CHI	20 CHI	21 CHI	22 CHI	23 CAL	24 CAL
25 CAL	26 CAL	27 OAK	28 OAK	29 OAK	30 TEX	

July

S	M	T	W	T	F	S
						1 TEX
2 TEX	3	4 DET	5 DET	6 CLE	7 CLE	8 CLE
9 CLE	10	11 ★	12	13 TOR	14 TOR	15 TOR
16 TOR	17 DET	18 DET	19 MIL	20 TOR	21 TOR	22 TOR
23 TOR	24 MIL	25 MIL	26 MIL	27 CLE	28 CLE	29 CLE
30 CLE	31					

August

S	M	T	W	T	F	S
		1 CAL	2 CAL	3 CAL	4 OAK	5 OAK
6 OAK	7 CHI	8 CHI	9 CHI	10	11 KC	12 KC
13 KC	14 MIN	15 MIN	16 MIN	17	18 BOS	19 BOS
20 BOS	21 BAL	22 BAL	23 BAL	24 NY	25 NY	26 NY
27 NY	28	29 BOS	30 BOS	31 BOS		

Sept/Oct

S	M	T	W	T	F	S
					1 BAL	2 BAL
3 BAL	4 NY	5 NY	6 NY	7	8 KC	9 KC
10 BAL	11 MIN	12 MIN	13 MIN	14	15 CHI	16 CHI
17 CHI	18 TEX	19 TEX	20 TEX	21 OAK	22 OAK	23 OAK
24 OAK	25 CAL	26 CAL	27 CAL	28 TEX	29 TEX	30 TEX
1 TEX	2					

 Home   ☐ Away   ★ All-Star Game

The Kingdome

Capacity: 58,879

Turf: Artificial

Dimensions:
LF Line: 331'
RF Line: 312'
Center: 405'
Left CF: 376'
Right CF: 352'

Tickets:
(206) 628-3555

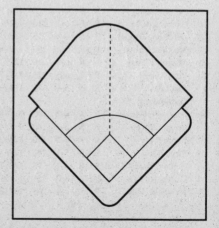

1994 Batting Order

1. Felix Fermin (Shortstop)
2. Eric Anthony (Left Field)
3. Ken Griffey, Jr. (Center Field)
4. Jay Buhner (Right Field)
5. Edgar Martinez (Third Base)
6. Reggie Jefferson (Designated Hitter)
7. Tino Martinez (First Base)
8. Dan Wilson (Catcher)
9. Luis Sojo (Second Base)

1994 Team Record
49–63 (.438); Third in AL West

AL East	W	L	AL Central	W	L	AL West	W	L
Baltimore	4	6	Chicago	1	9	California	7	2
Boston	6	6	Cleveland	2	3	Oakland	3	4
Detroit	3	6	Kansas City	4	6	Seattle	—	—
New York	4	8	Milwaukee	2	4	Texas	9	1
Toronto	1	5	Minnesota	3	3			
Total	18	31		12	25		19	7

1994 American League Team Rank Batting

Batting Average: Seventh (.269)
Runs Scored: Ninth (569)
Runs Batted In: Eighth (549)
Stolen Bases: Thirteenth (48)
Slugging Percentage: Fourth (.451)
On-Base Percentage: Eleventh (.335)

1994 American League Team Rank Pitching

Earned Run Average: Tenth (4.99)
Bases On Balls: Thirteenth (486)
Strikeouts: Second (763)
Wins: Thirteenth (49)
Saves: Tenth (21)
Complete Games: Third (13)

Seattle Mariners MVP

Ken Griffey, Jr.   No. 24/ OF

Born: 11/21/69, Donora, PA
Height: 6' 3"   **Weight:** 205
Bats: Left   **Throws:** Left
1994 OBP: .402   **SLG:** .674

More baffling than "What is the sound of one hand clapping?" is the eternal question: If Griffey were on your team, would you trade him for Frank Thomas? The primary differences between the two are on-base percentage (eighty-five-point advantage to Thomas) and fielding (Gold Glover Griffey versus potential DH Thomas). Okay, how about Ted Williams for Babe Ruth?

Griffey is a true phenomenon. At age twenty-five he's the M's all-time home run king. Last season he snapped numerous records for home run pace, including Ruth's mark of thirty HRs by June 30. *Junior hit one more homer in the month of May than the entire Montreal Expos team.* He made the AL top ten in home runs (first), total bases (second), batting average (eighth), runs scored (third), and slugging percentage (third).

For good measure, he collected twelve outfield assists (third most, behind Puckett and Lofton). Junior gets to the ball quickly, which is a key reason for his high assist totals, and his arm is extremely accurate. Having not reached his peak years, Junior's upward potential remains almost unlimited. Remember that in 1989, Griffey went deep just sixteen times in 455 at-bats. Our projected 1995 numbers for him are on a par with Babe Ruth circa 1927 or 1928. But we may be underestimating.

	G	AB	H	2B	3B	HR	RS	RBI	BB	SB	BA
1994	111	433	140	24	4	40	94	90	56	11	.323
Career	845	3180	972	194	19	172	518	543	374	88	.306
Projected	158	631	219	40	5	55	135	130	99	18	.331

Eric Anthony   No. 5/ OF

Born: 11/8/67, San Diego, CA
Height: 6' 2"   **Weight:** 195
Bats: Left   **Throws:** Left
1994 OBP: .297   **SLG:** .412

Anthony came out of the Astros' farm system in 1989, and he's never batted higher than .249. But he's managed to stay in the Show on the strength of his occassional power outbursts. He collected nine of his ten homers last year in two separate streaks that totaled 132 at-bats. Anthony made just two errors in left field, and his arm strength is above average.

	G	AB	H	2B	3B	HR	RS	RBI	BB	SB	BA
1994	79	262	62	14	1	10	31	30	23	6	.237
Career	509	1606	363	64	6	59	190	219	160	20	.226
Projected	133	463	122	21	3	16	65	62	46	6	.254

Bobby Ayala   No. 13/ P

Born: 7/8/69, Ventura, CA
Height: 6' 3"   **Weight:** 200
Bats: Right   **Throws:** Right
Opp. Batting Average: .203

Ayala had a huge season for the M's, who were sorely in need of a quality bullpen closer. The price was high; Seattle gave up Bret Boone and Erik Hanson in the deal for Ayala. Righthanders were pinned to a .183 batting average against Ayala's cruel split-finger fastball. He struggled in the strike-shortened second half, posting a 6.59 ERA after the All-Star break.

	G	GS	IP	ERA	H	BB	SO	W	L	SV
1994	46	0	56.2	2.86	42	26	76	4	3	18
Career	94	14	183.2	4.55	181	84	164	13	14	21
Projected	52	5	91.0	4.59	87	42	83	6	8	12

Chris Bosio   No. 29/ P

Born: 4/3/63, Carmichael, CA
Height: 6' 3"   **Weight:** 225
Bats: Right   **Throws:** Right
Opp. Batting Average: .277

Bosio is well known among big league batters for his diverse repertoire of nasty breaking pitches. Last season he was stung by poor run support, going 0–3 in April despite a 3.13 ERA. Bosio threw four complete games in just nineteen starts. His season was marred by knee surgery on July 19. He's not in great physical shape, but Bosio is a fine pitcher when healthy.

	G	GS	IP	ERA	H	BB	SO	W	L	SV
1994	19	19	125.0	4.32	137	40	67	4	10	0
Career	260	206	1479.1	3.77	1459	388	935	80	81	9
Projected	27	24	164.0	3.83	156	56	105	7	11	1

Jay Buhner   No. 19/ OF

Born: 8/13/64, Louisville, KY
Height: 6' 3"   **Weight:** 210
Bats: Right   **Throws:** Right
1994 OBP: .394   **SLG:** .542

The word among AL hurlers is that it's better to walk Buhner than to risk making a mistake over the plate. The burly slugger finished tied for ninth in the AL in walks. Buhner devastates lefties, punishing them at a .336 clip last season. He's also got a cannon arm, having gunned down eleven baserunners in '94, fourth most in the American League.

	G	AB	H	2B	3B	HR	RS	RBI	BB	SB	BA
1994	101	358	100	23	4	21	74	68	66	0	.279
Career	749	2520	646	123	16	129	377	427	355	6	.256
Projected	157	563	158	31	4	30	102	102	102	1	.277

Felix Fermin ⌐No. 10/ SS

Born: 10/9/63, Mao Valverde, DR
Height: 5' 11"   **Weight:** 170
Bats: Right   **Throws:** Right
1994 OBP: .338   **SLG:** .380

Fermin has an interesting mix of skills. He was the second-hardest AL hitter to fan, striking out just once in every 18.7 plate appearances. His total of twelve sacrifice bunts was also second in the league. Fermin's homer on May 9 at Chicago was his fourth in 4,529 at-bats as a professional (majors and minors). His primary value is with the glove.

	G	AB	H	2B	3B	HR	RS	RBI	BB	SB	BA
1994	101	379	120	21	0	1	52	35	11	4	.317
Career	819	2551	677	79	11	4	269	191	158	25	.265
Projected	148	532	155	23	1	2	63	50	22	5	.289

Dave Fleming   No. 35/ P

Born: 11/7/69, Queens, NY
Height: 6' 3"   **Weight:** 200
Bats: Left   **Throws:** Left
Opp. Batting Average: .311

Fleming is the prototype of a crafty left-hander. He changes speeds, moves the ball in and out of the strikezone, gives up his share of hits, and generally comes away with a win. In fact, Fleming already is the ninth-winningest pitcher in Seattle history. In '94, Fleming didn't get his stuff together till the season was nearly over, which is why his final numbers aren't good.

	G	GS	IP	ERA	H	BB	SO	W	L	SV
1994	23	23	117.0	6.46	152	65	65	7	11	0
Career	91	85	530.1	4.48	585	195	263	37	26	0
Projected	28	28	164.0	5.23	197	76	81	11	9	0

Greg Hibbard   No. 37/ P

Born: 9/13/64, New Orleans, LA
Height: 6' 0"   **Weight:** 185
Bats: Left   **Throws:** Left
Opp. Batting Average: .328

Hibbard is the definitive fourth starter. He's a workhorse who isn't likely to get blown out. He cuts off the running game and lets his infielders do most of the work. That is, when he's healthy. Last year Hibbard's season was cut short by shoulder surgery on July 8. Prior to the injury, Hibbard was tough on lefthanders, who hit just .240 against him.

	G	GS	IP	ERA	H	BB	SO	W	L	SV
1994	15	14	80.2	6.69	115	31	39	1	5	0
Career	165	158	990.0	4.05	1051	288	408	57	50	1
Projected	26	25	151.0	4.77	180	43	67	9	9	0

Randy Johnson   No. 51/ P

Born: 9/10/63, Walnut Creek, CA
Height: 6' 10"   **Weight:** 225
Bats: Right   **Throws:** Left
Opp. Batting Average: .216

Johnson does appear to be following Sandy Koufax's career pattern, but there's a big difference in the two pitchers' ages—Koufax entered the league at age nineteen, Johnson at twenty-four. It is likely that Johnson will once again be in the running for a Cy Young Award this season. Johnson has limited lefthanded hitters to a .198 batting average through his career.

	G	GS	IP	ERA	H	BB	SO	W	L	SV
1994	23	23	172.0	3.19	132	72	204	13	6	0
Career	188	186	1245.1	3.70	966	690	1330	81	62	1
Projected	33	33	242.0	3.22	179	97	290	18	8	0

Edgar Martinez   No. 11/ 3B

Born: 1/2/63, New York, NY
Height: 5' 11"   **Weight:** 190
Bats: Right   **Throws:** Right
1994 OBP: .387   **SLG:** .482

He lost the best years of his career drifting in the minors, but Martinez is a great professional hitter. He hit .329 against southpaws and grounded into just two doubleplays in 326 at-bats. Martinez has endured nagging injuries the past two seasons, but he's capable of winning a batting title, as he did in 1992. Martinez had a twenty-six game errorless streak in '94.

	G	AB	H	2B	3B	HR	RS	RBI	BB	SB	BA
1994	97	235	58	9	3	4	23	27	21	3	.247
Career	652	2266	686	152	9	62	362	268	316	23	.303
Projected	149	382	95	17	3	7	41	44	39	7	.246

Tino Martinez   No. 23/ 1B

Born: 12/7/67, Tampa, FL
Height: 6' 2"   **Weight:** 210
Bats: Left   **Throws:** Right
1994 OBP: .320   **SLG:** .508

The younger Martinez cornerman in Seattle started the '94 season with messed up mechanics (.104 BA in his first 106 at-bats), but he finished with the best homer total of his career. Martinez led the club in July with a .347 BA and six homers. He ranked second in fielding percentage among AL first basemen (.997) for the season. Piniella has been very patient with Martinez.

	G	AB	H	2B	3B	HR	RS	RBI	BB	SB	BA
1994	97	329	86	21	0	20	42	61	29	1	.261
Career	402	1377	350	71	3	57	158	201	136	3	.254
Projected	129	480	137	31	1	25	61	82	50	1	.274

Jeff Nelson   No. 43/ P

Born: 11/17/66, Baltimore, MD
Height: 6' 8"   **Weight:** 235
Bats: Right   **Throws:** Right
Opp. Batting Average: .226

If used correctly, Nelson is a very solid righthanded setup man. Righty hitters don't have a prayer against Nelson's slider; they hit just .168 against him in 1994, .213 in 461 at-bats through his career. Nelson was up and down between Seattle and Triple-A Calgary in 1994. He's not effective in pressure situations, allowing 52% of inherited runners to score.

	G	GS	IP	ERA	H	BB	SO	W	L	SV
1994	28	0	42.1	2.76	35	20	44	0	0	0
Career	165	0	183.1	3.58	163	98	151	6	10	7
Projected	54	0	56.0	3.71	50	30	57	3	2	1

Luis Sojo   No. 9/ 2B

Born: 1/3/66, Barquisimeto, Venezuela
Height: 5' 11"   **Weight:** 175
Bats: Right   **Throws:** Right
1994 OBP: .308   **SLG:** .423

Sojo was the last position player assigned to Triple-A Calgary by the Mariners coming out of spring training, but he was recalled May 6 and established himself as the M's second baseman. Sojo has some pop; he smacked a grand slam versus Texas in May and homered in back-to-back games in June. Sojo turns the doubleplay very well.

	G	AB	H	2B	3B	HR	RS	RBI	BB	SB	BA
1994	63	213	59	2	6	22	2	32	8	1	.277
Career	334	1072	279	33	10	33	96	110	37	13	.260
Projected	97	320	89	5	8	28	9	49	5	1	.268

Makoto Suzuki   No. 96/ P

Born: 5/31/75, Kobe, Japan
Height: 6' 3"   **Weight:** 195
Bats: Right   **Throws:** Right
Opp. Batting Average: —

Suzuki is a nineteen-year-old bundle of potential whose fastball reaches the high nineties. If he makes it to the majors, he'll become the first Japanese-born player to reach the big leagues without having started his pro career in Japan. He pitched relief in eight games at Double-A Jacksonville last season (1–0, 2.84), then had exploratory elbow surgery that showed no problems.

	G	GS	IP	ERA	H	BB	SO	W	L	SV
1994	0	0	0.0	0.00	0	0	0	0	0	0
Career	0	0	0.0	0.00	0	0	0	0	0	0
Projected			No projection. Player has not played in the majors.							

Dan Wilson   No. 6/ C

Born: 3/25/69, Arlington Heights, IL
Height: 6' 3"   **Weight:** 190
Bats: Right   **Throws:** Right
1994 OBP: .244   **SLG:** .312

The Reds drafted Wilson in the first round when Lou Pinella was manager in Cincinnati. Pinella obviously believes Wilson can learn to hit. There's no doubt that Wilson has a strong arm; he rang up 32.8% of would-be basestealers, the fifth-best rate in the American League. Wilson will need to generate some offense or he'll lose his starting job to rookie Chris Howard.

	G	AB	H	2B	3B	HR	RS	RBI	BB	SB	BA
1994	91	282	61	14	2	3	24	27	10	1	.216
Career	139	383	87	18	2	3	32	38	22	1	.227
Projected	140	410	97	20	2	4	36	42	23	1	.227

Texas
RANGERS

1995 Scouting Report

Outfielders: Potential MVP Juan Gonzalez (LF) had a disappointing season, partially due to nagging injuries. Rusty Greer (RF) topped all AL rookies in on-base percentage. The center field spot belongs to new acquisition Otis Nixon.

Infielders: Will Clark brought instant greatness to the Rangers' infield at first base. Across the diamond, Dean Palmer (3B) made twenty-two errors, but he sure has a knack for the longball. The shortstop situation is unstable, with prospect Esteban Beltre the primary option. At second base, Jeff Frye returned from knee surgery to post excellent numbers.

Catchers: All-Star backstop Ivan Rodriguez is getting better every year. His upward potential is almost limitless.

Starting Pitchers: The Rangers' stratospheric 5.45 ERA ranked twenty-seventh in the majors. Kenny Rogers was the staff's best, pitching a perfect game on July 28 versus California. Kevin Brown, the Rangers' ace in '93, gave up more hits than any other AL pitcher. The rest of the rotation could include any one of the following names (and '94 ERAs): Brian Bohanon (7.23), John Dettmer (4.33), Hector Fajardo (6.91), and Rick Helling (5.88).

Relief Pitchers: The Rangers will use Darren Oliver to replace Tom Henke. The rest of the pen is a committee featuring Matt Whiteside, and Cris Carpenter.

Designated Hitters: Jose Canseco was the Rangers' biggest bat last year. They'll need to find a new DH.

Manager: Johnny Oates (291–270) begins his tenure as Rangers manager this season.

1995 Outlook

The Rangers are a team of deep strengths and glaring weaknesses. If their pitching staff were merely average, they'd be a clear choice as the division favorite. If they weren't the AL's most porous defense, the Rangers would be playing .550 baseball.

The offense is potent. The Rangers seem to have people on base in almost every inning, and there's power in the heart of the order. The team's 3-4-5 hitters—Canseco, Clark, and Gonzalez—were the only trio in the big leagues that drove in at least eighty runs apiece. The Rangers got more production from the DH slot than any other team, thanks to the departed Canseco.

If anything, the Rangers disprove the myth that baseball is 90% pitching and defense. If that were true, Texas would be the majors' worst team instead of the AL West's winningest club in '94. The Rangers come to the ballpark knowing they may need to score at least six runs to win, and often they do just that. But a pitching staff that allows a 6.39 ERA on the road would be a problem even if the Rangers had Ruth and Gehrig in the batting order. The starting rotation doesn't figure to show much improvement in '95.

The AL West isn't a strong division—the first place Rangers finished ten games under .500—but it is the AL's most balanced division. The gap between first and last was only 5.5 games. The Rangers fared badly (8–22) against their divisional competition. Rangers players lost 660 days on the disabled list, but the injuries were generally not to key individuals.

Any team in the Western Division could come out on top over a full season, and the Rangers can score runs in bunches. But if pitching and defense count for anything, Texas isn't a championship team. The offense might be even more explosive in '95 than it was last season, but the pitching will be awful unless there's a significant change in personnel.

1995 Texas Rangers Roster

Manager: Johnny Oates
Coaches: Dick Bosman, Bucky Dent, Larry Hardy, Rudy Jaramillo, Ed Napoleon, Jerry Narron

No.	Pitchers	B	T	HT	WT	DOB	Birthplace
45	Bohanon, Brian	L	L	6–3	220	8/1/68	Houston, TX
53	Burrows, Terry	L	L	6–1	185	11/28/68	Lake Charles, LA
31	Carpenter, Cris	R	R	6–1	185	4/5/65	St. Augustine, FL
21	Dettmer, John	R	R	6–0	185	3/4/70	Glencoe, MO
24	Dreyer, Steve	R	R	6–3	180	11/19/69	Ames, IA
30	Fajardo, Hector	R	R	6–4	200	11/6/70	Michoacan, Mexico
57	Helling, Rick	R	R	6–3	215	12/15/70	West Fargo, ND
28	Oliver, Darren	R	L	6–0	170	10/6/70	Kansas City, MO
59	Pavlik, Roger	R	R	6–2	220	10/4/67	Houston, TX
37	Rogers, Kenny	L	L	6–1	205	11/10/64	Savannah, GA
35	Smith, Dan	L	L	6–5	195	4/20/69	St. Paul, MN
27	Whiteside, Matt	R	R	6–0	195	8/8/67	Charleston, MO
	Catchers						
—	Luce, Roger	R	R	6–4	215	5/7/69	Houston, TX
7	Rodriguez, Ivan	R	R	5–9	205	11/30/71	Vaga Baja, PR
	Infielders						
6	Beltre, Esteban	R	R	5–10	172	12/26/67	Ingenio Quisfuella, DR
22	Clark, Will	L	L	6–0	195	3/13/64	New Orleans, LA
1	Frye, Jeff	R	R	5–9	165	8/31/66	Oakland, CA
23	Gil, Benji	R	R	6–2	182	10/6/72	Tijuana, Mexico
9	Huson, Jeff	L	R	6–3	180	8/15/64	Scottsdale, AZ
—	Mercedes, Guillermo	R	R	5–11	155	1/17/74	La Romana, DR
16	Palmer, Dean	R	R	6–2	195	12/27/68	Tallahassee, FL
20	Strange, Doug	B	R	6–2	170	4/13/64	Greenville, SC
	Outfielders						
19	Gonzalez, Juan	R	R	6–3	210	10/16/69	Vaga Baja, PR
29	Greer, Rusty	L	L	6–0	190	1/21/69	Ft. Rucker, AL
15	Hulse, David	L	L	5–11	170	2/25/68	San Angelo, TX
32	Lowery, Terrell	R	R	6–3	175	10/25/70	Oakland, CA
—	Nixon, Otis	B	R	6–2	180	1/9/59	Evergreen, NC

1995 Schedule

April

S	M	T	W	T	F	S
						1
2	3 NY	4	5 NY	6	7 BAL	8 BAL
9 BAL	10 BOS	11	12 BOS	13 BAL	14 BAL	15 BAL
16 BAL	17	18 BOS	19 BOS	20 BOS	21 CLE	22 CLE
23 CLE	24 CLE	25 NY	26 NY	27 CLE	28 CLE	29 CLE
30 CLE						

May

S	M	T	W	T	F	S
	1 SEA	2 SEA	3 SEA	4	5 OAK	6 OAK
7 OAK	8 OAK	9 CAL	10 CAL	11 CAL	12 DET	13 DET
14 DET	15 TOR	16 TOR	17 TOR	18 MIL	19 MIL	20 MIL
21 MIL	22	23 CHI	24 CHI	25	26 MIN	27 MIN
28 MIN	29 KC	30 KC	31 KC			

June

S	M	T	W	T	F	S
				1 MIN	2 MIN	3 MIN
4 MIN	5 KC	6 KC	7 KC	8	9 CHI	10 CHI
11 CHI	12 MIL	13 MIL	14 MIL	15	16 TOR	17 TOR
18 TOR	19 DET	20 DET	21 DET	22	23 OAK	24 OAK
25 OAK	26 OAK	27 CAL	28 CAL	29 CAL	30 SEA	

July

S	M	T	W	T	F	S
						1 SEA
2 SEA	3	4 CLE	5 CLE	6 NY	7 NY	8 NY
9 NY	10	11 ★	12	13 BOS	14 BOS	15 BOS
16 BOS	17 BAL	18 BAL	19 CLE	20 CLE	21 NY	22 NY
23 NY	24 NY	25 BAL	26 BAL	27 BAL	28 BOS	29 BOS
30 BOS	31					

August

S	M	T	W	T	F	S
		1 OAK	2 OAK	3 OAK	4 CAL	5 CAL
6 CAL	7 CAL	8 DET	9 DET	10 DET	11 TOR	12 TOR
13 TOR	14	15 MIL	16 MIL	17 CHI	18 CHI	19 CHI
20 CHI	21 MIN	22 MIN	23 MIN	24 KC	25 KC	26 KC
27 KC	28 MIN	29 MIN	30 MIN	31		

Sept/Oct

S	M	T	W	T	F	S
					1 KC	2 KC
3 KC	4 CHI	5 CHI	6 CHI	7 CHI	8 MIL	9 MIL
10 MIL	11	12 TOR	13 TOR	14 TOR	15 DET	16 DET
17 DET	18 SEA	19 SEA	20 SEA	21	22 CAL	23 CAL
24 CAL	25	26 OAK	27 OAK	28 SEA	29 SEA	30 SEA
1 SEA						

☐ Home   ☐ Away   ★ All-Star Game

The Ballpark in Arlington

Capacity: 48,100

Turf: Grass

Dimensions:
LF Line: 334'
RF Line: 325'
Center: 400'
Left CF: 388'
Right CF: 377'–407'

Tickets:
(817) 273-5000

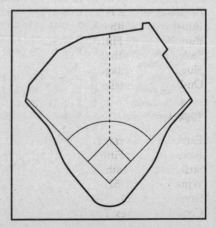

1994 Batting Order

1. David Hulse (Center Field)
2. Jeff Frye (Second Base)
3. Jose Canseco (Designated Hitter)
4. Will Clark (First Base)
5. Juan Gonzalez (Left Field)
6. Dean Palmer (Third Base)
7. Rusty Greer (Right Field)
8. Ivan Rodriguez (Catcher)
9. Manuel Lee (Shortstop)

1994 Team Record
52–62 (.456); First in AL West

AL East	W	L	AL Central	W	L	AL West	W	L
Baltimore	3	3	Chicago	5	4	California	4	6
Boston	5	1	Cleveland	7	5	Oakland	3	7
Detroit	7	5	Kansas City	3	4	Seattle	1	9
New York	2	3	Milwaukee	3	3	Texas	—	—
Toronto	4	8	Minnesota	5	4			
Total	21	20		23	20		8	22

1994 American League Team Rank Batting

Batting Average: Fourth (.280)
Runs Scored: Fifth (613)
Runs Batted In: Fifth (582)
Stolen Bases: Fifth (82)
Slugging Percentage: Seventh (.436)
On-Base Percentage: Third (.353)

1994 American League Team Rank Pitching

Earned Run Average: Thirteenth (5.45)
Bases On Balls: Fifth (394)
Strikeouts: Seventh (683)
Wins: Eleventh (52)
Saves: Sixth (26)
Complete Games: Tenth (10)

Texas Rangers MVP

Jose Canseco   No. 33/ DH

Born: 7/2/64, Havana, Cuba
Height: 6' 4"   **Weight:** 240
Bats: Right   **Throws:** Right
1994 OBP: .386   **SLG:** .552

The Rangers will sorely miss Canseco's power and personality. Returning from '93 elbow surgery, he was used exclusively in the DH role, freeing him to concentrate on hitting. Canseco is by far the youngest member of the majors' top ten active home run leaders. He's one of the game's most exciting sluggers.

Canseco has incredible tools—quick wrists, good batting eye, and great strength. But his mechanics are excellent as well. He does amass a ton of strikeouts (114, second in the AL), but Canseco ranked second in the league in number of pitches seen. He's got a big swing, but he isn't a wild swinger.

And of course, Canseco is tremendously productive. He finished among the AL leaders in home runs (fourth), runs (sixth), walks (seventh), RBIs (tied for seventh), and slugging (eighth). He hit .323 with runners in scoring position, .333 after the sixth inning. He crushed three homers versus Seattle on June 13, one of which traveled 480 feet.

Canseco has suffered back troubles, and he's been one of the game's least stable personalities, at times behaving erratically off the field. But there's no question that he could potentially hit sixty home runs for Boston if he can stay in the lineup and stay focused on baseball.

	G	AB	H	2B	3B	HR	RS	RBI	BB	SB	BA
1994	111	429	121	19	2	31	88	90	69	15	.282
Career	2175	4315	1154	204	11	276	732	870	518	149	.267
Projected	160	624	174	31	3	39	113	130	81	20	.275

Jack Armstrong   No. 77/ P

Born: 3/7/65, Englewood, NJ
Height: 6' 5"   **Weight:** 220
Bats: Right   **Throws:** Right
Opp. Batting Average: .231

The NL's starting pitcher in the 1990 All-Star Game, Armstrong is 23–52 since that start. He suffered a tear of the rotator cuff in his right shoulder after just two starts last year. Armstrong has great stuff and works hard, and his downfall is largely attributable to shoulder problems and poor pitch selection. It's tempting to write him off, but Armstrong could make a comeback.

	G	GS	IP	ERA	H	BB	SO	W	L	SV
1994	2	2	10.0	3.60	9	2	7	0	1	0
Career	152	130	786.2	4.58	807	319	510	40	65	0
Projected				No projection. Player was injured in 1994.						

Kevin Brown   No. 41/ P

Born: 3/14/65, McIntyre, GA
Height: 6' 4"   **Weight:** 195
Bats: Right   **Throws:** Right
Opp. Batting Average: .314

Brown won twenty-one games in 1992 and was compared favorably to Roger Clemens, but last year his performance dropped like a Bert Blyleven curveball. An extreme groundball pitcher, Brown led the AL in number of doubleplays induced (23). That was the only highlight of '94 for Brown, who tied for second in the league in runs allowed.

	G	GS	IP	ERA	H	BB	SO	W	L	SV
1994	26	25	170.0	4.82	218	50	123	7	9	0
Career	187	186	1278.2	3.81	1322	426	742	78	64	0
Projected	34	34	231.0	4.11	255	71	152	13	12	0

Cris Carpenter   No. 31/ P

Born: 4/5/65, St. Augustine, FL
Height: 6' 1"   **Weight:** 185
Bats: Right   **Throws:** Right
Opp. Batting Average: .291

Carpenter came to the Rangers in '93 as a pretty good setup man, but he's done little to help the Rangers' cause. He's become powerless to stop lefties, who lit him up for a .363 BA. Carpenter's ERA was a dismal 7.52 in his last seventeen appearances. He pitched in forty-seven games, sixth most in the league. Carpenter throws a moving fastball and a decent slider.

	G	GS	IP	ERA	H	BB	SO	W	L	SV
1994	47	0	59.0	5.03	69	20	39	2	5	5
Career	283	13	406.0	3.63	386	129	250	27	22	7
Projected	59	0	74.0	4.21	77	26	53	3	4	3

Will Clark   No. 22/ 1B

Born: 3/213/64, New Orleans, LA
Height: 6' 0"   **Weight:** 195
Bats: Left   **Throws:** Left
1994 OBP: .431   **SLG:** .501

The smooth-swinging ex-Giant sparked the Rangers' batting order with the AL's fifth-best on-base percentage. Clark hit very well in Arlington (.338) and came through in the clutch (.365 with runners in scoring position). He hit twelve of his thirteen homers off righthanded pitching. Clark's fielding has long been overrated; he ranked ninth in fielding percentage (.990).

	G	AB	H	2B	3B	HR	RS	RBI	BB	SB	BA
1994	110	389	128	24	2	13	73	80	71	5	.329
Career	1270	4658	1406	273	39	189	760	789	577	57	.302
Projected	146	536	166	31	2	17	95	94	82	4	.306

Jeff Frye   No. 1/ 2B

Born: 8/31/66, Oakland, CA
Height: 5' 9"   **Weight:** 165
Bats: Right   **Throws:** Right
1994 OBP: .408   **SLG:** .454

Frye is an exciting, hustling player who has had a hard time staying healthy. He's fast, but he's also had leg problems (knee, hamstring). Frye has hit at every level of pro ball, and he's a good bet to have a big year in '95, if he doesn't get hurt. He hit better at home (.407) than any other Ranger, and knocked two triples versus California May 10 to tie a club record.

	G	AB	H	2B	3B	HR	RS	RBI	BB	SB	BA
1994	57	205	67	20	3	0	37	18	29	6	.327
Career	124	404	118	29	4	1	61	30	45	7	.292
Projected				No projection. Player was injured in 1993.							

Juan Gonzalez   No. 19/ OF

Born: 10/16/69, Vaga Baja, PR
Height: 6' 3"   **Weight:** 210
Bats: Right   **Throws:** Right
1994 OBP: .330   **SLG:** .472

Gonzalez blew hot and cold in '94. His average stood at .250 through July 17, including a twenty-six game home run drought. Gonzalez hit at least twenty-seven homers in each of his first three full seasons; he has quickly become one of the majors' premier sluggers. He made the AL top ten in RBIs and intentional walks. He fielded .991 and had seven assists.

	G	AB	H	2B	3B	HR	RS	RBI	BB	SB	BA
1994	107	422	116	18	4	19	57	85	30	6	.275
Career	593	2237	613	119	9	140	334	433	152	14	.274
Projected	150	611	198	34	3	44	108	36	45	7	.309

Rusty Greer   No. 29/ OF

Born: 1/21/69, Fort Rucker, AL
Height: 6' 0"   **Weight:** 190
Bats: Left   **Throws:** Left
1994 OBP: .410   **SLG:** .487

Greer had a solid rookie campaign, finishing number one among first-year players in batting average and on-base percentage. He cuffed around lefties at a .332 rate. Greer preserved Kenny Rogers's perfect game with a diving catch in the ninth inning. He probably won't be a star, but he's got a fine batting eye and twenty-homer potential.

	G	AB	H	2B	3B	HR	RS	RBI	BB	SB	BA
1994	80	277	87	16	1	10	36	46	46	0	.314
Career	80	277	87	16	1	10	36	46	46	0	.314
Projected	No projection. Player was a rookie in 1994.										

Tom Henke   No. 50/ P

Born: 12/21/57, Kansas City, MO
Height: 6' 5"   **Weight:** 225
Bats: Right   **Throws:** Right
Opp. Batting Average: .232

Henke had a down year in '94, but the blame falls largely on a bulging disc in his lower back. He threw well after returning from the DL, and he's still got great movement on his fastball, striking out more than one batter per inning. Henke is seventh on the all-time saves list, and his ratio of 9.95 Ks per nine innings ranks number one in major league history.

	G	GS	IP	ERA	H	BB	SO	W	L	SV
1994	37	0	38.0	3.79	33	12	39	3	6	15
Career	590	0	735.1	2.73	565	237	858	43	41	275
Projected	58	0	63.0	3.22	49	22	66	4	6	31

Jay Howell   No. 52/ P

Born: 11/26/55, Miami, FL
Height: 6' 3"   **Weight:** 205
Bats: Right   **Throws:** Right
Opp. Batting Average: .262

Howell didn't pitch as poorly as his ERA, which was the highest of his career, would indicate. He allowed just three earned runs in nineteen innings after getting off to an awful start. He pitched great in Arlington (2.82 ERA), but was rocked on the road, compiling an 8.27 ERA in twenty appearances away from home. Howell has been a fine pitcher for a long time.

	G	GS	IP	ERA	H	BB	SO	W	L	SV
1994	40	0	43.0	5.44	44	16	22	4	1	2
Career	568	21	844.0	3.34	782	291	666	58	53	155
Projected	54	0	58.0	3.64	53	18	34	4	2	1

David Hulse   No. 15/ OF

Born: 2/25/68, San Angelo, TX
Height: 5' 11"   **Weight:** 170
Bats: Left   **Throws:** Left
1994 OBP: .305   **SLG:** .316

Hulse is a fast, smart baserunner. He compiled a 90% success rate in his twenty steal attempts. He grounded into just one DP all season, the AL's fourth-best ratio. But his hitting was streaky, and he wound up back in the minors in late July. The Rangers' right field and leadoff spots are in flux, and Hulse should get another chance to win the job.

	G	AB	H	2B	3B	HR	RS	RBI	BB	SB	BA
1994	77	310	79	8	4	1	58	19	21	18	.255
Career	223	809	225	21	14	2	143	50	50	50	.278
Projected	116	454	135	11	9	1	85	32	31	31	.286

Darren Oliver No. 28/ P

Born: 10/6/70, Kansas City, MO
Height: 6' 0" **Weight:** 170
Bats: Right **Throws:** Left
Opp. Batting Average: .223

He led American League rookie pitchers in appearances, then underwent elbow surgery in October. Oliver baffled lefthanders; they hit just .119 against him. And he didn't allow a home run in his last twenty outings. Oliver throws very hard, and the Rangers see him as the heir to Tom Henke's role of stopper, if his arm is sound.

	G	GS	IP	ERA	H	BB	SO	W	L	SV
1994	43	0	50.0	3.42	40	35	50	4	0	2
Career	45	0	53.1	3.38	42	36	54	4	0	2
Projected				No projection. Player was a rookie in 1994.						

Dean Palmer No. 16/ 3B

Born: 12/27/68, Tallahassee, FL
Height: 6' 2" **Weight:** 195
Bats: Right **Throws:** Right
1994 OBP: .302 **SLG:** .465

A professional home run hitter, Palmer can hit the ball to El Paso, but his game has some flaws. For starters, he led major league third basemen in errors, amassing ten in his final thirty-one games. Palmer ranks tenth all-time in Ranger history with ninety-three home runs. He tends to hit longballs in streaks, but when he's in a groove, things get exciting in a hurry.

	G	AB	H	2B	3B	HR	RS	RBI	BB	SB	BA
1994	93	342	84	14	2	19	50	59	26	3	.246
Career	490	1689	387	81	6	93	250	265	173	24	.229
Projected	146	541	143	29	3	34	90	101	52	9	.255

Ivan Rodriguez   No. 7/ C

Born: 11/30/71, Vaga Baja, PR
Height: 5' 9"   **Weight:** 205
Bats: Right   **Throws:** Right
1994 OBP: .360   **SLG:** .488

Rodriguez led AL qualifying catchers in batting average and set a team record for homers by a backstop. He's developing quickly as a hitter, and his defense is refined. Rodriguez gunned down 33.9% of would-be basestealers. He was slowed somewhat by minor injuries, which is typical for a catcher. Rodriguez caught all ten innings of the 1994 All-Star Game.

	G	AB	H	2B	3B	HR	RS	RBI	BB	SB	BA
1994	99	363	108	19	1	16	56	57	31	6	.298
Career	447	1536	420	79	6	37	175	187	89	14	.273
Projected	145	538	168	32	3	18	76	83	41	9	.298

Kenny Rogers   No. 37/ P

Born: 11/10/64, Savannah, GA
Height: 6' 1"   **Weight:** 205
Bats: Left   **Throws:** Left
Opp. Batting Average: .260

Beautiful and beastly. That describes a season in which Rogers hurled the eleventh regular season perfect game since 1900, then allowed thirteen runs in his next 10.1 innings. He's the winningest lefty in Rangers history, which says something interesting about the quality of Rangers pitching. Rogers ranked fourth in complete games (6) among AL hurlers.

	G	GS	IP	ERA	H	BB	SO	W	L	SV
1994	24	24	167.1	4.46	169	52	120	11	8	0
Career	345	69	735.1	4.03	733	294	540	53	44	28
Projected	34	32	213.0	4.27	215	70	148	15	10	0

Toronto
BLUE JAYS

1995 Scouting Report

Outfielders: The Blue Jays have a Gold Glover in center fielder Devon White. Joe Carter (RF) is a perennial All-Star and an RBI machine. Newcomer Mike Huff has shown intriguing potential in left field.

Infielders: The right side of the Jays' infield is superb. Second baseman Roberto Alomar is an annual Gold Glove fielder and a dynamic all-around offensive threat. John Olerud won a batting title in 1993 and figures to do so again before he turns thirty. Toronto isn't as strong on the left side. Ed Sprague does some things well, but he hasn't proven that he's a quality full-time major league third baseman. The shortstop position will probably be the sole domain of youngster Alex Gonzalez.

Catchers: Pat Borders kept his job when rookie Carlos Delgado faltered. Borders has a decent bat and a fine throwing arm.

Starting Pitchers: Toronto's starters throw wild and hard. The team's most reliable arm belongs to Pat Hentgen. Juan Guzman has great stuff, but he hasn't fully mastered it yet. The lower three-fifths of the rotation is thin. Todd Stottlemyre and Al Leiter haven't distinguished themselves. The fifth spot is open, so the Jays will probably test the free agent market.

Relief Pitchers: Top closer Duane Ward went down with a shoulder injury, but rookie Darren Hall stepped in to fill the gap. Journeyman lefty Tony Castillo had the best season of his career in a setup role.

Designated Hitters: Paul Molitor is a future Hall of Famer.

Manager: Cito Gaston (500–389) is popular among his players. He's the winningest manager in Blue Jays history.

1995 Outlook

The Blue Jays are a little bit like a person who has fallen off a cliff and landed on a ledge halfway to the bottom. Toronto still has enough talent to contend, but the Jays are a long way from the top of the division.

Toronto reminds us of another Canadian team, the Montreal Expos circa 1982. The Expos finished third in their division that year, despite sporting a roster that included Gary Carter, Tim Raines, Andre Dawson, Al Oliver, Jeff Reardon, and Steve Rogers—all in their prime. How could they have failed to win? For essentially the same reason that the Blue Jays tumbled from championship form in 1994: The team canceled out its great strengths with serious deficiencies.

The Blue Jays' lineup features All-Star quality at a minimum of five positions: Alomar (2B), Carter (RF), Olerud (1B), Molitor (DH), and Ward (RP). Unfortunately for the Jays, they received below-average production at third base, shortstop, and catcher. Toronto also got as little help from their bench as any team in the American League. Add in the league's most average starting pitching staff, and the result is a team that can appear to be both great and awful, depending on which element of the club is being considered.

It is likely that the Jays will be able to reverse their downfall to some degree this season. Neither of the club's youngest stars, Olerud and Alomar, were at their most productive in '94. Both are in their prime and can be expected to come back strong this year. The front office will almost certainly take steps to shore up the starting pitching. The minor league prospects haven't lived up to expectations, but it's too early to write them off.

Toronto is in a position to set the tone for the entire AL East. If the Jays are strong, the division will be one of baseball's most balanced. If Toronto is truly in decline, the East will be a two-horse race between Baltimore and New York, with the Jays and Boston battling for third place.

1995 Toronto Blue Jays Roster

Manager: Cito Gaston
Coaches: Bob Bailor, Galen Cisco, Larry Hisle, Dennis Holmberg,
Nick Leyva, Gene Tenace

No.	Pitchers	B	T	HT	WT	DOB	Birthplace
44	Brow, Scott	R	R	6–3	200	3/17/69	Butte, MT
49	Castillo, Tony	L	L	5–10	188	3/1/63	Lara, Venezuela
58	Cornett, Brad	R	R	6–3	190	2/4/69	Larnessa, TX
35	Gray, Dennis	L	L	6–6	215	12/24/69	Riverside, CA
66	Guzman, Juan	R	R	5–11	195	10/28/66	Santo Domingo, DR
36	Hall, Darren	R	R	6–3	205	7/14/64	Marysville, OH
41	Hentgen, Pat	R	R	6–2	200	11/13/68	Detroit, MI
28	Leiter, Al	L	L	6–3	215	10/23/65	Toms River, NJ
55	Menhart, Paul	R	R	6–2	190	3/25/69	St. Louis, MO
38	Small, Aaron	R	R	6–5	195	11/23/71	Oxnard, CA
46	Spoljaric, Paul	R	L	6–3	206	9/24/70	Kelowna, Canada
40	Timlin, Mike	R	R	6–4	210	3/10/66	Midland, TX
31	Ward, Duane	R	R	6–4	215	5/28/64	Parkview, NM
54	Williams, Woody	R	R	6–0	190	8/19/66	Houston, TX
	Catchers						
6	Delgado, Carlos	L	R	6–3	215	6/25/72	Aguadilla, PR
27	Knorr, Randy	R	R	6–2	218	11/12/68	San Gabriel, CA
53	Martinez, Angel	L	R	6–4	200	10/3/72	Villa Mella, DR
	Infielders						
12	Alomar, Roberto	B	R	6–0	185	2/5/68	Ponce, PR
70	Cedeno, Domingo	B	R	6–1	165	11/4/68	La Romana, DR
8	Gonzalez, Alex	R	R	6–0	186	4/8/73	Miami, FL
4	Molitor, Paul	R	R	6–0	185	8/22/56	St. Paul, MN
9	Olerud, John	L	L	6–5	218	8/5/68	Seattle, WA
33	Sprague, Ed	R	R	6–2	215	7/25/67	Castro Valley, CA
	Outfielders						
2	Butler, Rob	L	L	5–11	185	4/10/70	East York, Canada
29	Carter, Joe	R	R	6–3	225	3/7/60	Oklahoma City, OK
15	Green, Shawn	L	L	6–4	190	11/10/72	Des Plaines, IL
26	Huff, Mike	R	R	6–1	190	8/11/63	Honolulu, HI
17	Perez, Robert	R	R	6–3	205	6/4/69	Bolivar, Venezuela
25	White, Devon	B	R	6–2	180	12/29/62	Kingston, Jamaica

1995 Schedule

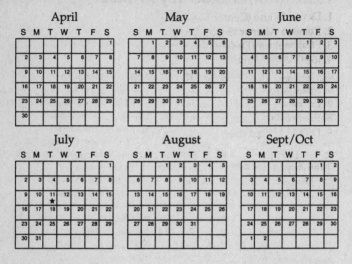

April

S	M	T	W	T	F	S
						1
2	3	4	5	6	7	8
9	10	11	12	13	14	15
16	17	18	19	20	21	22
23	24	25	26	27	28	29
30						

May

S	M	T	W	T	F	S
	1	2	3	4	5	6
7	8	9	10	11	12	13
14	15	16	17	18	19	20
21	22	23	24	25	26	27
28	29	30	31			

June

S	M	T	W	T	F	S
				1	2	3
4	5	6	7	8	9	10
11	12	13	14	15	16	17
18	19	20	21	22	23	24
25	26	27	28	29	30	

July

S	M	T	W	T	F	S
						1
2	3	4	5	6	7	8
9	10	11★	12	13	14	15
16	17	18	19	20	21	22
23	24	25	26	27	28	29
30	31					

August

S	M	T	W	T	F	S
		1	2	3	4	5
6	7	8	9	10	11	12
13	14	15	16	17	18	19
20	21	22	23	24	25	26
27	28	29	30	31		

Sept/Oct

S	M	T	W	T	F	S
					1	2
3	4	5	6	7	8	9
10	11	12	13	14	15	16
17	18	19	20	21	22	23
24	25	26	27	28	29	30
1	2					

The Blue Jays were unable to provide a schedule by press time.

SkyDome

Capacity: 52,268

Turf: Artificial

Dimensions:
LF Line: 328'
RF Line: 328'
Center: 400'
Alleys: 375'

Tickets:
(416) 341-1234

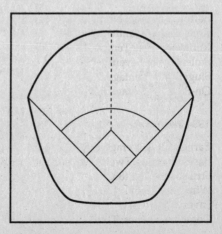

1994 Batting Order

1. Devon White (Center Field)
2. Roberto Alomar (Second Base)
3. Paul Molitor (Designated Hitter)
4. Joe Carter (Right Field)
5. John Olerud (First Base)
6. Mike Huff (Left Field)
7. Ed Sprague (Third Base)
8. Pat Borders (Catcher)
9. Dick Schofield (Shortstop)

1994 Team Record
55–60 (.478); Third in AL East

AL East	W	L	AL Central	W	L	AL West	W	L
Baltimore	2	7	Chicago	3	2	California	4	3
Boston	3	7	Cleveland	4	6	Oakland	1	5
Detroit	4	5	Kansas City	6	6	Seattle	5	1
New York	4	3	Milwaukee	3	7	Texas	8	4
Toronto	—	—	Minnesota	8	4			
Total	13	22		24	25		18	13

1994 American League Team Rank Batting

Batting Average: Ninth (.269)
Runs Scored: Tenth (566)
Runs Batted In: Tenth (534)
Stolen Bases: Seventh (79)
Slugging Percentage: Ninth (.424)
On-Base Percentage: Eighth (.336)

1994 American League Team Rank Pitching

Earned Run Average: Seventh (4.70)
Bases On Balls: Twelfth (482)
Strikeouts: First (832)
Wins: Sixth (55)
Saves: Sixth (26)
Complete Games: Third (13)

Toronto Blue Jays MVP

Paul Molitor   No. 4/ DH

Born: 8/22/56, St. Paul, MN
Height: 6' 0"   **Weight:** 185
Bats: Right   **Throws:** Right
1994 OBP: .410   **SLG:** .518

At age thirty-eight, the remarkably consistent Molitor continues making impressive additions to his Hall of Fame credentials. Once thought to be injury prone, Molitor had actually taken at least 500 at-bats in ten of his sixteen seasons prior to the strike-shortened 1994 campaign. He has been one of the most potent leadoff hitters in baseball history.

Molitor's bat speed hasn't decreased with age, thanks to the nature of his short, quick stroke. Molitor is dangerous when batting in any of the top three spots in the order. Last year, the Blue Jays' catalyst compiled the sixth-highest batting average in the American League, including forty-three multi-hit games (tied for fourth most in the league).

As dominant as Molitor was in 1993, he managed to increase his rate of production last season. He has taken offensive baseball to a higher level, combining a young player's athleticism with a sublime understanding of the game. Molitor made the AL's top ten in runs scored (seventh), total bases (eighth), doubles (ninth), and on-base percentage (tenth).

Deadly on the basepaths, Molitor will never run his team out of a rally, yet he's quick to take the extra base if an opposing fielder isn't alert. Molitor is a brilliant student of pitchers' moves; he swiped twenty bases last season without being caught once.

	G	AB	H	2B	3B	HR	RS	RBI	BB	SB	BA
1994	115	454	155	30	4	14	86	75	55	20	.341
Career	2131	8610	2647	472	95	196	1482	976	887	454	.337
Projected	160	621	200	37	5	20	116	104	74	23	.329

Roberto Alomar   No. 12/ 2B

Born: 2/5/68, Ponce, PR
Height: 6' 0"   **Weight:** 185
Bats: Both   **Throws:** Right
1994 OBP: .386   **SLG:** .452

A franchise player and one of the majors' most complete talents, Alomar is in his prime. Though he wasn't able to carry the troubled Blue Jays on his back last year, Alomar had a productive season and the plate and on the basepaths. At second base, Alomar put together a sparkling performance that culminated in his fourth consecutive Gold Glove Award.

	G	AB	H	2B	3B	HR	RS	RBI	BB	SB	BA
1994	107	392	120	25	4	8	78	38	51	19	.306
Career	1021	3943	1174	206	41	64	626	433	423	266	.298
Projected	160	613	202	40	6	12	124	64	84	35	.317

Pat Borders   No. 10/ C

Born: 5/14/63, Columbus, OH
Height: 6' 2"   **Weight:** 200
Bats: Right   **Throws:** Right
1994 OBP: .284   **SLG:** .329

The consensus opinion was that Borders would be losing his starting position in 1994, but Borders kept his job and played fine defense behind the plate. The Blue Jays' backstop threw out 31.6% of runners attempting to steal last year, the sixth-best rate in the American League. With the bat, Borders is still susceptible to swinging wildly at breaking pitches off the plate.

	G	AB	H	2B	3B	HR	RS	RBI	BB	SB	BA
1994	86	295	73	13	1	3	24	26	15	1	.247
Career	742	2295	587	127	9	53	204	269	111	6	.256
Projected	135	477	122	26	1	7	38	50	22	2	.254

Joe Carter No. 29/ OF

Born: 3/7/60, Oklahoma City, OK
Height: 6' 3" **Weight:** 225
Bats: Right **Throws:** Right
1994 OBP: .317 **SLG:** .524

Carter's gargantuan home run to win the 1992 World Series made him the most visible representative of Blue Jays' success. Carter was even more productive in '94, reaching the century mark in RBIs for the eighth time in the last nine seasons and finishing second in the league with 103 ribbies. Carter also reasserted himself stealing bases, going eleven-for-eleven.

	G	AB	H	2B	3B	HR	RS	RBI	BB	SB	BA
1994	111	435	118	25	2	27	70	103	33	11	.271
Career	1610	6239	1641	322	41	302	889	1097	382	200	.263
Projected	157	612	157	34	4	35	94	129	46	11	.257

Carlos Delgado No. 6/ OF

Born: 6/25/72, Aguadilla, PR
Height: 6' 3" **Weight:** 206
Bats: Left **Throws:** Right
1994 OBP: .352 **SLG:** .438

Delgado was perhaps the AL's most highly touted prospect last spring, and he came out swinging hard to start the season, collecting nine home runs by June. Despite the power output, Delgado's first season in the majors ended with a return to the minors for more seasoning, as his average hovered around .215 in his first extended major league trial.

	G	AB	H	2B	3B	HR	RS	RBI	BB	SB	BA
1994	43	130	28	2	0	9	17	24	25	1	.215
Career	45	131	28	2	0	9	17	24	26	1	.214
Projected	66	202	48	3	0	15	28	39	42	2	.224

Juan Guzman   No. 66/ P

Born: 10/28/66, Santo Domingo, DR
Height: 5' 11"   **Weight:** 195
Bats: Right   **Throws:** Right
Opp. Batting Average: .282

Guzman throws an array of nasty offerings, but his control is getting worse each year. Not only did he walk the seventh-most batters in the league, Guzman tied for the lead among AL hurlers in wild pitches. Despite his high ERA, Guzman managed to finish with a winning record. If he can somehow achieve command of his stuff, he could be a Cy Young winner.

	G	GS	IP	ERA	H	BB	SO	W	L	SV
1994	25	25	147.1	5.68	165	76	124	12	11	0
Career	109	109	687.2	3.79	609	324	606	52	22	0
Projected	33	33	210.0	4.67	215	106	182	15	8	0

Darren Hall   No. 36/ P

Born: 7/14/64, Irving, TX
Height: 6' 3"   **Weight:** 205
Bats: Right   **Throws:** Right
Opp. Batting Average: .226

Hall wasn't even rated as a top prospect in the Blue Jays' farm system, but he took over for injured closer Duane Ward and handled the job like a seasoned professional. Hall's 1993 ERA at Triple-A Syracuse was a portly 5.33, but he was tough on major leaguers, striking out nearly one batter per inning. Hall figures to be a solid closer this season.

	G	GS	IP	ERA	H	BB	SO	W	L	SV
1994	30	0	31.2	3.41	26	14	28	2	3	17
Career	30	0	31.2	3.41	26	14	28	2	3	17
Projected	No projection. Player was a rookie in 1994.									

Pat Hentgen
No. 41/ P

Born: 11/13/68, Detroit, MI
Height: 6' 2" **Weight:** 200
Bats: Right **Throws:** Right
Opp. Batting Average: .240

The only reliable starter on the Blue Jays' staff, Hentgen made great progress from his excellent 1993 debut. Hentgen has an impressive understanding of how to pitch. He uses his solid repertoire like a wily veteran, and his future looks bright. If Hentgen can reduce his frequency of bases on balls next year, he could join the AL's elite starters.

	G	GS	IP	ERA	H	BB	SO	W	L	SV
1994	24	24	174.2	3.40	158	59	147	13	8	0
Career	89	59	448.2	3.83	427	168	311	37	19	0
Projected	33	32	222.0	3.66	212	76	153	18	10	0

Mike Huff
No. 26/ OF

Born: 8/11/63, Honolulu, HI
Height: 6' 1" **Weight:** 190
Bats: Right **Throws:** Right
1994 OBP: .392 **SLG:** .449

Huff posted some decent numbers in the Chicago White Sox minor league system, but they dealt him to Toronto last year. Huff has good speed and an excellent batting eye, though he didn't show either of those qualities in 1994. He did make enough hard contact to hit over .300 with twenty-one extra-base hits, and he should get more playing time this season.

	G	AB	H	2B	3B	HR	RS	RBI	BB	SB	BA
1994	80	207	63	15	3	3	31	25	27	2	.304
Career	297	634	161	33	5	8	94	66	86	18	.254
Projected	123	254	73	17	3	4	36	32	37	3	.286

Al Leiter   No. 28/ P

Born: 10/23/65, Toms River, NJ
Height: 6' 3"   **Weight:** 215
Bats: Left   **Throws:** Left
Opp. Batting Average: .285

New York Yankees fans will remember Leiter from his days as a top prospect. His stuff is still pretty good, but arm injuries have kept Leiter from establishing himself. It seemed that Leiter was destined for the role of lefty setup man, a job for which he'd shown some adeptness in 1993, but the starter-starved Jays used him exclusively in the rotation, with mixed results.

	G	GS	IP	ERA	H	BB	SO	W	L	SV
1994	20	20	111.2	5.08	125	65	100	6	7	0
Career	85	55	339.0	4.75	328	201	286	22	21	2
Projected	30	18	122.0	4.60	122	68	93	8	7	1

John Olerud   No. 9/ 1B

Born: 8/5/68, Seattle, WA
Height: 6' 5"   **Weight:** 218
Bats: Left   **Throws:** Left
1994 OBP: .393   **SLG:** .477

Olerud is a study in pure hitting mechanics, with a gorgeous lefty swing that never varies. He's just entering his prime and figures to drive in 100+ runs this season. Olerud is one of only four major leaguers who have never played a game in the minor leagues. The Jays offered him to the Mets for Bret Saberhagen during the winter.

	G	AB	H	2B	3B	HR	RS	RBI	BB	SB	BA
1994	108	384	114	29	2	12	47	67	61	1	.297
Career	660	2213	658	156	6	83	333	356	370	2	.297
Projected	159	581	211	54	3	23	101	112	113	1	.349

Ed Sprague No. 33/ 3B

Born: 7/25/67, Castro Valley, CA
Height: 6' 2" **Weight:** 215
Bats: Right **Throws:** Right
1994 OBP: .296 **SLG:** .373

The Blue Jays have been searching for production at third base since Kelly Gruber began to decline in 1992. Toronto is hoping Sprague can develop into a consistent regular; he has the ability to hit twenty homers while keeping his average above the .250 mark. But Sprague's fielding is erratic, and his K/BB numbers (4/1) are a concern.

	G	AB	H	2B	3B	HR	RS	RBI	BB	SB	BA
1994	109	405	97	19	1	11	38	44	23	1	.240
Career	342	1158	294	59	2	28	111	144	77	2	.254
Projected	155	592	161	32	1	15	57	76	36	1	.261

Todd Stottlemyre No. 30/ P

Born: 5/20/65, Yakima, WA
Height: 6' 3" **Weight:** 200
Bats: Left **Throws:** Left
Opp. Batting Average: .276

Since entering the league in 1988, Stottlemyre has been riding a wave of expectations that have never been fulfilled. His arsenal is occasionally very effective, and he's been a reliable workhorse. Stottlemyer probably could have had a solid career as a middle reliever, but he was billed as a potential ace, and the Blue Jays haven't adjusted to the reality of his numbers.

	G	GS	IP	ERA	H	BB	SO	W	L	SV
1994	26	19	140.2	4.22	149	48	105	7	7	1
Career	206	175	1139.0	4.39	1182	414	662	69	70	1
Projected	28	24	158.0	4.56	176	58	101	9	10	0

Duane Ward   No. 31/ P

Born: 5/28/64, Parkview, NM
Height: 6' 4"   **Weight:** 215
Bats: Right   **Throws:** Right
Opp. Batting Average: —

One of the American League's most dominant closers in 1993 (forty-five saves), Ward was simply overused. Twenty-four of his seventy-one appearances in '93 were made without a single day of rest. Consequently, his entire 1994 season was lost to shoulder surgery on his pitching arm. When his arm is sound, Ward's slider can be unhittable.

	G	GS	IP	ERA	H	BB	SO	W	L	SV
1994	0	0	0.0	0.00	0	0	0	0	0	0
Career	458	2	664.0	3.19	540	281	676	32	36	121
Projected				No projection. Player was injured in 1994.						

Devon White   No. 25/ OF

Born: 12/29/62, Kingston, Jamaica
Height: 6' 2"   **Weight:** 180
Bats: Both   **Throws:** Right
1994 OBP: .313   **SLG:** .457

White's game has really improved since he batted .217 for California in 1990. His skills are well suited to playing in SkyDome, and he hits much better there than on the road. White is a super percentage basestealer with longball capabilities. But his greatest asset is defensive—last season was his sixth Gold Glove performance in center field.

	G	AB	H	2B	3B	HR	RS	RBI	BB	SB	BA
1994	100	403	109	24	6	13	67	49	21	11	.270
Career	1166	4515	1163	223	53	121	728	462	324	238	.258
Projected	150	616	171	41	7	17	114	63	48	28	.274

Individual Player Ratings

These ratings were conceived by the editors primarily as a help to members of fantasy/rotisserie leagues, but they should also prove intriguing to any fan who has ever argued the merits of Mo Vaughn versus Cecil Fielder, Moises Alou versus Sammy Sosa, or Mike Mussina versus Jimmy Key. It isn't possible to devise an all-encompassing number to simplify the complexities of a major leaguer's performance, but we can't resist trying to find an objective resolution to such comparisons.

The formulas employed are relatively basic. For hitters, the categories we chose to look at are batting average, runs scored, runs batted in, stolen bases minus failed attempts, and home runs. For starting pitchers, we utilized earned run average, strikeouts per innings pitched, hits plus walks divided by innings pitched, and wins minus losses. For relief pitchers, we employed the same stats as for starters, plus saves. The statistics under consideration are weighted so that, for example, steals aren't calculated as being equal to home runs. The method takes into account only 1994 performance, and it doesn't allow for age or fielding ability.

The computer gave a simulated nod to both leagues' MVP winners and the NL Cy Young recipient. But it rated Randy Johnson over David Cone among AL hurlers, which probably exposes a systemic flaw of "overweighting" strikeouts. The formula doesn't often concur with the Baseball Writers Association of America in regards to second- and third-place finishers. We haven't figured out whether Most Valuable Player means the player most important in the context of his team's season or simply the league's best player, but we do know that Barry Bonds had a better year with the bat than Matt Williams. Some head-to-head comparisons that really surprised us: Larry Walker over Moises Alou, Julio Franco ahead of Paul Molitor, and Chili Davis topping Paul O'Neill. We're fond of the ratings for relievers because the system gives setup men, such as Eric Plunk, their due by not overemphasizing high totals of saves.

AL Top 35 Hitters

1. Frank Thomas   Chicago White Sox
2. Albert Belle   Cleveland Indians
3. Ken Griffey, Jr.   Seattle Mariners
4. Kenny Lofton   Cleveland Indians
5. Jose Canseco   Texas Rangers
6. Kirby Puckett   Minnesota Twins
7. Joe Carter   Toronto Blue Jays
8. Ruben Sierra   Oakland A's
9. Julio Franco   Chicago White Sox
10. Paul Molitor   Toronto Blue Jays
11. Chili Davis   California Angels
12. Carlos Baerga   Cleveland Indians
13. Rafael Palmeiro   Baltimore Orioles
14. Paul O'Neill   New York Yankees
15. Cecil Fielder   Detroit Tigers
16. Mo Vaughn   Boston Red Sox
17. Tony Phillips   Detroit Tigers
18. Will Clark   Texas Rangers
19. Chuck Knoblauch   Minnesota Twins
20. Kirk Gibson   Detroit Tigers
21. Tim Salmon   California Angels
22. Cal Ripken, Jr.   Baltimore Orioles
23. Travis Fryman   Detroit Tigers
24. Juan Gonzalez   Texas Rangers
25. Jay Buhner   Seattle Mariners
26. Brady Anderson   Baltimore Orioles
27. Bob Hamelin   Kansas City Royals
28. Robin Ventura   Chicago White Sox
29. Bernie Williams   New York Yankees
30. Danny Tartabull   New York Yankees
31. Eddie Murray   Cleveland Indians
32. Tim Raines   Chicago White Sox
33. Shane Mack   Minnesota Twins
34. Geronimo Berroa   Oakland A's
35. Stan Javier   Oakland A's

AL Top 25 Starting Pitchers

1. Randy Johnson   Seattle Mariners
2. David Cone   Kansas City Royals
3. Mike Mussina   Baltimore Orioles
4. Roger Clemens   Boston Red Sox
5. Jimmy Key   New York Yankees
6. Jason Bere   Chicago White Sox
7. Pat Hentgen   Toronto Blue Jays
8. Alex Fernandez   Chicago White Sox
9. Dennis Martinez   Cleveland Indians
10. Wilson Alvarez   Chicago White Sox
11. Melido Perez   New York Yankees
12. Kevin Appier   Kansas City Royals
13. Ben McDonald   Baltimore Orioles
14. Steve Ontiveros   Oakland A's
15. Mark Clark   Cleveland Indians
16. Jack McDowell   Chicago White Sox
17. Charles Nagy   Cleveland Indians
18. Tom Gordon   Kansas City Royals
19. Kenny Rogers   Texas Rangers
20. Aaron Sele   Boston Red Sox
21. Chuck Finley   California Angels
22. Todd Stottlemyre   Toronto Blue Jays
23. Bill Wegman   Milwaukee Brewers
24. Kevin Tapani   Minnesota Twins
25. Sid Fernandez   Baltimore Orioles

AL Top 10 Relief Pitchers

1. Bobby Ayala   Seattle Mariners
2. Eric Plunk   Cleveland Indians
3. Steve Howe   New York Yankees
4. Bill Risley   Seattle Mariners
5. Lee Smith   Baltimore Orioles
6. Jeff Montgomery   Kansas City Royals
7. Dennis Eckersley   Oakland A's
8. Bob Wickman   New York Yankees
9. Tony Castillo   Toronto Blue Jays
10. Mark Eichhorn   Baltimore Orioles

NL Top 35 Hitters

1. Jeff Bagwell   Houston Astros
2. Barry Bonds   San Francisco Giants
3. Fred McGriff   Atlanta Braves
4. Matt Williams   San Francisco Giants
5. Dante Bichette   Colorado Rockies
6. Andres Galarraga   Colorado Rockies
7. Larry Walker   Montreal Expos
8. Moises Alou   Montreal Expos
9. Mike Piazza   Los Angeles Dodgers
10. Sammy Sosa   Chicago Cubs
11. Kevin Mitchell   Cincinnati Reds
12. Craig Biggio   Houston Astros
13. Tony Gwynn   San Diego Padres
14. Gary Sheffield   Florida Marlins
15. Tim Wallach   Los Angeles Dodgers
16. Jeff Conine   Florida Marlins
17. Ray Lankford   St. Louis Cardinals
18. Hal Morris   Cincinnati Reds
19. Wil Cordero   Montreal Expos
20. Ken Caminiti   Houston Astros
21. Barry Larkin   Cincinnati Reds
22. Reggie Sanders   Cincinnati Reds
23. Todd Zeile   St. Louis Cardinals
24. Bobby Bonilla   New York Mets
25. Derek Bell   San Diego Padres
26. David Justice   Atlanta Braves
27. Raul Mondesi   Los Angeles Dodgers
28. Bret Boone   Cincinnati Reds
29. Brett Butler   Los Angeles Dodgers
30. Gregg Jefferies   St. Louis Cardinals
31. Marquis Grissom   Montreal Expos
32. Jeff Kent   New York Mets
33. Roberto Kelly   Atlanta Braves
34. Mark Whiten   St. Louis Cardinals
35. Luis Gonzalez   Houston Astros

NL Top 25 Starting Pitchers

1. Greg Maddux	Atlanta Braves
2. Bret Saberhagen	New York Mets
3. Pedro J. Martinez	Montreal Expos
4. Doug Drabek	Houston Astros
5. Ken Hill	Montreal Expos
6. Danny Jackson	Philadelphia Phillies
7. Jose Rijo	Cincinnati Reds
8. Kent Mercker	Atlanta Braves
9. Marvin Freeman	Colorado Rockies
10. Butch Henry	Montreal Expos
11. Jeff Fassero	Montreal Expos
12. Shane Reynolds	Houston Astros
13. Steve Avery	Atlanta Braves
14. Ramon Martinez	Los Angeles Dodgers
15. Jim Bullinger	Chicago Cubs
16. Wm. VanLandingham	San Francisco Giants
17. Steve Trachsel	Chicago Cubs
18. Kevin Gross	Los Angeles Dodgers
19. Joey Hamilton	San Diego Padres
20. Tom Glavine	Atlanta Braves
21. Bobby Jones	New York Mets
22. Bobby Munoz	Philadelphia Phillies
23. Kevin Foster	Chicago Cubs
24. John Smiley	Cincinnati Reds
25. Andy Benes	San Diego Padres

NL Top 10 Relief Pitchers

1. Mel Rojas	Montreal Expos
2. Trevor Hoffman	San Diego Padres
3. Todd Jones	Houston Astros
4. John Wetteland	Montreal Expos
5. Jeff Brantley	Cincinnati Reds
6. Mike Jackson	San Francisco Giants
7. Robb Nen	Florida Marlins
8. Johnny Ruffin	Cincinnati Reds
9. Doug Jones	Philadelphia Phillies
10. Heathcliff Slocumb	Philadelphia Phillies

Pirates ace Zane Smith ranked tenth in NL ERA.

1994 Departmental Leaders

American League Batting

Batting Average

.359	O'Neill, Paul	New York Yankees
.357	Belle, Albert	Cleveland Indians
.353	Thomas, Frank	Chicago White Sox
.349	Lofton, Kenny	Cleveland Indians
.342	Boggs, Wade	New York Yankees
.341	Molitor, Paul	Toronto Blue Jays
.329	Clark, Will	Texas Rangers
.323	Griffey Jr., Ken	Seattle Mariners
.319	Palmeiro, Rafael	Baltimore Orioles
.319	Franco, Julio	Chicago White Sox

Home Runs

40	Griffey Jr., Ken	Seattle Mariners
38	Thomas, Frank	Chicago White Sox
36	Belle, Albert	Cleveland Indians
31	Canseco, Jose	Texas Rangers
28	Fielder, Cecil	Detroit Tigers
27	Carter, Joe	Toronto Blue Jays
26	Vaughn, Mo	Boston Red Sox
26	Davis, Chili	California Angels
24	Hamelin, Bob	Kansas City Royals
23	(04) Players Tied	

Runs Batted In

112	Puckett, Kirby	Minnesota Twins
103	Carter, Joe	Toronto Blue Jays
101	Thomas, Frank	Chicago White Sox
101	Belle, Albert	Cleveland Indians
98	Franco, Julio	Chicago White Sox
92	Sierra, Ruben	Oakland A's
90	Griffey Jr., Ken	Seattle Mariners
90	Fielder, Cecil	Detroit Tigers
90	Canseco, Jose	Texas Rangers
85	(02) Players Tied	

American League Pitching

Earned Run Average

2.65	Ontiveros, Steve	Oakland A's
2.85	Clemens, Roger	Boston Red Sox
2.94	Cone, David	Kansas City Royals
3.06	Mussina, Mike	Baltimore Orioles
3.19	Johnson, Randy	Seattle Mariners
3.27	Key, Jimmy	New York Yankees
3.40	Hentgen, Pat	Toronto Blue Jays
3.43	Bones, Ricky	Milwaukee Brewers
3.45	Alvarez, Wilson	Chicago White Sox
3.45	Nagy, Charles	Cleveland Indians

Wins

17	Key, Jimmy	New York Yankees
16	Mussina, Mike	Baltimore Orioles
16	Cone, David	Kansas City Royals
14	McDonald, Ben	Baltimore Orioles
13	Hentgen, Pat	Toronto Blue Jays
13	Johnson, Randy	Seattle Mariners
12	Alvarez, Wilson	Chicago White Sox
12	Guzman, Juan	Toronto Blue Jays
12	Bere, Jason	Chicago White Sox
11	(08) Players Tied	

Opp. Batting Average

.204	Clemens, Roger	Boston Red Sox
.209	Cone, David	Kansas City Royals
.216	Johnson, Randy	Seattle Mariners
.217	Ontiveros, Steve	Oakland A's
.229	Bere, Jason	Chicago White Sox
.236	Eldred, Cal	Milwaukee Brewers
.237	Gordon, Tom	Kansas City Royals
.238	Perez, Melido	New York Yankees
.240	Appier, Kevin	Kansas City Royals
.240	Hentgen, Pat	Toronto Blue Jays

National League Batting

Batting Average

.394	Gwynn, Tony	San Diego Padres
.368	Bagwell, Jeff	Houston Astros
.339	Alou, Moises	Montreal Expos
.335	Morris, Hal	Cincinnati Reds
.326	Mitchell, Kevin	Cincinnati Reds
.325	Jefferies, Gregg	St. Louis Cardinals
.322	Walker, Larry	Montreal Expos
.320	Boone, Bret	Cincinnati Reds
.320	Roberts, Bip	San Diego Padres
.319	Conine, Jeff	Florida Marlins

Home Runs

43	Williams, Matt	San Francisco Giants
39	Bagwell, Jeff	Houston Astros
37	Bonds, Barry	San Francisco Giants
34	McGriff, Fred	Atlanta Braves
31	Galarraga, Andres	Colorado Rockies
30	Mitchell, Kevin	Cincinnati Reds
27	Sheffield, Gary	Florida Marlins
27	Bichette, Dante	Colorado Rockies
25	Sosa, Sammy	Chicago Cubs
24	Piazza, Mike	Los Angeles Dodgers

Runs Batted In

116	Bagwell, Jeff	Houston Astros
96	Williams, Matt	San Francisco Giants
95	Bichette, Dante	Colorado Rockies
94	McGriff, Fred	Atlanta Braves
92	Piazza, Mike	Los Angeles Dodgers
86	Walker, Larry	Montreal Expos
85	Galarraga, Andres	Colorado Rockies
82	Conine, Jeff	Florida Marlins
81	Bonds, Barry	San Francisco Giants
78	(04) Players Tied	

National League Pitching

Earned Run Average

1.56	Maddux, Greg	Atlanta Braves
2.74	Saberhagen, Bret	New York Mets
2.84	Drabek, Doug	Houston Astros
2.99	Fassero, John	Montreal Expos
3.05	Reynolds, Shane	Houston Astros
3.08	Rijo, Jose	Cincinnati Reds
3.15	Jones, Bobby	New York Mets
3.21	Trachsel, Steve	Chicago Cubs
3.26	Jackson, Danny	Philadelphia Phillies
3.27	Smith, Zane	Pittsburgh Pirates

Wins

16	Hill, Ken	Montreal Expos
16	Maddux, Greg	Atlanta Braves
14	Saberhagen, Bret	New York Mets
14	Jackson, Danny	Philadelphia Phillies
13	Glavine, Tom	Atlanta Braves
12	Martinez, Ramon	Los Angeles Dodgers
12	Tewksbury, Bob	St. Louis Cardinals
12	Drabek, Doug	Houston Astros
11	Jones, Bobby	New York Mets

Opp. Batting Average

.207	Maddux, Greg	Atlanta Braves
.220	Martinez, Pedro J.	Montreal Expos
.220	Drabek, Doug	Houston Astros
.227	Avery, Steve	Atlanta Braves
.229	Fassero, Jeff	Montreal Expos
.233	Ashby, Andy	San Diego Padres
.237	Benes, Andy	San Diego Padres
.239	Smoltz, John	Atlanta Braves
.242	Trachsel, Steve	Chicago Cubs
.246	Young, Anthony	Chicago Cubs

1994 Individual Player Statistics

American League Hitters

	TEAM	POS	BA	G	AB	RS	H	2B	3B	HR	RBI	BB	SB
Aldrete, Mike	OAK	1B	.242	76	178	23	43	5	0	4	18	20	2
Alomar, Roberto	TOR	2B	.306	107	392	78	120	25	4	8	38	51	19
Alomar Jr., Sandy	CLE	C	.288	80	292	44	84	15	1	14	43	25	8
Amaral, Rich	SEA	2B	.263	77	228	37	60	10	2	4	18	24	5
Anderson, Brady	BAL	OF	.263	111	453	78	119	25	5	12	48	57	31
Anthony, Eric	SEA	OF	.237	79	262	31	62	14	1	10	30	23	6
Baerga, Carlos	CLE	2B	.314	103	442	81	139	32	2	19	80	10	8
Baines, Harold	BAL	DH	.294	94	326	44	96	12	1	16	54	30	0
Bautista, Danny	DET	OF	.232	31	99	12	23	4	1	4	15	3	1
Becker, Rich	MIN	OF	.265	28	98	12	26	3	0	1	8	13	6
Belle, Albert	CLE	OF	.357	106	412	90	147	35	2	36	101	58	9
Beltre, Esteban	TEX	SS	.282	48	131	12	37	5	0	0	12	16	2
Berroa, Geronimo	OAK	DH	.306	96	340	55	104	18	2	13	65	41	7
Berryhill, Damon	BOS	C	.263	82	255	30	67	17	2	6	34	19	0
Blowers, Mike	SEA	3B	.289	85	270	37	78	13	0	9	49	25	2
Boggs, Wade	NY	3B	.342	97	366	61	125	19	1	11	55	61	2
Borders, Pat	TOR	C	.247	85	295	24	73	13	1	3	26	15	1
Bordick, Mike	OAK	SS	.253	114	391	38	99	18	4	2	37	38	7
Boston, Darryl	NYY	OF	.182	52	77	11	14	2	0	1	14	6	0
Brooks, Hubie	KC	OF	.230	34	61	5	14	2	2	0	14	2	1
Brosius, Scott	OAK	3B	.238	96	324	31	77	14	1	14	49	24	2

	TEAM	POS	BA	G	AB	RS	H	2B	3B	HR	RBI	BB	SB
Brunansky, Tom	BOS	OF	.234	64	205	24	48	12	1	10	34	24	0
Buhner, Jay	SEA	OF	.279	101	358	74	100	23	4	21	68	66	0
Butler, Rob	TOR	OF	.176	41	74	13	13	0	1	0	5	7	0
Canseco, Jose	TEX	DH	.282	111	429	88	121	19	2	31	90	69	15
Carter, Joe	TOR	OF	.271	111	435	70	118	25	2	27	103	33	11
Cedeno, Domingo	TOR	SS	.196	47	97	14	19	2	3	0	10	10	1
Chamberlain, Wes	BOS	OF	.256	51	164	13	42	9	1	4	20	12	0
Cirillo, Jeff	MIL	3B	.238	39	126	17	30	9	0	3	12	11	0
Clark, Will	TEX	1B	.329	110	389	73	128	24	2	13	80	71	5
Cole, Alex	MIN	OF	.296	105	345	68	102	15	5	4	23	44	29
Coleman, Vince	KC	OF	.240	104	438	61	105	14	12	2	33	29	50
Coles, Darnell	TOR	OF	.210	48	143	15	30	6	1	4	15	10	0
Cooper, Scott	BOS	3B	.282	104	369	49	104	16	4	13	53	30	0
Cora, Joey	CWS	2B	.276	90	312	55	86	13	4	2	30	38	8
Curtis, Chad	CAL	OF	.256	114	453	67	116	23	4	11	50	37	25
Cuyler, Milt	DET	OF	.241	48	116	20	28	3	1	1	11	13	5
Davis, Chili	CAL	DH	.311	108	392	72	122	18	0	26	84	69	3
Davis, Eric	DET	OF	.183	37	120	19	22	4	0	3	13	18	5
Dawson, Andre	BOS	OF	.240	75	292	34	70	18	0	16	48	9	2
Delgado, Carlos	TOR	C	.215	43	130	17	28	2	0	9	24	25	1
Devereaux, Mike	BAL	OF	.203	85	301	35	61	8	2	9	33	22	1
Diaz, Alex	MIL	OF	.251	79	187	17	47	5	7	1	17	10	5
DiSarcina, Gary	CAL	SS	.260	112	389	53	101	14	2	3	33	18	3
Easley, Damion	CAL	2B	.215	88	316	41	68	16	1	6	30	29	4
Edmonds, Jim	CAL	OF	.273	94	289	35	79	13	1	5	37	30	4

	TEAM	POS	BA	G	AB	RS	H	2B	3B	HR	RBI	BB	SB
Espinoza, Alvaro	CLE	SS	.238	90	231	27	55	13	0	1	19	6	1
Fabregas, Jorge	CAL	C	.283	43	127	12	36	3	0	0	16	7	2
Felix, Junior	DET	OF	.306	86	301	54	92	25	1	13	49	26	1
Fermin, Felix	SEA	SS	.317	101	379	52	120	21	0	1	35	11	4
Fielder, Cecil	DET	1B	.259	109	425	67	110	16	2	28	90	50	0
Fletcher, Scott	BOS	2B	.227	63	185	31	42	9	1	3	11	16	8
Franco, Julio	CWS	DH	.319	112	433	72	138	19	2	20	98	62	8
Frye, Jeff	TEX	2B	.327	57	205	37	67	20	3	0	18	29	6
Fryman, Travis	DET	3B	.263	114	464	66	122	34	5	18	85	45	2
Gaetti, Gary	KC	3B	.287	90	327	53	94	15	3	12	57	19	0
Gagne, Greg	KC	SS	.259	107	375	39	97	23	3	7	51	27	10
Gallego, Mike	NYY	SS	.239	89	306	39	73	17	1	6	41	38	0
Gates, Brent	OAK	2B	.283	64	233	29	66	11	1	2	24	21	3
Gibson, Kirk	DET	OF	.276	98	330	71	91	17	2	23	72	42	4
Gomez, Chris	DET	SS	.257	84	296	32	76	19	0	8	53	33	5
Gomez, Leo	BAL	3B	.274	84	285	46	78	20	0	15	56	41	0
Gonzales, Alex	TOR	SS	.151	15	53	7	8	3	1	0	1	4	3
Gonzalez, Juan	TEX	OF	.275	107	422	57	116	18	4	19	85	30	6
Grebeck, Craig	CWS	3B	.309	35	97	17	30	5	0	0	5	12	0
Greenwell, Mike	BOS	OF	.269	95	327	60	88	25	1	11	45	38	2
Greer, Rusty	TEX	OF	.314	80	277	36	87	16	1	10	46	46	0
Griffey Jr., Ken	SEA	OF	.323	111	433	94	140	24	4	40	90	56	11
Guillen, Ozzie	CWS	SS	.288	100	365	46	105	9	5	1	39	14	5
Hale, Chip	MIN	2B	.263	67	118	13	31	9	0	1	11	16	0
Hamelin, Bob	KC	DH	.282	101	312	64	88	25	1	24	65	56	4

	TEAM	POS	BA	G	AB	RS	H	2B	3B	HR	RBI	BB	SB
Hamilton, Darryl	MIL	OF	.262	36	141	23	37	10	1	1	13	15	3
Hammonds, Jeffrey	BAL	OF	.296	68	250	45	74	18	2	8	31	17	5
Harper, Brian	MIL	OF	.291	64	251	23	73	15	0	4	32	9	0
Haselman, Bill	SEA	C	.193	38	83	11	16	7	1	1	8	3	1
Hatcher, Billy	BOS	OF	.244	44	164	24	40	9	1	1	18	11	4
Hemond, Scott	OAK	C	.222	91	198	23	44	11	0	3	20	16	7
Henderson, Dave	KC	OF	.247	56	198	27	49	14	1	5	31	16	2
Henderson, Rickey	OAK	OF	.260	87	296	66	77	13	0	6	20	72	22
Hoiles, Chris	BAL	C	.247	99	332	45	82	10	0	19	53	63	2
Howard, David	KC	2B	.229	46	83	9	19	4	0	1	13	11	3
Hrbek, Kent	MIN	1B	.270	81	274	34	74	11	0	10	53	37	0
Hudler, Rex	CAL	2B	.298	56	124	17	37	8	0	8	20	6	2
Huff, Mike	TOR	OF	.304	60	207	31	63	15	3	3	25	27	2
Hulett, Tim	BAL	3B	.228	35	92	11	21	2	1	2	15	12	0
Hulse, David	TEX	OF	.255	77	310	58	79	8	4	1	19	21	18
Jackson, Bo	CAL	OF	.279	75	201	23	56	7	0	13	43	20	1
Jackson, Darrin	CWS	OF	.312	104	369	43	115	17	3	10	51	27	7
Jaha, John	MIL	1B	.241	84	291	45	70	14	0	12	39	32	3
James, Chris	TEX	OF	.256	52	133	28	34	8	4	7	19	20	0
Javier, Stan	OAK	OF	.272	109	419	75	114	23	0	10	44	49	24
Jefferson, Reggie	SEA	1B	.327	63	162	24	53	11	0	8	32	17	0
Johnson, Lance	CWS	OF	.277	106	412	56	114	11	14	3	54	26	26
Jose, Felix	KC	OF	.303	99	366	56	111	28	1	11	55	35	10
Joyner, Wally	KC	1B	.311	97	363	52	113	20	3	8	57	47	3
Karkovice, Ron	CWS	C	.213	77	207	33	44	9	1	11	29	36	0

	TEAM	POS	BA	G	AB	RS	H	2B	3B	HR	RBI	BB	SB
Kelly, Pat	NYY	2B	.280	93	286	35	80	21	2	3	41	19	6
Kirby, Wayne	CLE	OF	.293	78	191	33	56	6	0	5	23	13	11
Knoblauch, Chuck	MIN	2B	.312	109	445	85	139	45	3	5	51	41	35
Knorr, Randy	TOR	C	.242	40	124	20	30	2	0	7	19	10	0
Kreuter, Chad	DET	C	.224	65	170	17	38	8	0	1	19	28	0
Lavalliere, Mike	CWS	C	.281	59	139	6	39	4	0	1	24	20	0
Lee, Manuel	TEX	SS	.278	95	335	41	93	18	2	2	38	21	3
Leius, Scott	MIN	3B	.246	97	350	57	86	16	1	14	49	37	2
Lewis, Mark	CLE	SS	.205	20	73	6	15	5	0	1	8	2	1
Leyritz, Jim	NY	C	.265	75	249	47	66	12	0	17	58	35	0
Lind, Jose	KC	2B	.269	85	290	34	78	16	2	1	31	16	9
Listach, Pat	MIL	SS	.296	16	54	8	16	3	0	0	2	3	2
Lofton, Kenny	CLE	OF	.349	112	459	105	160	32	9	12	57	52	60
Lovullo, Torey	SEA	2B	.222	36	72	9	16	5	0	2	7	9	1
Macfarlane, Mike	KC	C	.255	92	314	53	80	17	3	14	47	35	1
Mack, Shane	MIN	OF	.333	81	303	55	101	21	2	15	61	32	4
Maldonado, Candy	CLE	OF	.196	42	92	14	18	5	1	5	12	19	1
Martin, Norberto	CWS	2B	.275	45	131	19	36	7	1	1	16	9	4
Martinez, Edgar	SEA	3B	.285	89	326	47	93	23	1	13	51	53	6
Martinez, Tino	SEA	1B	.261	97	329	42	86	21	0	20	61	29	1
Matheny, Mike	MIL	C	.226	28	53	3	12	3	0	1	2	3	0
Mattingly, Don	NYY	1B	.304	97	372	62	113	20	1	6	51	60	0
Mayne, Brent	KC	C	.257	46	144	19	37	5	1	2	20	14	1
McCarty, Dave	MIN	OF	.260	44	131	21	34	8	2	1	12	7	2
McDowell, Oddibe	TEX	OF	.262	59	183	34	48	5	1	1	15	28	14

	TEAM	POS	BA	G	AB	RS	H	2B	3B	HR	RBI	BB	SB
McGwire, Mark	OAK	1B	.252	47	135	26	34	3	0	9	25	37	0
McLemore, Mark	BAL	2B	.257	104	343	44	88	11	1	3	29	51	20
McRae, Brian	KC	OF	.273	114	436	71	119	22	6	4	40	54	28
Meares, Pat	MIN	SS	.266	80	229	29	61	12	1	2	24	14	5
Mieske, Matt	MIL	OF	.259	84	259	36	67	13	1	10	38	21	3
Mitchell, Keith	SEA	OF	.227	46	128	21	29	2	0	5	15	18	0
Molitor, Paul	TOR	DH	.341	115	454	86	155	30	4	14	75	55	20
Munoz, Pedro	MIN	OF	.295	75	244	35	72	15	2	11	36	19	0
Murray, Eddie	CLE	DH	.254	108	433	57	110	21	1	17	76	31	8
Myers, Greg	CAL	C	.246	45	126	10	31	6	0	2	8	10	0
Naehring, Tim	BOS	2B	.276	80	297	41	82	18	1	7	42	30	1
Neel, Troy	OAK	1B	.266	83	278	43	74	13	0	15	48	38	2
Newson, Warren	CWS	OF	.255	63	102	16	26	5	0	2	7	14	1
Nilsson, Dave	MIL	C	.275	109	397	51	109	28	3	12	69	34	1
Nixon, Otis	BOS	OF	.274	103	398	60	109	15	1	0	25	55	42
Nokes, Matt	NYY	C	.291	28	79	11	23	3	0	7	19	5	0
O'Leary, Troy	MIL	OF	.273	27	66	9	18	1	1	2	7	5	1
Olerud, John	TOR	1B	.297	108	384	47	114	29	2	12	67	61	1
O'Neill, Paul	NYY	OF	.359	103	368	68	132	25	1	21	83	72	5
Ortiz, Junior	TEX	C	.276	29	76	3	21	2	0	0	9	5	0
Owen, Spike	CAL	3B	.310	82	268	30	83	17	2	3	37	49	2
Palmeiro, Rafael	BAL	1B	.319	111	436	82	139	32	0	23	76	54	7
Palmer, Dean	TEX	3B	.246	93	342	50	84	14	2	19	59	26	3
Parks, Derek	MIN	C	.191	31	89	6	17	6	0	1	9	4	0
Pena, Tony	CLE	C	.295	40	112	18	33	8	1	2	10	9	0

	TEAM	POS	BA	G	AB	RS	H	2B	3B	HR	RBI	BB	SB
Perez, Eduardo	CAL	3B	.209	38	129	10	27	7	0	5	16	12	3
Phillips, Tony	DET	OF	.281	114	438	91	123	19	3	19	61	95	13
Pirkl, Greg	SEA	1B	.264	19	53	7	14	3	0	6	11	1	0
Polonia, Luis	NYY	OF	.311	95	350	62	109	21	6	1	36	37	20
Puckett, Kirby	MIN	OF	.317	108	439	79	139	32	3	20	112	28	6
Raines, Tim	CWS	OF	.266	101	384	80	102	15	5	10	52	61	13
Ramirez, Manny	CLE	OF	.269	91	290	51	78	22	0	17	60	42	4
Reboulet, Jeff	MIN	SS	.259	74	189	28	49	11	1	3	23	18	0
Reed, Jody	MIL	2B	.271	108	399	48	108	22	0	2	37	57	5
Reynolds, Harold	CAL	2B	.232	74	207	33	48	10	1	0	11	23	10
Ripken, Billy	TEX	2B	.309	32	81	9	25	5	0	0	6	3	2
Ripken Jr., Cal	BAL	SS	.315	112	444	71	140	19	3	13	75	32	1
Rodriguez, Alex	SEA	SS	.204	17	54	4	11	0	0	0	2	3	3
Rodriguez, Carlos	BOS	SS	.287	57	174	15	50	14	1	0	13	11	1
Rodriguez, Ivan	TEX	C	.298	99	363	56	108	19	1	16	57	31	6
Rowland, Rich	BOS	C	.229	46	118	14	27	3	0	9	20	11	0
Sabo, Chris	BAL	3B	.256	68	258	41	66	15	3	11	42	20	1
Salmon, Tim	CAL	OF	.287	100	373	67	107	18	2	23	70	54	1
Samuel, Juan	DET	OF	.309	59	136	32	42	9	5	5	21	10	5
Schofield, Dick	TOR	SS	.255	95	325	38	83	14	1	4	32	34	7
Seitzer, Kevin	MIL	3B	.314	80	309	44	97	24	2	5	49	30	2
Shumpert, Terry	KC	2B	.240	64	183	28	44	6	2	8	24	13	18
Sierra, Ruben	OAK	OF	.268	110	426	71	114	21	1	23	92	23	8
Smith, Dwight	BAL	OF	.281	73	196	31	55	7	2	8	30	12	2
Smith, Lonnie	BAL	OF	.203	35	59	13	12	3	0	0	2	11	1

	TEAM	POS	BA	G	AB	RS	H	2B	3B	HR	RBI	BB	SB
Snow, J. T.	CAL	1B	.220	61	223	22	49	4	0	8	30	19	0
Sojo, Luis	SEA	SS	.277	63	213	32	59	9	2	6	22	8	2
Sorrento, Paul	CLE	1B	.280	95	322	43	90	14	0	14	62	34	0
Spiers, Bill	MIL	2B	.252	73	214	27	54	10	1	0	17	19	7
Sprague, Ed	TOR	3B	.240	109	405	38	97	19	1	11	44	23	1
Stanley, Mike	NYY	C	.300	82	290	54	87	20	0	17	57	39	0
Steinbach, Terry	OAK	C	.285	103	369	51	105	21	2	11	57	26	2
Strange, Doug	TEX	2B	.212	73	226	26	48	12	1	5	26	15	1
Surhoff, B. J.	MIL	3B	.261	40	134	20	35	11	2	5	22	16	0
Tackett, Jeff	BAL	C	.226	26	53	5	12	3	1	2	9	5	0
Tartabull, Danny	NYY	OF	.256	104	399	68	102	24	1	19	67	66	1
Tettleton, Mickey	DET	C	.248	107	339	57	84	18	2	17	51	97	0
Thomas, Frank	CWS	1B	.353	113	399	106	141	34	1	38	101	109	2
Thome, Jim	CLE	3B	.268	98	321	58	86	20	1	20	52	46	3
Tinsley, Lee	BOS	OF	.222	78	144	27	32	4	0	2	14	19	13
Trammell, Alan	DET	SS	.267	76	292	38	78	17	1	8	28	16	3
Turang, Brian	SEA	OF	.188	38	112	9	21	5	1	1	8	7	3
Turner, Chris	CAL	C	.242	58	149	23	36	7	1	1	12	10	3
Valentin, John	BOS	SS	.316	84	301	53	95	26	2	9	49	42	3
Valentin, Jose	MIL	SS	.239	97	285	47	68	19	0	11	46	38	12
Valle, Dave	BOS	C	.232	46	112	14	26	8	1	2	10	18	0
Vaughn, Greg	MIL	OF	.254	95	370	59	94	24	1	19	55	51	9
Vaughn, Mo	BOS	1B	.310	111	394	65	122	25	1	26	82	57	4
Velarde, Randy	NYY	SS	.279	77	280	47	78	16	1	9	34	22	4
Ventura, Robin	CWS	3B	.282	109	401	57	113	15	1	18	78	61	3

	TEAM	POS	BA	G	AB	RS	H	2B	3B	HR	RBI	BB	SB
Vizquel, Omar	CLE	SS	.273	69	286	39	78	10	1	1	33	23	13
Voigt, Jose	BAL	OF	.241	59	141	15	34	5	0	3	20	18	0
Walbeck, Matt	MIN	C	.204	97	338	31	69	12	0	5	35	17	1
Ward, Turner	MIL	OF	.232	102	367	55	85	15	2	9	45	52	6
Whitaker, Lou	DET	2B	.301	92	322	67	97	21	2	12	43	41	2
White, Devon	TOR	OF	.270	100	403	67	109	24	6	13	49	21	11
Williams, Bernie	NYY	OF	.289	108	408	80	118	29	1	12	57	61	16
Williams, Gerald	NYY	OF	.291	57	86	19	25	8	0	4	13	4	1
Wilson, Dan	SEA	C	.216	91	282	24	61	14	2	3	27	10	1
Winfield, Dave	MIN	DH	.252	77	294	35	74	15	3	10	43	31	2
Zupcic, Bob	BOS	OF	.196	36	92	10	18	4	1	1	8	4	0

American League Pitchers

	TEAM	W	L	ERA	RANK	G	GS	SV	IP	H	ER	BB	SO
Abbott, Jim	NY	9	8	4.55	30	24	24	0	160.1	167	81	64	90
Acre, Mark	OAK	5	1	3.41	—	34	0	0	34.1	24	13	23	21
Aguilera, Rick	MIN	1	4	3.63	—	44	0	23	44.2	57	18	10	46
Alvarez, Wilson	CWS	12	8	3.45	9	24	24	0	161.2	147	62	62	108
Anderson, Brian	CAL	7	5	5.22	—	18	18	0	101.2	120	59	27	47
Appier, Kevin	KC	7	6	3.83	17	23	23	0	155.0	137	66	63	145
Armstrong, Jack	TEX	0	1	3.60	—	2	2	0	10.0	9	4	2	7
Assenmacher, Paul	CWS	1	2	3.55	—	44	0	1	33.0	26	13	13	29
Ausanio, Joe	NYY	2	1	5.17	—	13	0	0	15.2	16	9	6	15
Ayala, Bobby	SEA	4	3	2.86	—	46	0	18	56.2	42	18	26	76

	TEAM	W	L	ERA	RANK	G	GS	SV	IP	H	ER	BB	SO
Bankhead, Scott	NYY	3	2	4.54	—	27	0	0	37.2	34	19	12	25
Barnes, Brian	CLE	0	1	5.40	—	6	0	0	13.1	12	8	15	5
Belcher, Tim	DET	7	15	5.89	45	25	25	0	162.0	192	106	78	76
Belinda, Stan	KC	2	2	5.14	—	37	0	1	49.0	47	28	24	37
Benitez, Armando	BAL	0	0	0.90	—	3	0	0	10.0	8	1	4	14
Bere, Jason	CWS	12	2	3.81	14	24	24	0	141.2	119	60	80	127
Bergman, Sean	DET	2	1	5.60	—	3	3	0	17.2	22	11	7	12
Boever, Joe	DET	9	2	3.98	—	46	0	3	81.1	80	36	37	49
Bohanon, Brian	TEX	2	2	7.23	—	11	5	0	37.1	51	30	8	26
Bolton, Tom	BAL	1	2	5.40	—	22	0	0	23.1	29	14	13	12
Bones, Ricky	MIL	10	9	3.43	8	24	24	0	170.2	166	65	45	57
Bosio, Chris	SEA	4	10	4.32	23	19	19	0	125.0	137	60	40	67
Brewer, Billy	KC	4	1	2.56	—	50	0	3	38.2	28	11	16	25
Briscoe, John	OAK	4	2	4.01	—	37	0	1	49.1	31	22	39	45
Bronkey, Jeff	MIL	1	1	4.35	—	16	0	1	20.2	20	10	12	13
Brow, Scott	TOR	0	3	5.90	—	18	0	2	29.0	34	19	19	15
Brown, Kevin	TEX	7	9	4.82	36	26	25	0	170.0	218	91	50	123
Butcher, Mike	CAL	2	1	6.67	—	33	0	0	29.2	31	22	23	19
Cadaret, Greg	DET	1	1	4.73	—	38	0	2	40.0	41	21	33	29
Campbell, Kevin	MIN	1	0	2.92	—	14	0	0	24.2	20	8	5	15
Carpenter, Cris	TEX	2	5	5.03	—	47	0	5	59.0	69	33	20	39
Casian, Larry	CLE	1	5	7.35	—	40	0	1	49.0	73	40	16	20
Castillo, Tony	TOR	5	2	2.51	—	41	0	1	68.0	66	19	28	43
Clark, Mark	CLE	11	3	3.82	15	20	20	0	127.1	133	54	40	60
Clemens, Roger	BOS	9	7	2.85	2	24	24	0	170.2	124	54	71	168

	TEAM	W	L	ERA	RANK	G	GS	SV	IP	H	ER	BB	SO
Cone, David	KC	16	5	2.94	3	23	23	0	171.2	130	56	54	132
Converse, Jim	SEA	0	5	8.69	—	13	8	0	48.2	73	47	40	39
Cook, Dennis	CWS	3	1	3.55	—	38	0	0	33.0	29	13	14	26
Cornett, Brad	TOR	1	3	6.68	—	9	4	0	31.0	40	23	11	22
Cox, Danny	TOR	1	1	1.45	—	10	0	3	18.2	7	3	7	14
Cummings, John	SEA	2	4	5.63	—	17	8	0	64.0	66	40	37	33
Darling, Ron	OAK	10	11	4.50	27	25	25	0	160.0	162	80	59	108
Darwin, Danny	BOS	7	5	6.30	—	13	13	0	75.2	101	53	24	54
Davis, Storm	DET	2	4	3.56	—	35	0	0	48.0	36	19	34	38
Davis, Tim	SEA	2	2	4.01	—	42	1	2	49.1	57	22	25	28
DeJesus, Jose	KC	3	1	4.73	—	5	4	0	26.2	27	14	13	12
DeLeon, Jose	CWS	3	2	3.36	—	42	0	2	67.0	48	25	31	67
Deshaies, Jim	MIN	6	12	7.39	50	25	25	0	130.1	170	107	54	78
Dettmer, John	TEX	0	6	4.33	—	11	9	0	54.0	63	26	20	27
DiPoto, Jerry	CLE	0	0	8.04	—	7	0	0	15.2	26	14	10	9
Doherty, John	DET	6	7	6.48	—	18	17	0	101.1	139	73	26	28
Dopson, John	CAL	1	4	6.14	—	21	5	1	58.2	67	40	26	33
Dreyer, Steve	TEX	1	1	5.71	—	5	3	0	17.1	19	11	8	11
Eckersley, Dennis	OAK	5	4	4.26	—	45	0	19	44.1	49	21	13	47
Eichhorn, Mark	BAL	6	5	2.15	—	43	0	1	71.0	62	17	19	35
Eldred, Cal	MIL	11	11	4.68	32	25	25	0	179.0	158	93	84	98
Erickson, Scott	MIN	8	11	5.44	40	23	23	0	144.0	173	87	59	104
Fajardo, Hector	TEX	5	7	6.91	—	18	12	0	83.1	95	64	26	45
Farr, Steve	BOS	2	1	5.72	—	30	0	4	28.1	41	18	18	20
Farrell, John	CAL	1	2	9.00	—	3	3	0	13.0	16	13	8	10

	TEAM	W	L	ERA	RANK	G	GS	SV	IP	H	ER	BB	SO
Fernandez, Alex	CWS	11	7	3.86	18	24	24	0	170.1	163	73	50	122
Fernandez, Sid	BAL	6	6	5.15	38	19	19	0	115.1	109	66	46	95
Fetters, Mike	MIL	1	4	2.54	—	42	0	17	46.0	41	13	27	31
Finley, Chuck	CAL	10	10	4.32	23	25	25	0	183.1	178	88	71	148
Finnvold, Gar	BOS	0	4	5.94	—	8	8	0	36.1	45	24	15	17
Fleming, Dave	SEA	7	11	6.46	48	23	23	0	117.0	152	84	65	65
Fossas, Tony	BOS	2	0	4.76	—	44	0	1	34.0	35	18	15	31
Frohwirth, Todd	BOS	0	3	10.80	—	22	0	1	26.2	40	32	17	13
Gardiner, Mike	DET	2	2	4.14	—	38	1	5	58.2	53	27	23	31
Gibson, Paul	MIL	1	1	4.97	—	30	0	0	29.0	26	16	17	21
Gohr, Greg	DET	2	2	4.50	—	8	6	0	34.0	36	17	21	21
Gordon, Tom	KC	11	7	4.35	25	24	24	0	155.1	136	75	87	126
Gossage, Rich	SEA	3	0	4.18	—	36	0	1	47.1	44	22	15	29
Grahe, Joe	CAL	2	5	6.65	—	40	0	13	43.1	68	32	18	26
Grimsley, Jason	CLE	5	2	4.57	—	14	13	0	82.2	91	42	34	59
Groom, Buddy	DET	0	2	3.94	—	40	0	1	32.0	31	14	13	27
Guardado, Eddie	MIN	0	2	8.47	—	4	4	0	17.0	26	16	4	8
Gubicza, Mark	KC	7	9	4.50	27	22	22	0	130.0	158	65	26	59
Gullickson, Bill	DET	4	5	5.93	46	21	19	0	115.1	156	76	25	65
Guthrie, Mark	MIN	4	2	6.14	—	50	2	1	51.1	65	35	18	38
Guzman, Juan	TOR	12	11	5.68	42	25	25	0	147.1	165	93	76	124
Hall, Darren	TOR	2	3	3.41	—	30	0	17	31.2	26	12	14	28
Haney, Chris	KC	2	2	7.31	—	6	6	0	28.1	36	23	11	18
Harris, Greg A.	NYY	3	5	7.99	—	38	0	2	50.2	64	45	26	48
Harris, Gene	DET	0	0	7.15	—	11	0	1	11.1	13	9	4	10

	TEAM	W	L	ERA	RANK	G	GS	SV	IP	H	ER	BB	SO
Helling, Rick	TEX	3	2	5.88	—	9	9	0	52.0	62	34	18	25
Henke, Tom	TEX	3	6	3.79	—	37	0	15	38.0	33	16	12	39
Henneman, Mike	DET	1	3	5.19	—	30	0	8	34.2	43	20	17	27
Henry, Doug	MIL	2	3	4.60	—	25	0	0	31.1	32	16	23	20
Hentgen, Pat	TOR	13	8	3.40	7	24	24	0	174.2	158	66	59	147
Hernandez, Roberto	CWS	4	4	4.91	—	45	0	14	47.2	44	26	19	50
Hernandez, Xavier	NYY	4	4	5.85	—	31	0	6	40.0	48	26	21	37
Hesketh, Joe	BOS	8	5	4.26	22	25	20	0	114.0	117	54	46	83
Hibbard, Greg	SEA	1	5	6.69	—	15	14	0	80.2	115	60	31	39
Higuera, Teddy	MIL	1	5	7.06	—	17	12	0	58.2	74	46	36	35
Hill, Milt	SEA	1	0	6.46	—	13	0	0	23.2	30	17	11	16
Hitchcock, Sterling	NYY	4	1	4.20	—	23	5	0	49.1	48	23	29	37
Honeycutt, Rick	TEX	1	2	7.20	—	42	0	2	25.0	37	20	9	18
Horsman, Vince	OAK	0	1	4.91	—	33	0	0	29.1	29	16	11	20
Howard, Chris	BOS	1	0	3.63	—	37	0	1	39.2	35	16	12	22
Howe, Steve	NYY	3	0	1.80	—	40	0	15	40.0	28	8	7	18
Howell, Jay	TEX	4	1	5.44	—	40	0	2	43.0	44	26	16	22
Hurst, Bruce	TEX	2	1	7.11	—	8	8	0	38.0	53	30	16	24
Hurst, James	TEX	0	0	10.13	—	8	0	0	10.2	17	12	8	5
Ignasiak, Mike	MIL	3	1	4.53	—	23	5	0	47.2	51	24	13	24
Jimenez, Miguel	OAK	1	4	7.41	—	8	7	0	34.0	38	28	32	22
Johnson, Dave	CWS	2	1	6.57	—	15	0	0	12.1	16	9	11	7
Johnson, Randy	SEA	13	6	3.19	5	23	23	0	172.0	132	61	72	204
Kamieniecki, Scott	NYY	8	6	3.76	13	22	16	0	117.1	115	49	59	71
Karsay, Steve	OAK	1	1	2.57	—	4	4	0	28.0	26	8	8	15

	TEAM	W	L	ERA	RANK	G	GS	SV	IP	H	ER	BB	SO
Key, Jimmy	NYY	17	4	3.27	6	25	25	0	168.0	177	61	52	97
Kiefer, Mark	MIL	1	0	8.44	—	7	0	0	10.2	15	10	8	8
King, Kevin	SEA	0	2	7.04	—	19	0	0	15.1	21	12	17	6
Krueger, Bill	DET	0	2	9.61	32	16	2	0	19.2	26	21	17	17
Langston, Mark	CAL	7	8	4.68	—	18	18	0	119.1	121	62	54	109
Leary, Tim	TEX	1	1	8.14	—	6	3	0	21.0	26	19	11	9
Lefferts, Craig	CAL	1	1	4.67	—	30	0	1	34.2	50	18	12	27
Leftwich, Phil	CAL	5	10	5.68	43	20	20	0	114.0	127	72	42	67
Leiper, Dave	OAK	0	0	1.93	—	26	0	1	18.2	13	4	6	14
Leiter, Al	TOR	6	7	5.08	—	20	20	0	111.2	125	63	65	100
Leiter, Mark	CAL	4	7	4.72	—	40	7	2	95.1	99	50	35	71
Lewis, Scott	CAL	0	1	6.10	—	20	0	0	31.0	46	21	10	10
Lilliquist, Derek	CLE	1	3	4.91	—	36	0	1	29.1	34	16	8	15
Lloyd, Graeme	MIL	2	3	5.17	—	43	0	3	47.0	49	27	15	31
Lopez, Albie	CLE	1	2	4.24	—	4	4	0	17.0	20	8	6	18
Lorraine, Andrew	CAL	0	2	10.61	—	4	3	0	18.2	30	22	11	10
Magnante, Mike	KC	2	3	4.60	—	36	1	0	47.0	55	24	16	21
Magrane, Joe	CAL	2	6	7.30	—	20	11	0	74.0	89	60	51	33
Mahomes, Pat	MIN	9	5	4.73	34	21	21	0	120.0	121	63	62	53
Martinez, Dennis	CLE	11	6	3.52	11	24	24	0	176.2	166	69	44	92
McCaskill, Kirk	CWS	1	4	3.42	—	40	0	3	52.2	51	20	22	37
McDonald, Ben	BAL	14	7	4.06	19	24	24	0	157.1	151	71	54	94
McDowell, Jack	CWS	10	9	3.73	12	25	25	0	181.0	186	75	42	127
Meacham, Rusty	KC	3	3	3.73	—	36	0	4	50.2	51	21	12	36
Melendez, Jose	BOS	0	1	6.06	—	10	0	0	16.1	20	11	8	9

	TEAM	W	L	ERA	RANK	G	GS	SV	IP	H	ER	BB	SO
Mercedes, Jose	MIL	2	0	2.32	—	19	0	0	31.0	22	8	16	11
Merriman, Brett	MIN	0	1	6.35	—	15	0	0	17.0	18	12	14	10
Mesa, Jose	CLE	7	5	3.83	—	51	0	2	73.0	71	31	26	63
Milacki, Bob	KC	0	5	6.14	—	10	10	0	55.2	68	38	20	17
Mills, Alan	BAL	3	3	5.16	—	47	0	2	45.1	43	26	24	44
Minchey, Nate	BOS	2	3	8.61	—	6	5	0	23.0	44	22	14	15
Miranda, Angel	MIL	2	5	5.28	—	8	8	0	46.0	39	27	27	24
Montgomery, Jeff	KC	2	3	4.03	—	42	0	27	44.2	48	20	15	50
Moore, Mike	DET	11	10	5.42	39	25	25	0	154.1	152	93	89	62
Morris, Jack	CLE	10	6	5.60	41	23	23	0	141.1	163	88	67	100
Moyer, Jamie	BAL	5	7	4.77	35	23	23	0	149.0	158	79	38	87
Mulholland, Terry	NYY	6	7	6.49	49	24	19	0	120.2	150	87	37	72
Mussina, Mike	BAL	16	5	3.06	4	24	24	0	176.1	163	60	42	99
Nabholz, Chris	BOS	3	5	7.64	—	14	12	0	53.0	67	45	38	28
Nagy, Charles	CLE	10	8	3.45	10	23	23	0	169.1	175	65	48	108
Navarro, Jaime	MIL	4	9	6.62	—	29	10	0	89.2	115	66	35	65
Nelson, Jeff	SEA	0	0	2.76	—	28	0	0	42.1	35	13	20	44
Nunez, Edwin	OAK	0	0	12.00	—	15	0	0	15.0	26	20	10	15
Ogea, Chad	CLE	0	1	6.06	—	4	1	0	16.1	21	11	10	11
Oliver, Darren	TEX	4	0	3.42	—	43	0	2	50.0	40	19	35	50
Ontiveros, Steve	OAK	6	4	2.65	1	27	13	0	115.1	93	34	26	56
Oquist, Mike	BAL	3	3	6.17	—	15	9	0	58.1	75	40	30	39
Orosco, Jesse	MIL	3	1	5.08	—	40	0	0	39.0	32	22	26	36
Pall, Donn	NYY	1	2	3.60	—	26	0	0	35.0	43	14	9	21
Patterson, Bob	CAL	2	3	4.07	—	47	0	1	42.0	35	19	15	30

	TEAM	W	L	ERA	RANK	G	GS	SV	IP	H	ER	BB	SO
Pavlik, Roger	TEX	2	5	7.69	—	11	11	0	50.1	61	43	30	31
Perez, Melido	NYY	9	4	4.10	20	22	22	0	151.1	134	69	58	109
Pichardo, Hipolito	KC	5	3	4.92	—	45	0	3	67.2	82	37	24	36
Plunk, Eric	CLE	7	2	2.54	—	41	0	3	71.0	61	20	37	73
Poole, Jim	BAL	1	0	6.64	—	38	0	0	20.1	32	15	11	18
Pulido, Carlos	MIN	3	7	5.98	—	19	14	0	84.1	87	56	40	32
Quantrill, Paul	BOS	1	1	3.52	—	17	0	0	23.0	25	9	5	15
Reed, Rick	TEX	1	1	5.94	—	4	3	0	16.2	17	11	7	12
Reyes, Carlos	OAK	0	3	4.15	—	27	9	1	78.0	71	36	44	57
Rhodes, Arthur	BAL	3	5	5.81	—	10	10	0	52.2	51	34	30	47
Righetti, Dave	TOR	0	1	10.18	—	20	0	0	20.1	22	23	19	14
Risley, Bill	SEA	9	6	3.44	—	37	0	0	52.1	31	20	19	61
Rogers, Kenny	TEX	11	8	4.46	26	24	24	0	167.1	169	83	52	120
Russell, Jeff	CLE	1	6	5.09	—	42	0	17	40.2	43	23	16	28
Ryan Jr., Ken	BOS	2	3	2.44	—	42	0	13	48.0	46	13	17	32
Salkeld, Roger	SEA	2	5	7.17	—	13	13	0	59.0	76	47	45	46
Sampen, Bill	CAL	1	1	6.46	—	10	0	0	15.1	14	11	13	9
Sanderson, Scott	CWS	8	4	5.09	—	18	14	0	92.0	110	52	12	36
Scanlan, Bob	MIL	2	6	4.11	—	30	12	2	103.0	117	47	28	65
Schullstrom, Erik	MIN	0	0	2.77	—	9	0	1	13.0	13	4	5	13
Schwarz, Jeff	CAL	0	0	5.50	—	13	0	0	18.0	14	11	22	18
Sele, Aaron	BOS	8	7	3.83	16	22	22	0	143.1	140	61	60	105
Shuey, Paul	CLE	0	1	8.49	—	14	0	5	11.2	14	11	12	16
Smith, Dan	TEX	1	2	4.30	—	13	0	0	14.2	18	7	12	9
Smith, Lee	BAL	1	4	3.29	—	41	0	33	38.1	34	14	11	42

	TEAM	W	L	ERA	RANK	G	GS	SV	IP	H	ER	BB	SO
Springer, Russ	CAL	2	2	5.52	—	18	5	2	45.2	53	28	14	28
Stevens, Dave	MIN	5	2	6.80	—	24	0	0	45.0	55	34	23	24
Stewart, Dave	TOR	7	8	5.87	44	22	22	0	133.1	151	87	62	111
Stottlemyre, Todd	TOR	7	7	4.22	21	26	19	1	140.2	149	66	48	105
Tapani, Kevin	MIN	11	7	4.62	31	24	24	0	156.0	181	80	39	91
Taylor, Billy	OAK	1	3	3.50	—	41	0	1	46.1	38	18	18	48
Timlin, Mike	TOR	0	1	5.18	—	34	0	2	40.0	41	23	20	38
Trlicek, Ricky	BOS	1	1	8.06	—	12	1	0	22.1	32	20	16	7
Trombley, Mike	MIN	2	0	6.33	—	24	0	0	48.1	56	34	18	32
Turner, Matt	CLE	1	0	2.13	—	9	0	1	12.2	13	3	7	5
Valdez, Sergio	BOS	0	1	8.16	—	12	1	0	14.1	25	13	8	4
Van Poppel, Todd	OAK	7	10	6.09	47	23	23	0	116.2	108	79	89	83
Vanegmond, Tim	BOS	2	3	6.34	—	7	7	0	38.1	38	27	21	22
Viola, Frank	BOS	1	1	4.65	—	6	6	0	31.0	34	16	17	9
Vosberg, Ed	OAK	0	2	3.95	—	16	0	0	13.2	16	6	5	12
Wegman, Bill	MIL	8	4	4.51	29	19	19	0	115.2	140	58	26	59
Welch, Bob	OAK	3	6	7.08	—	25	8	0	68.2	79	54	43	44
Wells, David	DET	5	7	3.96	—	16	16	0	111.1	113	49	24	71
Whiteside, Matt	TEX	2	2	5.02	—	47	0	1	61.0	68	34	28	37
Wickman, Bob	NYY	5	4	3.09	—	53	0	6	70.0	54	24	27	56
Williams, Woody	TOR	1	3	3.64	—	38	0	0	59.1	44	24	33	56
Williamson, Mark	BAL	3	1	4.01	—	28	2	1	67.1	75	30	17	28
Willis, Carl	MIN	2	4	5.92	—	49	0	3	59.1	89	39	12	37
Witt, Bobby	OAK	8	10	5.04	37	24	24	0	135.2	151	76	70	111

National League Hitters

	TEAM	POS	BA	G	AB	RS	H	2B	3B	HR	RBI	BB	SB
Abbott, Kurt	FLO	SS	.249	101	345	41	86	17	3	9	33	16	3
Alicea, Luis	STL	2B	.278	88	205	32	57	12	5	5	29	30	4
Alou, Moises	MON	OF	.339	107	422	81	143	31	5	22	78	42	7
Arias, Alex	FLO	2B	.239	59	113	4	27	5	0	0	15	9	0
Ausmus, Brad	SD	C	.251	101	327	45	82	12	1	7	24	30	5
Bagwell, Jeff	HOU	1B	.368	110	400	104	147	32	2	39	116	65	15
Barberie, Bret	FLO	2B	.301	107	372	40	112	20	2	5	31	23	2
Bass, Kevin	HOU	OF	.310	82	203	37	63	15	1	6	35	28	2
Batiste, Kim	PHI	3B	.234	64	209	17	49	6	0	1	13	1	1
Bean, Billy	SD	OF	.215	84	135	7	29	5	1	0	14	7	0
Bell, Derek	SD	OF	.311	108	434	54	135	20	0	14	54	29	24
Bell, Jay	PIT	SS	.276	110	424	68	117	35	4	9	45	49	2
Bell, Juan	MON	SS	.278	38	97	12	27	4	0	2	10	15	4
Belliard, Rafael	ATL	SS	.242	46	120	9	29	7	1	0	9	2	0
Benavides, Freddie	MON	SS	.188	47	85	8	16	5	1	0	6	3	0
Benjamin, Mike	SF	SS	.258	38	62	9	16	5	1	1	9	5	5
Benzinger, Todd	SF	1B	.265	107	328	32	87	13	2	9	31	17	2
Berry, Sean	MON	3B	.78	103	320	43	89	19	2	11	41	32	14
Bichette, Dante	COL	OF	.304	116	484	74	147	33	2	27	95	19	21
Biggio, Craig	HOU	2B	.318	114	437	88	139	44	5	6	56	62	39
Blauser, Jeff	ATL	SS	.258	96	380	56	98	21	4	6	45	38	1
Bogar, Tim	NYM	SS	.154	50	52	5	8	0	0	2	5	4	1
Bonds, Barry	SF	OF	.312	112	391	89	122	18	1	37	81	74	29

	TEAM	POS	BA	G	AB	RS	H	2B	3B	HR	RBI	BB	SB
Bonilla, Bobby	NYM	3B	.290	108	403	60	117	24	1	20	67	55	1
Boone, Bret	CIN	2B	.320	108	381	59	122	25	2	12	68	24	3
Bournigal, Rafael	LA	SS	.224	40	116	2	26	3	1	0	11	9	0
Branson, Jeff	CIN	SS	.284	58	109	18	31	4	1	6	16	5	0
Bream, Sid	ATL	1B	.344	46	61	7	21	5	0	0	7	9	0
Brogna, Rico	NYM	1B	.351	39	131	16	46	11	2	7	20	6	1
Browne, Jerry	FLO	3B	.295	101	329	42	97	17	4	3	30	52	3
Brumfield, Jacob	CIN	OF	.311	68	122	36	38	10	2	4	11	15	6
Buechele, Steve	CHC	3B	.242	104	339	33	82	11	1	14	52	39	1
Burkett, John	SF	P	.059	25	51	1	3	0	0	0	0	1	0
Burks, Ellis	COL	OF	.322	42	149	33	48	8	3	13	24	16	3
Burnitz, Jeromy	NYM	OF	.238	45	143	26	34	4	0	3	15	23	1
Butler, Brett	LA	OF	.314	111	417	79	131	13	9	8	33	68	27
Caminiti, Ken	HOU	3B	.283	111	406	63	115	28	2	18	75	43	4
Candiotti, Tom	LA	P	.140	23	50	2	7	1	0	0	3	1	0
Carr, Chuck	FLO	OF	.263	106	433	61	114	19	2	2	30	22	32
Carreon, Mark	SF	OF	.270	51	100	8	27	4	0	3	20	7	0
Carrillo, Matias	FLO	OF	.250	80	136	13	34	7	0	0	9	9	3
Castilla, Vinny	COL	SS	.331	52	130	16	43	11	1	3	18	7	2
Cedeno, Andujar	HOU	SS	.263	98	342	38	90	26	0	9	49	29	1
Chamberlain, Wes	PHI	OF	.275	24	69	7	19	5	0	2	6	3	0
Cianfrocco, Archi	SD	3B	.219	59	146	9	32	8	0	4	13	3	2
Clark, Dave	PIT	OF	.296	86	223	37	66	11	1	10	46	22	2
Clark, Phil	SD	OF	.215	61	149	14	32	6	0	5	20	5	2
Clayton, Royce	SF	SS	.236	108	385	38	91	14	6	3	30	30	23

	TEAM	POS	BA	G	AB	RS	H	2B	3B	HR	RBI	BB	SB
Colbrunn, Greg	FLO	1B	.303	47	155	17	47	10	0	6	31	9	1
Conine, Jeff	FLO	OF	.319	115	451	60	144	27	6	18	82	40	1
Cordero, Wil	MON	SS	.294	110	415	65	122	30	3	15	63	41	16
Cummings, Midre	PIT	OF	.244	24	86	11	21	4	0	1	12	4	0
Daulton, Darren	PHI	C	.300	69	257	43	77	17	1	15	56	33	4
DeShields, Delino	LA	2B	.250	89	320	51	80	11	3	2	33	54	27
Destrade, Orestes	FLO	1B	.208	39	130	12	27	4	0	5	15	19	1
Diaz, Mario	FLO	3B	.325	32	77	10	25	4	2	0	11	6	0
Donnels, Chris	HOU	3B	.267	54	86	12	23	5	0	3	5	13	1
Dorsett, Brian	CIN	C	.245	76	216	21	53	8	0	5	26	21	0
Drabek, Doug	HOU	P	.241	24	58	4	14	0	1	0	6	0	0
Duncan, Mariano	PHI	2B	.268	88	347	49	93	22	1	8	48	17	10
Dunston, Shawon	CHC	SS	.278	88	331	38	92	19	0	11	35	16	3
Dykstra, Lenny	PHI	OF	.273	84	315	68	86	26	5	5	24	68	15
Eisenreich, Jim	PHI	OF	.300	104	290	42	87	15	4	4	43	33	6
Eusebio, Tony	HOU	C	.296	55	159	18	47	9	1	5	30	8	0
Everett, Carl	FLO	OF	.216	16	51	7	11	1	0	2	6	3	4
Felder, Mike	HOU	OF	.239	58	117	10	28	2	2	0	13	4	3
Fernandez, Tony	CIN	3B	.279	104	366	50	102	18	6	8	50	44	12
Finley, Steve	HOU	OF	.276	94	373	64	103	16	5	11	33	28	13
Fletcher, Darrin	MON	C	.260	94	285	28	74	18	1	10	57	25	0
Floyd, Cliff	MON	1B	.281	100	334	43	94	19	4	4	41	24	10
Foley, Tom	PIT	2B	.236	59	123	13	29	7	0	3	15	13	0
Frazier, Lou	MON	OF	.271	76	140	25	38	3	1	0	14	18	20
Galarraga, Andres	COL	1B	.319	103	417	77	133	21	0	31	85	19	•8

	TEAM	POS	BA	G	AB	RS	H	2B	3B	HR	RBI	BB	SB
Gallagher, Dave	ATL	OF	.224	89	152	27	34	5	0	2	14	22	0
Garcia, Carlos	PIT	2B	.277	98	412	49	114	15	2	6	28	16	18
Gilkey, Bernard	STL	OF	.253	105	380	52	96	22	1	6	45	39	15
Girardi, Joe	COL	C	.276	93	330	47	91	9	4	4	34	21	3
Glavine, Tom	ATL	P	.179	26	56	4	10	1	0	0	3	5	0
Gonzalez, Luis	HOU	OF	.273	112	392	57	107	29	4	8	67	49	15
Grace, Mark	CHC	1B	.298	106	403	55	120	23	3	6	44	48	0
Grissom, Marquis	MON	OF	.288	110	475	96	137	25	4	11	45	41	36
Gutierrez, Ricky	SD	SS	.240	90	275	27	66	11	2	1	28	32	2
Gwynn, Chris	LA	OF	.268	58	71	9	19	0	0	3	13	7	0
Gwynn, Tony	SD	OF	.394	110	419	79	165	35	1	12	64	48	5
Harris, Lenny	CIN	3B	.310	66	100	13	31	3	1	0	14	5	7
Hatcher, Billy	PHI	OF	.246	43	134	15	33	5	1	2	13	6	4
Hayes, Charlie	COL	3B	.288	113	423	46	122	23	4	10	50	36	3
Hernandez, Carlos	LA	C	.219	32	64	6	14	2	0	2	6	1	0
Hernandez, Jose	CHC	3B	.242	56	132	18	32	2	3	1	9	8	2
Hill, Glenallen	CHC	OF	.297	89	269	48	80	12	1	10	38	29	19
Hollins, Dave	PHI	3B	.222	44	162	28	36	7	1	4	26	23	1
Howard, Thomas	CIN	OF	.264	83	178	24	47	11	0	5	24	10	4
Hundley, Todd	NYM	C	.237	91	291	45	69	10	1	16	42	25	2
Hunter, Brian R.	CIN	OF	.234	85	256	34	60	16	1	15	57	17	0
Hyers, Tim	SD	1B	.254	52	118	13	30	3	0	0	7	9	3
Incaviglia, Pete	PHI	OF	.230	80	244	28	56	10	1	13	32	16	1
Ingram, Garey	LA	2B	.282	26	78	10	22	1	0	3	8	7	0
Jackson, Danny	PHI	P	.158	26	57	3	9	2	1	0	7	2	0

	TEAM	POS	BA	G	AB	RS	H	2B	3B	HR	RBI	BB	SB
Jefferies, Gregg	STL	1B	.325	103	397	52	129	27	1	12	55	45	12
Jonhson, Brian	SD	C	.247	36	93	7	23	4	1	3	16	5	0
Johnson, Howard	COL	OF	.211	93	227	30	48	10	2	10	40	39	11
Jordan, Brian	STL	OF	.258	53	178	14	46	8	2	5	15	16	4
Jordan, Ricky	PHI	1B	.282	72	220	29	62	14	2	8	37	6	0
Justice, Dave	ATL	OF	.313	104	352	61	110	16	2	19	59	69	2
Karros, Eric	LA	1B	.266	111	406	51	108	21	1	14	46	29	2
Kelly, Mike	ATL	OF	.273	30	77	14	21	10	1	2	9	2	0
Kelly, Roberto	ATL	OF	.293	110	434	73	127	23	3	9	45	35	19
Kent, Jeff	NYM	2B	.292	107	415	53	121	24	5	14	68	23	1
King, Jeff	PIT	3B	.263	94	339	36	89	23	0	5	42	30	3
Kingery, Mike	COL	OF	.349	105	301	56	105	27	8	4	41	30	5
Klesko, Ryan	ATL	OF	.278	92	245	42	68	13	3	17	47	26	1
Kruk, John	PHI	1B	.302	75	255	35	77	17	0	5	38	42	4
Lankford, Ray	STL	OF	.267	109	416	89	111	25	5	19	57	58	11
Lansing, Mike	MON	3B	.266	106	394	44	105	21	2	5	35	30	12
Larkin, Barry	CIN	SS	.279	110	427	78	119	23	5	9	52	64	26
Lemke, Mark	ATL	2B	.294	104	350	40	103	15	0	3	31	38	0
Lewis, Darren	SF	OF	.257	114	451	70	116	15	9	4	29	53	30
Lieberthal, Mike	PHI	C	.266	24	79	6	21	3	1	1	5	3	0
Lindeman, Jim	NYM	1B	.270	52	137	18	37	8	1	7	20	6	0
Liriano, Nelson	COL	2B	.255	87	255	39	65	17	5	3	31	42	0
Livingstone, Scott	SD	3B	.272	57	180	11	49	12	1	2	10	6	2
Longmire, Tony	PHI	OF	.237	69	139	10	33	11	0	0	17	10	2
Lopez, Javier	ATL	C	.245	80	277	27	68	9	0	13	35	17	0

	TEAM	POS	BA	G	AB	RS	H	2B	3B	HR	RBI	BB	SB
Lopez, Luis	SD	SS	.277	77	235	29	65	16	1	2	20	15	3
Maddux, Greg	ATL	P	.222	25	63	5	14	2	0	0	2	1	0
Magadan, Dave	FLO	3B	.275	74	211	30	58	7	0	1	17	39	0
Manwaring, Kirt	SF	C	.250	97	316	30	79	17	1	1	29	25	1
Martin, Al	PIT	OF	.286	82	276	48	79	12	4	9	33	34	15
Martinez, Dave	SF	1B	.247	97	235	23	58	9	3	4	27	21	3
Martinez, Ramon	LA	P	.273	24	66	4	18	3	0	0	3	1	0
May, Derrick	CHC	OF	.284	100	345	43	98	19	2	8	51	30	3
McClendon, Lloyd	PIT	OF	.239	51	92	9	22	4	0	4	12	4	0
McGee, Willie	SF	OF	.282	45	156	19	44	3	0	5	23	15	3
McGriff, Fred	ATL	1B	.318	113	424	81	135	25	1	34	94	50	7
McGriff, Terry	STL	C	.219	42	114	10	25	6	0	0	13	13	0
McReynolds, Kevin	NYM	OF	.256	51	180	23	46	11	2	4	21	20	2
Mejia, Roberto	COL	2B	.241	38	116	11	28	8	1	4	14	15	3
Merced, Orlando	PIT	OF	.272	108	386	48	105	21	3	9	51	42	4
Milligan, Randy	MON	1B	.232	47	82	10	19	2	0	2	12	14	0
Mitchell, Kevin	CIN	OF	.326	95	310	57	101	18	1	30	77	59	2
Mondesi, Raul	LA	OF	.306	112	434	63	133	27	8	16	56	16	11
Morandini, Mickey	PHI	2B	.292	87	274	40	80	16	5	2	26	34	10
Morris, Hal	CIN	1B	.335	112	436	60	146	30	4	10	78	34	6
Mouton, James	HOU	OF	.245	99	310	43	76	11	0	2	16	27	24
O'Brien, Charlie	ATL	C	.243	51	152	24	37	11	0	8	28	15	0
Offerman, Jose	LA	SS	.210	72	243	27	51	8	4	1	25	38	2
Oliva, Jose	ATL	3B	.288	19	59	9	17	5	0	6	11	7	0
Oquendo, Jose	STL	SS	.264	55	129	13	34	2	2	0	9	21	1

	TEAM	POS	BA	G	AB	RS	H	2B	3B	HR	RBI	BB	SB
Orsulak, Joe	NYM	OF	.260	96	292	39	76	3	0	8	42	16	4
Pagnozzi, Tom	STL	C	.272	70	243	21	66	12	1	7	40	21	0
Parent, Mark	CHC	C	.263	44	99	8	26	4	0	3	16	13	0
Parrish, Lance	PIT	C	.270	40	126	10	34	5	0	3	16	18	1
Patterson, John	SF	2B	.238	85	240	36	57	10	1	3	32	16	13
Pecota, Bill	ATL	3B	.214	64	112	11	24	5	0	2	16	16	1
Pena, Geronimo	STL	2B	.254	83	213	33	54	13	1	11	34	24	9
Pendleton, Terry	ATL	3B	.252	77	309	25	78	18	3	7	30	12	2
Perry, Gerald	STL	1B	.325	60	77	12	25	7	0	3	18	15	1
Piazza, Mike	LA	C	.319	107	405	64	129	18	0	24	92	33	1
Plantier, Phil	SD	OF	.220	96	341	44	75	21	0	18	41	36	3
Pratt, Todd	PHI	C	.196	28	102	10	20	6	1	2	6	12	0
Reed, Jeff	SF	C	.175	50	103	11	18	3	0	1	7	11	0
Rhodes, Karl	CHC	OF	.234	95	269	39	63	17	0	8	19	33	6
Roberson, Kevin	CHC	OF	.218	44	55	8	12	4	0	4	9	2	0
Roberts, Bip	SD	2B	.320	105	403	52	129	15	5	2	31	39	21
Rodriguez, Henry	LA	OF	.268	104	306	33	82	14	2	8	49	17	0
Royer, Stan	STL	3B	.175	39	57	3	10	5	0	1	2	0	0
Saberhagen, Bret	NYM	P	.172	24	58	7	10	2	0	0	1	4	0
Sanchez, Rey	CHC	SS	.285	96	291	26	83	13	1	0	24	20	2
Sandberg, Ryne	CHC	2B	.238	57	223	36	53	9	5	5	24	23	2
Sanders, Deion	CIN	OF	.283	92	375	58	106	17	4	4	28	32	38
Sanders, Reggie	CIN	OF	.263	107	400	66	105	20	8	17	62	41	21
Santiago, Benito	FLO	C	.273	101	337	35	92	14	2	11	41	25	1
Scarsone, Steve	SF	2B	.272	52	103	21	28	8	0	2	13	10	0

	TEAM	POS	BA	G	AB	RS	H	2B	3B	HR	RBI	BB	SB
Segui, David	NYM	1B	.241	92	336	46	81	17	1	10	43	33	0
Servais, Scott	HOU	C	.195	78	251	27	49	15	1	9	41	10	0
Sheaffer, Danny	COL	C	.218	44	110	11	24	4	0	1	12	10	0
Sheffield, Gary	FLO	OF	.276	87	322	61	89	16	1	27	78	51	12
Shipley, Craig	SD	SS	.333	81	240	32	80	14	4	4	30	9	6
Slaught, Don	PIT	C	.288	76	240	21	69	7	0	2	21	34	0
Smiley, John	CIN	P	.200	24	55	5	11	3	0	0	2	4	0
Smith, Ozzie	STL	SS	.262	98	381	51	100	18	3	3	30	38	6
Smith, Zane	PIT	P	.211	26	57	2	12	1	0	0	2	0	0
Snyder, Cory	LA	OF	.235	73	153	18	36	6	0	6	18	14	1
Sosa, Sammy	CHC	OF	.300	105	426	59	128	17	6	25	70	25	22
Stankiewicz, Andy	HOU	SS	.259	37	54	10	14	3	0	1	5	12	1
Staton, Dave	SD	1B	.182	29	66	6	12	2	0	4	6	10	0
Stinnett, Kelly	NYM	C	.253	47	150	20	38	6	2	2	14	11	2
Stocker, Kevin	PHI	SS	.273	82	271	38	74	11	2	2	28	44	2
Strawberry, Darryl	SF	OF	.239	29	92	13	22	3	1	4	17	19	0
Tarasco, Tony	ATL	OF	.273	87	132	16	36	6	0	5	19	9	5
Taubensee, Eddie	HOU	C	.283	66	187	29	53	8	2	8	21	15	2
Tewksbury, Bob	STL	P	.185	24	54	4	10	2	1	0	3	2	0
Thompson, Milt	HOU	OF	.274	96	241	34	66	7	0	4	33	24	9
Thompson, Robby	SF	2B	.209	35	129	13	27	8	2	2	7	15	3
Thompson, Ryan	NYM	OF	.225	98	334	39	75	14	1	18	59	28	1
Tingley, Ron	FLO	C	.173	19	52	4	9	3	1	1	2	5	0
Treadway, Jeff	LA	2B	.299	52	67	14	20	3	0	0	5	5	1
Van Slyke, Andy	PIT	OF	.246	105	374	41	92	18	3	6	30	52	7

	TEAM	POS	BA	G	AB	RS	H	2B	3B	HR	RBI	BB	SB
VanderWal, John	COL	1B	.245	91	110	12	27	3	1	5	15	16	2
Varsho, Gary	PIT	OF	.256	67	82	15	21	6	3	0	5	4	0
Vina, Fernando	NYM	3B	.250	79	124	20	31	6	0	0	6	12	3
Vizcaino, Jose	NYM	SS	.256	103	410	47	105	13	3	3	33	33	1
Walker, Larry	MON	OF	.322	103	395	76	127	44	2	19	86	47	15
Wallach, Tim	LA	3B	.280	113	414	68	116	21	1	23	78	46	0
Walton, Jerome	CIN	OF	.309	46	68	10	21	4	0	1	9	4	1
Webster, Lenny	MON	C	.273	57	143	13	39	10	0	5	23	16	0
Webster, Mitch	LA	OF	.274	82	84	16	23	4	0	4	12	8	1
Weiss, Walt	COL	SS	.251	110	423	58	106	11	4	1	32	56	12
White, Rondell	MON	OF	.278	40	97	16	27	10	1	2	13	9	1
Whiten, Mark	STL	OF	.293	92	334	57	98	18	2	14	53	37	10
Wilkins, Rick	CHC	C	.227	100	313	44	71	25	2	7	39	40	4
Williams, Eddie	SD	1B	.331	49	175	32	58	11	1	11	42	15	0
Williams, Matt	SF	3B	.267	112	445	74	119	16	3	43	96	33	1
Young, Eric	COL	OF	.272	90	228	37	62	13	1	7	30	38	18
Young, Kevin	PIT	1B	.205	59	122	15	25	7	2	1	11	8	0
Zambrano, Eddie	CHC	OF	.259	67	116	17	30	7	0	6	18	16	2
Zeile, Todd	STL	3B	.267	113	415	62	111	25	1	19	75	52	1

National League Pitchers

	TEAM	W	L	ERA	RANK	G	GS	SV	IP	H	ER	BB	SO
Andersen, Larry	PHI	1	2	4.41	—	29	0	0	32.2	33	16	15	27
Aquino, Luis	FLO	2	1	3.73	—	29	1	0	50.2	39	21	22	224
Arocha, Rene	STL	4	4	4.01	—	45	7	11	83.0	94	37	21	62
Ashby, Andy	SD	6	11	3.40	12	24	24	0	164.1	145	62	43	121
Astacio, Pedro	LA	6	8	4.29	27	23	23	0	149.0	142	71	47	108
Avery, Steve	ATL	8	3	4.04	23	24	24	0	151.2	127	68	55	122
Ballard, Jeff	PIT	1	1	6.66	—	28	0	2	24.1	32	18	10	11
Banks, Willie	CHC	8	12	5.40	37	23	23	0	138.1	139	83	56	91
Bautista, Jose	CHC	4	5	3.89	—	58	0	1	69.1	75	30	17	45
Beck, Rod	SF	2	4	2.77	—	48	0	28	48.2	49	15	13	39
Bedrosian, Steve	ATL	0	2	3.33	—	46	0	0	46.0	41	17	18	43
Benes, Andy	SD	6	14	3.86	19	25	25	0	172.1	155	74	51	189
Bielecki, Mike	ATL	2	0	4.00	—	19	1	0	27.0	28	12	12	18
Black, Bud	SF	4	2	4.47	—	10	10	0	54.1	50	27	16	28
Blair, Willie	COL	0	5	5.79	—	47	1	3	77.2	98	50	39	68
Borland, Toby	PHI	1	0	2.36	—	24	0	1	34.1	31	9	14	26
Boskie, Shawn	PHI	4	6	5.01	—	20	14	0	88.1	88	49	29	61
Bottenfield, Kent	SF	3	1	6.15	—	16	1	1	24.2	33	18	10	15
Boucher, Denis	MON	0	1	6.75	—	10	2	0	18.2	24	14	7	17
Bowen, Ryan	FLO	1	5	4.94	—	8	8	0	47.1	50	26	19	32
Brantley, Jeff	CIN	6	6	2.48	—	50	0	15	65.1	46	18	28	63
Brocail, Doug	SD	0	0	5.82	—	12	0	0	17.0	21	11	5	11
Browning, Tom	CIN	3	1	4.20	—	7	7	0	40.2	34	19	13	22

	TEAM	W	L	ERA	RANK	G	GS	SV	IP	H	ER	BB	SO
Buckels, Gary	STL	0	1	2.25	—	10	0	0	12.0	8	3	7	9
Bullinger, Jim	CHC	6	2	3.60	—	33	10	2	100.0	87	40	34	72
Burba, Dave	SF	3	6	4.38	—	57	0	0	74.0	59	36	45	84
Burkett, John	SF	6	8	3.62	15	25	25	0	159.1	176	64	36	85
Candiotti, Tom	LA	7	7	4.12	25	23	22	0	153.0	149	70	54	102
Carrasco, Hector	CIN	5	6	2.24	—	45	0	6	56.1	42	14	30	41
Carter, Andy	PHI	0	2	4.46	—	20	0	0	34.1	34	17	12	18
Castillo, Frank	CHC	2	1	4.30	—	4	4	0	23.0	25	11	5	19
Castillo, Juan	NYM	0	0	6.94	—	2	2	0	11.2	17	9	5	1
Cimorelli, Frank	STL	0	0	8.78	—	11	0	1	13.1	20	13	10	1
Cooke, Steve	PIT	4	11	5.02	33	25	23	0	134.1	157	75	46	74
Cormier, Rheal	STL	3	2	5.45	—	7	7	0	39.2	40	24	7	26
Crim, Chuck	CHC	5	4	4.48	—	49	1	2	64.1	69	32	24	43
Daal, Omar	LA	0	0	3.29	—	24	0	0	13.2	12	5	5	9
Davis, Mark	SD	0	1	8.82	—	20	0	0	16.1	20	16	13	15
Delucia, Rich	CIN	0	0	4.22	—	8	0	0	10.2	9	5	5	15
Dewey, Mark	PIT	2	1	3.68	—	45	0	1	51.1	61	21	19	30
Drabek, Doug	HOU	12	6	2.84	3	23	23	0	164.2	132	52	45	121
Drahman, Brian	FLO	0	0	6.23	—	9	0	0	13.0	15	9	6	7
Dreifort, Darren	LA	0	5	6.21	—	27	0	6	29.0	45	20	15	22
Dyer, Mike	PIT	1	1	5.87	—	14	0	4	15.1	15	10	12	13
Edens, Tom	PHI	5	1	4.33	—	42	0	0	54.0	59	26	18	39
Elliott, Donnie	SD	0	1	3.27	—	30	1	0	33.0	31	12	21	24
Eversgerd, Bryan	STL	2	3	4.52	—	40	1	0	67.2	75	34	20	47
Fassero, Jeff	MON	8	6	2.99	4	21	21	0	138.2	119	46	40	119

	TEAM	W	L	ERA	RANK	G	GS	SV	IP	H	ER	BB	SO
Fortugno, Tim	CIN	1	0	4.20	—	25	0	0	30.0	32	14	14	29
Foster, Kevin	CHC	3	4	2.89	—	13	13	0	81.0	70	26	35	75
Franco, John	NYM	1	4	2.70	—	47	0	30	50.0	47	15	19	42
Fraser, Willy	FLO	2	0	5.84	—	9	0	0	12.1	20	8	6	7
Freeman, Marvin	COL	10	2	2.80	—	19	18	0	112.2	113	35	23	67
Frey, Steve	SF	1	0	4.94	—	44	0	0	31.0	37	17	15	20
Gardner, Mark	FLO	4	4	4.87	—	20	14	0	92.1	97	50	30	57
Glavine, Tom	ATL	13	9	3.97	22	25	25	0	165.1	173	73	70	140
Gomez, Pat	SF	0	1	3.78	—	26	0	0	33.1	23	14	20	14
Gooden, Dwight	NYM	3	4	6.31	—	7	7	0	41.1	46	29	15	40
Gott, Jim	LA	5	3	5.94	—	37	0	2	36.1	46	24	20	29
Gozzo, Mauro	NYM	3	5	4.83	—	23	8	0	69.0	86	37	28	33
Greene, Tommy	PHI	2	0	4.54	—	7	7	0	35.2	37	18	22	28
Gross, Kevin	LA	9	7	3.60	14	25	23	0	157.1	162	63	43	124
Guzman, Jose	CHC	2	2	9.15	—	4	4	0	29.2	22	20	13	11
Habyan, John	STL	1	0	3.23	—	52	0	1	47.1	50	17	20	46
Hamilton, Joey	SD	9	6	2.98	—	16	16	0	108.2	98	36	29	61
Hammond, Chris	FLO	4	4	3.07	—	13	13	0	73.1	79	25	23	40
Hampton, Mike	HOU	2	1	3.70	—	44	0	0	41.1	46	17	16	24
Hanson, Erik	CIN	5	5	4.11	24	22	21	0	122.2	137	56	23	101
Harkey, Mike	COL	1	6	5.79	—	24	13	0	91.2	125	59	35	39
Harnisch, Pete	HOU	8	5	5.40	—	17	17	0	95.0	100	57	39	62
Harris, Gene	SD	1	1	8.03	—	13	0	0	12.0	21	11	8	9
Harris, Greg W.	COL	3	12	6.65	40	29	19	1	130.1	154	96	52	82
Harvey, Bryan	FLO	0	0	5.23	—	12	0	6	10.1	12	6	4	10

	TEAM	W	L	ERA	RANK	G	GS	SV	IP	H	ER	BB	SO
Henry, Butch	MON	8	3	2.43	—	24	15	1	107.1	97	29	20	70
Heredia, Gil	MON	6	3	3.46	—	39	3	0	75.1	85	29	13	62
Hernandez, Jeremy	FLO	3	3	2.70	—	21	0	9	23.1	16	7	14	13
Hershiser, Orel	LA	6	6	3.79	16	21	21	1	135.1	146	57	42	72
Hickerson, Bryan	SF	4	8	5.40	—	28	14	1	98.1	118	59	38	59
Hill, Ken	MON	16	5	3.32	11	23	23	0	154.2	145	57	44	85
Hill, Milt	ATL	0	0	7.94	—	10	0	0	11.1	18	10	6	10
Hillman, Eric	NYM	0	3	7.79	—	11	6	0	34.2	45	30	11	20
Hoffman, Trevor	SD	4	4	2.57	—	47	0	20	56.0	39	16	20	68
Holmes, Darren	COL	0	3	6.35	—	29	0	3	28.1	35	20	24	33
Hope, John	PIT	0	0	5.79	—	9	0	0	14.0	18	9	4	6
Hough, Charlie	FLO	5	9	5.15	—	21	21	0	113.2	118	65	52	65
Hudek, John	HOU	0	2	2.97	—	42	0	16	39.1	24	13	18	39
Hurst, Jonathan	NYM	0	1	12.60	—	7	0	0	10.0	15	14	5	6
Ilsley, Blaise	CHC	0	0	7.80	—	10	0	0	15.0	25	13	9	9
Jackson, Danny	PHI	14	6	3.26	9	25	25	0	179.1	183	65	46	129
Jackson, Mike	SF	3	2	1.49	—	36	0	4	42.1	23	7	11	51
Jacome, Jason	NYM	4	3	2.67	—	8	8	0	54.0	54	16	17	30
Jarvis, Kevin	CIN	1	1	7.13	—	6	3	0	17.2	22	14	5	10
Johnstone, Jay	FLO	1	2	5.91	—	17	0	0	21.1	23	14	16	23
Jones, Bobby	NYM	12	7	3.15	7	24	24	0	160.0	157	56	56	80
Jones, Doug	PHI	2	4	2.17	—	47	0	27	54.0	55	13	6	38
Jones, Todd	HOU	5	2	2.72	—	48	0	5	72.2	52	22	26	63
Juden, Jeff	PHI	1	4	6.18	—	6	5	0	27.2	29	19	12	22
Kile, Darryl	HOU	9	6	4.57	30	24	24	0	147.2	153	75	82	105

	TEAM	W	L	ERA	RANK	G	GS	SV	IP	H	ER	BB	SO
Krueger, Bill	SD	3	2	4.83	—	8	7	0	41.0	42	22	7	30
Leskanic, Curt	COL	1	1	5.64	—	8	3	0	22.1	27	14	10	17
Lewis, Richie	FLO	1	4	5.67	—	45	0	0	54.0	62	34	38	45
Lieber, Jon	PIT	6	7	3.73	—	17	17	0	108.2	116	45	25	71
Linton, Doug	NYM	6	2	4.47	—	32	3	0	50.1	74	25	20	29
Maddux, Greg	ATL	16	6	1.56	1	25	25	0	202.0	150	35	31	156
Maddux, Mike	NYM	2	1	5.11	—	27	0	2	44.0	45	25	13	32
Manzanillo, Josias	NYM	3	2	2.66	—	37	14	2	47.1	34	14	13	48
Manzanillo, Ravelo	PIT	4	2	4.14	—	46	0	1	50.0	45	23	42	39
Martinez, Jose	SD	0	2	6.75	—	4	1	0	12.0	18	9	5	7
Martinez, Pedro A.	SD	3	2	2.90	—	48	1	3	68.1	52	22	49	52
Martinez, Pedro J.	MON	11	5	3.42	13	24	23	1	144.2	115	55	45	142
Martinez, Ramon	LA	12	7	3.97	21	24	24	0	170.0	160	75	56	119
Mason, Roger	NYM	3	5	3.75	—	47	0	1	60.0	55	25	25	33
Mattews, Terry	FLO	2	1	3.35	—	24	2	0	43.0	45	16	9	21
Mauser, Tim	SD	2	4	3.49	—	35	0	2	49.0	50	19	19	32
McDowell, Roger	LA	0	3	5.23	—	32	0	0	41.1	50	24	22	29
McElroy, Chuck	CIN	1	2	2.34	—	52	0	5	57.2	52	15	15	38
McMichael, Greg	ATL	4	6	3.84	—	51	0	21	58.2	66	25	19	47
Mercker, Kent	ATL	9	4	3.45	—	20	17	0	112.1	90	43	45	111
Miceli, Danny	PIT	2	1	5.93	—	28	0	2	27.1	28	18	11	27
Miller, Kurt	FLO	1	3	8.10	—	4	4	0	20.0	26	18	7	11
Minor, Blas	PIT	0	1	8.05	—	17	0	1	19.0	27	17	9	17
Monteleone, Rich	SF	4	3	3.18	—	39	0	0	45.1	43	16	13	16
Moore, Marcus	COL	1	1	6.15	—	29	0	0	33.2	33	23	21	33

	TEAM	W	L	ERA	RANK	G	GS	SV	IP	H	ER	BB	SO
Morgan, Mike	CHC	2	10	6.69	—	15	15	0	80.2	111	60	35	57
Munoz, Bobby	PHI	7	5	2.67	—	21	14	1	104.1	101	31	35	59
Munoz, Mike	COL	4	2	3.74	—	57	0	1	45.2	37	19	31	32
Murphy, Rob	STL	4	3	3.79	—	50	0	2	40.1	35	17	13	25
Mutis, Jeff	FLO	1	0	5.40	—	35	0	0	38.1	51	23	15	30
Myers, Randy	CHC	1	5	3.79	—	38	0	21	40.1	40	17	16	32
Neagle, Denny	PIT	9	10	5.12	34	24	24	0	137.0	135	78	49	122
Nen, Robb	FLO	5	5	2.95	—	44	0	15	58.0	46	19	17	60
Nied, David	COL	9	7	4.80	32	22	22	0	122.0	137	65	47	74
Olivares, Omar	STL	3	4	5.74	—	14	12	1	73.2	84	47	37	26
Olson, Gregg	ATL	0	2	9.20	—	16	0	1	14.2	19	15	13	10
Otto, Dave	CHC	0	1	3.80	—	36	0	0	45.0	49	19	22	19
Painter, Lance	COL	4	6	6.11	—	15	14	0	73.2	91	50	26	41
Palacios, Vicente	STL	3	8	4.44	29	31	17	1	117.2	104	58	43	95
Pena, Alejandro	PIT	3	2	5.02	—	22	0	7	28.2	22	16	10	27
Perez, Mike	STL	2	3	8.71	—	36	0	12	31.0	52	30	10	20
Perez, Yorkis	FLO	3	0	3.54	—	44	0	0	40.2	33	16	14	41
Plesac, Dan	CHC	2	3	4.61	—	54	0	1	54.2	61	28	13	53
Portugal, Mark	SF	10	8	3.93	20	21	21	0	137.1	135	60	45	87
Pugh, Tim	CIN	3	3	6.04	—	10	9	0	47.2	60	32	26	24
Quantrill, Paul	PHI	2	2	6.00	—	18	1	0	30.0	39	20	10	13
Rapp, Pat	FLO	7	8	3.85	17	24	23	0	133.1	132	57	69	75
Reed, Steve	COL	3	2	3.94	—	61	0	3	64.0	79	28	26	51
Remlinger, Mike	NYM	1	5	4.61	—	10	9	0	54.2	55	28	35	33
Reynolds, Shane	HOU	8	5	3.05	5	33	14	0	124.0	128	42	21	110

	TEAM	W	L	ERA	RANK	G	GS	SV	IP	H	ER	BB	SO
Reynoso, Armando	COL	3	4	4.82	—	9	9	0	52.1	54	28	22	25
Rijo, Jose	CIN	9	6	3.08	6	26	26	0	172.1	177	59	52	171
Ritz, Kevin	COL	5	6	5.62	—	15	15	0	73.2	88	46	35	53
Rivera, Ben	PHI	3	4	6.87	—	9	7	0	38.0	40	29	22	19
Robertson, Rich	PIT	0	0	6.89	—	8	0	0	15.2	20	12	10	8
Rodriguez, Rich	STL	3	5	4.03	—	56	0	0	60.1	62	27	26	43
Rogers, Kevin	SF	0	0	3.48	—	9	0	0	10.1	10	4	6	7
Rojas, Mel	MON	3	2	3.32	—	58	0	16	84.0	71	31	21	84
Roper, John	CIN	6	2	4.50	—	16	15	0	92.0	90	46	30	51
Rueter, Kirk	MON	7	3	5.17	—	20	20	0	92.1	106	53	23	50
Ruffin, Bruce	COL	4	5	4.04	—	56	0	16	55.2	55	25	30	65
Ruffin, Johnny	CIN	7	2	3.09	—	51	0	1	70.0	57	24	27	44
Saberhagen, Bret	NYM	14	4	2.74	2	24	24	0	177.1	169	54	13	143
Sager, A. J.	SD	1	4	5.98	—	22	3	0	46.2	62	31	16	26
Sanders, Scott	SD	4	8	4.78	—	23	20	1	111.0	103	59	48	109
Scheid, Rich	FLO	1	3	3.34	—	8	5	0	32.1	35	12	8	17
Schilling, Curt	PHI	2	8	4.48	—	13	13	0	82.1	87	41	28	58
Schourek, Pete	CIN	7	2	4.09	—	22	10	0	81.1	90	37	29	69
Scott, Tim	MON	5	2	2.70	—	40	0	1	53.1	51	16	18	37
Seanez, Rudy	LA	1	1	2.66	—	17	0	0	23.2	24	7	9	18
Seminara, Frank	NYM	0	2	5.82	—	10	1	0	17.0	20	11	8	7
Shaw, Jeff	MON	5	2	3.88	—	46	0	1	67.1	67	29	15	47
Slocumb, Heathcliff	PHI	5	1	2.86	—	52	0	0	72.1	75	23	28	58
Smiley, John	CIN	11	10	3.86	18	24	24	0	158.2	169	68	37	112
Smith, Pete	NYM	4	10	5.55	39	21	21	0	131.1	145	81	42	62

	TEAM	W	L	ERA	RANK	G	GS	SV	IP	H	ER	BB	SO
Smith, Zane	PIT	10	8	3.27	10	25	24	0	157.0	162	57	34	57
Smoltz, John	ATL	6	10	4.14	26	21	21	0	134.2	120	62	148	113
Stanton, Mike	ATL	3	1	3.55	—	49	0	3	45.2	41	18	26	35
Sutcliffe, Rick	STL	6	4	6.52	—	16	14	0	67.2	93	49	32	26
Swift, Bill	SF	8	7	3.38	28	17	17	0	109.1	109	41	31	62
Swindell, Greg	HOU	8	9	4.37	—	24	24	0	148.1	175	72	26	74
Tabaka, Jeff	SD	3	1	5.27	—	39	0	1	41.0	32	24	27	32
Telgheder, Dave	NYM	0	1	7.20	—	6	0	0	10.0	11	8	8	4
Tewksbury, Bob	STL	12	10	5.32	36	24	24	0	155.2	190	92	22	79
Tomlin, Randy	PIT	0	3	3.92	—	10	4	0	20.2	23	9	10	17
Torres, Salomon	SF	2	8	5.44	8	16	14	0	84.1	95	51	34	42
Trachsel, Steve	CHC	9	7	3.21	—	22	22	0	146.0	133	52	54	108
Urbani, Tom	STL	3	7	5.15	—	20	10	0	80.1	98	46	21	43
Valdes, Ismael	LA	3	1	3.18	—	21	1	0	28.1	21	10	10	28
Valenzuela, Fernando	PHI	1	2	3.00	—	8	7	0	45.0	42	15	7	19
VanLandingham, Wm.	SF	8	2	3.54	—	16	14	0	84.0	70	33	43	56
Veres, Dave	HOU	3	3	2.41	—	32	0	1	41.0	39	11	7	28
Veres, Randy	CHC	1	1	5.59	—	10	0	0	9.2	12	6	2	5
Wagner, Paul	PIT	7	8	4.59	31	29	17	0	119.2	136	61	50	86
Watson, Allen	STL	6	5	5.52	38	22	22	0	115.2	130	71	53	74
Wayne, Gary	LA	1	3	4.67	—	19	0	0	17.1	19	9	6	10
Weathers, Dave	FLO	8	12	5.27	35	24	24	0	135.0	166	79	59	72
Wendell, Turk	CHC	0	1	11.93	—	6	2	0	14.1	22	19	10	9
West, David	PHI	4	10	3.55	—	31	14	0	99.0	74	39	61	83
Wetteland, John	MON	4	6	2.83	—	52	0	25	63.2	46	20	21	68

	TEAM	W	L	ERA	RANK	G	GS	SV	IP	H	ER	BB	SO
White, Gabe	MON	1	1	6.08	—	7	5	1	23.2	24	16	11	17
White, Rick	PIT	4	5	3.82	—	43	5	6	75.1	79	32	17	38
Whitehurst, Wally	SD	4	7	4.92	—	13	13	0	64.0	84	35	26	43
Williams, Brian	HOU	6	5	5.74	—	20	13	0	78.1	112	50	41	49
Williams, Mike	PHI	2	4	5.01	—	12	8	0	50.0	61	28	20	29
Williams, Mitch	HOU	6	5	5.74	—	20	13	0	78.1	112	50	41	49
Wohlers, Mark	ATL	7	2	4.59	—	51	0	1	51.0	51	26	33	58
Worrell, Tim	SD	0	1	3.68	—	3	3	0	14.2	9	6	5	14
Worrell, Todd	LA	6	5	4.29	—	38	0	11	42.0	37	20	12	44
Young, Anthony	CHC	4	6	3.92	—	20	19	0	114.2	103	50	46	65

Rangers catcher Ivan Rodriguez won a 1994 Gold Glove.

Award Winners

Most Valuable Player

1931	AL	Lefty Grove, Philadelphia	P	31–4	2.06 ERA	5 SV
	NL	Frank Frisch, St. Louis	2B	.311 BA	4 HR	82 RBI
1932	AL	Jimmie Foxx, Philadelphia	1B	.364 BA	58 HR	169 RBI
	NL	Chuck Klein, Philadelphia	OF	.348 BA	38 HR	137 RBI
1933	AL	Jimmie Foxx, Philadelphia	1B	.356 BA	48 HR	163 RBI
	NL	Carl Hubbell, New York	P	21–12	2.30 ERA	5 SV
1934	AL	Mickey Cochrane, Detroit	C	.320 BA	2 HR	76 RBI
	NL	Dizzy Dean, St. Louis	P	30–7	2.66 ERA	7 SV
1935	AL	Hank Greenberg, Detroit	1B	.328 BA	36 HR	170 RBI
	NL	Gabby Hartnett, Chicago	C	.344 BA	13 HR	91 RBI
1936	AL	Lou Gehrig, New York	1B	.354 BA	49 HR	152 RBI
	NL	Carl Hubbell, New York	P	26–6	2.31 ERA	3 SV
1937	AL	Charley Gehringer, Detroit	2B	.371 BA	14 HR	96 RBI
	NL	Joe Medwick, St. Louis	OF	.374 BA	31 HR	154 RBI
1938	AL	Jimmie Foxx, Boston	1B	.349 BA	50 HR	175 RBI
	NL	Ernie Lombardi, Cincinnati	C	.342 BA	19 HR	95 RBI
1939	AL	Joe DiMaggio, New York	OF	.381 BA	31 HR	133 RBI
	NL	Bucky Walters, Cincinnati	P	27–11	2.29 ERA	0 SV
1940	AL	Hank Greenberg, Detroit	1B	.340 BA	41 HR	150 RBI
	NL	Frank McCormack, Cincinnati	1B	.309 BA	19 HR	127 RBI
1941	AL	Joe DiMaggio, New York	OF	.357 BA	30 HR	125 RBI
	NL	Dolph Camilli, Brooklyn	1B	.285 BA	34 HR	120 RBI
1942	AL	Joe Gordon, New York	2B	.322 BA	18 HR	103 RBI
	NL	Mort Cooper, St. Louis	P	22–7	1.78 ERA	0 SV
1943	AL	Spud Chandler, New York	P	20–4	1.64 ERA	0 SV
	NL	Stan Musial, St. Louis	OF	.357 BA	13 HR	81 RBI
1944	AL	Hal Newhouser, Detroit	P	29–9	2.22 ERA	2 SV
	NL	Marty Marion, St. Louis	SS	.267 BA	6 HR	63 RBI
1945	AL	Hal Newhouser, Detroit	P	25–9	1.81 ERA	2 SV
	NL	Phil Cavaretta, Chicago	1B	.355 BA	6 HR	97 RBI
1946	AL	Ted Williams, Boston	OF	.342 BA	38 HR	123 RBI
	NL	Stan Musial, St. Louis	1B	.365 BA	16 HR	103 RBI
1947	AL	Joe DiMaggio, New York	OF	.315 BA	20 HR	97 RBI
	NL	Bob Elliott, Boston	3B	.317 BA	22 HR	113 RBI
1948	AL	Lou Boudreau, Cleveland	SS	.355 BA	18 HR	106 RBI
	NL	Stan Musial, St. Louis	OF	.376 BA	39 HR	131 RBI
1949	AL	Ted Williams, Boston	OF	.343 BA	43 HR	159 RBI
	NL	Jackie Robinson, Brooklyn	2B	.342 BA	16 HR	124 RBI
1950	AL	Phil Rizzuto, New York	SS	.324 BA	7 HR	66 RBI
	NL	Jim Konstanty, Philadelphia	P	16–7	2.66 ERA	22 SV

Most Valuable Player (continued)

1951	AL	Yogi Berra, New York	C	.294 BA	27 HR	88 RBI
	NL	Roy Campanella, Brooklyn	C	.325 BA	33 HR	108 RBI
1952	AL	Bobby Shantz, Philadelphia	P	24–7	2.48 ERA	0 SV
	NL	Hank Sauer, Chicago	OF	.270 BA	37 HR	121 RBI
1953	AL	Al Rosen, Cleveland	3B	.336 BA	43 HR	145 RBI
	NL	Roy Campanella, Brooklyn	C	.312 BA	41 HR	142 RBI
1954	AL	Yogi Berra, New York	C	.307 BA	22 HR	125 RBI
	NL	Willie Mays, New York	OF	.345 BA	41 HR	110 RBI
1955	AL	Yogi Berra, New York	C	.272 BA	27 HR	108 RBI
	NL	Roy Campanella, Brooklyn	C	.318 BA	32 HR	107 RBI
1956	AL	Mickey Mantle, New York	OF	.353 BA	52 HR	130 RBI
	NL	Don Newcombe, Brooklyn	P	27–7	3.06 ERA	0 SV
1957	AL	Mickey Mantle, New York	OF	.365 BA	34 HR	94 RBI
	NL	Hank Aaron, Milwaukee	OF	.322 BA	44 HR	132 RBI
1958	AL	Jackie Jensen, Boston	OF	.286 BA	35 HR	122 RBI
	NL	Ernie Banks, Chicago	SS	.313 BA	47 HR	129 RBI
1959	AL	Nellie Fox, Chicago	2B	.306 BA	2 HR	70 RBI
	NL	Ernie Banks, Chicago	SS	.304 BA	45 HR	143 RBI
1960	AL	Roger Maris, New York	OF	.283 BA	39 HR	112 RBI
	NL	Dick Groat, Philadelphia	SS	.325 BA	2 HR	50 RBI
1961	AL	Roger Maris, New York	OF	.269 BA	61 HR	142 RBI
	NL	Frank Robinson, Cincinnati	OF	.323 BA	37 HR	124 RBI
1962	AL	Mickey Mantle, New York	OF	.321 BA	30 HR	89 RBI
	NL	Maury Wills, Los Angeles	SS	.299 BA	6 HR	48 RBI
1963	AL	Elston Howard, New York	C	.287 BA	28 HR	85 RBI
	NL	Sandy Koufax, Los Angeles	P	25–5	1.88 ERA	0 SV
1964	AL	Brooks Robinson, Baltimore	3B	.317 BA	28 HR	118 RBI
	NL	Ken Boyer, St. Louis	3B	.295 BA	24 HR	119 RBI
1965	NL	Willie Mays, San Francisco	OF	.317 BA	52 HR	112 RBI
	AL	Zoilo Versalles, Minnesota	SS	.273 BA	19 HR	77 RBI
1966	AL	Frank Robinson, Baltimore	OF	.316 BA	49 HR	122 RBI
	NL	Roberto Clemente, Pittsburgh	OF	.317 BA	29 HR	119 RBI
1967	AL	Carl Yastremski, Boston	OF	.326 BA	44 HR	121 RBI
	NL	Orlando Cepeda, St. Louis	1B	.325 BA	25 HR	111 RBI
1968	AL	Denny McLain, Detroit	P	31–6	1.96 ERA	0 SV
	NL	Bob Gibson, St. Louis	P	22–9	1.12 ERA	0 SV
1969	AL	Harmon Killebrew, Minn.	1B	.276 BA	49 HR	140 RBI
	NL	Willie McCovey, San Francisco	1B	.320 BA	45 HR	126 RBI
1970	AL	Boog Powell, Baltimore	1B	.297 BA	35 HR	114 RBI
	NL	Johnny Bench, Cincinnati	C	.293 BA	2 HR	27 RBI
1971	AL	Vida Blue, Oakland	P	24–8	1.82 ERA	0 SV
	NL	Joe Torre, St. Louis	3B	.363 BA	24 HR	137 RBI
1972	AL	Dick Allen, Chicago	1B	.308 BA	37 HR	113 RBI
	NL	Johnny Bench, Cincinnati	C	.270 BA	40 HR	125 RBI

1973	AL	Reggie Jackson, Oakland	OF	.293 BA	32 HR	117 RBI
	NL	Pete Rose, Cincinnati	OF	.338 BA	5 HR	64 RBI
1974	AL	Jeff Burroughs, Texas	OF	.301 BA	25 HR	118 RBI
	NL	Steve Garvey, Los Angeles	1B	.312 BA	21 HR	111 RBI
1975	AL	Fred Lynn, Boston	OF	.331 BA	21 HR	105 RBI
	NL	Joe Morgan, Cincinnati	2B	.327 BA	17 HR	94 RBI
1976	AL	Thurman Munson, New York	C	.302 BA	17 HR	105 RBI
	NL	Joe Morgan, Cincinnati	2B	.320 BA	27 HR	111 RBI
1977	AL	Rod Carew, Minnesota	1B	.388 BA	14 HR	100 RBI
	NL	George Foster, Cincinnati	OF	.32 BA	52 HR	149 RBI
1978	AL	Jim Rice, Boston	OF	.315 BA	46 HR	139 RBI
	NL	Dave Parker, Pittsburgh	OF	.334 BA	30 HR	117 RBI
1979	AL	Don Baylor, California	OF	.296 BA	36 HR	139 RBI
	NL	Keith Hernandez, St. Louis	1B	.344 BA	11 HR	105 RBI
	NL	Willie Stargell, Pittsburgh	1B	.281 BA	32 HR	82 RBI
1980	AL	George Brett, Kansas City	3B	.390 BA	24 HR	118 RBI
	NL	Mike Schmidt, Philadelphia	3B	.286 BA	48 HR	121 RBI
1981	AL	Rollie Fingers, Milwaukee	P	6–3	1.04 ERA	28 SV
	NL	Mike Schmidt, Philadelphia	3B	.316 BA	31 HR	91 RBI
1982	AL	Robin Yount, Milwaukee	OF	.331 BA	29 HR	114 RBI
	NL	Dale Murphy, Atlanta	OF	.281 BA	36 HR	109 RBI
1983	AL	Cal Ripken, Jr., Baltimore	SS	.318 BA	27 HR	102 RBI
	NL	Dale Murphy, Atlanta	OF	.302 BA	36 HR	121 RBI
1984	AL	Willie Hernandez, Detroit	P	9–3	1.92 ERA	32 SV
	NL	Ryne Sandberg, Chicago	2B	.314 BA	19 HR	84 RBI
1985	AL	Don Mattingly, New York	1B	.324 BA	35 HR	145 RBI
	NL	Willie McGee, St. Louis	OF	.353 BA	7 HR	48 RBI
1986	AL	Roger Clemens, Boston	P	24–4	2.48 ERA	0 SV
	NL	Mike Schmidt, Philadelphia	3B	.290 BA	37 HR	119 RBI
1987	AL	George Bell, Toronto	OF	.308 BA	47 HR	134 RBI
	NL	Andre Dawson, Chicago	OF	.287 BA	49 HR	137 RBI
1988	AL	Jose Canseco, Oakland	OF	.307 BA	42 HR	124 RBI
	NL	Kirk Gibson, Los Angeles	OF	.290 BA	25 HR	76 RBI
1989	AL	Robin Yount, Milwaukee	OF	.318 BA	21 HR	103 RBI
	NL	Kevin Mitchell, San Francisco	OF	.291 BA	47 HR	125 RBI
1990	AL	Rickey Henderson, Oakland	OF	.325 BA	28 HR	61 RBI
	NL	Barry Bonds, Pittsburgh	OF	.301 BA	33 HR	114 RBI
1991	AL	Cal Ripken, Jr., Baltimore	SS	.323 BA	34 HR	114 RBI
	NL	Terry Pendleton, Atlanta	3B	.319 BA	22 HR	86 RBI
1992	AL	Dennis Eckersley, Oakland	P	7–1	1.91 ERA	51 SV
	NL	Barry Bonds, Pittsburgh	OF	.311 BA	34 HR	103 RBI
1993	AL	Frank Thomas, Chicago	1B	.317 BA	41 HR	128 RBI
	NL	Barry Bonds, San Francisco	OF	.336 BA	46 HR	123 RBI
1994	AL	Frank Thomas, Chicago	1B	.353 BA	38 HR	101 RBI
	NL	Jeff Bagwell, Houston	1B	.368 BA	39 HR	116 RBI

Cy Young

1957		Warren Spahn, Milwaukee	21–11	2.69 ERA	3 SV
1958		Bob Turley, New York (AL)	21–7	2.97 ERA	1 SV
1959		Early Wynn, Chicago (AL)	22–10	3.17 ERA	0 SV
1960		Vernon Law, Pittsburgh	20–9	3.08 ERA	0 SV
1961		Whitey Ford, New York (AL)	25–4	3.21 ERA	0 SV
1962		Don Drysdale, Los Angeles	25–9	2.83 ERA	1 SV
1963		Sandy Koufax, Los Angeles	25–5	1.88 ERA	0 SV
1964		Dean Chance, Los Angeles	20–9	1.65 ERA	4 SV
1965		Sandy Koufax, Los Angeles	26–8	2.04 ERA	2 SV
1966		Sandy Koufax, Los Angeles	27–9	1.73 ERA	0 SV
1967	AL	Jim Lonborg, Boston	22–9	3.16 ERA	0 SV
	NL	Mike McCormick, San Francisco	22–10	2.85 ERA	0 SV
1968	AL	Denny McLain, Detroit	31–6	1.96 ERA	0 SV
	NL	Bob Gibson, St. Louis	22–9	1.12 ERA	0 SV
1969	AL	Denny McLain, Detroit	24–9	2.80 ERA	0 SV
	AL	Mike Cuellar, Baltimore	23–11	2.38 ERA	0 SV
	NL	Tom Seaver, New York	25–7	2.21 ERA	0 SV
1970	AL	Jim Perry, Minnesota	24–12	3.04 ERA	0 SV
	NL	Bob Gibson, St. Louis	23–7	3.12 ERA	0 SV
1971	AL	Vida Blue, Oakland	24–8	1.82 ERA	0 SV
	NL	Fergie Jenkins, Chicago	24–13	2.77 ERA	0 SV
1972	AL	Gaylord Perry, Cleveland	24–16	1.92 ERA	1 SV
	NL	Steve Carlton, Philadelphia	27–10	1.97 ERA	0 SV
1973	AL	Jim Palmer, Baltimore	22–9	2.40 ERA	1 SV
	NL	Tom Seaver, New York	19–10	2.08 ERA	0 SV
1974	AL	Jim Hunter, Oakland	25–12	2.49 ERA	0 SV
	NL	Mike Marshall, Los Angeles	15–12	2.42 ERA	21 SV
1975	AL	Jim Palmer, Baltimore	23–11	2.09 ERA	1 SV
	NL	Tom Seaver, New York	22–9	2.38 ERA	0 SV
1976	AL	Jim Palmer, Baltimore	22–13	2.51 ERA	0 SV
	NL	Randy Jones, San Diego	22–14	2.74 ERA	0 SV
1977	AL	Sparky Lyle, New York	13–5	2.17 ERA	26 SV
	NL	Steve Carlton, Philadelphia	23–10	2.64 ERA	0 SV
1978	AL	Ron Guidry, New York	25–3	1.74 ERA	0 SV
	NL	Gaylord Perry, San Diego	21–6	2.73 ERA	0 SV
1979	AL	Mike Flanagan, Baltimore	23–9	3.08 ERA	0 SV
	NL	Bruce Sutter, Chicago	6–6	2.22 ERA	37 SV
1980	AL	Steve Stone, Baltimore	25–7	3.23 ERA	0 SV
	NL	Steve Carlton, Philadelphia	24–9	2.34 ERA	0 SV
1981	AL	Rollie Fingers, Milwaukee	6–3	1.04 ERA	28 SV
	NL	Fernando Valenzuela, Los Angeles	13–7	2.48 ERA	0 SV
1982	AL	Pete Vuckovich, Milwaukee	18–6	3.34 ERA	0 SV
	NL	Steve Carlton, Philadelphia	23–11	3.10 ERA	0 SV

1983	AL	LaMarr Hoyt, Chicago	24–10	3.66 ERA	0 SV
	NL	John Denny, Philadelphia	19–6	2.37 ERA	0 SV
1984	AL	Willie Hernandez, Detroit	9–3	1.92 ERA	32 SV
	NL	Rick Sutcliffe, Chicago	20–6	3.97 ERA	0 SV
1985	AL	Bret Saberhagen, Kansas City	20–6	2.87 ERA	0 SV
	NL	Dwight Gooden, New York	24–4	1.53 ERA	0 SV
1986	AL	Roger Clemens, Boston	24–4	2.48 ERA	0 SV
	NL	Mike Scott, Houston	18–10	2.22 ERA	0 SV
1987	AL	Roger Clemens, Boston	20–9	2.97 ERA	0 SV
	NL	Steve Bedrosian, Philadelphia	5–3	2.83 ERA	40 SV
1988	AL	Frank Viola, Minnesota	24–7	2.64 ERA	0 SV
	NL	Orel Hershiser, Los Angeles	23–8	2.26 ERA	1 SV
1989	AL	Bret Saberhagen, Kansas City	23–6	2.16 ERA	0 SV
	NL	Mark Davis, San Diego	4–3	1.85 ERA	44 SV
1990	AL	Bob Welch, Oakland	27–6	2.95 ERA	0 SV
	NL	Doug Drabek, Pittsburgh	22–6	2.76 ERA	0 SV
1991	AL	Roger Clemens, Boston	18–10	2.62 ERA	0 SV
	NL	Tom Glavine, Atlanta	20–11	2.55 ERA	0 SV
1992	AL	Dennis Eckersley, Oakland	7–1	1.91 ERA	51 SV
	NL	Greg Maddux, Chicago	20–11	2.18 ERA	0 SV
1993	AL	Jack McDowell, Chicago	22–10	3.37 ERA	0 SV
	NL	Greg Maddux, Atlanta	20–10	2.36 ERA	0 SV
1994	AL	David Cone	16–5	2.94 ERA	0 SV
	NL	Greg Maddux	16–6	1.56 ERA	0 SV

Rookie of the Year

1949	AL	Roy Sievers, St. Louis	OF	.306 BA	16 HR	91 RBI
	NL	Don Newcombe, Brooklyn	P	17–8	3.17 ERA	1 SV
1950	AL	Walt Dropo, Boston	1B	.322 BA	34 HR	144 RBI
	NL	Sam Jethroe, Boston	OF	.273 BA	18 HR	58 RBI
1951	AL	Gil McDougald, New York	3B	.306 BA	14 HR	63 RBI
	NL	Willie Mays, New York	OF	.274 BA	20 HR	68 RBI
1952	AL	Harry Byrd, Philadelphia	P	15–15	3.31 ERA	2 SV
	NL	Joe Black, Brooklyn	P	15–4	2.15	15 SV
1953	AL	Harvey Kuenn, Detroit	SS	.308 BA	2 HR	48 RBI
	NL	Jim Gilliam, Brooklyn	2B	.278 BA	6 HR	63 RBI
1954	AL	Bob Grim, New York	P	20–6	3.26 ERA	0 SV
	NL	Wally Moon, St. Louis	OF	.304 BA	12 HR	76 RBI
1955	AL	Herb Score, Cleveland	P	16–10	2.85 ERA	0 SV
	NL	Bill Virdon, St. Louis	OF	.281 BA	17 HR	68 RBI
1956	AL	Luis Aparicio, Chicago	SS	.266 BA	3 HR	56 RBI
	NL	Frank Robinson, Cincinnati	OF	.290 BA	38 HR	83 RBI
1957	AL	Tony Kubek, New York	SS	.297 BA	3 HR	39 RBI
	NL	Jack Sanford, Philadelphia	P	19–8	3.08 ERA	1958

Rookie of the Year (continued)

AL	Albie Pearson, Washington	OF	.275 BA	3 HR	33 RBI	
NL	Orlando Cepeda, San Fran.	1B	.312 BA	25 HR	96 RBI	
1959 AL	Bob Allison, Washington	OF	.261 BA	30 HR	85 RBI	
NL	Willie McCovey, San Fran.	1B	.354 BA	13 HR	38 RBI	
1960 AL	Ron Hansen, Baltimore	SS	.255 BA	22 HR	86 RBI	
NL	Frank Howard, Los Angeles	OF	.268 BA	23 HR	77 RBI	
1961 AL	Don Schwall, Boston	P	15–7	3.22 ERA		
NL	Billy Williams, Chicago	OF	.278 BA	25 HR	86 RBI	
1962 AL	Tom Tresh, New York	SS	.286 BA	20 HR	93 RBI	
NL	Ken Hubbs, Chicago	2B	.260 BA	5 HR	49 RBI	
1963 AL	Gary Peters, Chicago	P	19–8	2.33 ERA		
NL	Pete Rose, Cinncinati	2B	.273 BA	6 HR	41 RBI	
1964 AL	Tony Oliva, Minnesota	OF	.323 BA	32 HR	94 RBI	
NL	Dick Allen, Philadelphia	3B	.318 BA	29 HR	91 RBI	
1965 AL	Curt Blefary, Baltimore	OF	.260 BA	22 HR	70 RBI	
NL	Jim Lefebvre, Los Angeles	2B	.250 BA	12 HR	69 RBI	
1966 AL	Tommie Agee, Chicago	OF	.273 BA	22 HR	86 RBI	
NL	Tommy Helms, Cincinnati	2B	.284 BA	9 HR	49 RBI	
1967 AL	Rod Carew, Minnesota	2B	.292 BA	8 HR	51 RBI	
NL	Tom Seaver, New York	P	16–13	2.76 ERA		
1968 AL	Stan Bahnsen, New York	P	17–12	2.05 ERA		
NL	Johnny Bench, Cincinnati	C	.275 BA	15 HR	82 RBI	
1969 AL	Lou Piniella, Kansas City	OF	.282 BA	11 HR	68 RBI	
NL	Ted Sizemore, Los Angeles	2B	.271 BA	4 HR	46 RBI	
1970 AL	Thurman Munson, New York	C	.302 BA	6 HR	53 RBI	
NL	Carl Morton, Montreal	P	18–11	3.60 ERA	0 SV	
1971 AL	Chris Chambliss, Cleveland	1B	.275 BA	9 HR	48 RBI	
NL	Earl Williams, Atlanta	C	.260 BA	33 HR	87 RBI	
1972 AL	Carlton Fisk, Boston	C	.293 BA	22 HR	61 RBI	
NL	Jon Matlack, New York	P	15–10	2.32 ERA		
1973 AL	Al Bumbry, Baltimore	OF	.337 BA	7 HR	34 RBI	
NL	Gary Matthews, San Fran.	OF	.300 BA	12 HR	58 RBI	
1974 AL	Mike Hargrove, Texas	1B	.323 BA	4 HR	66 RBI	
NL	Bake McBride, St. Louis	OF	.309 BA	6 HR	56 RBI	
1975 AL	Fred Lynn, Boston	OF	.331 BA	21 HR	105 RBI	
NL	John Montefusco, San Fran.	P	15–9	2.88 ERA	0 SV	
1976 AL	Mark Fidrych, Detroit	P	19–9	2.34 ERA	0 SV	
NL	Pat Zachry, Cincinnati	P	14–7	2.74 ERA	0 SV	
NL	Butch Metzger, San Diego	P	11–4	2.92 ERA	16 SV	
1977 AL	Eddie Murray, Baltimore	1B	.283 BA	27 HR	88 RBI	
NL	Andre Dawson, Montreal	OF	.282 BA	19 HR	65 RBI	
1978 AL	Lou Whitaker, Detroit	2B	.285 BA	3 HR	58 RBI	
NL	Bob Horner, Atlanta	3B	.266 BA	23 HR	63 RBI	

1979	AL	Alfredo Griffin, Toronto	SS	.287 BA	2 HR	31 RBI
	AL	John Castino, Minnesota	3B	.285 BA	5 HR	52 RBI
	NL	Rick Sutcliffe, Los Angeles	P	17–10	3.46 ERA	0 SV
1980	AL	Joe Charboneau, Cleveland	OF	.289 BA	23 HR	87 RBI
	NL	Steve Howe, Los Angeles	P	7–9	2.66 ERA	17 SV
1981	AL	Dave Righetti, New York	P	8–4	2.05 ERA	0 SV
	NL	Fernando Valenzuela, Los Angeles	P	13–7	2.48 ERA	0 SV
1982	AL	Cal Ripken, Baltimore	SS	.264 BA	28 HR	93 RBI
	NL	Steve Sax, Los Angeles	2B	.282 BA	4 HR	47 RBI
1983	AL	Ron Kittle, Chicago	OF	.254 BA	35 HR	100 RBI
	NL	Darryl Strawberry, New York	OF	.257 BA	26 HR	74 RBI
1984	AL	Alvin Davis, Seattle	1B	.284 BA	27 HR	116 RBI
	NL	Dwight Gooden, New York	P	17–9	2.60 ERA	0 SV
1985	AL	Ozzie Guillen, Chicago	SS	.273 BA	1 HR	33 RBI
	NL	Vince Coleman, St. Louis	OF	.267 BA	1 HR	40 RBI
1986	AL	Jose Canseco, Oakland	OF	.240 BA	33 HR	117 RBI
	NL	Todd Worrell, St. Louis	P	9–10	2.08 ERA	36 SV
1987	AL	Mark McGwire, Oakland	1B	.289 BA	49 HR	118 RBI
	NL	Benito Santiago, San Diego	C	.300 BA	18 HR	79 RBI
1988	AL	Walt Weiss, Oakland	SS	.250 BA	3 HR	39 RBI
	NL	Chris Sabo, Cincinnati	3B	.271 BA	11 HR	44 RBI
1989	AL	Gregg Olson, Baltimore	P	5–2	1.69 ERA	27 SV
	NL	Jerome Walton, Chicago	OF	.293 BA	5 HR	46 RBI
1990	AL	Sandy Alomar, Jr., Cleveland	C	.290 BA	9 HR	66 RBI
	NL	Dave Justice, Atlanta	OF	.282 BA	28 HR	78 RBI
1991	AL	Chuck Knoblauch, Cleveland	2B	.281 BA	1 HR	50 RBI
	NL	Jeff Bagwell, Houston	1B	.294 BA	15 HR	82 RBI
1992	AL	Pat Listach, Milwaukee	SS	.290 BA	1 HR	47 RBI
	NL	Eric Karros, Los Angeles	1B	.257 BA	20 HR	88 RBI
1993	AL	Tim Salmon, California	OF	.283 BA	31 HR	95 RBI
	NL	Mike Piazza, Los Angeles	C	.318 BA	35 HR	112 RBI
1994	AL	Bob Hamelin, Kansas City	DH	.282 BA	24 HR	65 RBI
	NL	Raul Mondesi, Los Angeles	OF	.306 BA	16 HR	56 RBI

Gold Glove

Pitchers

Year	National League	American League
1957	(no selection)	Bobby Shantz, New York
1958	Harvey Haddix, Cincinnati	Bobby Shantz, New York
1959	Harvey Haddix, Pittsburgh	Bobby Shantz, New York
1960	Harvey Haddix, Pittsburgh	Bobby Shantz, New York
1961	Bobby Shantz, Pittsburgh	Frank Lary, Detroit
1962	Bobby Shantz, St. Louis	Jim Kaat, Minnesota
1963	Bobby Shantz, St. Louis	Jim Kaat, Minnesota

Pitchers (continued)

Year	National League	American League
1964	Bobby Shantz, Philadelphia	Jim Kaat, Minnesota
1965	Bob Gibson, St. Louis	Jim Kaat, Minnesota
1966	Bob Gibson, St. Louis	Jim Kaat, Minnesota
1967	Bob Gibson, St. Louis	Jim Kaat, Minnesota
1968	Bob Gibson, St. Louis	Jim Kaat, Minnesota
1969	Bob Gibson, St. Louis	Jim Kaat, Minnesota
1970	Bob Gibson, St. Louis	Jim Kaat, Minnesota
1971	Bob Gibson, St. Louis	Jim Kaat, Minnesota
1972	Bob Gibson, St. Louis	Jim Kaat, Minnesota
1973	Bob Gibson, St. Louis	Jim Kaat, Minnesota
1974	Andy Messersmith, Los Angeles	Jim Kaat, Chicago
1975	Andy Messersmith, Los Angeles	Jim Kaat, Chicago
1976	Jim Kaat, Philadelphia	Jim Palmer, Baltimore
1977	Jim Kaat, Philadelphia	Jim Palmer, Baltimore
1978	Phil Niekro, Atlanta	Jim Palmer, Baltimore
1979	Phil Niekro, Atlanta	Jim Palmer, Baltimore
1980	Phil Niekro, Atlanta	Mike Norris, Oakland
1981	Steve Carlton, Philadelphia	Mike Norris, Oakland
1982	Phil Niekro, Atlanta	Ron Guidry, New York
1983	Phil Niekro, Atlanta	Ron Guidry, New York
1984	Joaquin Andujar, St. Louis	Ron Guidry, New York
1985	Rick Reuschel, Pittsburgh	Ron Guidry, New York
1986	Fernando Valenzuela, Los Angeles	Ron Guidry, New York
1987	Rick Reuschel, San Francisco	Mark Langston, Seattle
1988	Orel Hershiser, Los Angeles	Mark Langston, Seattle
1989	Ron Darling, New York	Bret Saberhagen, Kansas City
1990	Greg Maddux, Chicago	Mike Boddicker, Boston
1991	Greg Maddux, Chicago	Mark Langston, California
1992	Greg Maddux, Chicago	Mark Langston, California
1993	Greg Maddux, Atlanta	Mark Langston, California
1994	Greg Maddux, Atlanta	Mark Langston, California

Catchers

Year	National League	American League
1957	(no selection)	Sherm Lollar, Chicago
1958	Del Crandall, Milwaukee	Sherm Lollar, Chicago
1959	Del Crandall, Milwaukee	Sherm Lollar, Chicago
1960	Del Crandall, Milwaukee	Earl Battey, Washington
1961	John Roseboro, Los Angeles	Earl Battey, Minnesota
1962	Del Crandall, Milwaukee	Earl Battey, Minnesota
1963	Johnny Edwards, Cincinnati	Elston Howard, New York
1964	Johnny Edwards, Cincinnati	Elston Howard, New York
1965	Joe Torre, Milwaukee	Bill Freehan, Detroit

Year	National League	American League
1966	John Roseboro, Los Angeles	Bill Freehan, Detroit
1967	Randy Hundley, Chicago	Bill Freehan, Detroit
1968	Johnny Bench, Cincinnati	Bill Freehan, Detroit
1969	Johnny Bench, Cincinnati	Bill Freehan, Detroit
1970	Johnny Bench, Cincinnati	Ray Fosse, Cleveland
1971	Johnny Bench, Cincinnati	Ray Fosse, Cleveland
1972	Johnny Bench, Cincinnati	Carlton Fisk, Boston
1973	Johnny Bench, Cincinnati	Thurman Munson, New York
1974	Johnny Bench, Cincinnati	Thurman Munson, New York
1975	Johnny Bench, Cincinnati	Thurman Munson, New York
1976	Johnny Bench, Cincinnati	Jim Sundberg, Texas
1977	Johnny Bench, Cincinnati	Jim Sundberg, Texas
1978	Bob Boone, Philadelphia	Jim Sundberg, Texas
1979	Bob Boone, Philadelphia	Jim Sundberg, Texas
1980	Gary Carter, Montreal	Jim Sundberg, Texas
1981	Gary Carter, Montreal	Jim Sundberg, Texas
1982	Gary Carter, Montreal	Bob Boone, California
1983	Tony Pena, Pittsburgh	Lance Parrish, Detroit
1984	Tony Pena, Pittsburgh	Lance Parrish, Detroit
1985	Tony Pena, Pittsburgh	Lance Parrish, Detroit
1986	Jody Davis, Chicago	Bob Boone, California
1987	Mike LaValliere, Pittsburgh	Bob Boone, California
1988	Benito Santiago, San Diego	Bob Boone, California
1989	Benito Santiago, San Diego	Bob Boone, California
1990	Benito Santiago, San Diego	Sandy Alomar, Cleveland
1991	Tom Pagnozzi, St. Louis	Tony Pena, Boston
1992	Tom Pagnozzi, St. Louis	Ivan Rodriguez, Texas
1993	Kirt Manwaring, San Francisco	Ivan Rodriguez, Texas
1994	Tom Pagnozzi, St. Louis	Ivan Rodriguez, Texas

First Basemen

Year	National League	American League
1957	Gil Hodges, Brooklyn	(no selection)
1958	Gil Hodges, Los Angeles	Vic Power, Cleveland
1959	Gil Hodges, Los Angeles	Vic Power, Cleveland
1960	Bill White, St. Louis	Vic Power, Cleveland
1961	Bill White, St. Louis	Vic Power, Cleveland
1962	Bill White, St. Louis	Vic Power, Minnesota
1963	Bill White, St. Louis	Vic Power, Minnesota
1964	Bill White, St. Louis	Vic Power, Los Angeles
1965	Bill White, St. Louis	Joe Pepitone, New York
1966	Bill White, Philadelphia	Joe Pepitone, New York
1967	Wes Parker, Los Angeles	George Scott, Boston

First Basemen (continued)

Year	National League	American League
1968	Wes Parker, Los Angeles	George Scott, Boston
1969	Wes Parker, Los Angeles	Joe Pepitone, New York
1970	Wes Parker, Los Angeles	Jim Spencer, California
1971	Wes Parker, Los Angeles	George Scott, Boston
1972	Wes Parker, Los Angeles	George Scott, Milwaukee
1973	Mike Jorgenson, Montreal	George Scott, Milwaukee
1974	Steve Garvey, Los Angeles	George Scott, Milwaukee
1975	Steve Garvey, Los Angeles	George Scott, Milwaukee
1976	Steve Garvey, Los Angeles	George Scott, Milwaukee
1977	Steve Garvey, Los Angeles	Jim Spencer, Chicago
1978	Keith Hernandez, St. Louis	Chris Chambliss, New York
1979	Keith Hernandez, St. Louis	Cecil Cooper, Milwaukee
1980	Keith Hernandez, St. Louis	Cecil Cooper, Milwaukee
1981	Keith Hernandez, St. Louis	Mike Squires, Chicago
1982	Keith Hernandez, St. Louis	Eddie Murray, Baltimore
1983	Keith Hernandez, St. Louis-New York	Eddie Murray, Baltimore
1984	Keith Hernandez, New York	Eddie Murray, Baltimore
1985	Keith Hernandez, New York	Don Mattingly, New York
1986	Keith Hernandez, New York	Don Mattingly, New York
1987	Keith Hernandez, New York	Don Mattingly, New York
1988	Keith Hernandez, New York	Don Mattingly, New York
1989	Andres Galarraga, Montreal	Don Mattingly, New York
1990	Andres Galarraga, Montreal	Mark McGwire, Oakland
1991	Will Clark, San Francisco	Don Mattingly, New York
1992	Mark Grace, Chicago	Don Mattingly, New York
1993	Mark Grace, Chicago	Don Mattingly, New York
1994	Jeff Bagwell, Houston	Don Mattingly, New York

Second Basemen

Year	National League	American League
1957	(no selection)	Nellie Fox, Chicago
1958	Bill Mazeroski, Pittsburgh	Frank Bolling, Detroit
1959	Charlie Neal, Los Angeles	Nellie Fox, Chicago
1960	Bill Mazeroski, Pittsburgh	Nellie Fox, Chicago
1961	Bill Mazeroski, Pittsburgh	Bobby Richardson, New York
1962	Ken Hubbs, Chicago	Bobby Richardson, New York
1963	Bill Mazeroski, Pittsburgh	Bobby Richardson, New York
1964	Bill Mazeroski, Pittsburgh	Bobby Richardson, New York
1965	Bill Mazeroski, Pittsburgh	Bobby Richardson, New York
1966	Bill Mazeroski, Pittsburgh	Bobby Knoop, California
1967	Bill Mazeroski, Pittsburgh	Bobby Knoop, California
1968	Glenn Beckert, Chicago	Bobby Knoop, California
1969	Felix Millan, Atlanta	Dave Johnson, Baltimore

Year	National League	American League
1970	Tommy Helms, Cincinnati	Dave Johnson, Baltimore
1971	Tommy Helms, Cincinnati	Dave Johnson, Baltimore
1972	Felix Millan, Atlanta	Doug Griffin, Boston
1973	Joe Morgan, Cincinnati	Bobby Grich, Baltimore
1974	Joe Morgan, Cincinnati	Bobby Grich, Baltimore
1975	Joe Morgan, Cincinnati	Bobby Grich, Baltimore
1976	Joe Morgan, Cincinnati	Bobby Grich, Baltimore
1977	Joe Morgan, Cincinnati	Frank White, Kansas City
1978	Davey Lopes, Los Angeles	Frank White, Kansas City
1979	Manny Trillo, Philadelphia	Frank White, Kansas City
1980	Doug Flynn, New York	Frank White, Kansas City
1981	Manny Trillo, Philadelphia	Frank White, Kansas City
1982	Manny Trillo, Philadelphia	Frank White, Kansas City
1983	Ryne Sandberg, Chicago	Lou Whitaker, Detroit
1984	Ryne Sandberg, Chicago	Lou Whitaker, Detroit
1985	Ryne Sandberg, Chicago	Lou Whitaker, Detroit
1986	Ryne Sandberg, Chicago	Frank White, Kansas City
1987	Ryne Sandberg, Chicago	Frank White, Kansas City
1988	Ryne Sandberg, Chicago	Harold Reynolds, Seattle
1989	Ryne Sandberg, Chicago	Harold Reynolds, Seattle
1990	Ryne Sandberg, Chicago	Harold Reynolds, Seattle
1991	Ryne Sandberg, Chicago	Roberto Alomar, Toronto
1992	Jose Lind, Pittsburgh	Roberto Alomar, Toronto
1993	Robby Thompson, San Francisco	Roberto Alomar, Toronto
1994	Craig Biggio, Houston	Roberto Alomar, Toronto

Third Basemen

Year	National League	American League
1957	(no selection)	Frank Malzone, Boston
1958	Ken Boyer, St. Louis	Frank Malzone, Boston
1959	Ken Boyer, St. Louis	Frank Malzone, Boston
1960	Ken Boyer, St. Louis	Brooks Robinson, Baltimore
1961	Ken Boyer, St. Louis	Brooks Robinson, Baltimore
1962	Jim Davenport, San Francisco	Brooks Robinson, Baltimore
1963	Ken Boyer, St. Louis	Brooks Robinson, Baltimore
1964	Ron Santo, Chicago	Brooks Robinson, Baltimore
1965	Ron Santo, Chicago	Brooks Robinson, Baltimore
1966	Ron Santo, Chicago	Brooks Robinson, Baltimore
1967	Ron Santo, Chicago	Brooks Robinson, Baltimore
1968	Ron Santo, Chicago	Brooks Robinson, Baltimore
1969	Clete Boyer, Atlanta	Brooks Robinson, Baltimore
1970	Doug Rader, Houston	Brooks Robinson, Baltimore
1971	Doug Rader, Houston	Brooks Robinson, Baltimore

Third Basemen (continued)

Year	National League	American League
1972	Doug Rader, Houston	Brooks Robinson, Baltimore
1973	Doug Rader, Houston	Brooks Robinson, Baltimore
1974	Doug Rader, Houston	Brooks Robinson, Baltimore
1975	Ken Reitz, St. Louis	Brooks Robinson, Baltimore
1976	Mike Schmidt, Philadelphia	Aurelio Rodriguez, Detroit
1977	Mike Schmidt, Philadelphia	Graig Nettles, New York
1978	Mike Schmidt, Philadelphia	Graig Nettles, New York
1979	Mike Schmidt, Philadelphia	Buddy Bell, Texas
1980	Mike Schmidt, Philadelphia	Buddy Bell, Texas
1981	Mike Schmidt, Philadelphia	Buddy Bell, Texas
1982	Mike Schmidt, Philadelphia	Buddy Bell, Texas
1983	Mike Schmidt, Philadelphia	Buddy Bell, Texas
1984	Mike Schmidt, Philadelphia	Buddy Bell, Texas
1985	Tim Wallach, Montreal	George Brett, Kansas City
1986	Mike Schmidt, Philadelphia	Gary Gaetti, Minnesota
1987	Terry Pendleton, St. Louis	Gary Gaetti, Minnesota
1988	Tim Wallach, Montreal	Gary Gaetti, Minnesota
1989	Terry Pendleton, St. Louis	Gary Gaetti, Minnesota
1990	Tim Wallach, Montreal	Kelly Gruber, Toronto
1991	Matt Williams, San Francisco	Robin Ventura, Chicago
1992	Terry Pendleton, St. Louis	Robin Ventura, Chicago
1993	Matt Williams, San Francisco	Robin Ventura, Chicago
1994	Matt Williams, San Francisco	Wade Boggs, New York

Shortstops

Year	National League	American League
1957	Roy McMillan, Cincinnati	(no selection)
1958	Roy McMillan, Cincinnati	Luis Aparicio, Chicago
1959	Roy McMillan, Cincinnati	Luis Aparicio, Chicago
1960	Ernie Banks, Chicago	Luis Aparicio, Chicago
1961	Maury Wills, Los Angeles	Luis Aparicio, Chicago
1962	Maury Wills, Los Angeles	Luis Aparicio, Chicago
1963	Bobby Wine, Philadelphia	Zoilo Versalles, Minnesota
1964	Ruben Amaro, Philadelphia	Luis Aparicio, Baltimore
1965	Leo Cardenas, Cincinnati	Zoilo Versalles, Minnesota
1966	Gene Alley, Pittsburgh	Luis Aparicio, Baltimore
1967	Gene Alley, Pittsburgh	Jim Fregosi, California
1968	Dal Maxvill, St. Louis	Luis Aparicio, Chicago
1969	Don Kessinger, Chicago	Mark Belanger, Baltimore
1970	Don Kessinger, Chicago	Luis Aparicio, Chicago
1971	Buddy Harrelson, New York	Mark Belanger, Baltimore
1972	Larry Bowa, Philadelphia	Eddie Brinkman, Detroit
1973	Roger Metzger, Houston	Mark Belanger, Baltimore

Year	National League	American League
1974	Dave Concepcion, Cincinnati	Mark Belanger, Baltimore
1975	Dave Concepcion, Cincinnati	Mark Belanger, Baltimore
1976	Dave Concepcion, Cincinnati	Mark Belanger, Baltimore
1977	Dave Concepcion, Cincinnati	Mark Belanger, Baltimore
1978	Larry Bowa, Philadelphia	Mark Belanger, Baltimore
1979	Dave Concepcion, Cincinnati	Rick Burleson, Boston
1980	Ozzie Smith, San Diego	Alan Trammell, Detroit
1981	Ozzie Smith, San Diego	Alan Trammell, Detroit
1982	Ozzie Smith, St. Louis	Robin Yount, Milwaukee
1983	Ozzie Smith, St. Louis	Alan Trammell, Detroit
1984	Ozzie Smith, St. Louis	Alan Trammell, Detroit
1985	Ozzie Smith, St. Louis	Alfredo Griffin, Oakland
1986	Ozzie Smith, St. Louis	Tony Fernandez, Toronto
1987	Ozzie Smith, St. Louis	Tony Fernandez, Toronto
1988	Ozzie Smith, St. Louis	Tony Fernandez, Toronto
1989	Ozzie Smith, St. Louis	Tony Fernandez, Toronto
1990	Ozzie Smith, St. Louis	Ozzie Guillen, Chicago
1991	Ozzie Smith, St. Louis	Cal Ripken, Baltimore
1992	Ozzie Smith, St. Louis	Cal Ripken, Baltimore
1993	Jay Bell, Pittsburgh	Omar Vizquel, Seattle
1994	Barry Larkin, Cincinnati	Omar Vizquel, Cleveland

National League Outfielders

1957	Willie Mays, NY	(no other selection)	
1958	Frank Robinson, CIN	Willie Mays, SF	Hank Aaron, MIL
1959	J. Brandt, SF	Willie Mays, SF	Hank Aaron, MIL
1960	Wally Moon, LA	Willie Mays, SF	Hank Aaron, MIL
1961	Willie Mays, SF	Roberto Clemente, PIT	Vada Pinson, CIN
1962	Willie Mays, SF	Roberto Clemente, PIT	Bill Virdon, PIT
1963	Willie Mays, SF	Roberto Clemente, PIT	Curt Flood, STL
1964	Willie Mays, SF	Roberto Clemente, PIT	Curt Flood, STL
1965	Willie Mays, SF	Roberto Clemente, PIT	Curt Flood, STL
1966	Willie Mays, SF	Curt Flood, STL	Roberto Clemente, PIT
1967	Roberto Clemente, PIT	Curt Flood, STL	Willie Mays, SF
1968	Willie Mays, SF	Roberto Clemente, PIT	Curt Flood, STL
1969	Roberto Clemente, PIT	Curt Flood, STL	Pete Rose, CIN
1970	Roberto Clemente, PIT	Tommie Agee, NY	Pete Rose, CIN
1971	Roberto Clemente, PIT	Bobby Bonds, SF	Willie Davis, LA
1972	Roberto Clemente, PIT	Cesar Cedeno, HOU	Willie Davis, LA
1973	Bobby Bonds, SF	Cesar Cedeno, HOU	Willie Davis, LA
1974	Cesar Cedeno, HOU	Cesar Geronimo, CIN	Bobby Bonds, SF
1975	Cesar Cedeno, HOU	Cesar Geronimo, CIN	Garry Maddox, PHI
1976	Cesar Cedeno, HOU	Cesar Geronimo, CIN	Garry Maddox, PHI

National League Outfielders (continued)

1977	Cesar Geronimo, CIN	Garry Maddox, PHI	Dave Parker, PIT
1978	Garry Maddox, PHI	Dave Parker, PIT	E. Valentine, MON
1979	Garry Maddox, PHI	Dave Parker, PIT	Dave Winfield, SD
1980	Andre Dawson, MON	Garry Maddox, PHI	Dave Winfield, SD
1981	Andre Dawson, MON	Garry Maddox, PHI	Dusty Baker, LA
1982	Andre Dawson, MON	Dale Murphy, ATL	Garry Maddox, PHI
1983	Andre Dawson, MON	Dale Murphy, ATL	Willie McGee, STL
1984	Dale Murphy, ATL	Bob Dernier, CHI	Andre Dawson, MON
1985	Willie McGee, STL	Dale Murphy, ATL	Andre Dawson, MON
1986	Tony Gwynn, SD	Dale Murphy, ATL	Willie McGee, STL
1987	Eric Davis, Cin	Tony Gwynn, SD	Andre Dawson, CHI
1988	Andy Van Slyke, PIT	Eric Davis, Cincinnati	Andre Dawson, CHI
1989	Andy Van Slyke, PIT	Eric Davis, Cincinnati	Tony Gwynn, SD
1990	Andy Van Slyke, PIT	Tony Gwynn, SD	Barry Bonds, PIT
1991	Barry Bonds, PIT	Tony Gwynn, SD	Andy Van Slyke, PIT
1992	Barry Bonds, SF	Marquis Grissom, MON	Larry Walker, MON
1993	Barry Bonds, SF	Marquis Grissom, MON	Larry Walker, MON
1994	Barry Bonds, SF	Marquis Grissom, MON	Darren Lewis, SF

American League Outfielders

1957	Minnie Minoso, CHI	Al Kaline, DET	(no other selection)
1958	Norm Siebern, NY	Jim Piersall, BOS	Al Kaline, DET
1959	Minnie Minoso, CLE	Al Kaline, DET	Jackie Jensen, BOS
1960	Minnie Minoso, CHI	Jim Landis, CHI	Roger Maris, NY
1961	Al Kaline, DET	Jim Piersall, CLE	Jim Landis, CHI
1962	Jim Landis, CHI	Mickey Mantle, NY	Al Kaline, DET
1963	Al Kaline, DET	Carl Yastrzemski, BOS	Jim Landis, CHI
1964	Al Kaline, DET	Jim Landis, CHI	Vic Davalillo, CLE
1965	Al Kaline, DET	Tom Tresh, NY	Carl Yastrzemski, BOS
1966	Al Kaline, DET	Tommie Agee, CHI	Tony Oliva, MIN
1967	Carl Yastrzemski, BOS	Paul Blair, BAL	Al Kaline, DET
1968	Mickey Stanley, DET	Carl Yastrzemski, BOS	Reggie Smith, BOS
1969	Paul Blair, BAL	Mickey Stanley, DET	Carl Yastrzemski, BOS
1970	Mickey Stanley, DET	Paul Blair, BAL	Ken Berry, CHI
1971	Paul Blair, BAL	Amos Otis, KC	Carl Yastrzemski, BOS
1972	Paul Blair, BAL	Bobby Murcer, NY	Ken Berry, CAL
1973	Paul Blair, BAL	Amos Otis, KC	Mickey Stanley, DET
1974	Paul Blair, BAL	Amos Otis, KC	Joe Rudi, OAK
1975	Paul Blair, BAL	Joe Rudi, OAK	Fred Lynn, BOS
1976	Joe Rudi, OAK	Dwight Evans, BOS	Rick Manning, CLE
1977	J. Beniquez, TEX	Carl Yastrzemski, BOS	Al Cowens, KC
1978	Fred Lynn, BOS	Dwight Evans, BOS	Rick Miller, CAL
1979	Dwight Evans, BOS	Sixto Lezcano, MIL	Fred Lynn, BOS
1980	Fred Lynn, BOS	Dwayne Murphy, OAK	Willie Wilson, KC

1981	Dwayne Murphy, OAK	Dwight Evans, BOS	Rickey Henderson, OAK
1982	Dwight Evans, BOS	Dave Winfield, NY	Dwayne Murphy, OAK
1983	Dwight Evans, BOS	Dave Winfield, NY	Dwayne Murphy, OAK
1984	Dwight Evans, BOS	Dave Winfield, NY	Dwayne Murphy, OAK
1985	Gary Pettis, CAL	Dave Winfield, NY	Dwight Evans, BOS
			Dwayne Murphy, OAK
1986	Gary Pettis, CAL	Jesse Barfield, TOR	Kirby Puckett, MIN
1987	Jesse Barfield, TOR	Kirby Puckett, MIN	Dave Winfield, NY
1988	Kirby Puckett, MIN	Devon White, CAL	Gary Pettis, DET
1989	Devon White, CAL	Gary Pettis, DET	Kirby Puckett, MIN
1990	Gary Pettis, TEX	Ken Griffey Jr., SEA	Ellis Burks, BOS
1991	Ken Griffey, Jr., SEA	Devon White, TOR	Kirby Puckett, MIN
1992	Ken Griffey, Jr., SEA	Devon White, TOR	Kirby Puckett, MIN
1993	Ken Griffey, Jr., SEA	Devon White, TOR	Kenny Lofton, CLE
1994	Ken Griffey, Jr., SEA	Devon White, TOR	Kenny Lofton, CLE

World Series Winners

Year	AL Champion	NL Champion	World Series Champion		
1903	Boston Pilgrims	Pittsburgh Pirates	Boston Pilgrims	5	3
1905	Philadelphia Athletics	New York Giants	New York Giants	4	1
1906	Chicago White Sox	Chicago Cubs	Chicago White Sox	4	2
1907	Detroit Tigers	Chicago Cubs	Chicago Cubs	4	0
1908	Detroit Tigers	Chicago Cubs	Chicago Cubs	4	1
1909	Detroit Tigers	Pittsburgh Pirates	Pittsburgh Pirates	4	3
1910	Philadelphia Athletics	Chicago Cubs	Philadelphia Athletics	4	1
1911	Philadelphia Athletics	New York Giants	Philadelphia Athletics	4	2
1912	Boston Red Sox	New York Giants	Boston Red Sox	4	3
1913	Philadelphia Athletics	New York Giants	Philadelphia Athletics	4	1
1914	Philadelphia Athletics	Boston Braves	Boston Braves	4	0
1915	Boston Red Sox	Philadelphia Phillies	Boston Red Sox	4	1
1916	Boston Red Sox	Brooklyn Robins	Boston Red Sox	4	1
1917	Chicago White Sox	New York Giants	Chicago White Sox	4	2
1918	Boston Red Sox	Chicago Cubs	Boston Red Sox	4	2
1919	Chicago White Sox	Cincinnati Reds	Cincinnati Reds	5	3
1920	Cleveland Indians	Brooklyn Robins	Cleveland Indians	5	2
1921	New York Yankees	New York Giants	New York Yankees	5	3
1922	New York Yankees	New York Giants	New York Yankees	4	0
1923	New York Yankees	New York Giants	New York Yankees	4	2
1924	Washington Senators	New York Giants	Washington Senators	4	2
1925	Washington Senators	Pittsburgh Pirates	Pittsburgh Pirates	4	3
1926	New York Yankees	St. Louis Cardinals	St. Louis Cardinals	4	3
1927	New York Yankees	Pittsburgh Pirates	New York Yankees	4	0
1928	New York Yankees	St. Louis Cardinals	New York Yankees	4	0

World Series Winners (continued)

Year	AL Champion	NL Champion	World Series Champion		
1929	Philadelphia Athletics	Chicago Cubs	Philadelphia Athletics	4	2
1930	Philadelphia Athletics	St. Louis Cardinals	Philadelphia Athletics	4	2
1931	Philadelphia Athletics	St. Louis Cardinals	St. Louis Cardinals	4	3
1932	New York Yankees	Chicago Cubs	New York Yankees	4	0
1933	Washington Senators	New York Giants	New York Giants	4	1
1934	Detroit Tigers	St. Louis Cardinals	St. Louis Cardinals	4	3
1935	Detroit Tigers	Chicago Cubs	Detroit Tigers	4	2
1936	New York Yankees	New York Giants	New York Yankees	4	2
1937	New York Yankees	New York Giants	New York Yankees	4	1
1938	New York Yankees	Chicago Cubs	New York Yankees	4	0
1939	New York Yankees	Cincinnati Reds	New York Yankees	4	0
1940	Detroit Tigers	Cincinnati Reds	Cincinnati Reds	4	3
1941	New York Yankees	Brooklyn Dodgers	New York Yankees	4	1
1942	New York Yankees	St. Louis Cardinals	St. Louis Cardinals	4	1
1943	New York Yankees	St. Louis Cardinals	New York Yankees	4	1
1944	St. Louis Browns	St. Louis Cardinals	St. Louis Cardinals	4	2
1945	Detroit Tigers	Chicago Cubs	Detroit Tigers	4	3
1946	Boston Red Sox	St. Louis Cardinals	St. Louis Cardinals	4	3
1947	New York Yankees	Chicago Cubs	New York Yankees	4	3
1948	Cleveland Indians	Boston Braves	Cleveland Indians	4	2
1949	New York Yankees	Brooklyn Dodgers	New York Yankees	4	1
1950	New York Yankees	Philadelphia Phillies	New York Yankees	4	0
1951	New York Yankees	New York Giants	New York Yankees	4	2
1952	New York Yankees	Brooklyn Dodgers	New York Yankees	4	3
1953	New York Yankees	Brooklyn Dodgers	New York Yankees	4	2
1954	Cleveland Indians	New York Giants	New York Giants	4	0
1955	New York Yankees	Brooklyn Dodgers	Brooklyn Dodgers	4	3
1956	New York Yankees	Brooklyn Dodgers	New York Yankees	4	3
1957	New York Yankees	Milwaukee Braves	Milwaukee Braves	4	3
1958	New York Yankees	Milwaukee Braves	New York Yankees	4	3
1959	Chicago White Sox	Los Angeles Dodgers	Los Angeles Dodgers	4	2
1960	New York Yankees	Pittsburgh Pirates	Pittsburgh Pirates	4	3
1961	New York Yankees	Cincinnati Reds	New York Yankees	4	1
1962	New York Yankees	San Francisco Giants	New York Yankees	4	3
1963	New York Yankees	Los Angeles Dodgers	Los Angeles Dodgers	4	2
1964	New York Yankees	St. Louis Cardinals	St. Louis Cardinals	4	3
1965	Minnesota Twins	Los Angeles Dodgers	Los Angeles Dodgers	4	3
1966	Baltimore Orioles	Los Angeles Dodgers	Baltimore Orioles	4	0
1967	Boston Red Sox	St. Louis Cardinals	St. Louis Cardinals	4	3
1968	Detroit Tigers	St. Louis Cardinals	Detroit Tigers	4	3
1969	Baltimore Orioles	New York Mets	New York Mets	4	1
1970	Baltimore Orioles	Cincinnati Reds	Baltimore Orioles	4	1

Year	AL Champion	NL Champion	World Series Champion		
1971	Baltimore Orioles	Pittsburgh Pirates	Pittsburgh Pirates	4	3
1972	Oakland A's	Cincinnati Reds	Oakland A's	4	3
1973	Oakland A's	New York Mets	Oakland A's	4	3
1974	Oakland A's	Los Angeles Dodgers	Oakland A's	4	1
1975	Boston Red Sox	Cincinnati Reds	Cincinnati Reds	4	3
1976	New York Yankees	Cincinnati Reds	Cincinnati Reds	4	0
1977	New York Yankees	Los Angeles Dodgers	New York Yankees	4	2
1978	New York Yankees	Los Angeles Dodgers	New York Yankees	4	2
1979	Baltimore Orioles	Pittsburgh Pirates	Pittsburgh Pirates	4	3
1980	Kansas City Royals	Philadelphia Phillies	Philadelphia Phillies	4	2
1981	New York Yankees	Los Angeles Dodgers	Los Angeles Dodgers	4	2
1982	Milwaukee Brewers	St. Louis Cardinals	St. Louis Cardinals	4	3
1983	Baltimore Orioles	Philadelphia Phillies	Baltimore Orioles	4	1
1984	Detroit Tigers	San Diego Padres	Detroit Tigers	4	1
1985	Kansas City Royals	St. Louis Cardinals	Kansas City Royals	4	3
1986	Boston Red Sox	New York Mets	New York Mets	4	3
1987	Minnesota Twins	St. Louis Cardinals	Minnesota Twins	4	3
1988	Oakland A's	Los Angeles Dodgers	Los Angeles Dodgers	4	1
1989	Oakland A's	San Francisco Giants	Oakland A's	4	0
1990	Oakland A's	Cincinnati Reds	Cincinnati Reds	4	0
1991	Minnesota Twins	Atlanta Braves	Minnesota Twins	4	3
1992	Toronto Blue Jays	Atlanta Braves	Toronto Blue Jays	4	2
1993	Toronto Blue Jays	Philadelphia Phillies	Toronto Blue Jays	4	2
1994	Playoffs were canceled due to work stoppage.				

Career Records

Runs

1.	Ty Cobb	2,245
2.	Hank Aaron	2,174
	Babe Ruth	2,174
4.	Pete Rose	2,165
5.	Willie Mays	2,062
6.	Stan Musial	1,949
7.	Lou Gehrig	1,888
8.	Tris Speaker	1,882
9.	Mel Ott	1,859
10.	Frank Robinson	1,829

Hits

1.	Pete Rose	4,256
2.	Ty Cobb	4,190
3.	Hank Aaron	3,771
4.	Stan Musial	3,630
5.	Tris Speaker	3,514
6.	Carl Yastrzemski	3,419
7.	Honus Wagner	3,415
8.	Eddie Collins	3,310
9.	Willie Mays	3,283
10.	Nap Lajoie	3,242

Home Runs

1.	Hank Aaron	755
2.	Babe Ruth	714
3.	Willie Mays	660
4.	Frank Robinson	586
5.	Harmon Killebrew	573
6.	Reggie Jackson	563
7.	Mike Schmidt	548
8.	Mickey Mantle	536
9.	Jimmie Foxx	534
10.	Willie McCovey	521
	Ted Williams	521

Total Bases

1.	Hank Aaron	6,856
2.	Stan Musial	6,134
3.	Willie Mays	6,066
4.	Ty Cobb	5,855
5.	Babe Ruth	5,793
6.	Pete Rose	5,752
7.	Carl Yastrzemski	5,539
8.	Frank Robinson	5,373
9.	Tris Speaker	5,101
10.	Lou Gehrig	5,060

Runs Batted In

1.	Hank Aaron	2,297
2.	Babe Ruth	2,213
3.	Lou Gehrig	1,995
4.	Stan Musial	1,951
5.	Ty Cobb	1,937
6.	Jimmie Foxx	1,922
7.	Willie Mays	1,903
8.	Cap Anson	1,879
9.	Mel Ott	1,860
10.	Carl Yastrzemski	1,844

Walks

1.	Babe Ruth	2,056
2.	Ted Williams	2,019
3.	Joe Morgan	1,865
4.	Carl Yastrzemski	1,845
5.	Mickey Mantle	1,733
6.	Mel Ott	1,708
7.	Eddie Yost	1,614
8.	Darrell Evans	1,605
9.	Stan Musial	1,599
10.	Pete Rose	1,566

Batting Average

1.	Ty Cobb	.366
2.	Rogers Hornsby	.358
3.	Joe Jackson	.356
4.	Ed Delahanty	.346
5.	Tris Speaker	.345
6.	Ted Williams	.344
7.	Billy Hamilton	.344
8.	Dan Brouthers	.342
9.	Babe Ruth	.342
10.	Harry Heilmann	.342

Slugging Percentage

1.	Babe Ruth	.690
2.	Ted Williams	.634
3.	Lou Gehrig	.632
4.	Jimmie Foxx	.609
5.	Hank Greenberg	.605
6.	Joe DiMaggio	.579
7.	Rogers Hornsby	.577
8.	Johnny Mize	.562
9.	Stan Musial	.559
10.	Willie Mays	.557

Stolen Bases

1.	Rickey Henderson	1,117
2.	Lou Brock	938
3.	Billy Hamilton	912
4.	Ty Cobb	891
5.	Tim Raines	764
6.	Eddie Collins	744
7.	Arlie Latham	739
8.	Max Carey	738
9.	Honus Wagner	722
10.	Joe Morgan	689

Wins

1.	Cy Young	511
2.	Walter Johnson	417
3.	Pete Alexander	373
	Christy Mathewson	373
5.	Warren Spahn	363
6.	Kid Nichols	361
7.	Jim Galvin	360
8.	Tim Keefe	342
9.	Steve Carlton	329
10.	John Clarkson	328

Losses

1.	Cy Young	316
2.	Jim Galvin	308
3.	Nolan Ryan	292
4.	Walter Johnson	279
5.	Phil Niekro	274
6.	Gaylord Perry	265
7.	Don Sutton	256
8.	Jack Powell	254
9.	Eppa Rixey	251
10.	Bert Blyleven	250

Games

1.	Hoyt Wilhelm	1,070
2.	Kent Tekulve	1,050
3.	Rich Gossage	1,002
4.	Lindy McDaniel	987
5.	Rollie Fingers	944
6.	Gene Garber	931
7.	Cy Young	906
8.	Sparky Lyle	899
9.	Jim Kaat	898
10.	Don McMahon	874

Games Started

1.	Cy Young	815
2.	Nolan Ryan	773
3.	Don Sutton	756
4.	Phil Niekro	716
5.	Steve Carlton	709
6.	Tommy John	700
7.	Gaylord Perry	690
8.	Bert Blyleven	685
9.	Jim Galvin	682
10.	Walter Johnson	665
	Warren Spahn	665

Shutouts

1.	Walter Johnson	110
2.	Pete Alexander	90
3.	Christy Mathewson	79
4.	Cy Young	76
5.	Eddie Plank	69
6.	Warren Spahn	63
7.	Nolan Ryan	61
	Tom Seaver	61
9.	Bert Blyleven	60
10.	Don Sutton	58

Saves

1.	Lee Smith	434
2.	Jeff Reardon	367
3.	Rollie Fingers	341
4.	Rich Gossage	310
5.	Bruce Sutter	300
6.	Dennis Eckersley	294
7.	Tom Henke	275
8.	Dave Righetti	252
9.	Dan Quisenberry	244
10.	Sparky Lyle	238

Innings Pitched

1.	Cy Young	7,354.2
2.	Jim Galvin	5,941.1
3.	Walter Johnson	5,923.2
4.	Phil Niekro	5,404.1
5.	Nolan Ryan	5,387.0
6.	Gaylord Perry	5,350.1
7.	Don Sutton	5,282.1
8.	Warren Spahn	5,243.2
9.	Steve Carlton	5,217.1
10.	Pete Alexander	5,189.1

Strikeouts

1.	Nolan Ryan	5,714
2.	Steve Carlton	4,136
3.	Bert Blyleven	3,701
4.	Tom Seaver	3,640
5.	Don Sutton	3,574
6.	Gaylord Perry	3,534
7.	Walter Johnson	3,509
8.	Phil Niekro	3,342
9.	Fergie Jenkins	3,192
10.	Bob Gibson	3,117

Earned Run Average

1.	Ed Walsh	1.82
2.	Addie Joss	1.89
3.	Mordecai Brown	2.06
4.	Monte Ward	2.10
5.	Christy Mathewson	2.13
6.	Rube Waddell	2.16
7.	Walter Johnson	2.17
8.	Orval Overall	2.23
9.	Tommy Bond	2.25
10.	Ed Reulbach	2.28

Single Season Records

Runs

1.	Billy Hamilton	1894	192
2.	Tom Brown	1891	177
	Babe Ruth	1921	177
4.	Tip O'Neill	1887	167
	Lou Gehrig	1936	167
6.	Billy Hamilton	1895	166
7.	Willie Keeler	1894	165
	Joe Kelley	1894	165
9.	Arlie Latham	1887	163
	Babe Ruth	1928	163
	Lou Gehrig	1931	163

Hits

1.	George Sisler	1920	257
2.	Lefty O'Doul	1929	254
	Bill Terry	1930	254
4.	Al Simmons	1925	253
5.	Rogers Hornsby	1922	250
	Chuck Klein	1930	250
7.	Ty Cobb	1911	248
8.	George Sisler	1922	246
9.	Heinie Manush	1928	241
	Babe Herman	1930	241

Home Runs

1.	Roger Maris	1961	61
2.	Babe Ruth	1927	60
3.	Babe Ruth	1921	59
4.	Jimmie Foxx	1932	58
	Hank Greenberg	1938	58
6.	Hack Wilson	1930	56
7.	Babe Ruth	1920	54
	Babe Ruth	1928	54
	Ralph Kiner	1949	54
	Mickey Mantle	1961	54

Total Bases

1.	Babe Ruth	1921	457
2.	Rogers Hornsby	1922	450
3.	Lou Gehrig	1927	447
4.	Chuck Klein	1930	445
5.	Jimmie Foxx	1932	438
6.	Stan Musial	1948	429
7.	Hack Wilson	1930	423
8.	Chuck Klein	1932	420
9.	Lou Gehrig	1930	419
10.	Joe DiMaggio	1937	418

Runs Batted In

1.	Hack Wilson	1930	190
2.	Lou Gehrig	1931	184
3.	Hank Greenberg	1937	183
4.	Lou Gehrig	1927	175
	Jimmie Fox	1938	175
6.	Lou Gehrig	1930	174
7.	Babe Ruth	1921	171
8.	Chuck Klein	1930	170
	Hank Greenberg	1935	170
10.	Jimmie Fox	1932	169

Walks

1.	Babe Ruth	1923	170
2.	Ted Williams	1947	162
	Ted Williams	1949	162
4.	Ted Williams	1946	156
5.	Eddie Yost	1956	151
6.	Eddie Joost	1949	149
7.	Babe Ruth	1920	148
	Eddie Stanky	1945	148
9.	Jim Wynn	1969	148
10.	Jimmy Sheckard	1911	147

Batting Average

1.	Hugh Duffy	1894	.440
2.	Tip O'Neill	1887	.435
3.	Ross Barnes	1876	.429
4.	Nap Lajoie	1901	.426
5.	Willie Keeler	1897	.424
6.	Rogers Hornsby	1924	.424
7.	George Sisler	1922	.420
8.	Ty Cobb	1911	.420
9.	Fred Dunlap	1884	.412
10.	Ty Cobb	1912	.410

Slugging Percentage

1.	Babe Ruth	1920	.847
2.	Babe Ruth	1921	.846
3.	Babe Ruth	1927	.772
4.	Lou Gehrig	1927	.765
5.	Babe Ruth	1923	.764
6.	Rogers Hornsby	1925	.756
7.	Jimmie Foxx	1932	.749
8.	Jeff Bagwell	1994	.750
9.	Babe Ruth	1924	.739
10.	Babe Ruth	1926	.737

Stolen Bases

1.	Hugh Nicol	1887	138
2.	Rickey Henderson	1982	130
3.	Arlie Latham	1887	129
4.	Lou Brock	1974	118
5.	Charlie Comiskey	1887	117
6.	Monte Ward	1887	111
	Billy Hamilton	1889	111
	Billy Hamilton	1891	111
9.	Vince Coleman	1985	110
10.	Arlie Latham	1888	109
	Vince Coleman	1987	109

Year-by-Year Statistical Leaders

NL Batting Average   AL Batting Average

Year	Player, Team	BA	Player, Team	BA
1876	Ross Barnes, CHI	.429	——	—
1877	James "Deacon" White, BOS	.387	——	—
1878	Paul Hines, PRO	.358	——	—
1879	Paul Hines, PRO	.357	——	—
1880	George Gore, CHI	.360	——	—
1881	Adrian "Cap" Anson, CHI	.399	——	—
1882	"Big Dan" Brouthers, BUF	.368	——	—
1883	"Big Dan" Brouthers, BUF	.374	——	—
1884	Mike "King" Kelly, CHI	.354	——	—
1885	Roger Connor, NYG	.371	——	—
1886	Mike "King" Kelly, CHI	.388	——	—
1887	Sam Thompson, DET	.372	——	—
1888	Adrian "Cap" Anson, CHI	.344	——	—
1889	"Big Dan" Brouthers, BOS	.373	——	—
1890	Jack Glasscock, NYG	.336	——	—
1891	Billy Hamilton, PHI	.340	——	—
1892	"Big Dan" Brouthers, BRO	.335	——	—
1893	Billy Hamilton, PHI	.380	——	—
1894	Hugh Duffy, BOS	.440	——	—
1895	Jesse Burkett, CLE	.409	——	—
1896	Jesse Burkett, CLE	.410	——	—
1897	"Wee Willie" Keeler, BAL	.424	——	—
1898	"Wee Willie" Keeler, BAL	.385	——	—
1899	Big Ed" Delahanty, PHI	.410	——	—
1900	"Honus" Wagner, PIT	.381	——	—
1901	Jesse Burkett, STL	.376	Napoleon Lajoie, PHI	.422
1902	Ginger Beaumont, PIT	.357	Ed Delahanty, WAS	.376
1903	"Honus" Wagner, PIT	.355	Napoleon Lajoie, CLE	.355
1904	"Honus" Wagner, PIT	.349	Napoleon Lajoie, CLE	.381
1905	Cy Seymour, CIN	.377	Elmer Flick, CLE	.306
1906	"Honus" Wagner, PIT	.339	George Stone, STL	.358
1907	"Honus" Wagner, PIT	.350	Ty Cobb, DET	.350
1908	"Honus" Wagner, PIT	.354	Ty Cobb, DET	.324
1909	"Honus" Wagner, PIT	.339	Ty Cobb, DET	.377
1910	Sherry Magee, PHI	.331	Ty Cobb, DET	.385
1911	"Honus" Wagner, PIT	.334	Ty Cobb, DET	.420
1912	Heinie Zimmerman, CHI	.372	Ty Cobb, DET	.410
1913	Jake Daubert, BRO	.350	Ty Cobb, DET	.390
1914	Jake Daubert, BRO	.329	Ty Cobb, DET	.368
1915	Larry Doyle, NYG	.320	Ty Cobb, DET	.369

NL Batting Average

AL Batting Average

Year	Player, Team	BA	Player, Team	BA
1916	Hal Chase, CIN	.339	Tris Speaker, CLE	.386
1917	Edd Roush, CIN	.341	Ty Cobb, DET	.383
1918	Zack Wheat, BRO	.335	Ty Cobb, DET	.382
1919	Edd Roush, CIN	.321	Ty Cobb, DET	.384
1920	Rogers Hornsby, STL	.370	George Sisler, STL	.407
1921	Rogers Hornsby, STL	.397	Harry Heilmann, DET	.394
1922	Rogers Hornsby, STL	.401	George Sisler, STL	.420
1923	Rogers Hornsby, STL	.384	Harry Heilmann, DET	.403
1924	Rogers Hornsby, STL	.424	Babe Ruth, NYY	.378
1925	Rogers Hornsby, STL	.403	Harry Heilmann, DET	.393
1926	Paul "Big Poison" Waner, PIT	.336	Heinie Manush, DET	.378
1927	Paul "Big Poison" Waner, PIT	.380	Harry Heilmann, DET	.398
1928	Rogers Hornsby, STL	.387	Goose Goslin, WAS	.379
1929	"Lefty" O'Doul, PHI	.398	Lew Fonseca, CLE	.369
1930	Bill Terry, NYG	.401	Al Simmons, PHI	.381
1931	Chick Hafey, STL	.349	Al Simmons, PHI	.390
1932	"Lefty" O'Doul, BRO	.368	Dale Alexander, BOS–DET	.367
1933	Chuck Klein, PHI	.368	Jimmy Foxx, PHI	.356
1934	Paul "Big Poison" Waner, PIT	.362	Lou Gehrig, NYY	.363
1935	Floyd "Arky" Vaughan, PIT	.385	Buddy Myer, WAS	.349
1936	Paul "Big Poison" Waner, PIT	.373	Luke Appling, CHI	.388
1937	Joe "Ducky" Medwick, STL	.374	Charlie Gehringer, DET	.371
1938	Ernie Lombardi, CIN	.342	Jimmie Foxx, BOS	.349
1939	Johnny Mize, STL	.349	Joe DiMaggio, NYY	.381
1940	Stan Hack, CHI	.317	Joe DiMaggio, NYY	.352
1941	Pete Reiser, BRO	.343	Ted Williams, BOS	.406
1942	Enos "Country" Slaughter, STL	.318	Ted Williams, BOS	.356
1943	Stan Musial, STL	.357	Luke Appling, CHI	.328
1944	Fred "Dixie" Walker, BRO	.357	Lou Boudreau, CLE	.327
1945	Phil Cavarretta, CHI	.355	Snuffy Stirnweiss, NYY	.309
1946	Stan Musial, STL	.365	Mickey Vernon, WAS	.353
1947	Harry Walker, STL–PHI	.363	Ted Williams, BOS	.343
1948	Stan Musial, STL	.376	Ted Williams, BOS	.369
1949	Jackie Robinson, BRO	.342	Ted Williams, BOS	.343
			George Kell, DET	.343
1950	Stan Musial, STL	.346	Billy Goodman, BOS	.354
1951	Stan Musial, STL	.355	Ferris Fain, PHI	.344
1952	Stan Musial, STL	.336	Ferris Fain, PHI	.327
1953	Carl Furillo, BRO	.344	Mickey Vernon, WAS	.337
1954	Willie Mays, NYG	.345	Bobby Avila, CLE	.341
1955	Richie Ashburn, PHI	.338	Al Kaline, DET	.340
1956	Hank Aaron, MIL	.328	Mickey Mantle, NYY	.353

NL Batting Average

Year	Player, Team	BA
1957	Stan Musial, STL	.351
1958	Richie Ashburn, PHI	.350
1959	Hank Aaron, MIL	.355
1960	Dick Groat, PIT	.325
1961	Roberto Clemente, PIT	.351
1962	Tommy Davis, LA	.346
1963	Tommy Davis, LA	.326
1964	Roberto Clemente, PIT	.339
1965	Roberto Clemente, PIT	.329
1966	Matty Alou, PIT	.342
1967	Roberto Clemente, PIT	.357
1968	Pete Rose, CIN	.335
1969	Pete Rose, CIN	.348
1970	Rico Carty, ATL	.366
1971	Joe Torre, STL	.363
1972	Billy Williams, CHI	.333
1973	Pete Rose, CIN	.338
1974	Ralph Garr, ATL	.353
1975	Bill Madlock, CHI	.354
1976	Bill Madlock, CHI	.339
1977	Dave Parker, PIT	.338
1978	Dave Parker, PIT	.334
1979	Keith Hernandez, STL	.344
1980	Bill Buckner, CHI	.324
1981	Pete Rose, PHI	.325
1982	Al Oliver, MON	.331
1983	Bill Madlock, PHI	.323
1984	Tony Gwynn, SD	.351
1985	Willie McGee, STL	.353
1986	Tim Raines, MON	.334
1987	Tony Gwynn, SD	.370
1988	Tony Gwynn, SD	.313
1989	Tony Gwynn, SD	.336
1990	Willie McGee, STL	.335
1991	Terry Pendleton, ATL	.319
1992	Gary Sheffield, SD	.330
1993	Andres Galarraga, COL	.370
1994	Tony Gwynn, SD	.394

AL Batting Average

Player, Team	BA
Ted Williams, BOS	.388
Ted Williams, BOS	.328
Harvey Kuenn, DET	.353
Pete Runnels, BOS	.320
Norm Cash, DET	.361
Pete Runnels, BOS	.326
Carl Yastrzemski, BOS	.321
Tony Oliva, MIN	.323
Tony Oliva, MIN	.321
Frank Robinson, BAL	.316
Carl Yastrzemski, BOS	.326
Carl Yastrzemski, BOS	.301
Rod Carew, MIN	.332
Alex Johnson, CAL	.329
Tony Oliva, MIN	.337
Rod Carew, MIN	.318
Rod Carew, MIN	.350
Rod Carew, MIN	.364
Rod Carew, MIN	.359
George Brett, KC	.333
Rod Carew, MIN	.388
Rod Carew, MIN	.333
Fred Lynn, BOS	.333
George Brett, KC	.390
Carney Lansford, BOS	.326
Tom Paciorek, SEA	.326
Willie Wilson, KC	.332
Wade Boggs, BOS	.361
Don Mattingly, NYY	.343
Wade Boggs, BOS	.368
Wade Boggs, BOS	.357
Wade Boggs, BOS	.363
Wade Boggs, BOS	.366
Kirby Puckett, MIN	.339
George Brett, KC	.329
Julio Franco, TEX	.341
Edgar Martinez, SEA	.343
John Olerud, TOR	.363
Paul O'Neill, NYY	.359

NL Home Runs

AL Home Runs

Year	Player, Team	HR	Player, Team	HR
1876	George Hall, PHI	5	——	—
1877	Lip Pike, CIN	4	——	—
1878	Paul Hines, PRO	4	——	—
1879	Charley Jones, BOS	9	——	—
1880	Jim O'Rourke, BOS	6	——	—
	Harry Stovey, WOR	6		
1881	"Big Dan" Brouthers, BUF	8	——	—
1882	George Wood, DET	7	——	—
1883	"Buck" Ewing, NYG	10	——	—
1884	Ned Williamson, CHI	27	——	—
1885	Abner Dalrymple, CHI	11	——	—
1886	"Big Dan" Brouthers, DET	11	——	—
	Hardy Richardson, DET	11		
1887	Billy O'Brien, WAS	19	——	—
1888	Jimmy Ryan, CHI	16	——	—
1889	Sam Thompson, PHI	20	——	—
1890	"Oyster" Burns, BRO	13	——	—
	Walt Wilmot, CHI	13		
1890	Mike Tiernan, NYG	13		
1891	Mike Tiernan, NYG	17	——	—
1892	"Bug" Holliday, CIN	13	——	—
1893	"Big Ed" Delahanty, PHI	19	——	—
1894	Hugh Duffy, BOS	18	——	—
1895	Sam Thompson, PHI	18	——	—
1896	"Big Ed" Delahanty, PHI	13	——	—
	Bill Joyce, WAS–NYG	13		
1897	Hugh Duffy, BOS	11	——	—
1898	Jimmy Collins, BOS	15	——	—
1899	"Buck" Freeman, WAS	25	——	—
1900	Herman Long, BOS	12	——	—
1901	Sam Crawford, CIN	16	Napoleon Lajoie, PHI	13
1902	Tommy Leach, PIT	6	Socks Seybold, PHI	16
1903	Jimmy Sheckard, BRO	9	Buck Freeman, BOS	13
1904	Harry Lumley, BRO	9	Harry Davis, PHI	10
1905	Fred Odwell, CIN	9	Harry Davis, PHI	8
1906	Tim Jordan, BRO	12	Harry Davis, PHI	12
1907	Dave Brain, BOS	10	Harry Davis, PHI	8
1908	Tim Jordan, BRO	12	Sam Crawford, DET	7
1909	John "Red" Murray, NYG	7	Ty Cobb, DET	9
1910	Fred Beck, BOS	10	Jake Stahl, BOS	10
	Frank Schulte, CHI	10		
1911	Frank Schulte, CHI	21	Frank Baker, PHI	11

NL Home Runs

Year	Player, Team	HR
1912	Heinie Zimmerman, CHI	14
1913	"Gavvy" Cravath, PHI	19
1914	"Gavvy" Cravath, PHI	19
1915	"Gavvy" Cravath, PHI	24
1916	"Cy" Williams, CHI	12
	Dave Robertson, NYG	12
1917	Dave Robertson, NYG	12
1918	"Gavvy" Cravath, PHI	8
1919	"Gavvy" Cravath, PHI	12
1920	"Cy" Williams, PHI	15
1921	George Kelly, NYG	23
1922	Rogers Hornsby, STL	42
1923	"Cy" Williams, PHI	41
1924	Jack Fournier, BRO	27
1925	Rogers Hornsby, STL	39
1926	Lewis "Hack" Wilson, CHI	21
1927	Lewis "Hack" Wilson, CHI	30
	"Cy" Williams, PHI	30
1928	Lewis "Hack" Wilson, CHI	31
	"Sunny Jim" Bottomley, STL	31
1929	Chuck Klein, PHI	43
1930	Lewis "Hack" Wilson, CHI	56
1931	Chuck Klein, PHI	31
1932	Mel Ott, NYG	38
	Chuck Klein, PHI	38
1933	Chuck Klein, PHI	28
1934	Mel Ott, NYG	35
	"Ripper" Collins, STL	35
1935	Wally Barger, BOS	34
1936	Mel Ott, NYG	33
1937	Mel Ott, NYG	31
	Joe "Ducky" Medwick, STL	31
1938	Mel Ott, NYG	36
1939	Johnny Mize, STL	28
1940	Johnny Mize, STL	43
1941	Dolph Camilli, BRO	34
1942	Mel Ott, NYG	30
1943	Bill Nicholson, CHI	29

AL Home Runs

Player, Team	HR
Frank Baker, PHI	10
Tris Speaker, BOS	10
Frank Baker, PHI	12
Frank Baker, PHI	9
Braggo Roth, CHI–CLE	7
Wally Pipp, NYY	12
Wally Pipp, NYY	9
Babe Ruth, BOS	11
Tilly Walker, PHI	11
Babe Ruth, BOS	29
Babe Ruth, NYY	54
Babe Ruth, NYY	59
Ken Williams, STL	39
Babe Ruth, NYY	41
Babe Ruth, NYY	46
Bob Meusel, NYY	33
Babe Ruth, NYY	47
Babe Ruth, NYY	60
Babe Ruth, NYY	54
Babe Ruth, NYY	46
Babe Ruth, NYY	49
Babe Ruth, NYY	46
Lou Gehrig, NYY	46
Jimmy Foxx, PHI	58
Jimmy Foxx, PHI	48
Lou Gehrig, NYY	49
Jimmy Foxx, PHI	36
Hank Greenberg, DET	36
Lou Gehrig, NYY	49
Joe DiMaggio, NYY	46
Hank Greenberg, DET	58
Jimmie Foxx, BOS	35
Hank Greenberg, DET	41
Ted Williams, BOS	37
Ted Williams, BOS	36
Rudy York, DET	34

NL Home Runs   ## AL Home Runs

Year	Player, Team	HR	Player, Team	HR
1944	Bill Nicholson, CHI	33	Nick Etten, NYY	22
1945	Tommy Holmes, BOS	28	Vern Stephens, STL	24
1946	Ralph Kiner, PIT	23	Hank Greenberg, DET	44
1947	Johnny Mize, NYG	51	Ted Williams, BOS	32
	Ralph Kiner, PIT	51		
1948	Johnny Mize, NYG	40	Joe DiMaggio, NYY	39
	Ralph Kiner, PIT	40		
1949	Ralph Kiner, PIT	54	Ted Williams, BOS	43
1950	Ralph Kiner, PIT	47	Al Rosen, CLE	37
1951	Ralph Kiner, PIT	42	Gus Zernial, CHI–PHI	33
1952	Hank Sauer, CHI	37	Larry Doby, CLE	32
	Ralph Kiner, PIT	37		
1953	Eddie Matthews, MIL	47	Al Rosen, CLE	43
1954	Ted Kluszewski, CIN	49	Larry Doby, CLE	32
1955	Willie Mays, NYG	51	Mickey Mantle, NYY	37
1956	Duke Snider, BRO	43	Mickey Mantle, NYY	52
1957	Hank Aaron, MIL	44	Roy Sievers, WAS	42
1958	Ernie Banks, CHI	47	Mickey Mantle, NYY	42
1959	Eddie Matthews, MIL	46	Harmon Killebrew, WAS	42
			Rocky Colavito, CLE	42
1960	Ernie Banks, CHI	41	Mickey Mantle, NYY	40
1961	Orlando Cepeda, SF	46	Roger Maris, NYY	61
1962	Willie Mays, SF	49	Harmon Killebrew, MIN	48
1963	Hank Aaron, MIL	44	Harmon Killebrew, MIN	45
	Willie McCovey, SF	44		
1964	Willie Mays, SF	47	Harmon Killebrew, MIN	49
1965	Willie Mays, SF	52	Tony Conigliaro, BOS	32
1966	Hank Aaron, ATL	44	Frank Robinson, BAL	49
1967	Hank Aaron, ATL	39	Carl Yastrzemski, BOS	44
			Harmon Killebrew, MIN	44
1968	Willie McCovey, SF	36	Frank Howard, WAS	44
1969	Willie McCovey, SF	46	Harmon Killebrew, MIN	49
1970	Johnny Bench, CIN	45	Frank Howard, WAS	44
1971	Willie Stargell, PIT	48	Bill Melton, CHI	33
1972	Johnny Bench, CIN	40	Dick Allen, CHI	37
1973	Willie Stargell, PIT	44	Reggie Jackson, OAK	32
1974	Mike Schmidt, PHI	36	Dick Allen, CHI	32
1975	Mike Schmidt, PHI	38	Reggie Jackson, OAK	36
			George Scott, MIL	36
1976	Mike Schmidt, PHI	38	Graig Nettles, NYY	32
1977	George Foster, CIN	52	Jim Rice, BOS	39
1978	George Foster, CIN	40	Jim Rice, BOS	46

NL Home Runs

Year	Player, Team	HR
1979	Dave Kingman, CHI	48
1980	Mike Schmidt, PHI	48
1981	Mike Schmidt, PHI	31
1982	Dave Kingman, NYM	37
1983	Mike Schmidt, PHI	40
1984	Dale Murphy, ATL	36
	Mike Schmidt, PHI	36
1985	Dale Murphy, ATL	37
1986	Mike Schmidt, PHI	37
1987	Andre Dawson, CHI	49
1988	Darryl Strawberry, NYM	39
1989	Kevin Mitchell, SF	47
1990	Ryne Sandberg, CHI	40
1991	Howard Johnson, NYM	38
1992	Fred McGriff, SD	35
1993	Barry Bonds, SF	46
1994	Matt Williams, SF	43

AL Home Runs

Player, Team	HR
Gorman Thomas, MIL	45
Reggie Jackson, NYY	41
Ben Oglivie, MIL	41
Bobby Grich, CAL	22
Tony Armas, OAK	22
Dwight Evans, BOS	22
Eddie Murray, BAL	22
Reggie Jackson, CAL	39
Gorman Thomas, MIL	39
Jim Rice, BOS	39
Tony Armas, BOS	43
Darrell Evans, DET	40
Jesse Barfield, TOR	40
Mark McGwire, OAK	49
Jose Canseco, OAK	42
Fred McGriff, TOR	36
Cecil Fielder, DET	51
Cecil Fielder, DET	44
Jose Canseco, OAK	44
Juan Gonzalez, TEX	43
Juan Gonzalez, TEX	46
Ken Griffey, Jr., SEA	40

NL Runs Batted In

Year	Player, Team	RBI
1876	James "Deacon" White, CHI	60
1877	James "Deacon" White, BOS	49
1878	Paul Hines, PRO	50
1879	John O'Rourke, BOS	62
1880	Adrian "Cap" Anson, CHI	74
1881	Adrian "Cap" Anson, CHI	82
1882	Adrian "Cap" Anson, CHI	83
1883	"Big Dan" Brouthers, BUF	97
1884	Adrian "Cap" Anson, CHI	102
1885	Adrian "Cap" Anson, CHI	108
1886	Adrian "Cap" Anson, CHI	147
1887	Sam Thompson, DET	166
1888	Adrian "Cap" Anson, CHI	84
1889	Roger Connor, NYG	130
1890	"Oyster" Burns, BRO	128

AL Runs Batted In

Player, Team	RBI
——	—
——	—
——	—
——	—
——	—
——	—
——	—
——	—
——	—
——	—
——	—
——	—
——	—
——	—
——	—

NL Runs Batted In

Year	Player, Team	RBI
1891	Adrian "Cap" Anson, CHI	120
1892	"Big Dan" Brouthers, BRO	124
1893	"Big Ed" Delahanty, PHI	146
1894	Hugh Duffy, BOS	145
1895	Sam Thompson, PHI	165
1896	"Big Ed" Delahanty, PHI	126
1897	George Davis, NYG	136
1898	Nap Lajoie, PHI	127
1899	"Big Ed" Delahanty, PHI	137
1900	Elmer Flick, PHI	110
1901	"Honus" Wagner, PIT	126
1902	"Honus" Wagner, PIT	91
1903	Sam Mertes, NYG	104
1904	Bill Dahlen, NYG	80
1905	Cy Seymour, CIN	121
1906	Harry Steinfeldt, CHI	83
	Jim Nealon, PIT	83
1907	Sherry Magee, PHI	85
1908	"Honus" Wagner, PIT	109
1909	"Honus" Wagner, PIT	100
1910	Sherry Magee, PHI	123
1911	Frank Schulte, CHI	107
	"Chief" Wilson, PIT	107
1912	"Honus" Wagner, PIT	102
1913	"Gavvy" Cravath, PHI	128
1914	Sherry Magee, PHI	103
1915	"Gavvy" Cravath, PHI	115
1916	Heinie Zimmerman, CHI-NYY	83
1917	Heinie Zimmerman, NYY	102
1918	Sherry Magee, CIN	76
1919	Hy Myers, BRO	73
1920	George Kelly, NYG	94
	Rogers Hornsby, STL	94
1921	Rogers Hornsby, STL	126
1922	Rogers Hornsby, STL	152
1923	Emil Meusel, NYG	125
1924	George Kelly, NYG	136
1925	Rogers Hornsby, STL	143
1926	Sunny Jim" Bottomley, STL	120
1927	Paul "Big Poison" Waner, PIT	131

AL Runs Batted In

Player, Team	RBI
——	—
——	—
——	—
——	—
——	—
——	—
——	—
——	—
——	—
——	—
Napoleon Lajoie, PHI	125
Buck Freeman, BOS	121
Buck Freeman, BOS	104
Napoleon Lajoie, CLE	102
Harry Davis, PHI	83
Harry Davis, PHI	96
Ty Cobb, DET	116
Ty Cobb, DET	108
Ty Cobb, DET	107
Sam Crawford, DET	120
Ty Cobb, DET	144
Frank Baker, PHI	133
Frank Baker, PHI	126
Sam Crawford, DET	104
B. Veach, DET	112
Sam Crawford, DET	112
Del Pratt, STL	103
Bobby Veach, DET	103
Bobby Veach, DET	78
Babe Ruth, BOS	114
Babe Ruth, NYY	137
Babe Ruth, NYY	171
Ken Williams, STL	155
Babe Ruth, NYY	130
Tris Speaker, CLE	130
Goose Goslin, WAS	129
Bob Meusel, NYY	138
Babe Ruth, NYY	145
Lou Gehrig, NYY	175

NL Runs Batted In

AL Runs Batted In

Year	Player, Team	RBI	Player, Team	RBI
1928	"Sunny Jim" Bottomley, STL	136	Babe Ruth, NYY	142
			Lou Gehrig, NYY	142
1929	Lewis "Hack" Wilson, CHI	159	Al Simmons, PHI	157
1930	Lewis "Hack" Wilson, CHI	190	Lou Gehrig, NYY	174
1931	Chuck Klein, PHI	121	Lou Gehrig, NYY	184
1932	Don Hurst, PHI	143	Jimmy Foxx, PHI	169
1933	Chuck Klein, PHI	120	Jimmy Foxx, PHI	163
1934	Mel Ott, NYG	135	Lou Gehrig, NYY	165
1935	Wally Berger, BOS	130	Hank Greenberg, DET	170
1936	Joe "Ducky" Medwick, STL	138	Hal Trosky, CLE	162
1937	Joe "Ducky" Medwick, STL	154	Hank Greenberg, DET	183
1938	Joe "Ducky" Medwick, STL	122	Jimmie Foxx, BOS	175
1939	Frank McCormick, CIN	128	Ted Williams, BOS	145
1940	Johnny Mize, STL	137	Hank Greenberg, DET	150
1941	Dolph Camilli, BRO	120	Joe DiMaggio, NYY	125
1942	Johnny Mize, NYG	110	Ted Williams, BOS	137
1943	Bill Nicholson, CHI	128	Rudy York, DET	118
1944	Bill Nicholson, CHI	122	Vern Stephens, STL	109
1945	Fred "Dixie" Walker, BRO	124	Nick Etten, NYY	111
1946	Enos Slaughter, STL	130	Hank Greenberg, DET	127
1947	Johnny Mize, NYG	138	Ted Williams, BOS	114
1948	Stan Musial, STL	131	Joe DiMaggio, NYY	155
1949	Ralph Kiner, PIT	127	Ted Williams, BOS	159
			Vern Stephens, BOS	159
1950	Del Ennis, PHI	126	Walt Dropo, BOS	144
			Vern Stephens, BOS	144
1951	Monte Irvin, NYG	121	Gus Zernial, CHI-PHI	129
1952	Hank Sauer, CHI	121	Al Rosen, CLE	105
1953	Roy Campanella, BRO	142	Al Rosen, CLE	145
1954	Ted Kluszewski, CIN	141	Larry Doby, CLE	126
1955	Duke Snider, BRO	136	Ray Boone, DET	116
			Jackie Jensen, BOS	116
1956	Stan Musial, STL	109	Mickey Mantle, NYY	130
1957	Hank Aaron, MIL	132	Roy Sievers, WAS	114
1958	Ernie Banks, CHI	129	Jackie Jensen, BOS	122
1959	Ernie Banks, CHI	143	Jackie Jensen, BOS	112
1960	Hank Aaron, MIL	126	Roger Maris, NYY	112
1961	Orlando Cepeda, SF	142	Roger Maris, NYY	142
1962	Tommy Davis, LA	153	Harmon Killebrew, MIN	126
1963	Hank Aaron, MIL	130	Dick Stuart, BOS	118
1964	Ken Boyer, STL	119	Brooks Robinson, BAL	118
1965	Deron Johnson, CIN	130	Rocky Colavito, CLE	108

NL Runs Batted In

Year	Player, Team	RBI
1966	Hank Aaron, ATL	127
1967	Orlando Cepeda, STL	111
1968	Willie McCovey, SF	105
1969	Willie McCovey, SF	126
1970	Johnny Bench, CIN	148
1971	Joe Torre, STL	137
1972	Johnny Bench, CIN	125
1973	Willie Stargell, PIT	119
1974	Johnny Bench, CIN	129
1975	Greg Luzinski, PHI	120
1976	George Foster, CIN	121
1977	George Foster, CIN	149
1978	George Foster, CIN	120
1979	Dave Winfield, SD	118
1980	Mike Schmidt, PHI	121
1981	Mike Schmidt, PHI	91
1982	Dale Murphy, ATL	109
	Al Oliver, MON	109
1983	Dale Murphy, ATL	121
1984	Gary Carter, MON	106
	Mike Schmidt, PHI	106
1985	Dave Parker, CIN	125
1986	Mike Schmidt, PHI	119
1987	Andre Dawson, CHI	137
1988	Will Clark, SF	109
1989	Kevin Mitchell, SF	125
1990	Matt Williams, SF	122
1991	Howard Johnson, NYG	117
1992	Darren Daulton, PHI	109
1993	Barry Bonds, SF	123
1994	Jeff Bagwell, HOU	116

AL Runs Batted In

Player, Team	RBI
Frank Robinson, BAL	122
Carl Yastrzemski, BOS	121
Ken Harrelson, BOS	109
Harmon Killebrew, MIN	140
Frank Howard, WAS	126
Harmon Killebrew, MIN	119
Dick Allen, CHI	113
Reggie Jackson, OAK	117
Jeff Burroughs, TEX	118
George Scott, MIL	109
Lee May, BAL	109
Larry Hisle, MIN	119
Jim Rice, BOS	139
Don Baylor, CAL	139
Cecil Cooper, MIL	122
Eddie Murray, BAL	78
Hal McRae, KC	133
Jim Rice, BOS	126
Cecil Cooper, MIL	126
Tony Armas, BOS	123
Don Mattingly, NYY	145
Joe Carter, CLE	121
George Bell, TOR	134
Jose Canseco, OAK	124
Ruben Sierra, TEX	119
Cecil Fielder, DET	132
Cecil Fielder, DET	133
Cecil Fielder, DET	124
Albert Belle, CLE	129
Kirby Puckett, MIN	112

NL Stolen Bases

Year	Player, Team	SB
1886	Ed Andrews, PHI	56
1887	John "Monte" Ward, NYG	111
1888	"Dummy" Hoy, WAS	82
1889	Jim Fogarty, PHI	99
1890	Billy Hamilton, PHI	102
1891	Billy Hamilton, PHI	111

AL Stolen Bases

Player, Team	SB
—	—
—	—
—	—
—	—
—	—
—	—

NL Stolen Bases

AL Stolen Bases

Year	Player, Team	SB	Player, Team	SB
1892	John "Monte" Ward, BRO	88	——	—
1893	Tom Brown, LOU	66	——	—
1894	Billy Hamilton, PHI	98	——	—
1895	Billy Hamilton, PHI	97	——	—
1896	Joe Kelley, BAL	87	——	—
1897	Bill Lange, CHI	73	——	—
1898	"Big Ed" Delahanty, PHI	58	——	—
1899	Jimmy Sheckard, BAL	77	——	—
1900	George Van Haltren, NYG	45	——	—
	"Patsy" Donovan, STL	45		
1901	"Honus" Wagner, PIT	49	Frank Isbell, CHI	52
1902	"Honus" Wagner, PIT	42	Topsy Hartsel, PHI	47
1903	Jimmy Sheckard, BRO	67	Harry Bay, CLE	45
	Frank "Husk" Chance, CHI	67		
1904	"Honus" Wagner, PIT	53	Elmer Flick, CLE	42
1905	Billy Maloney, CHI	59	Danny Hoffman, PHI	46
	Art Devlin, NYG	59		
1906	Frank "Husk" Chance, CHI	57	John Anderson, WAS	39
			Elmer Flick, WAS	39
1907	"Honus" Wagner, PIT	61	Ty Cobb, DET	49
1908	"Honus" Wagner, PIT	53	Patsy Dougherty, CHI	47
1909	Bob Bescher, CIN	54	Ty Cobb, DET	76
1910	Bob Bescher, CIN	70	Eddie Collins, PHI	81
1911	Bob Bescher, CIN	80	Ty Cobb, DET	83
1912	Bob Bescher, CIN	67	Clyde Milan, WAS	88
1913	Max "Scoops" Carey, PIT	61	Clyde Milan, WAS	75
1914	George J. Burns, NYG	62	Fritz Maisel, NYY	74
1915	Max "Scoops" Carey, PIT	36	Ty Cobb, DET	96
1916	Max "Scoops" Carey, PIT	63	Ty Cobb, DET	68
1917	Max "Scoops" Carey, PIT	46	Ty Cobb, DET	55
1918	Max "Scoops" Carey, PIT	58	George Sisler, STL	45
1919	George J. Burns, NYG	40	Eddie Collins, CHI	33
1920	Max "Scoops" Carey, PIT	52	Sam Rice, WAS	63
1921	Frankie Frisch, NYG	49	George Sisler, STL	35
1922	Max "Scoops" Carey, PIT	51	George Sisler, STL	51
1923	Max "Scoops" Carey, PIT	51	Eddie Collins, CHI	47
1924	Max "Scoops" Carey, PIT	49	Eddie Collins, CHI	42
1925	Max "Scoops" Carey, PIT	46	Johnny Mostil, CHI	43
1926	Hazen "Kiki" Cuyler, PIT	35	Johnny Mostil, CHI	35
1927	Frankie Frisch, STL	48	George Sisler, STL	27
1928	Hazen "Kiki" Cuyler, CHI	37	Buddy Myer, BOS	30
1929	Hazen "Kiki" Cuyler, CHI	43	Charlie Gehringer, DET	28

NL Stolen Bases   AL Stolen Bases

Year	Player, Team	SB	Player, Team	SB
1930	Hazen "Kiki" Cuyler, CHI	37	Marty McManus, DET	23
1931	Frankie Frisch, STL	28	Ben Chapman, NYY	61
1932	Chuck Klein, PHI	20	Ben Chapman, NYY	38
1933	John "Pepper" Martin, STL	26	Ben Chapman, NYY	27
1934	John "Pepper" Martin, STL	23	Billy Werber, BOS	40
1935	Augie Galan, CHI	22	Billy Werber, BOS	29
1936	John "Pepper" Martin, STL	23	Lyn Lary, STL	37
1937	Augie Galan, CHI	23	Billy Werber, PHI	35
			Ben Chapman, BOS-WAS	35
1938	Stan Hack, CHI	16	Frank Crosetti, NYY	27
1939	Stan Hack, CHI	17	George Case, WAS	51
	Lee Handley, PIT	17		
1940	Lonny Frey, CIN	22	George Case, WAS	35
1941	Danny Murtaugh, PHI	18	George Case, WAS	33
1942	Pete Reiser, BRO	20	George Case, WAS	44
1943	Floyd "Arky" Vaughan, BRO	20	George Case, WAS	61
1944	Johnny Barrett, PIT	28	Snuffy Stirnweiss, NYY	55
1945	"Red" Schoendienst, STL	26	Snuffy Stirnweiss, NYY	33
1946	Pete Reiser, BRO	34	George Case, CLE	28
1947	Jackie Robinson, BRO	29	Bob Dillinger, STL	34
1948	Richie Ashburn, PHI	32	Bob Dillinger, STL	28
1949	Jackie Robinson, BRO	37	Bob Dillinger, STL	20
1950	Sam Jethroe, BOS	35	Dom DiMaggio, BOS	15
1951	Sam Jethroe, BOS	35	Minnie Minoso, CHI-CLE	31
1952	"Pee Wee" Reese, BRO	30	Minnie Minoso, CHI	22
1953	Bill Bruton, MIL	26	Minnie Minoso, CHI	25
1954	Bill Bruton, MIL	34	Jackie Jensen, BOS	22
1955	Bill Bruton, MIL	25	Jim Rivera, CHI	25
1956	Willie Mays, NYG	40	Luis Aparicio, CHI	21
1957	Willie Mays, NYG	38	Luis Aparicio, CHI	28
1958	Willie Mays, SF	31	Luis Aparicio, CHI	29
1959	Willie Mays, SF	27	Luis Aparicio, CHI	56
1960	Maury Wills, LA	50	Luis Aparicio, CHI	51
1961	Maury Wills, LA	35	Luis Aparicio, CHI	53
1962	Maury Wills, LA	104	Luis Aparicio, CHI	31
1963	Maury Wills, LA	40	Luis Aparicio, BAL	40
1964	Maury Wills, LA	53	Luis Aparicio, BAL	57
1965	Maury Wills, LA	94	Bert Campaneris, KC	51
1966	Lou Brock, STL	74	Bert Campaneris, KC	52
1967	Lou Brock, STL	52	Bert Campaneris, KC	55
1968	Lou Brock, STL	62	Bert Campaneris, OAK	62
1969	Lou Brock, STL	53	Tommy Harper, SEA	73

NL Stolen Bases

Year	Player, Team	SB
1970	Bobby Tolan, CIN	57
1971	Lou Brock, STL	64
1972	Lou Brock, STL	63
1973	Lou Brock, STL	70
1974	Lou Brock, STL	118
1975	Davey Lopes, LA	77
1976	Davey Lopes, LA	63
1977	Frank Taveras, PIT	70
1978	Omar Moreno, PIT	71
1979	Omar Moreno, PIT	77
1980	Ron LeFlore, MON	97
1981	Tim Raines, MON	71
1982	Tim Raines, MON	78
1983	Tim Raines, MON	90
1984	Tim Raines, MON	75
1985	Vince Coleman, STL	110
1986	Vince Coleman, STL	107
1987	Vince Coleman, STL	109
1988	Vince Coleman, STL	81
1989	Vince Coleman, STL	65
1990	Vince Coleman, STL	77
1991	Marquis Grissom, MON	76
1992	Marquis Grissom, MON	78
1993	Chuck Carr, FLO	58
1994	Craig Biggio, HOU	39

AL Stolen Bases

Player, Team	SB
Bert Campaneris, OAK	42
Amos Otis, KC	52
Bert Campaneris, OAK	52
Tommy Harper, BOS	54
Billy North, OAK	54
Mickey Rivers, CAL	70
Billy North, OAK	75
Fred Patek, KC	53
Ron LeFlore, DET	68
Willie Wilson, KC	83
Rickey Henderson, OAK	100
Rickey Henderson, OAK	56
Rickey Henderson, OAK	130
Rickey Henderson, OAK	108
Rickey Henderson, OAK	66
Rickey Henderson, NYY	80
Rickey Henderson, NYY	87
Harold Reynolds, SEA	60
Rickey Henderson, NYY	93
Rickey Henderson, NYY-OAK	77
Rickey Henderson, OAK	65
Rickey Henderson, OAK	58
Kenny Lofton, CLE	66
Kenny Lofton, CLE	70
Kenny Lofton, CLE	60

NL Wins

Year	Player, Team	Wins
1876	Al Spalding, CHI	47
1877	Tommy Bond, BOS	40
1878	Tommy Bond, BOS	40
1879	John "Monte" Ward, PRO	47
1880	Jim McCormick, CLE	45
1881	Jim Whitney, BOS	31
	Larry Corcoran, CHI	31
1882	Jim McCormick, CLE	36
1883	"Ol' Hoss" Radbourn, PRO	.48
1884	"Ol' Hoss" Radbourn, PRO	59
1885	John Clarkson, CHI	53
1886	Charles "Lady" Baldwin, DET	42
	Tim Keefe, NYG	42

AL Wins

Player, Team	Wins
——	—
——	—
——	—
——	—
——	—
——	—
——	—
——	—
——	—
——	—

NL Wins   AL Wins

Year	Player, Team	Wins	Player, Team	Wins
1887	John Clarkson, CHI	38	——	—
1888	Tim Keefe, NYG	35	——	—
1889	John Clarkson, BOS	49	——	—
1890	Bill Hutchinson, CHI	42	——	—
1891	Bill Hutchinson, CHI	44	——	—
1892	Bill Hutchinson, CHI	37	——	—
1893	Frank Killen, PIT	36	——	—
1894	Amos Rusie, NYG	36	——	—
1895	Cy Young, CLE	35	——	—
1896	Nichols, BOS	30	——	—
1896	Frank Killen, PIT	30	——	—
1897	Nichols, BOS	31	——	—
1898	Nichols, BOS	31	——	—
1899	McGinnity, BAL	28	——	—
1899	Jim Hughes, BRO	28	——	—
1900	Joe McGinnity, BRO	28	——	—
1901	Bill Donovan, BRO	25	Cy Young, BOS	33
1902	Jack Chesbro, PIT	28	Cy Young, BOS	32
1903	Joe McGinnity, NYG	31	Cy Young, BOS	28
1904	Joe McGinnity, NYG	35	Jack Chesbro, NYY	41
1905	Christy Mathewson, NYG	31	Rube Waddell, PHI	26
1906	Joe McGinnity, NYG	27	Al Orth, NYY	27
1907	Christy Mathewson, NYG	24	Addie Joss, CLE	27
			Doc White, CHI	27
1908	Christy Mathewson, NYG	37	Ed Walsh, CHI	40
1909	"Three Finger" Brown, CHI	27	George Mullin, DET	29
1910	Christy Mathewson, NYG	27	Jack Coombs, PHI	31
1911	Grover C. Alexander, PHI	28	Jack Coombs, PHI	28
1912	Larry Cheney, CHI	26	"Smokey" Joe Wood, BOS	34
	Rube Marquard, NYG	26		
1913	Tom Seaton, PHI	27	Walter Johnson, WAS	36
1914	Richard Rudolph, BOS	27	Walter Johnson, WAS	28
	Grover C. Alexander, PHI	27		
1915	Grover C. Alexander, PHI	31	Walter Johnson, WAS	28
1916	Grover C. Alexander, PHI	33	Walter Johnson, WAS	25
1917	Grover C. Alexander, PHI	30	Eddie Cicotte, CHI	28
1918	James "Hippo" Vaughn, CHI	22	Walter Johnson, WAS	23
1919	Jesse Barnes, NYG	25	Eddie Cicotte, CHI	29
1920	Grover C. Alexander, CHI	27	Jim Bagby, CLE	31
1921	Burleigh Grimes, BRO	22	Carl Mays, NYY	27
	Wilbur Cooper, PIT	22	Urban Shocker, STL	27
1922	Eppa Rixey, CIN	25	Eddie Rommel, PHI	27

NL Wins

AL Wins

Year	Player, Team	Wins	Player, Team	Wins
1923	Dolf Luque, CIN	27	George Uhle, CLE	26
1924	Arthur "Dazzy" Vance, BRO	28	Walter Johnson, WAS	23
1925	Arthur "Dazzy" Vance, BRO	22	Eddie Rommel, PHI	21
1926	Pete Donahue, CIN	20	George Uhle, CLE	27
	Remy "Ray" Kremer, PIT	20		
	Lee Meadows, PIT	20		
	Flint Rhem, STL	20		
1927	Charlie Root, CHI	26	Waite Hoyt, NYY	22
			Ted Lyons, CHI	22
1928	Rube Benton, NYG	25	Lefty Grove, PHI	24
	Burleigh Grimes, PIT	25	George Pipgras, NYY	24
1929	Perce "Pat" Malone, CHI	22	George Earnshaw, PHI	24
1930	Perce "Pat" Malone, CHI	20	Lefty Grove, PHI	28
	Remy "Ray" Kremer, PIT	20		
1931	J. Elliott, PHI	19	Lefty Grove, PHI	31
	Henry "Heinie" Meine, PIT	19		
	Billy Hallahan, STL	19		
1932	Lonnie Warneke, CHI	22	General Crowder, WAS	26
1933	Carl Hubbell, NYG	23	General Crowder, WAS	24
			Lefty Grove, PHI	24
1934	Jay "Dizzy" Dean, STL	30	Lefty Gomez, NYY	26
1935	Jay "Dizzy" Dean, STL	28	Wes Ferrell, BOS	25
1936	Carl Hubbell, NYG	26	Tommy Bridges, DET	23
1937	Carl Hubbell, NYG	22	Lefty Gomez, NYY	21
1938	Bill Lee, CHI	22	Red Ruffing, NYY	21
1939	Bucky Walters, CIN	27	Bob Feller, CLE	24
1940	Bucky Walters, CIN	22	Bob Feller, CLE	27
1941	Whit Wyatt, BRO	22	Bob Feller, CLE	25
	Kirby Higbe, BRO	22		
1942	Mort Cooper, STL	22	Tex Hughson, BOS	22
1943	Elmer Riddle, CIN	21	Spud Chandler, NYY	20
	Truett "Rip" Sewell, PIT	21	Dizzy Trout, DET	20
	Mort Cooper, STL	21		
1944	Bucky Walters, CIN	23	Hal Newhouser, DET	29
1945	Red Barrett, BOS–STL	23	Hal Newhouser, DET	25
1946	Howie Pollet, STL	21	Hal Newhouser, DET	26
			Bob Feller, CLE	26
1947	Ewell Blackwell, CIN	22	Bob Feller, CLE	20
1948	Johnny Sain, BOS	24	Hal Newhouser, DET	21
1949	Warren Spahn, BOS	21	Mel Parnell, BOS	25
1950	Warren Spahn, BOS	21	Bob Lemon, CLE	23
1951	Sal Maglie, NYG	23	Bob Feller, CLE	22

NL Wins			AL Wins	
Year	Player, Team	Wins	Player, Team	Wins
	Larry Jansen, NYG	23		
1952	Robin Roberts, PHI	28	Bobby Shantz, PHI	24
1953	Warren Spahn, MIL	23	Bob Porterfield, WAS	22
	Robin Roberts, PHI	23		
1954	Robin Roberts, PHI	23	Bob Lemon, CLE	23
			Early Wynn, CLE	23
1955	Robin Roberts, PHI	23	Bob Lemon, CLE	18
			Frank Sullivan, BOS	18
			Whitey Ford, NYY	18
1956	Don Newcombe, BRO	27	Frank Lary, DET	21
1957	Warren Spahn, MIL	21	Jim Bunning, DET	20
			Billy Pierce, CHI	20
1958	Warren Spahn, MIL	22	Bob Turley, NYY	21
	Bob Friend, PIT	22		
1959	Warren Spahn, MIL	21	Early Wynn, CHI	22
	Lew Burdette, MIL	21		
	Sam Jones, SF	21		
1960	Warren Spahn, MIL	21	Jim Perry, CLE	18
	Ernie Broglio, STL	21	Chuck Estrada, BAL	18
1961	Warren Spahn, MIL	21	Whitey Ford, NYY	25
1962	Don Drysdale, LA	25	Ralph Terry, NYY	23
1963	Sandy Koufax, LA	25	Whitey Ford, NYY	24
	Juan Marichal, SF	25		
1964	Larry Jackson, CHI	24	Gary Peters, CHI	20
			Dean Chance, LA	20
1965	Sandy Koufax, LA	26	Mudcat Grant, MIN	21
1966	Sandy Koufax, LA	27	Jim Kaat, MIN	25
1967	Mike McCormick, SF	22	Jim Lonborg, BOS	22
			Earl Wilson, DET	22
1968	Juan Marichal, SF	26	Denny McLain, DET	31
1969	Tom Seaver, NYM	25	Denny McLain, DET	24
1970	Gaylord Perry, SF	23	Mike Cuellar, BAL	24
	Bob Gibson, STL	23	Jim Perry, MIN	24
			Dave McNally, BAL	24
1971	Ferguson Jenkins, CHI	24	Mickey Lolich, DET	25
1972	Steve Carlton, PHI	27	Gaylord Perry, CLE	24
			Wilbur Wood, CHI	24
1973	Ron Bryant, SF	24	Wilbur Wood, CHI	24
1974	Phil Niekro, ATL	20	Catfish Hunter, OAK	25
	Andy Messersmith, LA	20	Ferguson Jenkins, TEX	25
1975	Tom Seaver, NYM	22	Catfish Hunter, NYY	23
			Jim Palmer, BAL	23

NL Wins

Year	Player, Team	ERA
1976	Randy Jones, SD	22
1977	Steve Carlton, PHI	23
1978	Gaylord Perry, SD	21
1979	Phil Niekro, ATL	21
	Joe Niekro, HOU	21
1980	Steve Carlton, PHI	24
1981	Tom Seaver, CIN	14
1982	Steve Carlton, PHI	23
1983	John Denny, PHI	19
1984	Joaquin Andujar, STL	20
1985	Dwight Gooden, NYM	24
1986	Fernando Valenzuela, LA	21
1987	Rick Sutcliffe, CHI	18
1988	Danny Jackson, CIN	23
	Orel Hershiser, LA	23
1989	Mike Scott, HOU	20
1990	Doug Drabek, PIT	22
1991	Tom Glavine, ATL	20
	John Smiley, PIT	20
1992	Tom Glavine, ATL	20
	Greg Maddux, CHI	20
1993	John Burkett, SF	22
	Tom Glavine, ATL	22
1994	Ken Hill, MON	16
	Greg Maddux, ATL	16

AL Wins

Player, Team	ERA
Jim Palmer, BAL	22
Jim Palmer, BAL	20
Dennis Leonard, KC	20
Dave Goltz, MIN	20
Ron Guidry, NYY	25
Mike Flanagan, BAL	23
Steve Stone, BAL	25
Pete Vuckovich, MIL	14
Dennis Martinez, BAL	14
Steve McCatty, OAK	14
Jack Morris, DET	14
LaMarr Hoyt, CHI	19
LaMarr Hoyt, CHI	24
Mike Boddicker, BAL	20
Ron Guidry, NYY	22
Roger Clemens, BOS	24
Roger Clemens, BOS	20
Dave Stewart, OAK	20
Frank Viola, MIN	24
Bret Saberhagen, KC	23
Bob Welch, OAK	27
Scott Erickson, MIN	20
Bill Gullickson, DET	20
Kevin Brown, TEX	21
Jack Morris, TOR	21
Jack McDowell, CHI	22
Jimmy Key, NYY	17

NL ERA

Year	Player, Team	ERA
1876	"Foghorn" Bradley, STL	1.23
1877	Tommy Bond, BOS	2.11
1878	"Monte" Ward, PRO	1.51
1879	Tommy Bond, BOS	1.96
1880	Tim Keefe, Troy	0.86
1881	"Stump" Weidman, DET	1.80
1882	Larry Corcoran, CHI	1.95

AL ERA

Player, Team	ERA
——	—
——	—
——	—
——	—
——	—
——	—
——	—

NL ERA

Year	Player, Team	ERA
1883	Jim McCormick, CLE	1.84
1884	"Ol' Hoss" Radbourn, PRO	1.38
1885	Tim Keefe, NYG	1.58
1886	Charlie Ferguson, PHI	1.98
1887	Dan Casey, PHI	2.86
1888	Tim Keefe, NYG	1.74
1889	John Clarkson, BOS	2.73
1890	Billy Rhines, CIN	1.95
1891	John Ewing, NYG	2.27
1892	Cy Young, CLE	1.93
1893	Ted Breitenstein, STL	3.18
1894	Amos Rusie, NYG	2.78
1895	Al Maul, WAS	2.45
1896	Billy Rhines, CIN	2.45
1897	Amos Rusie, NYG	2.54
1898	Clark Griffith, CHI	1.88
1899	Vic Willis, BOS	2.50
1900	"Rube" Waddell, PIT	2.37
1901	Jesse Tannehill, PIT	2.18
1902	Jack Taylor, CHI	1.33
1903	Sam Leever, PIT	2.06
1904	Joe McGinnity, NYG	1.61
1905	Christy Mathewson, NY	1.27
1906	"Three Fingers" Brown, CHI	1.04
1907	Jack Pfiester, CHI	1.15
1908	Christy Mathewson, NY	1.43
1909	Christy Mathewson, NY	1.14
1910	King Cole, CHI	1.80
1911	Christy Mathewson, NY	1.99
1912	"Jeff" Tesreau, NYG	1.96
1913	Christy Mathewson, NY	2.06
1914	Bill Doak, STL	1.72
1915	Grover C. Alexander, PHI	1.22
1916	Grover C. Alexander, PHI	1.55
1917	Fred Anderson, NYG	1.44
1918	James "Hippo" Vaughn, CHI	1.74
1919	Grover C. Alexander, CHI	1.72
1920	Grover C. Alexander, CHI	1.91
1921	Bill Doak, STL	2.59
1922	Phil Douglas, NYG	2.63
1923	Dolf Luque, CIN	1.93
1924	"Dazzy" Vance, BRO	2.16

AL ERA

Player, Team	ERA
——	—
——	—
——	—
——	—
——	—
——	—
——	—
——	—
——	—
——	—
——	—
——	—
——	—
——	—
——	—
——	—
——	—
——	—
Cy Young, BOS	1.62
Ed Siever, DET	1.91
Earl Moore, CLE	1.77
Addie Joss, CLE	1.59
Rube Waddell, PHI	1.48
Doc White, CHI	1.52
Ed Walsh, CHI	1.60
Addie Joss, CLE	1.16
Harry Krause, PHI	1.39
Ed Walsh, CHI	1.27
Vean Gregg, CLE	1.81
Walter Johnson, WAS	1.39
Walter Johnson, WAS	1.09
Dutch Leonard, BOS	1.01
"Smokey" Joe Wood, BOS	1.49
Babe Ruth, BOS	1.75
Eddie Cicotte, CHI	1.53
Walter Johnson, WAS	1.27
Walter Johnson, WAS	1.49
Bob Shawkey, NYY	2.45
Red Faber, CHI	2.48
Red Faber, CHI	2.80
Stan Coveleski, CLE	2.76
Walter Johnson, WAS	2.72

Year	Player, Team	SO	Player, Team	SO
1885	John Clarkson, CHI	308	——	—
1886	"Lady" Baldwin, DET	323	——	—
1887	John Clarkson, CHI	237	——	—
1888	Tim Keefe, NYG	333	——	—
1889	John Clarkson, BOS	284	——	—
1890	Amos Rusie, NYG	341	——	—
1891	Amos Rusie, NYG	337	——	—
1892	Bill Hutchinson, CHI	316	——	—
1893	Amos Rusie, NYG	208	——	—
1894	Amos Rusie, NYG	195	——	—
1895	Amos Rusie, NYG	201	——	—
1896	Cy Young, CLE	140	——	—
1897	James "Doc" McJames, WAS	156	——	—
1898	Cy Seymour, NYG	239	——	—
1899	Frank "Noodles" Hahn, CIN	145	——	—
1900	Rube Waddell, PIT	130	——	—
1901	Frank "Noodles" Hahn, CIN	239	Cy Young, BOS	158
1902	Vic Willis, BOS	225	Rube Waddell, PHI	210
1903	Christy Mathewson, NY	267	Rube Waddell, PHI	302
1904	Christy Mathewson, NY	212	Rube Waddell, PHI	349
1905	Christy Mathewson, NY	206	Rube Waddell, PHI	287
1906	Fred Beebe, CHI–STL	171	Rube Waddell, PHI	196
1907	Christy Mathewson, NY	178	Rube Waddell, PHI	232
1908	Christy Mathewson, NY	259	Ed Walsh, CHI	269
1909	Orval Overall, CHI	205	F. Smith, CHI	177
1910	Earl Moore, PHI	185	Walter Johnson, WAS	313
1911	Rube Marquard, NYG	237	Ed Walsh, CHI	255
1912	Grover C. Alexander, PHI	195	Walter Johnson, WAS	303
1913	Tom Seaton, PHI	168	Walter Johnson, WAS	243
1914	Grover C. Alexander, PHI	214	Walter Johnson, WAS	225
1915	Grover C. Alexander, PHI	241	Walter Johnson, WAS	203
1916	Grover C. Alexander, PHI	167	Walter Johnson, WAS	228
1917	Grover C. Alexander, PHI	200	Walter Johnson, WAS	188
1918	James "Hippo" Vaughn, CHI	148	Walter Johnson, WAS	162
1919	James "Hippo" Vaughn, CHI	141	Walter Johnson, WAS	147
1920	Grover C. Alexander, CHI	173	Stan Coveleski, CLE	133
1921	Burleigh Grimes, BRO	136	Walter Johnson, WAS	143
1922	Arthur "Dazzy" Vance, BRO	134	Urban Shocker, STL	149
1923	Arthur "Dazzy" Vance, BRO	197	Walter Johnson, WAS	130
1924	Arthur "Dazzy" Vance, BRO	262	Walter Johnson, WAS	158
1925	Arthur "Dazzy" Vance, BRO	221	Lefty Grove, PHI	116
1926	Arthur "Dazzy" Vance, BRO	140	Lefty Grove, PHI	194

Year	Player, Team	SO	Player, Team	SO
1927	Arthur "Dazzy" Vance, BRO	184	Lefty Grove, PHI	174
1928	Arthur "Dazzy" Vance, BRO	200	Lefty Grove, PHI	183
1929	Perce "Pat" Malone, CHI	166	Lefty Grove, PHI	170
1930	Bill Hallahan, STL	177	Lefty Grove, PHI	209
1931	Billy Hallahan, STL	159	Lefty Grove, PHI	175
1932	Jay "Dizzy" Dean, STL	191	Red Ruffing, NYY	190
1933	Jay "Dizzy" Dean, STL	199	Lefty Gomez, NYY	163
1934	Jay "Dizzy" Dean, STL	195	Lefty Gomez, NYY	158
1935	Jay "Dizzy" Dean, STL	182	Tommy Bridges, DET	163
1936	Van Lingle Mungo, BRO	238	Tommy Bridges, DET	175
1937	Carl Hubbell, NYG	159	Lefty Gomez, NYY	194
1938	Clay Bryant, CHI	135	Bob Feller, CLE	240
1939	Claude Passeau, PHI–CIN	137	Bob Feller, CLE	246
1940	Kirby Higbe, PHI	137	Bob Feller, CLE	261
1941	Johnny Vander Meer, CIN	202	Bob Feller, CLE	260
1942	Johnny Vander Meer, CIN	186	Bobo Newsom, WAS	113
			Tex Hughson, BOS	113
1943	Johnny Vander Meer, CIN	174	Allie Reynolds, CLE	151
1944	Bill Voiselle, NYG	161	Hal Newhouser, DET	187
1945	Elwin "Preacher" Roe, PIT	148	Hal Newhouser, DET	212
1946	Johnny Schmitz, CHI	135	Bob Feller, CLE	348
1947	Ewell Blackwell, CIN	193	Bob Feller, CLE	196
1948	Harry Brecheen, STL	149	Bob Feller, CLE	164
1949	Warren Spahn, BOS	151	Virgil Trucks, DET	153
1950	Warren Spahn, BOS	191	Bob Lemon, CLE	170
1951	Warren Spahn, BOS	164	Vic Raschi, NYY	164
	Don Newcombe, BRO	164		
1952	Warren Spahn, BOS	183	Allie Reynolds, NYY	160
1953	Robin Roberts, PHI	198	Billy Pierce, CHI	186
1954	Robin Roberts, PHI	185	Bob Turley, BAL	185
1955	Sam Jones, CHI	198	Herb Score, CLE	245
1956	Sam Jones, CHI	176	Herb Score, CLE	263
1957	Jack Sanford, PHI	188	Early Wynn, CLE	184
1958	Sam Jones, STL	225	Early Wynn, CHI	179
1959	Don Drysdale, LA	242	Jim Bunning, DET	201
1960	Don Drysdale, LA	246	Jim Bunning, DET	201
1961	Sandy Koufax, LA	269	Camilo Pascual, MIN	221
1962	Don Drysdale, LA	232	Camilo Pascual, MIN	206
1963	Sandy Koufax, LA	306	Camilo Pascual, MIN	202
1964	Bob Veale, PIT	250	Al Downing, NYY	217
1965	Sandy Koufax, LA	382	Sam McDowell, CLE	325
1966	Sandy Koufax, LA	317	Sam McDowell, CLE	225

NL Strikeouts

AL Strikeouts

Year	Player, Team	SO	Player, Team	SO
1967	Jim Bunning, PHI	253	Jim Lonborg, BOS	246
1968	Bob Gibson, STL	268	Sam McDowell, CLE	283
1969	Ferguson Jenkins, CHI	273	Sam McDowell, CLE	279
1970	Tom Seaver, NYM	283	Sam McDowell, CLE	304
1971	Tom Seaver, NYM	289	Mickey Lolich, DET	308
1972	Steve Carlton, PHI	310	Nolan Ryan, CAL	329
1973	Tom Seaver, NYM	251	Nolan Ryan, CAL	383
1974	Steve Carlton, PHI	240	Nolan Ryan, CAL	367
1975	Tom Seaver, NYM	243	Frank Tanana, CAL	269
1976	Tom Seaver, NYM	235	Nolan Ryan, CAL	327
1977	Phil Niekro, ATL	262	Nolan Ryan, CAL	341
1978	J. R. Richard, HOU	303	Nolan Ryan, CAL	260
1979	J. R. Richard, HOU	313	Nolan Ryan, CAL	223
1980	Steve Carlton, PHI	286	Len Barker, CLE	187
1981	Fernando Valenzuela, LA	180	Len Barker, CLE	127
1982	Steve Carlton, PHI	286	Floyd Bannister, SEA	209
1983	Steve Carlton, PHI	275	Jack Morris, DET	232
1984	Dwight Gooden, NYM	276	Mark Langston, SEA	204
1985	Dwight Gooden, NYM	268	Bert Blyleven, CLE–MIN	206
1986	Mike Scott, HOU	306	Mark Langston, SEA	245
1987	Nolan Ryan, HOU	270	Mark Langston, SEA	262
1988	Nolan Ryan, HOU	228	Roger Clemens, BOS	291
1989	Jose DeLeon, STL	201	Nolan Ryan, TEX	301
1990	David Cone, NYM	233	Nolan Ryan, TEX	232
1991	David Cone, NYM	241	Roger Clemens, BOS	241
1992	John Smoltz, ATL	215	Randy Johnson, SEA	241
1993	Jose Rijo, CIN	227	Randy Johnson, SEA	308
1994	Andy Benes, SD	189	Randy Johnson, SEA	204

Index of Featured Players

Fungoes

Before the modern era, non-star baseball players were often the objects of some less-than-flattering nicknames. Here's a list of some of the classic handles of pre-1940s ballplayers, along with the date of each player's first season in the majors. Perhaps the current crop of .270-hitting millionaires would be able to achieve a rational perspective if fans began referring to them by such expressions of affection as the following.

Goat Anderson	(1907)	Wheezer Dell	(1912)
Footsie Blair	(1929)	Turkey Gross	(1925)
Coonie Blank	(1909)	Mule Hass	(1925)
Ping Bodie	(1911)	Bunny High	(1913)
Stub Brown	(1893)	Slats Jordan	(1901)
Oyster Burns	(1884)	Rube Lutzke	(1923)
Bunk Congalton	(1902)	Waddy MacPhee	(1922)
Boob Fowler	(1923)	Simmy Murch	(1904)
Daff Gammons	(1901)	Pid Purdy	(1926)
Orator Shaffer	(1874)	Possum Whitted	(1912)

Okay, before we let you go, allow us to test your knowledge of modern baseball history with the following stumpers.

1. Which player is the only National Leaguer to win two Triple Crowns?

2. Who has been honored with MVP Awards in both leagues?

3. Nolan Ryan's pitching career spanned twenty-seven seasons, a major league record. Who's mark of twenty-six seasons did Ryan top?

4. Which active player hit two homers in the same inning, one lefthanded and one righthanded?

Answers: 1. Rogers Hornsby; 2. Frank Robinson; 3. Tommy John; 4. Carlos Baerga